D101 09
2

D0470990

THE GRAIL

ALSO BY ANDREW SINCLAIR

FICTION

The Breaking of Bumbo
My Friend Judas
The Raker
The Facts in the Case of E.A. Poe
Gog
Magog
King Ludd
Blood & Kin

NON-FICTION

Prohibition: The Era of Excess
The Better Half: The Emancipation of the American Woman
The Concise History of the United States
Che Guevara
Dylan: Poet of His People
Jack London
John Ford
Corsair: The Life of J.P. Morgan
The Other Victoria
The Red and the Blue
Francis Bacon: His Life and Violent Times
Spiegel: The Man Behind the Pictures
War Like a Wasp: The Lost Decade of the Forties
In Love and Anger: A View of the Sixties
The Need to Give: The Patron and the Arts
Arts and Cultures
Jerusalem: The Endless Crusade
The Sword and the Grail
The Discovery of the Grail
The Secret Scroll
Rosslyn
Viva Che!

ANTHOLOGIES

Selections from the Greek Anthology
The War Decade

THE
GRAIL

The Quest
for a Legend

ANDREW SINCLAIR

SUTTON PUBLISHING

First published in the United Kingdom in 2007 by
Sutton Publishing Limited · Phoenix Mill
Thrupp · Stroud · Gloucestershire · GL5 2BU

Copyright © Andrew Sinclair, 2007

All rights reserved. No part of this publication may be reproduced,
stored in a retrieval system, or transmitted, in any form, or by any
means, electronic, mechanical, photocopying, recording or otherwise,
without the prior permission of the publisher and copyright holder.

Andrew Sinclair has asserted the moral right to be identified as the
author of this work.

British Library Cataloguing in Publication Data
A catalogue record for this book is available from the British Library.

Hardback ISBN 978-0-7509-4472-4
Paperback ISBN 978-0-7509-4473-1

Typeset in Bembo Mono.
Typesetting and origination by
Sutton Publishing Limited.
Printed and bound in England.

CONTENTS

But the marvel that he found
Terrified him time after time.
No man may speak or tell of it.
Whoever does so is in trouble.
For it is the sign of the Grail
Those who tell of it to others
Will be punished for their pride.

Gawain's vision in
The History of the Grail, *c.* 1200

ONE

THE NAMES OF THE GRAIL

Truth consisteth in the right ordering of names in our affirmations.

Thomas Hobbes, *Leviathan*

he womb has always made children. The horn and the cup have served drink. The cauldron and the bowl have given food. From these facts of life comes the quest for the Grail. The word itself derived from classical times, as did the Christian religion and some of its ceremonies. Its roots lay in the Greek κράτήρ or *krater*. Very like the later communion chalice, a *krater* was a bowl or cup with two handles, in which wine was mixed with water. Other meanings were a basin in the rock or the open mouth of a volcano. The Romans took over the word as *cratera*, which also signified for Virgil an oil-holder, used in anointing, and for Ovid, a starry constellation in the shape of a cup. Yet these were only bygone roots of the later term 'Grail', a chameleon in its shape, an enigma in its meaning as well as its ancestry.

In early Catalonia, Gascony and the Langue d'Oc, the Silver Latin word *gradalis* signified, by the 9th century, a vessel or platter. Yet also *gradale*, translated into Old French as *grael*, meant 'gradual', as a rise in rank or the slow progress of a long search. The will of Ermengarde, the daughter of Count Borell, mentioned in 1030 two *gradales* among her gold and silver vessels, while an early *Chanson de Geste*, 'Girart de Roussillon', sung of a castle hoard containing gold and coins, *grasals* and candelabra. And in the *Roman d'Alexandre*, a pilgrim ate from a large *grasal* dish, large enough to hold a joint of meat or a big fish. And so, before the Grail of the medieval romances became holy in whatever shape it appeared, some classical and religious elements were attached to its form – a communal wine cup, a vessel for anointing with

oil, a heavenly pattern of stars, a fiery crater, and a prolonged quest for betterment.

In the first Grail romance, *Perceval*, Chrétien de Troyes certainly thought of a Grail as a large metal server, carried by a maiden, who was followed by another maiden bearing a *tailleor* or small carving dish. His contemporary Helinand, the abbot of Froidmont, described the Grail as a wide shallow dish, which held rare meats for rich people. A following romance, *The Quest of the Holy Grail*, saw the sacred container as the platter from the Last Supper, holding the Paschal Lamb and its juices. In early versions of the legend, there was no question of the Grail being a chalice or a cup, but rather a metal dinner tray, as in the Welsh *Peredur*, where the Grail proffered a severed and gory head on its base.

In both the Welsh Arthurian romances, the *Perlesvaus* and *Peredur*, the prefix *per* signified a basin used to bring forth some boiled food. In a history of Breton folktales, written in 1842, the magical bard Taliesin was said to have placed the jewelled vessel in a temple, dedicated to the Sophia or a Muse. He declared: 'This vase inspires poetic genius; it confers wisdom; it reveals to its worshippers the knowledge of the future, the mysteries of the world, the entire treasury of human knowledge.' In Welsh tradition, which predated the Grail romances and contained Celtic and Irish pagan references, the Grail referred to ancient rituals in search of enlightenment as well as to the cauldron of regeneration and the horn of plenty.

The question is how these classical beliefs reached Brittany and the early troubadours, who made popular the Arthurian legends in the Middle Ages. The beliefs in an Earth Mother and in the

france morref albanie or [...] hirland norkbay

danmark germen dortingale nauerne armori angeon

ysland ducthland almain gruffom galis gres

aragon espayne mede libbe arge egipte

turrie babiloine surrie beethie tones rome

sun-worship of Zoroaster and Mithras came to Britain in Roman times. These cults preached a vision of the universe as a bowl with the cosmos hovering over the rim of the infinite. Early Christianity, with its Gnostic Eastern beliefs in the Sophia as the messenger to heaven, flourished until the 4th century, when Byzantine strictures against heresy closed down the concept of the direct approach to divine intelligence in favour of the need for the intervention of Church and state. Curiously enough, the Irish monasteries were converted to the Greek rite and its texts; they were the shining lights of Britain from the 6th to the 9th centuries, in what were called the Dark Ages; they passed on some classical learning to the offshore islands of Europe. And the *Corpus Hermeticum*, attributed to the god of Wisdom, Mercury, and the legendary Hermes Trismegistus, was translated into Latin and available to those proto-scientists who were interested in alchemy.

The most misleading of the names of the sacred vessel was a wrong reading of *San Grael*, or Holy Grael, for *Sang Real*, or Holy and Royal Blood. The confusion began in the 12th century with *The History of the Holy Grail* by Robert de Boron, who also wrote the works *Joseph of Arimathea* and *Merlin* for a knightly audience. His Grail was a *veissel* or vase, which Joseph used to catch the flow from the wounds of Jesus, once he was taken down from the Cross. This spawned the medieval legends of Joseph and Mary Magdalene bringing the container of the Blood of Christ to Sarrazis or Sarras, the south of France, and on to Logres or the west of England.

At this stage, the Grail was being identified with the communion *calice* or chalice, which King Arthur saw in the *Perlesvaus* as the last of five visionary and changing shapes at a consecration ceremony, conducted by a wandering hermit.

Later, the Grail Quest was transfused into a royal bloodline, dating back to the appearance in St John's Gospel of the risen Jesus to the beloved Mary Magdalene in the garden. This was the doing of John Hardyng, a contemporary of Sir Thomas Malory, whose *Morte D'Arthur*, printed by Caxton in 1485, informed Tudor times of the medieval romances of Camelot. In his version, Hardyng conventionally began the quest for the Grail with its appearance at the Round Table; but then he misread *San Grael* for 'Sanke Roiall', the title of a military Order of twelve knights, who represented the Knights Templars and the Apostles in a messianic conquest on behalf of the true faith. The shield with the red cross of St George, the English patron saint, which had belonged to Joseph of Arimathea and to Galahad, was brought back by Perceval after many adventures to hang in Glastonbury Abbey. This timely romance buttressed the Tudor claim to the throne; the Welsh King Henry the Seventh even called his eldest son Arthur in memory of the legendary king, and, if the royal heir had not died young, an Arthur the Second would have been crowned.

This confusion of names in their right ordering created a Holy Blood, which would lead to a modern publishing industry, without proof or truth. Mary Magdalene was said to have had an affair with the living Jesus. Carrying a Grail holding the flow from his wounds, she would sail with their children to the South of France. Through the Levites, the divine seed would be sown in the heritage of the French Merovingian kings, who would join Christ in the flowering leaves from the Stem of Jesse and the Song and Temple of Solomon. All of these legends were based on the misreading of two words, taken from a series of medieval myths; it would produce an enduring romance, which even the troubadours, let alone the Holy Spirit, would have blushed to conceive.

King Arthur and his kingdoms. From the 14th-century *Chronicle of England* by Peter Langtoft. *(British Library, London)*

TWO

THE GRAILS FROM THE
EAST AND THE NORTH

Do not think that the Resurrection is an illusion. It is no illusion, but it is truth. It is
more suitable to say, then, that the world is an illusion.

The Epistle to Rheginus, c. 320

The earliest records of the West came from the Near East. Water power ruled the first cities and kingdoms of Meso-potamia. A wise god of the underworld called Enki sent his freshwater ocean up to the *apsû* tanks in the first Assyrian temples. This water was carried in buckets by fish man-gods to humankind. Persian worshippers then poured libations from jars into bowls set before the altars of their gods. In these original scenes of religion, the water tank and the bucket, the jug and the bowl were depicted as the source of life, which should be given back to the divine. They were prophecies of the Grail.

The theocracy of ancient Egypt was equally dependent on the River Nile, which could make the desert green. Thoth was the god of wisdom and science, who invented letters and became the Greek Hermes. Both divine messengers had the serpent of wisdom as their symbol. As Herodotus declared in his *Histories*, 'the names of almost all the gods came from Egypt into Greece'. He then added that 'the Egyptians were the first who introduced public festivals, processing and solemn supplication'. These rites were introduced into the mysteries at Eleusis, the primal ceremonies of birth and death in Greece, while the oracles of Apollo at Claros and of the Pythia at Delphi provided the prophecies of the future. The very Greek myths of creation also had an Egyptian basis, although some of them derived from the original inhabitants called the Pelasgians, influenced by the primary cults of a goddess of Mother Earth and fertility.

In the beginning was Chaos. Eurynome, the maker of everything, was caught in the coils of the great serpent Ophion. She was changed into a dove, a later symbol of the Grail, and produced the Egg of Creation, which split in two in the serpent's grasp to produce the universe and our world. Later, the great god Zeus was born. His father was Kronos, who had married his own sister, Rhea. Told that he would be dethroned by one of his sons, Kronos swallowed them all except for Zeus, for Rhea had substituted a stone for her son. She gave him to the nymph Amalthea to rear in the shape of a goat. Amalthea kept him fed from the corn-ucopia, a horn of plenty, so famous in legend that Gelon, the tyrant hero of Syra-cuse, reproduced it in the 5th century BC in a grotto in his palace garden.

A human god, dressed in a fish skin and holding a bucket and a cone. From Sir Austen Henry Layard's drawing of a monumental stone relief from the Assyrian city of Nimrod, about 9th century BC.

Opposite and above: Greek pictures of the religious mysteries. *(From the pottery collection of Sir William Hamilton)*

Right: An Egyptian fresco of Thoth or Hermes Trismegistus.

Zeus became the cupbearer of Kronos and gave him an emetic, which made him vomit out Zeus's brothers and sisters as well as the substitute stone. Kronos was then defeated with his allies, the Titans, and exiled to farthest Britain: he would later be worshipped in the shape of a black stone. Zeus was said to have given his stone to serve as an altar at Delphi, where the oracle pronounced his wisdom and held the cup that was the mouth and the womb of the gods. Aeschylus, Pindar and Pausanias all wrote that the Delphians considered that divine white stone as the navel and the centre of the world. When Rome occupied Greece, the strongest oath would be *Per Jovem Lapidem*, 'By Jupiter the Stone'. Both Poseidon and Neptune were worshipped as a square stone, while Hermes and Mercury were represented by a plain standing stone or a head placed on a square column. A black meteoric stone representing the female principle of creation, as it would in the original pagan Ka'aba at Mecca, was delivered by King Attalos of Pergamon and installed in the temple of Rhea, the Greek mother of the gods, on the Palatine. A precedent was set for the medieval Grail romance *Parzival*, which saw divine grace as a stone fallen from heaven.

In these Creation myths, many of the later themes of the Grail appeared: the wise serpent, the split egg-bowl of Creation, the stone of prophecy, the cornucopia or giver of plenty; the cup and its godlike bearer, the replacement of the ruler, the divine altar still on earth. In the important mysteries at Eleusis, none of the rituals were foretold. Leaving the soil of Greece from there, Demeter rescued her daughter Persephone from the underworld of Hades, only to lose her each year to winter in the everlasting cycle of the seasons. Demeter had made the earth the Waste Land of the Grail Castle fables, before she recovered her daughter and allowed again the greenery of spring and the harvests of autumn.

During the dramas and celebrations over nine days at Eleusis, sacred vessels were shown. Clement of Alexandria and Plato both mentioned a ritual speech of the worshippers: 'I fasted, I drank the potion. I took it from the chest. Having tasted it, I put it away in the basket and from the basket into the chest.' These sacraments were followed on the fourth day of the festival by a procession with a basket containing pomegranates and poppy seeds, cakes and salt, and a live serpent. On the last day, two jars filled with water and wine were placed to the east and to the west. These were overturned to the words *ue kue*, 'rain' and 'conceive'.

These fertility rites were matched in the contemporary Orphic mysteries of Dionysus, the god of wine and the spirit. His celebrants ate the raw flesh of animals, as he was said to have done in his role of the savage hunter. When his follower Orpheus, with his lyre, was torn apart by the frenzied Bacchantes, his sacrifice was a prelude to eating the divine flesh and drinking the blood in an orgiastic mystery. The singing head of the Greek bard was said to have been washed up at Lesbos, an event celebrated by Milton in his *Lycidas* – another version of the speaking heads of the Celtic gods and Christian martyrs.

The way to heaven was through an ecstatic vision of God. An ascetic life of penance culminated in a religious celebration, in which wine and narcotics were used to induce the vision of the divine. The early ceremonies of the Orphic cult may have included Minoan and Anatolian sacrifices, where the blood of sheep and goats was poured from a jug into a cauldron in the ground. Later Orphics in Roman times were attracted by the Christian community, where wine was translated into Holy Blood as a means of absolution, of freeing the spirit from the flesh.

In Homer, the cult of Apollo, whose anger devastated the Greek camp outside Troy at the start of the *Iliad*, was associated with Κλάρος, a method of prophecy that used marked twigs taken from a bowl to show the divine will. Moreover, this was a way of dividing the spoils among the warlords by seeing who drew the long end, and not the short. At Delphi and Claros (probably the origin of its name), such a means of divination was common. It passed on to western Europe, for the Roman historian Tacitus noted that the Celtic and Germanic peoples divined the future by casting marked twigs. Also at Claros stood a blue-marble navel stone, the ὀμφαλος, the origin of this earth.

The temple there was so famous as an oracle that the Latin poet Ovid, in exile by the Black Sea, wrote of Clarian Apollo. The enquirers went underground to a sacred spring, where a male priest drank from the holy water and answered the question he was posed in a gnomic way. His trance may have been aided by the opium poppy or hemp or methane gas from the neighbouring marshes. Four rows of a hundred sacrificial stone blocks are buried there by the stubs of the fallen columns and headless statues of the ruined temple. They are the testament to a mass slaughter in a sacrament, involving a baptism and a communion of blood. Through that butchery, an insight might be reached on the divine will about the future.

The *taurobolium*, or bath in the gore of the great beast, would be adopted by the cult of the sun-god Mithras. The initiate was baptised above a perforated platform. Accused of stealing communion ceremonies about the Blood of Jesus from this pagan ritual, the Christian poet Prudentius left a full account of this crimson practice. The novice was put in a trench below some planks, which supported the slaughter of the bull.

He exposed his head and all his garments to be saturated with the blood; then he turned round and held up his neck that the blood might trickle upon his lips, ears, eyes, and nostrils; he moistened his tongue and the blood, which he then drank as a sacramental act. Greeted by the spectators, he came forth from this bloody baptism believing that he was purified from his sin and 'born again for eternity'. He was cleansed from the past and endowed with the principle of immortality.

After this ceremony, the initiate passed through seven grades, as in many later rituals. Jerome listed these as the Raven, the Hidden One, the Soldier, the Lion, the Persian, the Heliodromus or Sun-chaser, and the Father. Progress through the hierarchy was marked by branding and symbolic deaths, still a rite of passage of modern Masonry. The worship of the sun-god was the luminous spirit of the cult, which flourished in Rome under

Aurelian, who proclaimed the 'Invincible Sun', *Sol invictus*, as the protector of the imperial house.

Worship of the bull had derived from India and the Persian Mazdaists, who saw the world as a battleground between the forces of light and good and the powers of darkness and evil. Mithras was identified with the sun, the bringer of light to humanity, the mediator in the cosmic struggle. Other sources came from the Assyrians and the earth mother Cybele, whose lover Attis was castrated. The vengeful Bull of Heaven, sent by another primal earth goddess Ishtar, had been killed by the Babylonian hero and king Gilgamesh, who had spurned her divinity and lust. The genitals of the beast were eaten by many worshippers, while one ancient text stated, 'Reborn into eternity through bull sacrifice.'

The bovine head was held to represent the sun with its fiery eye, its horns spreading in rays of divine light. Herodotus described Apis as a bullock, whose godly mother could only conceive him from lightning, flashing from heaven. Moloch was depicted with a bestial head, and in the Orphic hymns, Bacchus was styled 'the deity with two horns, having the head of a bull'. The biblical Moses in medieval sculpture would even be given spikes of stone bone sprouting from his brow to represent twin rays of grace.

The widespread Mithraic chapels of the Roman Empire were often built underground or in caves

The upper section of a limestone stele from the Serapeum at Saqqara shows the Persian king Cambyses in the guise of an Egyptian pharaoh kneeling before the Apis bull.

with the signs of the zodiac set on mosaic floors. Part of the service was a communion with a consecrated cup and a loaf, symbols of the holy supper, which Mithras had taken with the sun after his time on earth. The Christians claimed that the followers of Mithras had stolen their Eucharist, although the reverse might have been true. A recent discovery in a cave beneath the ruins of a house in the Bosnian town of Jayce revealed some of the rites of the solar cult. In a carving, the god could be seen at the ritual sacrifice of a bull with a sun-disc behind his loose tunic. A dog was swallowing the blood of the beast as a symbol of the immortality of the soul. The reptile of resurrection, because it sloughed its skin from a renewed body, the Serpent of Wisdom was also shown, turning about the sword-arm of this divine killer.

As a religion that appealed mainly to the army, the Mithraic creed was similar to those of later medieval and modern military secret societies. They met in grottos that symbolised the universe; they used astrology and heavenly symbols; and they practised a form of equality, in which a sergeant could command a general. In Roman times, legates and *clarissimi* could find themselves the subordinates of legionaries in the brotherhood. Preferment from the ranks by mutual aid was an inducement to join in such classical mysteries, which appeared to solve the problematic passage between life and the hereafter. Apuleius wrote of his exalted invitation, that he approached the

A bronze Roman figure of Apis, showing on his horns the sun-disc and the Serpent of Wisdom.

confines of death: 'After being carried through all the elements, I returned to earth. At midnight I beheld the sun shining with its bright splendour. I penetrated into the very presence of the gods below and the gods above, where I worshipped face to face.'

The empires of Alexander the Great and of the Roman emperors were the conditions for the diaspora of modern religion in the West. The Persian cult of Mithras, the hermetic literature from Egypt and Babylon, the Stoic heritage and the Platonic influence, and the Jewish Torah with its stress on a single God, all met in the mixing-bowl of Alexandria. There the Cabbala encountered Gnosticism, alchemy fused with astrology, the Essenes-influenced Christianity. In a letter of 118 AC from the Emperor Hadrian to the Consul Servianus, the early Christians were even connected with the bull-worship of the pharaohs and the Romans:

> Those who call themselves Bishops of Christ are vowed to Serapis; there is no ruler of the Jewish Synagogue, no Samaritan, no priest of the Christians, who is not an astrologer, a diviner, and a charlatan. Their Patriarch himself, when he comes to Egypt, is by some forced to adore Serapis, and by others Christ. They have all but one God, Him the Christians worship, Him the Jews, Him all the Egyptians and those of all other nations.

One citizen, Philo of Alexandria, would combine the various sources of the divine Word or *Logos* into the Gospels, as the Grail romances would do. Plato had taught a doctrine of the human soul and an inscrutable Creator of the essence within all things. After his example, Posidonius wrote that the knowledge of God was transcendent, but possibly might be understood through a personal inquest into the divine. He influenced Lucretius and Virgil, Cicero and Seneca, the hermetic scribes and the Jewish Philo, who tried to reconcile the concept of a God, attainable by reason, yet also only by belief. As he commented on the revelation of Jehovah to Moses, 'Is it to be wondered at, if the Being defies the comprehension of men, when the spirit that is in each one is unknown?'

As with the later quest for the Grail, the search for the knowledge of God, which would ensure a life after death, preoccupied the Mediterranean peoples for the four centuries after the death of Christ upon the Cross. Against the knowledge and understanding of early Greek philosophy and science stood the faiths and the enlightened visions of the Near East. A deep inner experience opposed enquiry within defined limits. Only through a sense of connection with the divine intelligence might the many excursions towards a revelation, as St Paul had on the road to Damascus, be resolved.

These many routes to the hereafter explained the success of the flourishing Mystery religions of the time, before the Byzantine Empire instituted a state Christian Church and so condemned as heresies the hydra-headed variants on the official creed. Under severe penalty, all individual probes towards heaven would have to pass the scrutiny of bishop and priest-king. So spiritual adventures became the recitations of a set text.

After 372, the emperors Valentinian and Theodosius the First and the Second all proscribed the assemblies of Gnostics and Neoplatonists and other arcane religions. These went underground; yet the Byzantine Psellos affirmed that the Eleusinian Mysteries were still being practised in Athens in the 8th century and, even then, continued in secrecy. In Persia, the Mazdaists and other cultists were put to the sword by early Islam, while after St Augustine, the Church of Rome was credited with the deaths of 100,000 Manichees within 300 years. Further heretics such as the Cathari would imitate the Manichees in their three grades – Disciples and Auditors and Perfecti, an Elect group that was the priestly order of the sect, serving under twelve *Magistri* as a council. Like the Masons later, according to Epiphanus, the hidden members recognised each other by scratching the palm of a stranger's hand with a fingernail.

Along with Eastern doctrines, the cult of Mithras also brought to Europe the early knowledge of astrology. In the sourcebook of the Arthurian legend, Geoffrey of Monmouth would claim that at Carleon (or Camelot), there was 'a college of two hundred philosophers, who studied astronomy and other sciences; and who were particularly employed in watching the course of the stars, and predicting events to the King from these observations'. In the 6th-century poem *Lludd the Great*, the legendary Taliesin dealt with many prophecies, such as:

> Astronomers are predicting
> Misfortune in the land.

Two centuries on, the astrologer and logician Adhelm appeared; he had been taught in Greek and Latin by Theodore, the Archbishop of Canterbury, who came from Tarsus in Asia Minor. And Alcuin of York, the teacher of Charlemagne, advised the Holy Roman Emperor on 'the harmony of the sky', and how the stars and the planets might affect human actions. These ancient strands of enquiry would all inform the later Grail romances.

The Mithraic cult was also brought to Britain by the passage of 5,000 Sarmatian horsemen in 175 AC from the steppes through the Balkans as far as Hadrian's Wall with its barracks. With them was brought the worship of the patron sun-god of the whole Roman Empire, proclaimed by the Emperor Aurelian. Four Mithras altars and two legionary standards bearing the heads of bulls are still preserved in the museum at Maryport in Cumbria. Rudyard Kipling himself wrote a hymn to the beliefs of the 30th Legion, quartered on the Wall.

> Mithras, God of the Midnight, here where the
> great bull dies,
> Look on thy children in darkness. Oh take our
> sacrifice!
> Many roads thou has fashioned – all of them lead
> to the Light:
> Mithras, also a soldier, teach us to die aright!

In pagan and Celtic Britain, two major cults were already those of the severed head and the horned god. Along with the serpent and the stag, the bull and the ram were the divine symbols. Bulls' heads were also linked with hawks or eagles. The greatest of the supernatural bulls, the Donn of

Cuálnge in Ulster, had fifty youths playing on its back or leaping over it as in ancient Crete. An effort to rustle the mighty beast resulted in an Irish civil war.

Another creed from Persia provided a primary symbolism for the Grail. This was the preaching of Zoroaster, who believed that we all have a spark of the divine fire within us, a message that would pass through the Balkans to influence the later Cathar heretics in Provence. Born in Shiz, the capital of the Sassanian Empire, the Persian magus told of the Gohar. Above the bowl of the heavens, the globe or cosmos hovered in space. Representations of such a shape for the Grail exist in a painting in Nuremberg of Mary Magdalene dropping a pearl into a golden vase for the benefit of the infant Christ, also on a Templar chalice tombstone with an Arabic inscription in the church in Corstorphine in Scotland.

In the medieval romance *The Young Titurel*, the Temple of the Grail stood on an onyx Mount of Salvation, built in the round beneath a golden dome on which jewelled constellations blazed above a mechanical gold sun and silver moon. In the early 7th century, the Persian King Chosroes the Second had built just such a palace on the holy mountain of Shiz, where there was a previous circular sanctuary of sacred fire in memory of Zoroaster, whose Manichean beliefs influenced the Gnostics and the alchemists. This circular palace of precious metals and stones showed the heavens, which were rotated by teams of horses pulling ropes from sunken pits below. Mineral deposits from a crater lake made the mountain gleam as if onyx. This early planetarium was called the Throne of Arches, the Takt-i-Taqdis; twenty-two ornate arches surrounded the central mound, the same number of lesser temples that encircled the main hall of the Grail Castle in *The Young Titurel*. Unfortunately, the Byzantine Emperor Heraclius defeated Chosroes, tore down the Takt and took back the True Cross, which Chosroes had removed there after his seizure of Jerusalem. An early crusade to recapture the True Cross was well known in medieval Europe and served as material for the songs of the troubadours.

Prehistoric bull-god painting from the grotto of Trois Frères, Ariège, Pyrénées, France.

The courts of Charlemagne and the Norman kings could read in Latin translation some of the old Greek romances about the career of Alexander the Great. By the 12th century, particularly in the *Alexandreis* of Walter of Châtillon, the deeds of the Greek hero rivalled the tales of Troy as sources for parts of the Grail romances. Alexander was legendary as a universal ruler in the Near East long before the crusaders arrived, and his empire was presented as superior to the Roman one. He had wished to be worshipped as divine, and the stories about him made him appear both as a warrior and a god.

As a matter of fact, when Alexander had died in Babylon, his embalmed body was placed in a temple on wheels to be dragged back to Greece. His divine remains were diverted to Alexandria, where a mausoleum was built to house them. He had expressed the wish to be buried at the Oracle of Siwa, where another meteorite – as in the Ka'aba at Mecca – was the stone of prophecy. This one was beset with local emeralds, exactly as the green *lapis exilis* fallen from heaven would be represented as the Grail in Wolfram von Eschenbach's *Parzival*. When the Alexandria mausoleum was burned, the holy corpse was said to have been spirited away to Siwa, where the oracle had prophesied that the Greek general would become a god.

Certainly, the legend of Alexander would join those of Arthur and Charlemagne to represent the three paladins of medieval chivalry. And another common source, the fall of Troy, was accessible in *The Aeneid* of Virgil, who had taken some of his poem from Homer's *Iliad* and *Odyssey* as well as the exploits of Alexander. His Latin epic dealt less with the trials of the soul than with a particular quest in order to fulfil a divine purpose. Although Aeneas also reached the Land of the Dead, he discovered there the answer to his life's work, the creation of the Roman Empire. So fable was turned into the forecast of history. This epic would serve as an inspiration for the later Holy Roman Empire and the unity of Christendom.

At her feast for Aeneas, Queen Dido of Carthage produced 'a golden bowl, that shone with gems divine'. Filled with wine, it was used by all the priestly rulers of her country. Jupiter and Bacchus were invoked by its presence. In John Dryden's translation, the ceremony was described thus:

> The goblet then she took, with nectar crowned
> (Sprinkling the first libations on the ground),
> And raised it to her mouth with sober grace,
> Then, sipping, offered to the next in place.

This cup of worship and peace was passed round all the guests in a form of communion, and was later used by Dido to pour wine in marriage vows to Aeneas before other oaths to Juno, Bacchus and Ceres, holding a cornucopia, a horn of plenty, in her hand. Deserted by Aeneas on his mission towards Rome, Dido committed suicide, only to encounter her lost lover again in Hades, which he had penetrated by nipping off a golden bough of mistletoe in a sacred oak grove, led there by two doves. All these later symbols of the Grail culminated in the curing of the wound of Aeneas, who had been pierced by a dart, at the touch of the goddess mother Venus. She had brought dittany from Crete and brewed it with ambrosia:

> Unseen she stands,
> Tempering the mixture with her heavenly hands,
> And pours it in a bowl, already crowned.

The holy and healing cups and bowls of Virgil derived from the Greek Mysteries, as did so many of the Latin gods. Some of the central myths of the Norse gods also seemed to originate from Greece, as well as the prehistoric cults of an earth goddess. In the accounts of Valhalla, the *Prose Edda* of the Icelander Snorri Sturluson told of a steaming cauldron named Eldhrímnir, which always served the pork of the everlasting boar Sæhrímnir with his renewable flesh, while the eternal goat Heiórún gave bubbling mead from her teats for the drinking horns of the gods at their perpetual feast. Other Nordic sagas told of great feasts, at which cattle were sacrificed; their blood was splattered over the food, and toasts were given in ale to the goddess Freyr and the supreme Odin. At the annual gathering of the Althing in Iceland, a bull was sacrificed and its blood was sprinkled within the sacred circle, used for binding oaths.

When Thor, the mighty thunder god, was challenged to a drinking bout by the underworld Loki, he could not drain his horn because its end was in the ocean; but he created the tides and the foreshore by his swallowings. The mead cauldron of Ymir inspired strength and wisdom in all who drank from it. These legends of gargantuan bounty were supported by earlier charms to the northern goddess of fertility:

Aeneas is healed by the sacred cup and bowl of the mother goddess. *(From engravings designed by Francis Cleyn and executed by Wenceslaus Hollar and Pierre Lambert for John Dryden's translations of Vergil's* Aeneid, London, 1692)

Erce, Erce, Erce, Mother of Earth . . .
Hail to thee, Earth, mother of men!
Be fruitful in God's embrace,
Filled with food for the use of men.

Although the Nordic Frigg or Freyr was not more powerful than Odin, the ruler of the gods, she was similar to Ceres as the goddess of birth and the seasons. And the northern Adonis, the god Balder, had strange affinities with the crucified Christ and the legend of the Fisher King. All things were asked never to harm him, but the blind Hodhr threw a shaft of mistletoe at him and pierced him, so that he died until he was resurrected at the end of the world.

In the 10th-century poem *The Dream of the Rood*, Christ was portrayed on a jewelled cross brilliant with light. He was being killed by many men piercing him with shafts until His Blood flowed. His Body was raised by his followers and

The prehistoric figure of the Venus
of Willendorf.

encased in gold and silver, as His Blood would be
in a multitude of reliquaries. Earlier runes on the
Ruthwell Cross quoted *The Dream of the Rood* in
reference to the killing of Balder by missiles
thrown into His Body.

The similarity between the myth of
Balder bleeding from the shaft sent by the
blind Hodhr, and the Gospel account of
Christ pierced in his side by the Holy
Lance of the blind centurion, later called
St Longinus, was remarkable. And so was
the myth of the bleeding wound of the
Fisher King that was made by a lance
and incurable except by the right
answer of a Knight of the Grail. Such
Nordic beliefs may well have derived
from the teaching of the Druids or
from the older cult of an earth
goddess, as shown in the obese figurine
of the Aurignacian Venus of Willendorf.

Certainly, Celtic cults were developed
from Druid worship and influenced the
sagas of the Arthurian court, which would in
turn have their effect on the later Norse sagas.
Blessed vessels were created by the metalwork
expertise of the Celtic smiths. The Cimbri sent to
the Emperor Augustus as a gift 'the most sacred
cauldron in their country'. As part of a series of
Belgic pit burials in Kent at the time of Caesar's
invasion of Britain, the ornamental Aylesford
Bucket was used in the ceremonies of death and
rebirth.

Moreover, the famous silver-plated bowl of the
1st century, the Gunderstrup Cauldron, was em-
bossed with a Druidic scene of sacrifice and
regeneration. Dead warriors from an underworld
formed a queue to be given life by a mediatory
god, who was plunging a prisoner head first into a
vessel shaped like the female pudenda. Contemporary Roman writers told of Celtic human
sacrifices, who were suffocated in a tub of blood,

over which others had their heads severed, but the
Gunderstrup scene may only represent a ritual
baptism for the resurrection of the departed.

The most ancient sacrificial stones of all, such as
the Knowth Stone in County Meath dating from
2500 BC, were used for the ritual slaughter of
beasts and people, as they were in classical antiquity.

The Irish Druids believed that the soul resided in the brain, an organ so venerated in early myth that the wounded Bran the Blessed asked his companions to sever his head and bury it in Britain to act as a talking oracle – the role of Mimir from his well in Norse legend. And the Dagda, the father of the ancient Irish gods, had a cauldron of plenty named Undri, which fed all the hungry. His gigantic club also had the property of the Holy Lance: it could heal as well as kill.

Other forefathers of the children of Danu, who were said to have populated Ireland from four fabulous cities, were Nuada or Nodens, and Lug or Ludd. These legendary settlers brought with them other symbols of the Grail as well as the magic cauldron: Lia Fa'il or the Stone of Destiny; the Gorian sword which was forged before Excalibur; and the Finian Spear of Victory. Lug, who may have given his name to London, where Bran's head was believed to live on Tower Hill, was a sun-god such as Mithras. The seizing of the fiery Spear by the Irish hero Brian was another prophecy of the Grail legends, for he killed the royal owner and took the weapon from a boiling cauldron.

The last stand of the Druids took place on Holy Island, off Anglesey, and Irish and Welsh traditions

Dead warriors lining up to be plunged into the cauldron of rebirth. From the silver-gilt Gunderstrup Cauldron, about 1st century AD. *(National Museum, Copenhagen, Denmark)*

would inform most of the Arthurian legends. The summary by the great authority, Roger Sherman Loomis, defined the ancient Celtic roots of the Grail:

> It is possible on the Celtic hypothesis to account for the precise form of the vessel, namely a deep platter – its properties of miraculous feeding, of selecting those whom it will feed, of prolongation of youth and life; the bleeding spear and adventures connected with it; the broken sword miraculously mended; the magic ship in which Galahad, Perceval and Bors voyaged; Perceval's sister; the Loathly Damsel; the Siege Perilous; the Maimed King; the visits of Gawain and Perceval to his castle; the question test; Gawain's wakening in the open; the names of the Grail Kings and Grail heroes; the introduction of Joseph of Arimathea, and many other details.

Ancient and pagan beliefs were the sources that filled the many Grails in their genesis.

THREE

KING ARTHUR: WHERE FACT MET LEGEND

I have heaped together all that I have found from the annals of the Romans, the writings of the Holy Fathers, and the traditions of our own old men.

Nennius, *Historia Britonum, c.* 800

The enduring tragedy of the early Christian Church was the imposition in the 5th century of state control by Byzantium and Rome. The consequences would be catastrophic. Faiths were upended into heresies. For a thousand years, Greek and Latin orthodoxy would force a hundred sects into two ways of worship; but when the Reformation came, thousands of rebellious creeds would proliferate, as bees from the honey-trap of the skull of the lion, slain by Samson. What was lost by imperial control were the beliefs of the martyred saints and slaves in a victim saviour Christ like the Fisher King, not a militant one; in a free congregation, which elected its own priests, who might be women; and in the direct contact of each person in the flock with the divine.

During the spread of early Christianity, there was a multitude of interpretations of what the Gospels meant. Many of the Gnostic texts were excluded from the final Bible. One of them, *The Epistle to Rheginos*, began by stating that there were some who wanted to learn much, but they were occupied with questions that had no answers. They had not stood within the Word or *Logos* of Truth. They sought their own solution, which could only come through Jesus Christ, who had denied death, although that was the law of humankind. 'Those who are living shall die. How do they live in an illusion? The rich have become poor and the kings have been overthrown, everything has to change. The cosmos is an illusion.' All was a process, the

transformation of things into newness, which would create a heaven from a corrupt society.

The authors of the Gnostic texts chose insight rather than the sermons of early Christian bishops as the way to interpret the Gospels and reach revelation. On this count, they were denounced in the late 2nd century by St Irenaeus for 'inventing something new every day'. His chief target was Justin Martyr, who had been a Stoic and a Platonist before becoming a Christian philosopher. Justin praised the heresies of Simon Magus, the magician and enemy of St Paul, while Christ was treated as the Word, who mediated between the sinful earth and the light of paradise.

These inspirations were called Gnosis, which now came to mean a personal vision, a direct and individual perception of truth. The first appearance of Jesus to Mary Magdalene in the garden after his crucifixion was interpreted in her apocryphal Gospel as no actual event or even a spiritual flash; she saw him in her mind. This vision she reported to his disciples. They could now see the risen Christ as she had; any believer could see him. Of course, the direct approach to Christian revelation put in doubt all religious authority. Why listen to a bishop if an inner voice told you what Christ wanted you to hear?

In St Mark's Gospel, it was stated that Jesus had given the disciples the secret of the kingdom of God, while he spoke to the rest of the world in parables. While St Peter and St Paul professed to pass on these secrets to the Churches later established in Rome and Byzantium, the Gnostic gospels claimed that the living Jesus could at any time reveal his hidden mysteries to a woman who was not even a disciple. He could appear to Mary Magdalene, who represented the ancient female principle of generation, and to the Sophia, the goddess of wisdom. He would show himself to the person who was fit to see and hear the divine message.

For the Gnostics, there were two distinct worlds, split by a war zone and a veil between heaven and earth. On the shining and dividing screen were the pictures of things, created by the *Logos* and interpreted by Christ. Flaming walls separated wisdom from matter with angels as messengers across the horizon between sky and sea and land. The problem of evil allowed by a just God was solved, for life below was already a hell.

While the Christians were still secret sects persecuted by the Roman Empire, such heresies could flourish among a larger heresy. Yet after Constantine established Christianity as the official faith, these subversive cults, which declared that authority was evil, had to be extirpated. Yet the Byzantine emperor would call his new basilica Sancta Sophia, not after any saint, but after the wise goddess.

The more extreme of the sects were persecuted – the Ophites, who worshipped the wise serpent; the Adamites, who held their ceremonies in the nude; and the Cainites, who cast aside all civil authority for the veneration of Cain, who was carrying out the divine will by killing his brother Abel, as well as of Judas, who was ordained to denounce Jesus. As St Irenaeus wrote of the teaching of the Gnostic 'Gospel of Judas', 'He alone was acquainted with the truth as no others were, and so accomplished the mystery of betrayal. By him all things, both earthly and heavenly, were thrown into dissolution.'

For the philosophers of the Cabbala, the Shekinah was the Sophia, the principle of the Divine Mother united with God, and eternal and indivisible. As St Irenaeus also wrote of the Gnostics, they said that the Sophia spoke of Jesus descending from 'the incorruptible light of heaven'. The Sophia was also the serpent in the Garden of Eden, which brought wisdom with the apple to Eve and Adam, and led to their expulsion from paradise to a Satanic earth.

A wise religion has always adopted the pagan. Deviant beliefs and old myths can be converted into a divine creed. In the Grail legends, the ancient tales of cauldrons of creation and horns of plenty and female bearers of all bounty would be transmuted in the Middle Ages to Christian chalices without bottom in their giving of food and drink. Yet the Greek and Latin Churches would never quite swallow the quest for the Grail. For this search derived from the worst of heresies, which was preached in the Near East and in Britain before the time of King Arthur.

The great offence to the Bishop of Rome was the idea of a direct approach to God without the intercession of the Church. In the early 5th century, two Celtic monks, Pelagius and Coelestius, were banished from the Holy City for preaching that through their deeds, human beings could perfect themselves. There was no original sin, as St Augustine was arguing. Therefore a priest, who might absolve sins, was unnecessary. The believer could reach heaven by his acts alone on a sinful earth. 'Everything good, and everything evil,' Pelagius wrote, 'for which we are either praised or blamed, is not born with us, but done by us.'

This doctrine was condemned by the Council of Ephesus, because it denied state authority over the Church. In Celtic countries, about 540, the monk Gildas wrote in *The Loss and Conquest of Britain* of 'the general destruction of everything good and the general growth of everything evil throughout the land'. Yet one hero led the resistance, a cavalry commander with a Roman name, Ambrosius Aurelianus. Although he was brave on foot, Gildas wrote, Ambrosius was braver still on horseback. He defeated the Saxons in the northeast, but he could not drive them from their southern territories and downs. The counter-attack

Christ in the garden with Mary Magdalene. A grail lies beside her. (*Church of St Lawrence, Strasbourg*)

ended in the siege of Mons Badonicus. The commander at this battle was not named by Gildas, but in the contemporary *Easter Annals*, a historical miscellany that still survives in the British Museum; an entry in about 518 reads: 'Battle of Badon, in which Arthur carried the cross of our Lord Jesus Christ on his shoulders for three days and three nights, and the Britons triumphed.'

King Arthur was a Celtic war commander and a hero among the native peoples of Cornwall, Wales, Ireland and southern Scotland. A different Byzantine rite had passed from the Mediterranean along the old tin trade routes to these Celtic civilisations. From that Greek learning, the Irish monasteries were becoming the leading lights of what were later miscalled the Dark Ages. They were sending missionaries, pilgrim saints and hermits after the example of the desert Christian Fathers to Wales, the Isle of Man and Scotland. St Petroc carried the faith to the west of England and Brittany where Celtic refugees had already fled from the Anglo-Saxons: many churches were named after him. St Samson also sailed to Cornwall and Brittany with his Irish chariot; his voyage was commemorated on a stained-glass window in the Cathedral of Dol. St Columba brought the Irish Word of God to the west of Scotland and the north of England; St Guillermus carried it to what would be called Normandy.

Other pilgrim saints reached Galicia in Spain, and Orkney, the Shetlands, the Faroes and even Iceland. And St Columbanus took the Irish influence deep into France and Italy itself. His foundation of the original monastery of St Etienne in Nevers in about 600 is commemorated there: though it was taken over by Benedictines during the Cluniac reform of the 11th century, a magnificent Grail window still shows a holy lamp burning above the sun-disc at the back of the head of Christ at the Last Supper, blessing the bread of His Body on a golden platter, and a bowl of wine.

The most ancient church in England, the wattle building at Glastonbury, was traditionally founded in 433 by St Patrick himself; his supposed bones were placed in a stone pyramid covered with gold and silver by the high altar of the first abbey. Other Celtic saints followed him there – notably Columba, Brigit and Benignus – and Glastonbury, or 'the glassy isle', became a mirror for the faith of pilgrims crossing the Irish Sea. The influence of the Greek rite there was proved by the recent excavation of a Byzantine censer on the edge of the abbey precinct, also the presence of Gnostic heresy in the jasper episcopal ring carved with a serpent god, belonging to the Abbot Seffrid Pelochin and still on display at Chichester Cathedral.

Although Glastonbury gave way to the Roman influence after the Synod of Whitby, its Celtic past made it continually revered. The Chalice Well and the Tor were held by the Welsh to be manifestations of Annwn, the Otherworld, while St David was also said to have been a visitor. Certainly, the *Anglo-Saxon Chronicle* reported that the Pope sent a piece of the True Cross to King Alfred, who then reputedly presented it to the abbey. Its relics would make it, in William of Malmesbury's words, a 'heavenly sanctuary on earth'. Among them would be manna and parts of the rods of Moses and Aaron; the bones of St John the Baptist and the milk of the Virgin Mary; and many sacred remains of the Passion, including a nail from the Cross. There was no Grail in early times, however, in spite of the abbey's later identification with the coming of Joseph of Arimathea to Britain, and with Avalon and the death of King Arthur.

An old Cornish legend asserted that Joseph arrived there with his relative, the boy Jesus, and taught him how to extract tin and purge it of its wolfram. According to Herodotus and Diodorus Siculus, the tin trade did exist between Phoenicia and Cornwall in those times. Certainly, the guild of the Cornish tinners used to shout after the metal was flashed: 'Joseph was in the trade.' In Somerset the story was that Christ and Joseph came by ship from Tarshish and stayed in Summerland, another name for the county, and in a place called Paradise. The people of Priddy on the top of the Mendip Hills, the centre of ancient copper and lead mining, also believed that the two holy men spent time in the village. And there was the enduring creed at Glastonbury of the final visit of Joseph with the Grail containing Christ's Blood, which he is meant to have dropped into the prehistoric Chalice Well. His grave was conveniently discovered there in medieval times, as were the tombs of King Arthur and Guinevere. Over the Arimathean's bones was an inscription: I CAME TO THE BRITONS AFTER I BURIED CHRIST. I TAUGHT. I REST.

To this faith was added the legend of another visit by Joseph with the young Jesus. St Augustine believed the story well enough to write to Pope Gregory that on 'a royal island' to the west, the first missionaries from Rome found a wattle church 'constructed by no human art, but by the hands of Christ Himself, for the salvation of His people'. Allegedly, Joseph had been granted twelve hides of land by the local pagan king, Arviragus, to build his church. This grant appeared to be confirmed by folios from the Norman Domesday Book: 'The Home of God, in the great Monastery of Glastonbury, called the secret of The Lord. This Glastonbury church possesses in its own Villa XII hides of land which have never paid tax.'

The Celtic religious renaissance was based on the Atlantic sea routes, and was set against the authority of Mediterranean Rome. It was spread by holy pilgrims and hermits, the apostles of the later Grail romances, preaching resistance to the Nordic, Germanic and later Arabic assaults on the Celtic folk. It demanded a political hero, who would defend his people and their independent faith from their enemies. It chose Arthur, the *dux bellorum* or war leader mentioned in the 8th century by the Welsh monk Nennius as the victor of twelve battles, ending in a final defeat in 539 described in the *Easter Annals*: 'The Battle of Camlann, in which Arthur and

Joseph of Arimathea holding two sacred vessels, depicted in a 15th-century stained-glass window in All Saints' Church, Langport, Somerset.

Medraut [Mordred] perished. And there was a plague in Britain and Ireland.'

In centuries of Grail studies, the actual process of Christian belief in Arthur's Britain has been ignored. If he carried the image of Jesus on his banner at the siege of Badon, what might the Son of God say to him? If he were a Pelagian, if he rode with the contemporary Celts for their independence against the Anglo-Saxons who were being converted to Rome, then he might have followed the words from the Sermon on the Mount in the Gospel of St Matthew: 'Be ye therefore perfect, even as your Father which is in heaven is perfect.'

For the heresy of salvation through good works was the inspiration for the knights on the quest for the Grail. By his virtue, each member of the Round Table might reach the light of God and the Holy Spirit without the need of a priest to absolve his sins. These wandering mailed horsemen were advised on their way to the Grail Castle by holy men, modelled on the travelling Celtic preachers who were spreading their independent faith over the northern Atlantic seaboard.

In the first Grail romance by Chrétien de Troyes, Perceval was put on the right path for his return to the Grail Castle by his hermit uncle, who told him that the wounded Fisher King lived only on the communion host, which reached him directly from heaven and the Holy Spirit, not through the Church of Rome. The legends of Arthur and the Grail were to enshrine the resistance of many peoples to the authority of the Holy See. That is why they would prove so popular in their spread across Europe, until by the 12th century, the Prior of Tewkesbury could state that the praise of Arthur had reached even the Near East.

Above: The mysteries of Dionysus, pictured on the Romano-British Great Bowl of Mildenhall. *(British Museum)*

Right: King Arthur bids farewell to his knights as they leave on the quest for the Grail, and he greets them on their return. *(13th-century French illustration)*

Mary Magdalene depicted on an 8th century Ruthwell Cross washing the feet of Christ. *(By an unknown Anglo-Saxon sculptor)*

Rome was to try and take over the legend of King Arthur and the Grail, although it was heretical. This was because the stories of Camelot and chivalry would inspire the crusaders to the Levant. Pope Gregory the Great had been happy to substitute the pagan for the Christian in England. As he wrote to his envoy Abbot Mellitus:

> I have come to the conclusion that the temples of the idols in England should not on any account be destroyed. Augustine must smash the idols, but the temples themselves should be sprinkled with holy water and altars set up in them in which relics are to be enclosed. For we ought to take advantage of well-built temples by purifying them from devil-worship and dedicating them to the service of the true God. In this way, I hope the people (seeing their temples are not destroyed) will leave their idolatry and yet continue to frequent the places as formerly, so coming to know and revere the true God.

Perhaps the Great Bowl of the silver Mildenhall Treasure, now in the British Museum, exemplified the papal wisdom. Among its 4th-century praise of Dionysus and Pan and the demigods and nymphs pouring pitchers of plenty or opening the lids of vases of bounty, Christian fish symbols already burst from the beard and locks of the central sun-god Mithras. The one religion used the other to infiltrate the new faith.

Yet in the later case of the Grail, the attempt of Rome to sanctify the legends would be half-hearted. Arthur and the Knights of the Round Table would not be ingested, as were other cults of protest. At the time of the historical Arthur, his stance as the Celtic leader in war and faith was clear. He stood against the authority of imperial Rome, which had abandoned its dominions to the ravages of the pagans, although these might later be converted by Christian Rome. To all the emperors and kings who would need to

He is only a little less known to the people of Asia than to the Britons, as we are informed by the pilgrims who return from the Eastern lands. The peoples of the East speak of him, as they do in the West . . . Rome, queen of cities, sings of his acts, while his wars are known in its former rival Carthage. Antioch, Armenia and Palestine celebrate his deeds.

resist the Holy See, Arthur would become the symbol of that opposition.

The roles of the Irish saints Columba and Columbanus, as bearers of the Greek and Gnostic doctrines of the divine light, are wreathed in history. In his early account, Adamman, the Abbot of Iona, who died in 704, declared that St Brendan saw 'a most brilliant pillar wreathed with fiery flares' preceding his fellow saint. A side chapel was filled with light by Columba, and nobody could look on him any more than on the midday sun. As the saint told another novice, 'Take care of one thing, my child, that you do not attempt to spy out and pry too closely into the nature of that heavenly light which was not granted thee.' And another peeper through the keyhole of the saint's cell was told that if prayers had not been said for him, he would have fallen dead before the door, or had his blinded eyes torn from their sockets. With Columba's death, the whole vault of heaven was illuminated, while an immense pillar of fire rose to the stars at midnight, so that the earth was as bright as under the summer sun at noon.

Such a confusion of the Irish missionary Columba with the sun-god Mithras heralded his coming to his famous monastery in Iona. There, the saint was also meant to have blessed a knife for the slaughter of bulls, although he hoped that it would not injure man or beast. Equally in the 6th century, from St Andrews to the Orcadian Isles, an anchorite and monastic movement of Irish monks, the Célidé or Culdees, established early Christian and Eastern Greek practices in the first Scottish church, independent of Rome, before the Reformation. Their Greek names as priests, *papas*, are still commemorated on Papa Stour in Shetland and Papa Westray in Orkney.

These early differences were backed by later letters to the Pope, written by the Celtic St Columbanus, who took his mission from Ireland through Burgundy to Bobbio in Italy. He told Gregory the Great and Boniface the Fourth that they had limited authority, which did not extend to the Celtic Christian ways of worship. In his most famous letter, Columbanus disagreed on the dates of Easter. He was grieved at the ill repute of

the contemporary chair of St Peter in Rome. 'It may be that in this affair, a living dog is better than a dead lion. For a living saint may correct the errors that have not been corrected by another greater one.' He also protested that the Celts were the recipients of pure and early Christianity. 'For all we Irish living at the uttermost ends of the earth are the disciples of Saint Peter and Saint Paul and of all the disciples who wrote the sacred canon under the inspiration of the Holy Spirit: receiving nothing outside the evangelical and apostolical doctrine.'

What is certain is that the tradition of Arthur was taken up by the Celtic bards to create the legend of a conquering hero, who would reflect his fame on to his people. Already by the 7th century, four British royal families had given a son the name of Arthur. He became the Matter of Britain, as opposed to the Matter of France, which glorified Charlemagne, the supreme emperor. And there was also the Matter of the classical age of Homer and Virgil, the heroes of Troy and Rome, and of Alexander the Great. These bardic tales would provide the synthesis of the European romances of the Middle Ages, where the Mediterranean heritage met the British, French and German to create the stories of the personal search for the divine.

The actual Celtic Grails which existed from Arthur's time were hanging bowls, not communion chalices in the hands of priests. These round bronze pendants, ornamented with enamel and scrollwork, have been discovered in Warwickshire and Lincolnshire; also three at the sumptuous ship burial at Sutton Hoo, made by a master smith for the East Anglian court. On one bowl, there are six red enamel medallions on the sides, while on the lid appears an emblem of early Christianity – the fish, a Greek acronym of the name Jesus Christ. Simpler metal vessels, which hung over hearths and fires, had held the daily food of hunting and gathering peoples for dozens of centuries. Pieces of game and roots were added to the top of the stockpot, which, if replenished, provided an inexhaustible supply of soup and stew. This was the material origin of the Celtic Grails, which would feed all who came to them. Perhaps the last vestige of that tradition of a flowing bowl is the stirrup cup, still passed round from saddle to saddle at a modern hunt.

In the early Welsh legends of Arthur, however, the King led his knights on a raid to seize the Spoils of Annwn, including a magic cauldron of rebirth. This lay in another world, or Faerie Fortress, as the Grail Castle would lie. The rim of the cauldron was ornamented in the style of contemporary hanging bowls with dark-blue enamel and pearls. As a bardic poem of the time, *Culhwch and Olwen*, declared, the cauldron could provide meat and drink for everybody. Yet in this version, Arthur filled it with the treasures of Ireland and took it back from that country to his own. And in the Taliesin poems, another cauldron, that of Ceridwen, gave him divine inspiration and wisdom, when he licked three drops of the boiling brew in the iron vessel off his fingers.

In later imperial times, trade would follow the flag. But in the 12th century, song followed the sword. The few who could read in the age of Arthur and in the successive centuries were mainly priests, and the language was Latin. Most people were illiterate. They saw or heard what they thought, and they thought that was what they knew. In ancient Greece, Homer and the bards, who succeeded him at the courts of the later warlords of Europe, sang of the exploits of past heroes, whose deeds were already swaddled in legend. In the French and British fiefdoms of the Normans, the Welsh and Breton bards and troubadours were predominant. They were like Widsith in the early English poem of the Far Traveller, who claimed to have sung all over Europe and the Near East. He glorified his peers:

> Thus wandering, the minstrels travel as chance will have it through the lands of many different peoples. Always they are bound to come across, in the north or the south, some person who is touched by their song and is generous with his gifts, who will increase his reputation in front of his henchmen showing his nobility of spirit before worldly things pass away, the light and the life. He who works for his own good

name will be rewarded on earth by a strong and steady fame.

After the Dark Ages, Celtic minstrels were moving through the Atlantic areas, spreading the legends of Arthur and his companions. Transcendent among them at the court of Poitou was the Welshman Bleheris. He was the 'fabulous translator' of Arthurian legend into Norman French, and he was commemorated by two rivals as someone who knew the history of all the counts and all the kings of Britain, and 'all the stories of the Grail'.

The term troubadour derived from the Provençal word *trobar*, to compose, to seek and to find. In that sense, the lays of the minstrels were quests for the Grail put to words and music. Certainly, their art was influenced by oriental singers from Spain as much as by Celtic bards or classical legends. Arabesques, with their tantalising sadness, became part of their technique, and the pilgrims and knights who set out for Palestine repeated the refrains. The wandering minstrels were the entertainers and reporters of their age, which could not always distinguish between fancy and fact.

The pilgrim Celtic saints had converted the Atlantic seaboard to the Greek rite. Now the Welsh and Breton troubadours spread the word of King Arthur, his exploits and his empire from the ocean through the continent by word of mouth. A written French text, derived from the Welsh or Breton Geoffrey of Monmouth's Latin version of *The History of the Kings of Britain*, was set down by Wace of Jersey in the Channel Islands. He dedicated his creative translation of the Matter of Britain, *Roman de Brut*, to Eleanor of Aquitaine, the wife of Henry the Second of England and Normandy. With her possessions, the King could be the sovereign of an Anglo-French empire almost as large as that of Arthur, which Monmouth's text

The adventurous romances of the Quest of the Grail, as would be written by a monk, quill and horn inkwell in hand. *(Ebbo Gospels, c. 835)*

claimed as stretching from Britain to the Rhine. Wace added to the story the legend of the Round Table, which he had heard from other Celtic sources, and ended his account with the hope that the undying King Arthur would be resurrected when his people might need him.

These two seminal texts were copied out hundreds of times in the next centuries before the arrival of printing. But in this illiterate era, it was the wandering minstrels who spread the word of Arthur, using Geoffrey of Monmouth and Wace as cue sheets. Since the time of Homer, flattering bards had been the chief entertainers of the courts. From Poitou and Aquitaine, the fame of Arthur reached Italy, probably with the Breton contingent assembling at Bari for the First Crusade. The early 12th-century arch over the north door of Modena Cathedral portrayed Arthur of Britain, called Artus, and his knights as they rode to deliver the Queen of Camelot from the Dolorous Tower.

In 1165, a mosaic was laid in the cathedral of Otranto, near Bari, showing Arturus Rex carrying a sceptre and riding a goat. At the end of the century, Gervase of Tilbury visited the Norman court in Sicily and reported that King Arthur had been sighted living in the fiery crater of Mount Etna, that natural Cauldron of Annwn. Again, the Normans of the time were struggling with the papacy for control of southern Italy, and the myth of Arthur's return suited their aggressive diplomacy.

The spreading of the stories of Arthur and his knights over Europe and the Near East was the seedbed of the Grail. The age of the crusades yearned for a holy mission as well as a justification for taking over new lands in the Mediterranean. Papal blessing for the counter-attack on Islam and the capture of the Kingdom of Jerusalem was not enough, for the Norman, Frankish and German emperors, kings, dukes and counts were often opposed to the political aims of the papacy, which strove to assert its authority over all secular powers. What the chivalry of Europe demanded was a sacred quest that sanctified individual bloody actions without the need for absolution from the Catholic Church, which might withhold the shriving of sins for the benefit of its wily strategy.

For Rome denied the giving of communion to lay people in the 13th century. The Body and Blood of Christ, the host and the chalice were reserved for the priest. In the *Perlesvaus*, King Arthur saw a vision of the Grail in five forms, but its true shape was withheld from him by religious prohibition. 'For the secrets of the sacrament none should tell, save he whom God has granted grace.' As Synesius, the Bishop of Ptolemais, had written: 'The truth must be kept secret, and the masses need a teaching proportioned to their imperfect reason.'

FOUR

THE KRATER OF ALCHEMY

What else can we see in the Grail but a bundle of paradoxes?

It is visible and invisible; an object – cup, vessel, or stone – and not an object; a person and not a person – neither male nor female; it dispenses earthly food or celestial; it inspires love, it inspires terror; it embodies predestination, but requires, nevertheless, individual effort. These, of course, are the paradoxes of the Divine, and they have found in the Grail symbol a perfect representation – so perfect, indeed, that the Grail, like the Divine, baffles description, remaining an imageless image.

Helen Adolf, *Visio Pacis*

he antecedents of the Grail legends grew through folk consciousness and the power of myths as role models. As the faithful may try to imitate Christ, so the peoples of past ages sought inspiration in the examples of Apollo and Alexander, King Arthur and Charlemagne, and Hermes Trismegistus. The historical truth of their lives was insignificant in traditional ages, which fed on fables and magic and dreams. Reason had little to do with such glitter for the mind. The cutting edge of early science was alchemy. Like so many early faiths, the art developed in the eastern Mediterranean. Mercury was distilled from cinnabar, but its changeable nature allowed it to make an amalgam with other metals, and yet again to be distilled from them. It appeared to be as the divine intelligence, and so it became a property of the wise Hermes, the messenger of the gods, and of the legendary Trismegistus, who was said to have inscribed on an Emerald Tablet the mystery of this scientific enquiry. The troops of Alexander the Great were meant to have discovered the Phoenician text in a cave near Hebron or in the Great Pyramid at Gîza; but the only translations to survive are medieval versions. One of the best is from the 12th-century *The Emerald Tablet of Hermes*:

True it is, without falsehood, certain most true. That which is above is like to that which is below, and that which is below is like to that which is above, to accomplish the miracles of one thing. And as all things come from the contemplation of one, so all things arose from this one thing by a single act of adaptation.

The father thereof is the Sun, the mother the Moon.

The Emerald Tablet of Hermes Trismegistus. At the top of the medallion of the Order of the Rosy Cross, the sun and the moon pour fire and the elixir of life into the cosmic cup. *(From Geheime Figuren der Rosenkreuzer, Altona, 1785)*

The wind carried its womb, the earth is the source thereof. It is the father of all works of wonder throughout the world.

The power thereof is perfect.

If it be cast on to earth, it will separate the element of earth from that of fire, the subtle from the gross.

With great sagacity it ascends gently from earth to heaven. Again it descends to earth and unites in itself the force from things superior and things inferior.

Thus you will possess the brightness of the world, and all obscurity will fly far from you.

This thing is the strong fortitude of all strength, for it overcomes every subtle thing and penetrates every solid substance.

Thus was this world created.

Hence will there be marvellous adaptations achieved of which the manner is this.

For this reason I am called Hermes Trismegistus because I hold three parts of the wisdom of the whole world.

That which I had to say about the operation of the Sun is completed.

An alchemical furnace.
(*Geber*, De alchimia, *1529*)

Illustrations from Henry and Renée
Kahane, *The Krater and the Grail:
Hermetic Sources of the Parzival.*
(University of Illinois Press, 1966)

Based on the ancient solar cults of Zoroaster and Mithras, also on the concept of Aristotle that human beings were generated from man and the sun, the Emerald Tablet connected alchemy to astrology. The whole of Creation was made from earth and air, fire and water. These four humours were applied to all nature and living things, also to the six known metals that might combine with mercury. These were allied to the seven planets – gold from the Sun, silver from the Moon, lead from Saturn, iron from Mars, tin from Jupiter, copper from Venus and quicksilver from Mercury. The Zodiac itself governed the twelve parts of the human body, with Aquarius, in a medieval woodcut, pouring life-giving water onto Pisces, the symbol of Christianity.

The two leading alchemists of the 5th century were Bishop Synesius of Ptolemais and the Gnostic Zosimos of Panopolis. This was the time when the great heresy of alchemy, the direct communication with the divine intelligence through Hermes and Mercury, was being brought within the intervention of emperor and Church. Yet even Synesius, in an apocryphal work, declared of the metals: 'Take from them that living silver and you will make it the medicine or quintessence, the imperishable and permanent power, the bond of all elements which contained within itself the spirit which unites all things.'

The idea of the whole cosmos, permeated by a sacred spirit, attracted the mystic Jews of the Cabbala and the Stoics as well as the alchemists, whose symbols began appearing – the fire-breathing winged dragon, the Serpent of Wisdom, and the Philosopher's Egg or Stone. The curved retorts, in which the metals were fused, became the symbols of purification and the transfusion of the divine essence.

In these processes, the Hellenistic scientist Zosimos was a master. Lead and copper ingots were laid on ledges above metallic sulphur and arsenic sulphide along with water in a pot over the heated floor of the still. The fumes made sulphuric acid, which condensed and fell on the copper and lead. The acid and salts first blackened the two metals, then whitened them, and finally made them red, before they were melted into yellow brass, which looked like gold.

A work of Zosimos, *The Visions*, seemed to describe a dream of achieving the Grail:

I saw a sacrificing priest standing before me at the top of an altar in the form of a bowl. This altar had fifteen steps leading up to it. Then the priest stood up and I heard a voice from above saying to me, 'I have accomplished the descent of the fifteen steps of darkness and the ascent of the steps of light and it is he who sacrifices, that renews me, casting away the coarseness of the body; and being consecrated priest by necessity, I become a spirit.' And having heard the voice of him who stood on the bowl-shaped altar, I questioned him, wishing to find out who he was. He answered me in a weak voice, saying, 'I am Ion, the priest of the sanctuary, and I have survived intolerable violence. For one came headlong in the morning, dismembering me with a sword, and tearing me asunder according to the rigour of harmony. And

flaying my head with the sword which he held fast, he mingled my bones with my flesh and burned them in the fire of the treatment, until I learnt by the transformation of the body to become a spirit.'

Zosimos was probably referring to the *krater* in the alchemical text *Corpus Hermeticum*, the holy bowl where each individual soul mixed with the universal mind and the Word of God. In his fifth vision of the priest at the sacred altar celebrating the fearful mysteries, he was told that the holy man wished to put blood into the many bodies in the bowl, 'to make clear the eyes, and to raise up the dead'. This process of regeneration was paralleled not only in other hermetic texts, but in Nordic and Celtic rites, as depicted on the Danish sacrificial Gunderstrup bowl.

Such ascents towards a cauldron-altar of knowledge were similar to the quests for the Cauldron of Annwn in Celtic mythology. As an expert on alchemy noted of the appearances of the figures in *The Visions*:

A priest is cut to pieces and before the remains are destroyed in the fire he vomits himself out as a manikin. A man of copper is destroyed and revives as a small man clothed in red. An old prophetic figure is taken and, white with age, is thrown into the cauldron. Finally the bearer of the Meridian of the Sun is himself dismembered and the visionary can then behold the mystery. For the alchemist this was all a poetic vision which held an inner truth about the world and the soul. It seems that the idea was also closely associated with the stage by stage development of the embryo from fertilization to birth. . . .

The study of alchemy in Europe was undermined by Byzantine orthodoxy. Neither Church nor state could allow the human understanding of the divine mysteries. The Gnostic gospels and other speculations were doomed as heresies. On the borders of Syria and Persia, however, the alchemic tradition continued with the Manichees and the Nestorians, until Islam conquered the Middle East and inherited the esoteric writings of the Hellenistic world.

In the hermetic doctrines, God the Father was the essence of all things; his Son was within the essential forms; and the Holy Spirit was the action and energy of the whole. The eternal and divine Unity was the principle of Creation. The wisdom of the cosmos lay in the Father; everlasting understanding came from the Son; the eternal agent in the Trinity was the Holy Spirit, who was both Love and the Divine Will. These Gnostic beliefs permeated the studies of the Grail with its Christian connotations. In the romances, God the Father gave the blessings of the Grail; God the Son was the messenger between heaven and earth in the visions of many a Grail; and the Holy Spirit was Grailness, or the process and power within the veins of mortal beings.

In the time of the early Christian Church, the alchemist Simon Magus claimed to be the direct representative of the supreme power of God, a rival messiah to Christ. His wisdom was the immediate Word of the Lord. 'He was the first to declare,' wrote St Irenaeus, 'that he himself was the God who is over all things, and that the world was made by his angels.' The divine principle was fire, which emanated in six elements: heaven and earth, the sun and the moon, air and water – a doctrine that also derived from the Persian fire and sun worshippers who followed Zoroaster. By hearsay and magic, Simon Magus had himself raised in Rome towards heaven as the Antichrist in a demonic chariot of fire, only to be brought down by the prayers of St Peter and St Paul. In his fall, Magus broke both of his legs and another Christian Father had the heretic buried alive.

Among the Gnostic sects, the Nassenes believed in a Cup of Anacreon, which represented the world. In it God mixed the four elements of earth and air, fire and water, in order to create the world of forms. A contemporary Persian legend told of a Cup of Jamshid, in which all the mysteries of nature could be discerned. In the hermetic tradition, a vessel filled with *νǒus*, or consciousness, had been sent down from heaven to bathe mankind in divine understanding.

St Mary Magdalene with Grail and the hand of the Risen Christ on her brow. *(From the Renaissance Resurrection window in Auch Cathedral)*

As Carl Gustav Jung wrote of these three legends in his *Alchemical Studies*, the vessels were early fonts, 'in which the immersion takes place and transformation into a spiritual renewal or rebirth'. Even in the most Christian Grail romance of Robert de Boron, Jesus had esoteric learning taught to Joseph of Arimathea, who established the mysteries of the Grail under the guardianship of its hereditary knights. Classical and Eastern mysticism and alchemy would always be elements in the signs and wonders, which would meet the seekers of the true way.

Left: Mary Magdalene holds the Grail as a chalice and a stone from heaven in front of the Krell'scher high altar, Church of St Lawrence, Nuremberg.

Right: 'And here the great teacher Augustine through the grace of God was christened by St Ambrose. . . . And confounding the teachings of Fortunatus the Heretic, teaching the rules of the Manichees. . . .' *(From the choir stalls of Carlisle Cathedral, painted in the late 15th century)*

At the opening of *Perceval*, the first Grail romance about the holy fool, the season of the year was given as 'when fields grow green'. The Welsh youth picked up his three javelins and met five knights, who shone in the sunlight in red, white, silver, blue and gold. The four elements of the classical and medieval cosmos were earth, air, fire and water. Their colours were blue, golden-yellow, red and green. To explain the changes within an alchemic vessel that might convert base metal into gold, earth was seen as blue and lead, air as yellow and sulphur, fire as red and arsenic, while water was green and copper.

The colours worn by the knights in the Grail romances attested to the power of alchemy in the imagination of the Middle Ages. In *Perceval*, the fool's first act after visiting King Arthur was to slay the Red Knight, who had struck him with his lance. He then returned the gold cup stolen by the Red Knight to the travelling court at Carduel or Carlisle. This deed was not only a material forecast of Perceval's destiny, but also a symbol of the reddening fire of alchemy, which transmuted the base into the precious.

Throughout the succeeding Grail romances, the colours of the elements and alchemic changes – particularly green, black and red – appeared in the costumes and heraldry of the various heroes of chivalry. The references would culminate in Wolfram von Eschenbach's *Parzival*, where the Grail was revealed as a green stone or water fallen as manna from heaven, the secret of a wise Jewish astronomer named Flegetanis, who knew of the mysteries of the alchemy of the eastern Mediterranean.

In the medieval romances, such heresies, particularly the Pelagian and the Gnostic, would play a major role along with alchemy in the Quest for the Grail, which was the direct search for the divine. The three great sins of Gnosticism – the separation of the Creator from God the Father, the denial of the divinity of Christ on earth, and the hatred of flesh and matter as the source of all evil – were inspirations of that poetic mission. And for both the Gnostics and the authors of *The Lives of the Saints*, Mary Magdalene was the legendary bearer of a Grail that held the mystery of the Risen Christ. Until modern times, that myth of the Magdalene carrying the Holy Blood in her womb as well as carrying it in her hands, was rank heresy and blasphemy. The concept was the product of the active imagination of Jung, using a technique that he based on the visionary practices of ancient oriental and Western mystics. He had become interested in the Grail by reading the alchemical text of the Emerald Tablet. Despite his fame as a collaborator with Freud in analytic psychology, he remained a psychic and a romantic with a particular interest in Gnosticism and the Grail. He thought that the metaphysical language of the oriental sages matched his psychological terms. He was particularly fascinated by alchemy, which seemed to prophesy the modern examination of the unconscious. 'The experiences of the alchemists were, in a sense, my experiences, and their world was my world. . . . The uninterrupted intellectual chain back to Gnosticism gave substance to my psychology.'

For Jung, the procedures of his active imagination closely resembled the methods of the alchemists, who had tried to control and interpret what the Greeks had called *hypnagogia* or the waking dream. In fact, the directed reverie was a way of attaining visions of the divine. As Jung's wife Emma defined it in her work with Marie-Louise von Franz, *The Grail Legend*, 'the individual became like a vessel for the inflowing contents of the unconscious'. Her husband had agreed with the legendary writer of antiquity, Maria Prophetissa, that 'the whole secret lies in knowing about the Hermetic vessel'. Maria was called the sister of Moses and was connected with the Sophia of Wisdom of Gnostic tradition. Jung also quoted the teachings of Herakleon that a dying man should pray to the demiurgic powers: 'I am a vessel more precious than the feminine being who made you. Whereas your mother knew not her own roots, I know of myself, and I know whence I have come.'

So Jung used the language of alchemy and the classical origins of the Grail as the mixing-bowl of wisdom and self-knowledge to create a process of depth psychology. The mysterious vessel was a fiery womb, which transformed the being within it. Although it might enlighten the spirit, it could also destroy the unworthy viewer, as when Lancelot was scorched and fell into a deathly coma in *The Quest of the Holy Grail*. The Holy Ghost had been interpreted by the Gnostics as the female Sophia, for the Spirit of God was the mediator of the Virgin Birth in the flesh, bringing out Christ to illuminate the darkness of this world.

Furthermore, Jung linked the ancient healing horn cups with the chalice of the Eucharist. He quoted Hippolytus on the Greek cup of Anacreon, which was dumb.

Yet Anacreon affirms that it tells him in mute language what he must become, that is, spiritual and not carnal, if he will hear the secret hidden in silence. And this secret is the water which Jesus, at that fair marriage, changed into wine. That was the great and true beginning of the miracles which Jesus wrought in Cana in Galilee, and thus he showed forth the kingdom of heaven.

That cup was also an alchemical retort as well as the lower half of the world, made of water and earth. It gave out life and healing, as did the sacred vessels of gold and silver, taken from the Temple of Jerusalem to Babylon and returned to the Second Temple built by Zerubbabel, described in the Book of Ezra and the Apocryphal Ezra:

Then I opened my mouth, and lo! there was
               reached unto me a full cup
Which was full as it were with water, but the
               colour of it was like fire.

And I took it and drank; and when I had drunk
My heart poured forth understanding.
Wisdom grew in my breast
And my spirit retained its memory.

Jung emphasised the interpretation of the Holy Vessel as the womb. He cited Saint Ambrose, declaring that God 'chose for himself this vessel, through which he should descend to sanctify the temple of shame'. He continued: 'In the womb of the virgin, grace increased like a heap of wheat and the flowers of the lily.' In Gnostic literature, the 'vase of sins' was contrasted with the 'vessel of virtue' of the Mother of God. When Jung considered how strongly the Fathers of the Church were influenced by Gnostic and heretical ideas, he conceived that the symbolism of the vessel might be a pagan relic which was adapted by Christianity. The worship of Mary secured for Rome the heritage of the Earth Mother, and Isis and other ancient goddesses. 'The image of the *vas Sapientiae*, vessel of wisdom, likewise recalls its Gnostic prototype, Sophia.'

What Jung wanted to do was to elucidate the psychological relations between the veneration of woman and the legend of the Grail, so characteristic of the early Middle Ages. The central Holy Vessel seemed to Jung to be a 'thoroughly non-Christian image . . . a genuine relic of Gnosticism'. The feminine principle, as in the demonstrated cult of St Mary Magdalene, was strengthened in the masculine psychology of that time. 'Its symbolisation in an enigmatic image must be interpreted as a spiritualisation of the eroticism aroused by the worship of woman.'

Jung became convinced that the Grail legend might have been 'the germ of a new orientation to life'. The Gnostic basis of the Grail took him back to the early Christian heresies, in which the unconscious psychology of man was in the full and luxuriant flower of its perversity. For it strongly resisted the rules of the Church and society. It represented 'that Promethean and creative spirit which will bow only to the individual soul and to no collective ruling . . . a belief in the efficacy of individual revelation and individual knowledge.

This belief was rooted in the proud feeling of man's affinity with the gods, subject to no human law, and so overmastering that it may even subdue the gods by the sheer power of Gnosis.'

The genius of Jung wedded early medieval heresy and the Quest for the Grail to modern depth psychology and the analysis of self. He also related the sacred vessel to nascent feminism. 'It is always the knight,' one guardian of her sex wrote, 'the masculine representative of the Quest, who goes in search of the divine vessel – perhaps because it is a feminine symbol to begin with, but also because women do not *need* the quest, are already vessels of the Holy Blood, their archetype the Virgin, and are therefore Grail *bearers* rather than seekers. Each may give birth, therefore, to the new Grail Lord.'

Such stimulating works of cultural history as Riane Eisler's *The Chalice and the Blade* stressed that much of human history was essentially a male domination over producing women. The Garden of Eden was an allegory of Neolithic times, when women cultivated the soil with men. In Mesopotamian legends the supreme deity was the Queen of Heaven. The Earth Goddess had been worshipped since the beginnings of civilisation. But the blade or the phallus, the Holy Lance or Spear or Sword of Destiny, these had become the nuclear warheads, the supreme weapons of destruction. Against them in Marian and psychological terms stood the chalice and the womb, the Grail and rebirth, the Spirit and regeneration. Jung, indeed, also quoted the Cistercian prior of Châlis, Guillaume de Digulleville, on the alchemical colour of the Holy Ghost, which was green because 'it sprang forth and gave comfort'. So should future societies be for the feminist social scientists, looking for places 'where the power to give and nurture, which the Chalice symbolises, was supreme'.

This was not so in the medieval legends of the Grail. There the male knight by bloody deeds had looked for the divine. In a sense, if the Grail was the feminine symbol of the womb that gave birth to all men, then the Galahad and Perceval who achieved that goal were returning to their source.

Yet such an interpretation was no longer the Matter of Britain nor of France, but the psychology of Jung and the feminists. The search for the Grail had always been a heresy, a personal enquiry after God; but only now was it reduced to self-analysis or a version of cultural history, indoctrinated with some modern perceptions. Hermes Trismegistus may have been percipient in his *Rosarium*, when he declared: 'And thus the Philosopher is not the Master of the Stone, but rather its Minister.'

For Jung, there was no actual Holy Bloodline, no children of Jesus by his beloved one. He had planted, however, such a misconception in modern sensationalist minds by linking the myths of the Grail to the womb and the Earth Mother and the cult of Mary Magdalene. For him, the Grail was a pervasive symbol of creation and a perpetual quest after a divine spirit – the pursuit of the alchemists. This was the true heritage of the Grail romancers, and not the product of the active imagination of Chrétien de Troyes and his followers. From the well of ancient wisdom, from which Mímir drank out of his Gjallarhorn in the Norse sagas, the remembrance of Grail was drawn in a golden bucket to surface in the enduring medieval legends of humankind.

FIVE

THE GARDEN OF THE GRAIL

Were not God's laws
His Gospel laws, in olden time held forth
By types, shadows, and metaphors?
John Bunyan, Apology to *The Pilgrim's Progress*, 1678

rucial to *Perceval* and the later Grail romances was the story of the Fisher King and the Waste Land, surrounding his castle on Munsalvaesche, the Mount of Salvation, the peak of paradise. The questing knight should have demanded of the ruler the reason why he was wounded in the groin. If Perceval had asked the question, the fertility of the royal person and the barren earth would have been restored. For the early Christian secret symbol was a fish, signifying ἰχθεός or Jesus Christ God in Greek; Jesus recruited the fisherman Peter as His primary disciple, who then became the fisher of men's souls; He could feed, as the Grail, a host of people with thousands of loaves and fishes; and He was also wounded by St Longinus in the side by the Holy Lance, the key symbol in the Grail procession. Moreover, the Fisher King represented the pagan Green Man, carved in so many Gothic cathedrals, as well as the biblical Garden of Eden and paradise and all creation in nature and the human spirit.

The hope of those existing in poor and stunted societies has lain both in nostalgia for a Golden Age and in a reverie about an easeful afterdeath. From the earliest recorded times of agricultural peoples, divine help has been invoked for the sprouting of the crops and the bounty of the harvest. A Waste Land, devastated by drought or locusts or the harrying of war, has demanded the intercession of priest-kings, who might plant again a green growth in the soil. Any harm done to the ruler would call forth pestilence and famine. Only

his cure would restore the bloom on living things.

The concept of a garden that poured forth delicacies and delights derived from Persia and was hallowed in the Torah. The original word 'paradise' came from *pairi* or 'around' and *daeza* or 'wall', and it signified the bounty within an enclosed green space. When Xenephon first turned the word into the Greek *paradeisos*, he made the Athenian sage Socrates praise the Persian king for his love of pleasure gardens, 'filled with all the fine and good things that the earth wishes to bestow, and in these he himself spends most of his time'. These were the rare preserves of the very rich.

The idea of a garden of paradise dated back to the founding city of Mesopotamia, the Sumerian State of Uruk with its seminal epic of King Gilgamesh, who wandered to the immortal Dilmun of the Gods, where stood 'the Tree with trunk of gold, and beautiful to see'. In that idyllic surround of delight, there were no widows and no sicknesses, no old age and no grief. Such a dream of plenty was re-created in one of the wonders of the world, the Hanging Gardens of Babylon, where Queen Semiramis tried to reproduce paradise. The creations made for her were suspended because they were built on *ziggurats* or stepped pyramids. As always, water was their necessity; indeed, the control of great rivers had created the first civilisations of Egypt, China and India. A hydraulic system and aqueducts brought water to the top enclosure of the Hanging Gardens, from where it flowed down through channels to irrigate all the flowers, fruit and trees below.

After the return of the Jews from their captivity by the waters of Babylon, where they had sat down and wept, their rebuilt Jerusalem was often confused with an urban paradise, now given the Hebrew name of *pordes*. Ezekiel's warning of the fate of the King of Tyre equated 'Eden, the garden of God' with a holy mountain covered with precious stones of fire. The irrigated orchard, however, was the practical garden of paradise of ancient Israel rather than the onyx and crystal mount of vision and tradition; yet even in the apocryphal Book of Enoch, fragrant trees encircled the divine throne on the top of the seventh mountain.

Early Jewish tradition held the earth to be a disc arising from the waters, while paradise itself was an enclosed garden or a small park. This blessed place was located at various times at the head of the Persian Gulf, at Mount Saphon in Syria, and at Hebron, but more usually in Jerusalem. There was the site of the original Garden of Eden, which was related to the Hebrew word *gan-eden* or sweetness or delight. In its more erotic verses, the Song of Solomon compared the beloved to a scented paradise:

A garden inclosed is my sister, my spouse; a spring shut up, a fountain sealed.

Thy plants are an orchard of pomegranates, with pleasant fruits; camphire with spikenard.

Spikenard and saffron; calamus and cinnamon, with all trees of frankincense; myrrh and aloes, with all the chief spices:

A fountain of gardens, a well of living waters, and streams from Lebanon.

Awake, O north wind; and come, thou south; blow upon my garden, that the spices thereof may flow out. Let my beloved come into his garden, and eat his pleasant fruits.

The Greeks divided their gardens of paradise into Arcadia for the living, the Fortunate Isles of the Hesperides for the heroes and the Elysian Fields for the virtuous dead. The route there along the Acheron and the Styx joined the third stream of Lethe, which brought forgetfulness. In the green Elysian Fields, all was peace. But the return from there was much more difficult than the going down. Even the supreme Christian poet Dante would place the Elysian Fields outside his *Inferno*, so that celebrated pagans including Homer could rest for ever by meadow and stream without having to suffer the torments of the damned. In the fourth book of the *Odyssey*, indeed, Proteus informed Menelaos of his destiny:

You shall not die in Argos with its meadows.
The divine will grants you the Elysian Fields
With golden mighty heroes at world's end,
Where all of living is a dream of ease.
The fall of snow is hardly known, nor winter
Long with frost, nor rain in buckets,
But only sleepy breezes from the ocean
With cups like waters for the souls of men.

In his early poem *Works and Days*, Hesiod imagined a Golden Age, when the fruitful earth bore abundant crops for mortals, who existed like gods in peace among their flocks. As Adam and Eve before the Fall, they lived without sorrow and were given all the riches of nature. They were the friends of the immortal gods in peace among their flocks under the rule of the creator Kronos, who was to be called Saturn by the Romans. Pindar also celebrated the same theme in his second *Olympiad*, when he wrote of a mislaid paradise, where golden flowers shone on the branches of magnificent trees, while their roots were fed by brilliant waters. All of these plants provided garlands and crowns for everyone. And Telecides took up that nostalgic paean, describing streams flowing with wine and fishes baking themselves in order to be served at table. 'Men were fat then.'

Beyond the dreams of literature, Greeks created practical shady places. Laurels and vines were planted outside the temples of the gods, and the ancient oracle of Dodona was set in an oak grove. The gardens of the Academia in Athens were

HESPERIDVM HORTI

In this picture, Hercules kills the dragon to reach the golden apples of the garden of the Hesperides, plucked by the three goddesses. From the title page of Rembert Dodoens, *Cruydenboeck*, 1554, illustrated by Hans Liefrinck.

transformed from blessed places into walks for philosophers beneath the olive trees, sacred to Athene, the goddess of wisdom. The tyrant Hero of Syracuse built a park with its feature the horn of plenty, an altar or a grotto, given by the nymph Amalthea to nourish Zeus as a child. In the history by the Stoic philosopher Diodorus Siculus, the sun passed directly over the seven Fortunate Isles, where all the people were beautiful and healthy and peaceful, living in free love as long as they wished. These visions of bliss on earth were placed towards North Africa or the Atlantic Ocean.

The description by Homer of the Grotto of Calypso would be matched by the seventh *Idyll* of Theocritos. In that, grasses and woods and streams would blend together in harmony and peace. This poetry of nature would recall a lost paradise, but also one of human wants and need. These settings would become the bowers of lovers, where Adam and Eve were not ashamed, but gloried in their nakedness. Moreover, paradise was again placed on the peak of a mountain. In the *Achilleid*, Statius would describe a blessed grove that grew so high that its top branches scraped at heaven, while

Claudian would set the sunlit gardens of Venus on a crag near to the gods.

When Virgil became the Homer of Rome in *The Aeneid*, Aeneas, his founder of the city, with his Sibyl passed through the Mournful Fields to the Elysian ones. As Dryden wrote:

These holy rites performed, they took their way,
Where long extended plains of pleasure lay;
The verdant fields with those of heaven may vie,
With either vested, and a purple sky –
The blissful seats of happy souls below.

The Roman poet Ovid in his *Metamorphoses* took up the theme of a lost Golden Age, when the untilled earth had grown all the food needed by humanity. 'Streams of milk and sweet nectar flowed, and yellow honey was distilled from the green-leaved oak.' And Horace wrote:

The ocean round us waits. Set the sail
For the Elysian Fields and the Fortunate Isles.
No plough is needed for the abundant corn,
No pruning-hook for vine or budding olive,
The figs push black along the heavy tree . . .
Jupiter gave these shores for men of right.

As important as the sacred grove had been to the Romans was the Tree of Life all over the world. The taste of its sap gave the gift of eternal bliss to

Left: A walled Moghul Paradise Garden, irrigated by a bullock turning a waterwheel, *c.* 1620.

Right: Yggdrasil, the world tree which supports heaven from hell and is encircled by the Midgard serpent, which holds our Middle Earth together. *(Frontispiece of Bishop Percy,* Northern Antiquities, *1847)*

the Persians, while the Chinese revered a huge trunk with evergreen branches in their Elysian Fields at Kuen-Luen. The Tree of Wisdom of the Buddhists was also that of the Knowledge of Good and Evil; and holy rivers flowed from its four branches. For the Nordic peoples, the ash Yggdrasil held the earth in the middle between Valhalla and the underworld; upon it, Odin had been crucified for nine nights to retrieve the Runes and so give to humanity all understanding. The oak was sacred to Zeus for the Greeks and to Andastra for the Druids. Laurels crowned the brows of Apollo and the classical poets, and the olive was the fruit of the wisdom of Athene.

The problem of the vision of a Golden Age and a lost paradise was that it excluded the pleasures of the rich and forgot the sufferings of the poor. Addressing the Creator in heaven, Lucian had complained that the ancient poets had talked of a fruitful earth and rivers flowing with wine, milk and honey. People themselves were golden. Now most of the Romans were leaden, 'eating our crusts of bread with the sweat of our brow, forever bowed with poverty and want and helplessness'. This condition would obviously be more endurable if the rich were apparently not having such a fine time. The preaching of paradise was no panacea for the social ills of earth.

Such biblical and classical descriptions of the Garden of Eden would be the inspiration for the 'paradises' within the cloisters of medieval Christian monasteries, enclosed green spaces for prayer and meditation. Their squares would be quartered by four paths meeting in a central fountain, while a tree or herbs or grass would fill each segment. For had not God told Adam before the creation of Eve: 'Of every tree of the garden thou mayest freely eat: but of the Tree of the Knowledge of Good and Evil, thou shalt not eat of it.' The sustaining Tree of Life was held to be the date palm or the olive tree, the cedar or the cypress, while the serpent's deadly tree of the Knowledge of Good and Evil and of the Fall of Man was the oak apple or poisonous yew.

Although wary of adopting pagan beliefs, Christianity would incorporate as much nature worship as it could in pictures from the pages of the Bible. The fertile Tree of Jesse bore the kings of Israel up to God the Father in many medieval windows of stained glass. A trunk, blasted on one side and leafy on the other, divided the Fall from the Passion in the works of Cranach the Elder and Holbein. The Cross itself in many early illuminated manuscripts was shown to be sprouting young leaves, as though the agony of Christ were making the dead wood bud.

For the Christian faith, three fundamental events occurred in a green place – the Fall of Man, the Agony in the Garden, and the evidence of the Resurrection with the risen Christ first appearing

A monastic Garden of Paradise.

to St Mary Magdalene. As the Gospel according to St John declared:

> Jesus saith unto her, Woman why weepest thou? Whom seekest thou? She, supposing him to be a gardener, saith unto him, Sir, if thou have borne him hence, tell me where thou hast laid him, and I will take him away.

> Jesus saith unto her, Mary. She turned herself, and saith unto him, Rabboni, which is to say, Master.

> Jesus saith unto her, Touch me not, for I am not yet ascended to my Father; but go to my brethren and say unto them, I ascend unto my Father, and your Father; and to my God, and your God.

So the image of Christ the gardener of paradise was established. He was shown resting on his spade in medieval illuminations. His work of Creation with his Father was finished. The two Trees of Eden were enclosed within the pale. The Grail of his Blood was now a golden bucket of holy water, set in front of the Magdalene, to whom he chose first to discover himself. In that garden, according to the Book of Revelation, 'the leaves of the tree were for the healing of the nations'.

A literal demonstration of Christ in the garden with St Mary Magdalene survives at her basilica and nunnery at St-Maximin La Sainte-Baume. Here, in the apocryphal gospels, she brought his Blood in a Grail to Provence; here she was carried by angels from her hermitage in a cave to be buried; here a bone of hers is still revered. A fresco shows her covered only by her red hair, carrying

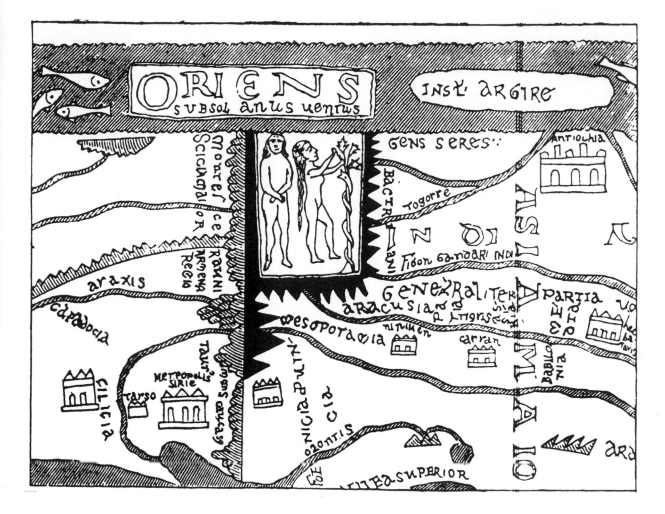

Adam and Eve in an Eden surrounded by fire near India and China. *(From the* Mappa mundi *of St Severus, as redrawn by Eduardo Coli,* Il Paradiso Terrestre Dantesco, *1897)*

the Holy Blood in a golden pot in her hand. A painting shows her kissing the nail through the feet of Jesus on the Cross. And another painting of the 15th century shows Christ by the Tree of Life with his spade, declaring to her of the wound in his side, '*Noli me tangere*' (Do not touch me): it is similar to the picture of St Wolfgang on the altarpiece in the St Lawrence Church at Nuremberg.

After the collapse of the Roman Empire and during the centuries to come that were to be miscalled the Dark Ages, the concept of the garden hardly existed. The Christian Fathers resorted to Virgil's *Eclogue*, as much as to Genesis, in order to keep alive the vision of paradise during the Gothic

invasions. In the 4th century, Lactantius argued that the classical myths of a golden age should be interpreted as a poetic vision of a primitive Eden. Athanasius of Alexandria and St Basil in his *Hexameron*, depicted a world of the riches of nature before the Fall. Yet, two other philosophers of Alexandria, the cultivated Jew Philo and the unorthodox Origen, both questioned the literal truth of the primal garden. 'Do not let fables that God tills the soil or plants a paradise enter our mind,' Philo declared. 'Never yet have Trees of Life and of Knowledge appeared on earth, nor is it likely that they will appear hereafter.' Eden was a Platonic allegory, a myth of innocence lost in experience, the spirit erring in its struggle to escape the flesh. Paradise lay within the individual soul, where God had planted a garden of virtues: if cultivated by a good life, the harvest would be perfect happiness.

Christ in the Garden with his spade and Mary Magdalene with a golden Grail. *(From the Church of St Lorenz, Nuremberg)*

This stained-glass west window in Canterbury Cathedral shows Adam digging outside the Garden of Eden with the Tree of Jesse in the background, *c.* 1178.

perpetual fruits and flowers, 'no strong winds, no storms, no hail, no turbulence, no bolts of thunder, no ice in winter, no damp in spring, no heat in summer, no drought in autumn'. The climate was always mild, the birds and the beasts were tame, and all was bliss and peace.

Such divergent views of the truths of Genesis were reconciled and defined by the two great saints and bishops, Ambrose of Milan and Augustine of Hippo in North Africa. Familiar with classical and biblical belief, Ambrose equated the Elysian Fields and Eden with the terrestrial paradise shown to St Paul and promised by Christ to the penitent thief. Before the Fall, Adam was a kind of angel in a state of bliss, suspended halfway between heaven and earth. Augustine followed this interpretation by discerning a paradise of the spirit as well as the soil. The Tree of Life signified the dominion of the soul over nature, the Tree of the Knowledge of Good and Evil was the choice between the delights of the spirit and the pleasures of the flesh. In his most important work, *The City of God*, Augustine saw a more illuminating paradise as the symbol of the Church; its four rivers were the four Gospels, while the Tree of Life was Christ and the meaning of the Cross. Yet he was adamant that Eden had once existed, stating that 'our first parents were indeed upon the earth in a place full of trees and fruits, which was called Paradise'.

Another test of early Christianity became celebrated for its descriptions of a garden eastward towards Eden. In the apocryphal Apocalypse of Paul, an angel took the saint to the land promised to the meek, 'for they shall inherit the earth'. A river of milk and honey flowed through orchards, which bore a variety of fruits twelve times a year. Each vine had 10,000 branches and a million grapes. The earth glittered seven times more brightly than polished silver. This territory was the reward of the blessed and would replace the world when it was destroyed in the final war against

Origen was harsher on the parable of Creation. Who could be so silly as to believe that God was a farmer? Who could have eaten the fruit of real Trees of Life and of Knowledge? The drama of Eden was still enacted in every man and woman, given daily the serpent's apple to tempt their spirit. Yet even Origen admitted that the saints, as they departed from the world, would stay in some place, 'which the divine scripture calls paradise'. This was a strict school for souls, which, after due discipline, graduated the worthy to ascend sphere by sphere to heaven. An actual description was given in the works of Pseudo-Basil, in which paradise was put on top of a mountain and was fed by a winding river. The land was full of milk and honey and

Satan, which would result in the rule of Christ and his saints for a thousand years.

The Spanish St Isidore followed the allegories of Augustine in describing paradise as the Church and the Gospels, but he surrounded it with mystical fire reaching to heaven. The first English description, that of the Venerable Bede in the 8th century, reverted to the concept of Eden on the ground with its four rivers, two of which were the Nile and the Ganges, already known in Europe. The quartet of waters had many significances: the cardinal virtues and the rites of baptism, the four humours of the body of the classical doctor Galen as well as the sum of the Evangelists. The Tree of Life was not only Christ and the doctrine of the Church, but wisdom in the corporal body. And through Alcuin, the British head of the School of Charlemagne in Aachen, these doctrines would reach the imperial court, which was to revive the garden in Europe after its practical loss for 500 years.

Jewish tradition had also asserted that Eden never disappeared from earth. Noah had given it to Shem with Mount Zion and Sinai and all Asia. Although it was still the source of the four rivers of life, it was inaccessible and lay behind a wall of fire to the east beyond the horizon. Isidore of Seville had further declared that the Latin *hortus* was the equivalent of the Greek word for paradise, while *deliciae* was the equivalent of the Hebrew word for Eden. So the term *hortus deliciarum* would be created for medieval herbals, describing walled orchards of fruit trees containing the Tree of Life and a source that split into a cross of streams.

In the 12th-century *Hortus Deliciarum* by Herrade de Landsberg, the abbess of St Odile in Alsace, lay the perfect expression of St Augustine's pronunciation of Eden, declared to be a historical

Illustrations from the 12th-century *Hortus Deliciarum* by Herrade de Landsberg.

fact. He had called Jesus the Tree of Life, while the other saints were fruit trees, and the four Gospels were the flowing rivers of Eden.

The *Hortus Deliciarum* portrayed these concepts. Its creation of Adam and Eve showed God on his throne breathing the Holy Spirit into the primal man, then plucking the original woman from his rib under the Tree of Life. Other pictures showed the serpent and Eve and the apple with the Tree of the Knowledge of Good and Evil, while Eden itself was portrayed under a wrought dome, resting on the two pillars of the Temple of Solomon, its four rivers gushing out of pitchers to water the Tree of Life with its leaves of the Trinity, and two other seedlings sprouting crosses. Finally, Abraham was shown on his throne, his bosom filled with the blessed. Two pairs of water-bearers poured the rivers of paradise onto his two

Eden as a walled garden in the
Cologne Bible, 1478.

The fountain of life as a *fons mercurialis*.
(Rosarium philosophorum, *1550*)

Christ in the middle of the four rivers of paradise.
(13th-century manuscript of Peregrinus, Speculum
Virginum*)*

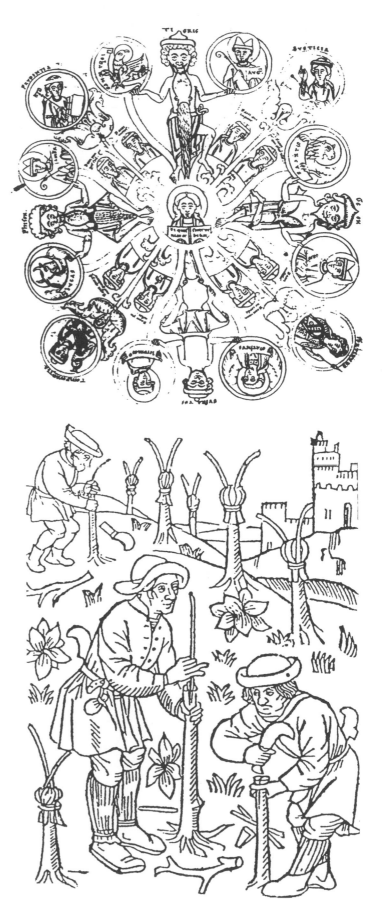

Medieval gardeners grafting trees. *(15th-century
French illustration)*

date palms, all crowned by the three hanging lamps of divine grace.

Such were the antecedents of the Grail romances in visions of a heavenly bower or an earthly paradise on a Mount of Salvation, where every wish-fulfilment was gratified in the passage of a blessed vessel in a procession through the castle of the Fisher King. The troubadours and scribes of the active imagination were the heirs of a long tradition of ancient, classical and biblical tradition. They were culling the herbs and flowers of the millennia, which brought forth the Garden of Eden and the benign hereafter, the cornucopia and the Celtic Cauldron of Regeneration, the Sophia and the Risen Saviour. All these juices bore fruit in the Quest for the Grail.

SIX

A GRAIL OR THE GRAIL

> There has been a succession of attempts to force the Grail to yield a monolithic meaning, to determine for it a precise synonym. To some it is the chalice of the Eucharist, to others a misinterpretation of the horn of plenty of Celtic mythology, and to still others a phallic symbol when taken in conjunction with the Lance. . . . Was its content the Trinity, the Eucharist, or the *manna* of the Hebrews?
>
> Frederick W. Locke, *The Quest for the Holy Grail*, 1960

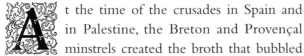

At the time of the crusades in Spain and in Palestine, the Breton and Provençal minstrels created the broth that bubbled into the legend of the Grail. The Norman conquest of England allowed the traditions of King Arthur to pass over in song to the continent; the Welsh Bleheris was held to have performed at the court of the original troubadour Guillem, the seventh Conte de Peiteus, and the ninth Duke of Aquitaine. In the modern Poitiers, his domain, Celtic myths and strains met Arabic rhymes and refrains. From this cross-culture of Britain and the 'Muslim lake' of the Mediterranean arose the Grail sagas, originally phrased in Occitan, the Romance language once spoken in the South of France. A century before the first *Story of the Grail*, the *Perceval* of Chrétien de Troyes, the crusader Guillem and his heirs mixed many ingredients in their verses. This period saw the capture and the loss of Jerusalem, also the advance of the petty Christian kings of northern Spain against the Saracens, as Charlemagne had previously met the Moors, leaving behind the *Chanson* of Roland to rival the quests of the knights, searching for the Grail from Arthur's Round Table.

The catalyst of the legends was Guillem's granddaughter, the forceful Eleanor of Aquitaine. She first wed King Louis the Seventh of France and went with him on the disastrous Second Crusade to the Holy Land. She had the marriage annulled and then became the wife of the later King Henry the Second of England; their lands now stretched from the Borders of Scotland to the Pyrenees of Spain. With the patronage of her court, and that of her daughter, the Countess Marie of Champagne, the troubadours became the songbirds of the Frankish aristocracy. Under the wing of the Countess Marie, Chrétien de Troyes was to write two Arthurian romances about Tristan and Lancelot, and later to dedicate his masterpiece *Perceval* to the widowed Marie's proposed husband, Philippe of Alsace, the Count of Flanders, who died of the plague in Palestine on the Third Crusade.

The early troubadours spread their messages through *joglars*, who were the wandering choirs of the creators of song. The texts spoke of chivalry and courtly love and the Gnostic heresies that would lead to the campaign against fellow Albigensian Christians. Jaune Rudel went on a crusade to prove his love for the Countess of Tripoli, and he wrote:

> Gladly I'd lie, at her command,
> A captive in a Moorish land
> Her precious bidding to fulfil.

And Guillem Figueira of Toulouse could not stand the conception of the Catholic Church, nor its assaults on his countrymen:

Rome, the evil I point out is easy to see:
You martyr Christians and you do it scornfully.
But tell me what words, what book do you read,
    Saying man should kill those who
    Believe in God? It's to
Him who is the true and daily bread, I plead:
    Give to Rome what it's due.

Those troubadours who supported the Cathars and the Albigensian rebels escaped from the ravaging of Provence to the court of the sympathetic Alfonso the Second, the King of Aragon, who died in 1213 at the Battle of Muret. Religious romances were written as allegories, with titles such as *Celestial Chivalry* or the *Knight of the Bright Star* or *The Leaves of the Rose*. The apocryphal and Gnostic Gospel of Nicodemus was translated into Occitan; it told of the Grail legend of the transfer of the Holy Vessel containing the Blood of Christ to the south of France. And the probable Cathar Peire Cardenal even wrote of a healing unguent contained in a golden holder, adorned with most precious stones, 'none other than the holy grail itself, or the book of the Gospels, as the Albigenses had adopted and translated it; the Golden Book, the vessel containing the true light, visible only to the Initiated'. And in his despair about the crushing of the Cathars by fire and sword, Cardenal declared:

God's wisdom is called lunacy,
While the Lord's friend, where'er he be,
Knows they're all mad, the whole damned horde
Who've lost the good sense of the Lord,
While they know he's just crazy: he
Refused this world's mad sanity.

The Norman poet Wace had already translated the fanciful British history of Geoffrey of Monmouth into French verse. To the legendary victories of King Arthur, Wace added the concept of the Round Table, where each noble knight was equal to his neighbour in a brotherhood of chivalry. Arthur even killed the giant of the Mont St Michel before defeating Roman armies in France, and dying at a final battle in Britain at

Camble, perhaps to return again. Wace testified to the oral versions of Arthur's exploits, already flying from mouth to mouth around the Celtic bards and Provençal *joglars*. Wondrous events were 'so often told about Arthur that they have become the stuff of fiction . . . The *raconteurs* have spun so many yarns, the minstrels have sung so many tall stories to glitter in their tales; that they have made all appear unreal.'

An invention has components. Yet these bits do not cohere before the assembly. They are merely sources without a stream, shreds without a shape. Chrétien de Troyes created the story of the Grail in his *Perceval*, putting it together from many ancient and contemporary tales, as well as from his own imagination. His was a synthesis of genius, making molten many myths to forge for the chivalry of his time a justification for the search for glory and for God.

For his trade, Chrétien was fortunate in his birth and career. He was probably born about 1135 at Troyes in Champagne in France. The city was a crossroads of Eastern beliefs returning with the crusades to jostle with the Christian faith; also a frontier where the Matter of Britain and Arthur met the Matter of France and Charlemagne. Chrétien was trained in Latin to be a priest, but became instead a translator of Ovid, particularly the *Art of Love and Remedy for Love*, and two stories from the *Metamorphoses*, the changing of men and women into beasts and birds.

Moreover, Chrétien is believed to have composed *Erec and Enide*, a tale of Camelot, and he wrote three more romances for the cultivated Marie, the Countess of Champagne, the daughter of the French king. His next manuscript was called *Cligès* and dealt with Tristan, although Chrétien set it in Greek Byzantium. *Yvain* or *The Knight with the Lion* was penned in praise of noble love and marriage, while the adultery of Queen Guinevere was recounted in *Lancelot* or *The Knight in the Cart*. Chrétien declared that his patron, the Countess Marie, gave him the *matière et san*, the matter and

The Emperor Charlemagne on crusade.

charles lempereur d'alemaino
Charles Maigne

la ueille de la pentedu
ste qñt tout li compaig
non de la table rounde fu
rent uenu a camaelot ┐ il orent
en le seruice/il fisent mettre les ta

The golden cup at the feast of King Arthur at Camelot, before it was recovered from the Red Knight by Perceval. *(14th-century French manuscript, British Library, London)*

of France. He died of the plague on the Third Crusade without recapturing Jerusalem, now lost to the Muslim armies of Saladin. In one sense, the invention of the Quest for the Grail would symbolise other crusades to regain the Holy City in Palestine.

Chrétien dedicated his last unfinished romance, *Perceval* or *The Story of the Grail*, to this Count of Flanders, whose father, Thierry of Alsace, had even bequeathed a Chapel of the Holy Blood of Christ – the sacred relic was his reward from the King of Jerusalem for valour shown on the Second Crusade and on three other expeditions against the forces of Islam. In a great procession in 1150, he had donated the precious fluid to the city of Bruges. The chapel built to house the relic still exists; round dark brick arches lead to a shadowy altar, over which a golden pelican now settles. The bird was a symbol of the Redeemer, as it was meant to feed its young with its own blood, as shown on the mosaic in Charlemagne's chapel at Aachen; it also represented a distilling vessel for the process of alchemy.

Influenced by the mass faith in the Holy Blood and the fierce stance against heresy taken by Philip of Flanders, Chrétien de Troyes turned the Celtic Grail myths of pagan cauldrons into Christian symbols. In fact, he claimed that he had merely put into verse a lost book loaned to him by his patron.

> He tried and tried time after time
> The best tale ever told to rhyme
> The royal courts recount the tale:
> It is the story of the grail.

the sense of that romance. He only shaped the work, which concentrated on the love triangle that ruined Camelot.

Countess Marie and her mother, indeed, were said to have presided at a Court of Love, which insisted – as did King Arthur's Round Table – on a knightly code of chaste behaviour to women. Marie made Champagne the vineyard of the culture of courtesy and chivalry, but when her husband, Count Henry, went away to the Holy Land and died a week after his return to Troyes, she left public life, refusing to marry the new patron of her poet Chrétien. This was the widowed Philip of Alsace, Count of Flanders and a temporary Regent

Count Philip had fallen out with the King of France before going to the Holy Land. Chrétien also presented Perceval as a rebel against authority. A simple Welsh youth with a lethal proficiency with javelins, he badgered passing knights to find out what they did, and then deserted his mother to

In this 13th-century French illustration of the Grail Procession towards Joseph of Arimathea *(left)*, the Holy Lance is carried by an angel *(right)*.

make his way to the court of Arthur. There he discovered that a Red Knight had insulted the King and had stolen a gold cup. He pursued the knight and killed him with a javelin through his eye, taking his armour and his horse. He also had the gold cup returned to Arthur. Untaught, Perceval went on his way towards the Grail Castle.

This ingenious opening prophesied the mysteries of the mission. Perceval was then too simple to see the Quest for the Holy Grail as more than a fight to recover a stolen precious object. And so he was unaware, when he met the crippled King of the Grail Castle, fishing in a boat nearby. Directed to that place, Perceval found himself in the finest fortress this side of Beirut in the Near East. There he was given a sword of Arabian, Grecian and

Venetian work. The following procession of the Grail was also associated with the East and the crusaders. It was led by a squire carrying a white lance with a tip that bled drops of crimson blood.

The discovery of the Holy Lance below the cathedral of Antioch had saved the First Crusade from disaster. This relic was held to be the iron point, which the blind centurion Longinus had put into the side of Christ, only to have his sight restored by the blood and water of the Saviour running down into his eyes. That sacred flow was also said to have been collected by Joseph of Arimathea in the cup used at the Last Supper, a vessel which was to become the chief symbol of the Grail.

In Chrétien's Grail Castle, Perceval next saw two squires bearing candle-holders, each with ten lights, as if in a Byzantine or Jewish ceremony. These also represented the ever-burning twin golden chandeliers, which shone above the tomb of the Prophet Muhammad at Medina. In other

Left: A ritual sacrifice beneath the Crucifixion, with St Longinus and the Holy Lance, also the sponge on the reed being offered to Christ. *(Floreffe Bible, c. 1170, British Library, London)*

Right: A woodcut by Dürer of St John the Divine's apocalyptic vision of the Son of Man with the Grail symbols of the sunburst and the seven stars, the sword and the seven golden candles in their holders.

This blessed vision of Perceval was nearer to pantheism than to the doctrine of the Roman Catholic Church. Although the bleeding lance was associated with the death of Christ, it also had a parallel in the magic spear of Welsh and Irish literature. This belonged to the god Lug, and was both lethal and life-giving. It could kill as well as make the desert green. It could destroy all the royal enemies, but also a whole kingdom. Its prick could ravage as well as regenerate. The harm of its point could only be blunted in a cauldron or bowl of boiling blood and water, the male principle creating birth from the female. Otherwise, its wounds might lay waste to the land of the Fisher King, who was incurably castrated by its thrust between his thighs.

Chrétien de Troyes went further by combining the Celtic and Nordic cauldron and horn of plenty with the communion wafer. He was not, however, the first to use the word 'Grail'. Meaning a 'dish', *grail* had occurred previously in a romance about Alexander the Great, and earlier as *gradalis*, or a bowl to serve delicacies. In the dialects of the south of France, it was called *li graaus, grazal, greel* or *grial*. Significantly, Chrétien referred to *un graal*, which resembled a small tureen in the first vision of Perceval, 'a Grail' among many others, rather than 'the Grail' of later Continuations, based on his unending story.

As the inventor of Arthurian romances about the Grail, Chrétien was not responsible for making singular the many guises of a holy vessel. Observed most carefully, the initial vision seen by Perceval in the procession was of a covered dish, borne in both hands by a maiden. To the knights there, it was a cornucopia, which supplied all the food and drink

romances, *The Song of Antioch* and *The Conquest of Jerusalem*, the champion of the First Crusade, Godfrey de Bouillon, swore that he would seize these two candelabra and place them in their rightful place by the Tomb of Christ. Then in *Perceval*, a maiden appeared with a jewelled Grail, shining with brilliant light as in the Holy Fire ceremony at Easter in the Church of the Holy Sepulchre. She was followed by another maiden with a silver platter, who passed by the bed of the maimed Fisher King.

they wanted – venison and bread, rare fruit and wine. It also represented the Welsh *dysgl*, a giver of plenty and one of the legendary Thirteen Treasures of Britain. Moreover, it was not in the shape of a Christian bowl or chalice; at the time, women were forbidden to touch the Catholic *ciborium* or lidded communion cup. Only later in the *Story of the Grail* did Perceval's hermit uncle speak of 'the Grail . . . such a holy thing' that it could feed the wounded Fisher King on one mass wafer every day for twelve years:

> He is so very spiritual
> That he has required no food at all
> Except the host the Grail contained.

To the Church of Rome, a communion vessel could only be held in the hands of a male priest. The elevation of the host to the congregation remained a sacred mystery that would not be unveiled. Yet to Chrétien, all those in search of

Above: The Fisher King is maimed by the bleeding lance. *(14th-century French manuscript,* Le Roman du Saint-Graal*)*

Right: The elevation of the host in front of the King of France, by the Master of St Giles. *(National Gallery, London)*

perfection might see the Grail themselves. He was associating the giving by Christ of His Body and Blood with pagan goddesses of fertility, the chalice representing the womb. He was also alluding to the Gnostic heresies from the Near East that were spreading across Flanders, Brittany, Champagne, Provence and Italy. These spoke of a Sophia, who embodied divine wisdom. The Grail in her hands was the Word and the Light of God, which blazed like the sun on the darkness of this earth, where Satan was fighting for mastery of the flesh.

For the Gnostics, the most significant of biblical texts came from St John the Evangelist: 'God is Light, and in Him is no darkness at all.' Their

preachers saw themselves as John the Baptist in the Gospel of St John: 'He was not that Light, but was sent to bear witness of that Light. That was the true Light, which lighteth every man that cometh into the world.' This was the Light that shone from Chrétien's Grail, carried in the female hands of wisdom and rebirth. The Gospel also contained the stories of Nicodemus and Joseph of Arimathea, so significant in the medieval romances about King Arthur and his knights.

The fault of Perceval was not to understand or ask a question about who was served by the Grail; such a query would have cured the Fisher King. He never returned to put right his error that there was only a Grail of lesser purpose. Yet the error of the later Grail romances was not to heed Chrétien and to write about a unique Grail, without recognising a multitude of sources and appearances of 'the Grail'. They should have survived to see a play by Tom Stoppard, *The Real Thing*, in which a character says, 'This is the life', only to hear, 'This is a life among other lives.'

There was 'a Grail' among many other Grails. 'The Grail' appeared to the questing knights in a *mélange* of shapes or forms, ranging from a vase to a bloody platter with a severed head on it, and even to a meteorite; yet it was named as one vision seen through separate eyes, or even as five visions in the *Perlesvaus* in the sight of King Arthur. The various symbols of 'a Grail', carved on medieval tombstones or sculptures or surrounded by lead on stained-glass windows, showed its changing facets. And in the prevalent cult of relics, there was an abundance of actual Grails to visit. There were silver, gold and jewelled holders of scraps, splinters and nails from the True Cross or the Holy Lance, or what was claimed to be parts of them. Anything that was held to have touched the Body and Blood of Jesus was a tangible Grail, although the Risen Christ had said to Mary Magdalene in the Gospel garden, *Noli me tangere*, 'Do not touch me.'

In Gnostic understanding, as all of Creation derived from One Being, so all the divine blessings emanated from 'the Grail', the grace of God, received on earth through his messenger, the Son, and infused with all the gifts of the Holy Spirit.

This was another version of the mystery of the Trinity, the Three Gods in One. As Alan Bennett perfectly expressed the philosophy of G.E. Moore in *Beyond the Fringe*, there was 'An Apple', 'The Apple', and 'Apple' or 'Appleness', so there was 'A Grail', 'The Grail', and 'Grail' or the essence of the word, most significant to those who believed in the Father, the Son and the Holy Ghost.

The host within a Grail seen by Perceval was not wholly the communion wafer of Catholic absolution, but the blessed bread distributed among all believers at the feasts of the early Christian communities and later the Cathar heretics. As well as the Body of Christ, it was a remembrance of the miracle of the loaves and the fishes, when Jesus fed the multitude – the fish was a Greek sign of Christianity, while the Fisher King symbolised the search for salvation within his castle. In *Perceval*, the maiden carrying the covered bowl of the Grail was followed by another young woman with a silver platter. They were serving sacred food to the Knights of the Grail, but it was not the Eucharist. And Perceval saw no priest, altar or cross inside the castle walls.

Although Chrétien de Troyes was a French-speaking cleric and poet, his influence came from Britain, Rome, Byzantium and the Jerusalem of the crusades. He might have visited the first two places; he knew of the history and creeds of all four. In the sacred objects of the Grail procession, he combined the Celtic and the Nordic with the Christian, the Cabbala and Islam. The bleeding white lance derived from the castle of the god Lug, as well as the hand of St Longinus, who had let out the blood of Christ with it.

There was, indeed, a famous school of the Cabbala at Troyes in Chrétien's time, led by the re-nowned Rashi. A golden Grail set with gems was a Celtic cornucopia and a Christian chalice. The silver platter represented a cauldron of plenty and the dish on which was once set both the head of John the Baptist and the Lamb of the Last Supper. The Grail held many sources and had many shapes. That was only to be expected from the imagination of a poet, who had translated Ovid's *Metamorphoses*. Stirring and blending was natural to the chef of *Perceval*.

St John the Evangelist is struck by the divine intelligence as he reads the *Logos*, the Word of God. *(From a vellum gospel, Constantinople, c. 1400)*

Chrétien's last romance contributed to the spiritual awakening of Western Christendom at the time. There were discoveries or rediscoveries in science, mathematics and philosophy; the founding of convents, monasteries and military Orders; the flowering of chivalry and courtly love; the building of the Gothic cathedrals; and the arrival of the crusades in Jerusalem, there to build a holy and heavenly city on earth. The quest of the crusaders fed on the Quest for the Grail. Both were martial pilgrimages in search of the place of the Holy

Spirit, also of peace and plenty on earth before a vision of heaven.

During the reign of King Henry the Second and Eleanor of Aquitaine, the Arthurian Matter of Britain had been conceived. Both Geoffrey of Monmouth and William of Malmesbury dedicated their chronicles to Robert, Duke of Gloucester, an amateur of Arabic astronomy, who also patronised in 1158 a polymath in the arts and sciences, the Jewish sage Abenezra from Toledo on his tour of England. A model for the later Flegitanis, said to

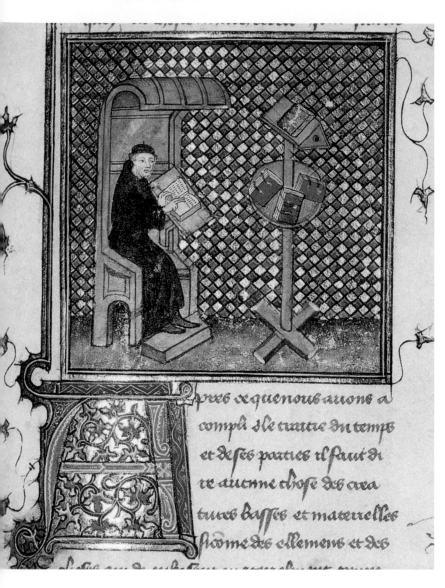

This picture of a medieval illuminator and librarian comes from a Troyes manuscript of the late 15th century.

have inspired *Parzival*, Abenezra also lectured in France and Provence, Lombardy and the Near East. His learning and fame were spread by the troubadours at the court of Marie de Champagne. Also a poet, Abenczra tended to deprecate his influence on astral studies or quests for the Grail:

> The planets and stars from their courses
>   Swerved when I first saw the light.
> Were I dealer in candles
>   The Sun would then shine all right.
>
> I strive to succeed, but I cannot,
>   For the spheres of the heavens oppose;
> If making the shrouds were my trade,
>   No one would die – I suppose.

Another model in *Perceval* for the wise hermits, interpreting the will of the heavens, was Maimonides of Cordoba. Born in 1135 of a mathematical father, he studied Arabic learning in the Near East and became the physician and astrologer to Saladin. Offered the same post by King Richard, the Cœur de Lion, on the Third Crusade, Maimonides wisely refused. His work as a bridge between the mystic inclinations of Judaism and Islam and Christianity was taken up by the catalyst of time, the translator Gerard of Cremona. He and his assistants put into Latin over eighty manuscripts, written in Greek and Arabic, including the works of Avicenna and Albumazar, Hippocrates and Hayyán, Galen and Geber and Ptolemy. Then, as now, the rendering of one speech into another tongue was the comet of knowledge.

When King Richard came within sight of Jerusalem, he hid his eyes under his shield and turned his crusading army away, as Lancelot did before his Grail. He did not feel fit to achieve his desire. For only a knight without sin could reach the divine Light, which ministered to the needs of its guardians on the Holy Mount of Salvation. The way to the Grail was by trial and test, in fact as well as in fiction.

SEVEN

THE JOSEPH GRAILS

Then Joseph of Arimathea took a *gresal*, in which he put the Blood of Jesus Christ, and he kept the lance; and all returned to the city, save for the kin of the mother of Jesus Christ and the others who were with her.

Pasqual, Bishop of Jaén, *Libre de Gamaliel c.* 1290, from the Gospel of Nicodemus

The Grail romances became so popular with the crusaders that the French demanded a Christian and a Norman purpose. Robert de Boron added the biblical legend of Joseph of Arimathea, who brought the Grail from Jerusalem to Britain and France, and who provided the lineage of the Fisher King and the heroic knights. Two particular prose stories, *The Quest of the Holy Grail* and *The History of the Grail*, confirmed the links between the white Cistercian monks and the Templars of the red cross,

Joseph of Arimathea.

giving the conquests of chivalry the sanction of the chalice. Yet in these professions of Christian faith, paganism, heresy and alchemy were never quite transmuted into the true faith.

The Celtic sources of the Grail were anathema to Robert de Boron, although he may have added corroboration to the claims of the monks of Glastonbury Abbey, who declared at the end of the 12th century that they had unearthed the bones of King Arthur and his Queen. The abbey had been burned down in 1184 and King Henry the Second had died five years later. Abbot Henry de Sully needed a miracle to raise funds and restore the holy place. As his contemporary Gerald of Wales recorded, he read the leaden cross found by the graves, which was inscribed in Latin: HERE IN THE ISLE OF AVALON LIES BURIED THE RENOWNED KING ARTHUR, WITH GUINE-VERE, HIS SECOND WIFE. As for the discovery:

> The body was reduced to dust, but it was lifted up into the fresh air from the depths of the grave and carried with the [huge] bones to a more proper place of burial. In the same grave was found a tress of woman's hair, yellow and lovely to see, plaited and coiled with exquisite art, and belonging no doubt to Arthur's wife.

These relics provided for the rebuilding of Glastonbury. Under the inspired leadership of Henry of Blois, the nephew of the English King Henry the First, the abbey went through a Cluniac reform before it fell into the hands of the

Cistercians, the white monks established by St Bernard. A mystical 'sapphire' altar, probably of porphyry, was installed, covered with gold and silver and gemstones. The cult of King Arthur and the Round Table was encouraged, although the only surviving carvings of knights in armour in the ruined abbey are over the north doorway of the Lady Chapel in a sequence depicting the Massacre of the Innocents. One of the murderous warriors even bears a shield with a flowering cross upon it. The bones of King Arthur and his Queen were housed in a black marble mausoleum with two pairs of lions at their heads and their feet.

The family of Abbot Henry de Sully would claim a similar miracle to secure the future of the Norman Abbey of Fécamp. There, the Holy Blood collected by Joseph of Arimathea was meant to have been washed up, concealed in two lead caskets within a fig-tree trunk. Both events had to do with the bringing of the Grail by Joseph of Arimathea to Sarras in France and Avalon in Britain. This was the subject of the Burgundian poet, Robert de Boron, who may himself have served time in a Saracen gaol in the Holy Land. Although he claimed that his source was an original Latin text, he appeared to borrow from the *Perceval* of Chrétien de Troyes, as well as from its later prologues, one of which told how the kingdom of Logres became the Waste Land.

In his *Joseph of Arimathea*, Robert de Boron put his original questing knight in the service of Pontius Pilate as a centurion. He was given the vessels which had caught the Blood of Christ on the Cross, and also permission to bury his Body. With Nicodemus, Joseph prepared the corpse, beginning the tradition of the Grail as a stone, on which the dead Jesus bled.

While they were washing it, the wounds began to bleed, which made them very afraid, for they remembered the stone at the foot of the Cross that was split open by the falling blood. Then Joseph thought of his vessel and decided that the drops would be better preserved there than in any other place. So he took it and collected the blood from the wounds. He wrapped the body in a fine cloth and laid it in a stone sarcophagus which he had long possessed, meaning to be buried in it himself one day. He concealed the sarcophagus with a large flat rock so that Christ's disciples might not be able to steal the Body. But he took the vessel with the blood home with him.

Imprisoned by the Jews, Joseph was visited by Christ, who gave him back the vessel holding most of the Holy Blood that had fallen from his Body at the funeral preparations. 'You shall have it and preserve it,' Christ said, 'and all they into whose charge you shall commit it. . . . Whoever knows about it will be better loved in this world, and the company of those who have news of it and write books about it will be more sought after than other people.' When Joseph asked why the Grail had been given to him, Christ answered:

You did take Me down from the Cross and lay Me in your sepulchre, after I had sat by Simon Peter at the meal and said that I would be betrayed. Because this happened at table, tables will be set up in the future, so that I may be sacrificed. The table signifies the Cross; the vessels in which the sacrifice and consecration will be made signify the grave where you laid Me. This is the cup in which My Body will be consecrated in the form of the Host. The paten that will be put upon it signifies the stone with which you closed the mouth of the tomb, the cloth that will be spread over it signifies the linen that you wound round My Body. Thus the meaning of your action will be known to Christendom for all time, until the end of the world.

For Robert de Boron, the Grail was a 'vase' which contained the Holy Blood of Jesus. It was the holder and the dish for the bread and the Paschal Lamb at the Last Supper; also for catching the fluid from the wounds of Christ on the Cross. So it was a giver of sacred food and drink as well as a container of suffering and judgement. When Joseph was later imprisoned, the Grail kept him alive for forty years. Only when he gave it to Bron, another version of the Celtic god Bran, could he depart from the earth, while Bron took this talisman of immortality to the West.

Bron later caught a fish and laid it beside the Grail. So he became the Rich Fisher of the Grail Castle of Corbenic. This Christian symbolism was also a signal of bounty and life. 'IXΘEOS or FISH was the Greek acronym for JESUS CHRIST GOD. It represented the miracles of food for all – the loaves and the fishes – and of living in the great waters of birth. De Boron even compared the joy of those who saw the Grail to a fish escaping from guddling fingers:

> It is like the ease of the fish
> Which a man holds in his hand
> And from that hand it swims free . . .

Joseph and Bron took the Grail to Sarras and Avalon, where it was kept on a table beside a cup and a book, which was the Word of God in the New Testament. This passage made the Holy Vessel become the allegory of the conversion of France and England to the Roman Catholic faith. The Grail Castle was located at Glastonbury, thus joining Christianity to the bones of the legendary British Arthur. De Boron's poem confirmed a precious legend in the apocryphal Gospel of Nicodemus, but it added that Joseph of Arimathea brought the Grail to the most ancient Christian abbey in the south-west of England. And for all of its elevation of the Passion and the Eucharist, it still upheld the Celtic myth of the magic cauldron of plenty and of judgement.

The pagan residues of the Grail myths were being given a Christian gloss, just as the contemporary alchemical process was meant to turn base lead into spiritual gold. The veil, used by St Veronica to wipe the sweat off the face of Jesus on his torment towards Golgotha, had not only become a medieval relic, but was declared by de Boron to have cured the leper Vespasian, the son of the persecuting Roman Emperor Titus. The Round Table was said to be modelled after the table of the Last Supper, again copied by Joseph of Arimathea when he first instituted a company of twelve Knights of the Grail. One seat, to become the Siege Perilous, was left empty, as if for the apostate Judas. Ever the original crusader, King Arthur was given triumphs over the Emperor of Rome and the Sultan with his horde of 50,000 Saracens, in order to make himself master of Europe, before being recalled to Britain to meet his death in Mordred's rebellion.

Written about 1200 by Gautier de Doulens, the *First Continuation* of the stories *Perceval* and *Joseph of Arimathea* told of the peerless Gawain. He reached the Grail Castle, saw the mysterious procession and failed in his task when the maimed king required the mending of a broken sword. Gawain could not do so because he had not achieved 'enough as a knight to be able to know the truth about these things'. The shattered weapon symbolised aborted crusades and the loss of Jerusalem, which must be recaptured. Only if chivalry was united in the reconquest of the Holy Land would 'The Grail' be seen again. This unfortunate definition of One Sacred Vessel would bedevil all future romances about that vision of Grace and the Holy Spirit. The task was now a single armed mission, directed by a kind of Jehovah or vengeful God, whose gift to human endeavour and sacrifice was a luminous route to heaven.

In Manessier's further *Continuation*, written some thirty years later, the ignorant knight Perceval learned that the Holy Lance, seen in the Grail procession, was the one used by the Roman centurion St Longinus to pierce the crucified Christ in the ribs, and that the Grail was the holder used by Joseph of Arimathea to catch the blood flowing from the wound made by the Lance. The sword, which Perceval mended, had broken in the killing of the brother of the Fisher King, who had then thrust himself in the thighs. He could find no cure until his brother's death was avenged, which Perceval achieved, and so was crowned as the next Fisher King, before becoming a hermit and having the Grail and the Lance taken with his soul to heaven.

There was no ending to the embellishment of the Grail messages, particularly in the vulgate cycle, beginning with *The History* and *The Quest of the Holy Grail*. Written in the thirty years after the end of the 12th century, most of these prose sagas were probably designed by one author from Champagne. He could well have attended St Bernard's school at Clairvaux, near the Troyes of the Chrétien who composed the original *Perceval*. Certainly the cycle was French in bias, a concentration on the exploits of Lancelot, appropriated by the Normans as their knight from the Ban de Benoic, and stressing the return of the Grail from Avalon at Glastonbury to Sarras in the south of France. The works of the cycle – particularly the lengthy *Lancelot*, in which the Grail cured the knight of his madness – made cross-references to the other texts in the series, while the *Mort d'Artu* followed Wace in using the conquests of Arthur and Lancelot to prefigure the Norman empire in France and Britain.

Enamel shoulderpiece of the Crucifixion with the Holy Lance and the Grail of Joseph of Arimathea, *c*. 1180.

Jesus Christ eating fish on a Grail platter at the Last Supper.
*(From a mosaic in the Church of S. Apollinare Nuovo
in Ravenna)*

The author of *The History of the Grail* claimed to have received the Word of God in 717, more than 500 years before the French text was written. He declared that he was an anonymous hermit who found himself in the wild part of a heathen land on Good Friday night and fell asleep. A voice from heaven called to him four times, and told him to wake and learn of three things in one and one in three.

He saw a man of surpassing beauty, who represented the Trinity. He could not stand the blazing brightness of this vision, so the man blew light into his eyes, gave him the gift of tongues and put a torch in his mouth. He said he was the Fountain of Wisdom and the Perfect Master, identified by Nicodemus, who had brought to Joseph of Arimathea the myrrh and aloes for embalming the body of Jesus.

The man took the hermit's hand and gave him a book no larger than his palm. The man declared that he had written the marvels in the book, then he disappeared in thunder, earthquake and blinding sunburst. The hermit fell to the ground after his mystic vision, but he woke to find the book and read its beginning:

> Here is the book of Thy Descent,
> Here is the Book of the Sangreal,
> Here begin the terrors,
> Here begin the miracles.

The hermit hid the book in a cabinet by his altar, only to find it gone the next day, in the manner that Christ had risen from his tomb. He was told to walk on a path to the Stone and the Valley of the Dead, or the Otherworld, and the Cross of the Seven Roads. On the altar of a forest chapel, he discovered again the divine book and was ordered by Christ to make a copy. This was *The*

An angel brings down a scroll of the Grail to a hermit. This drawing is taken from the oldest fresco of the Grail in France in the Church of St Nicholas at Civray, built in the 12th century on the pilgrim route to Santiago de Compostela.

History of the Grail. As the author said, he would not have dared to write it, if it had not been revealed to him.

So the *History* was the first description of the Grail as the literal Word of God. It gave the authority of the Almighty to the legend of Joseph of Arimathea, as well as creating a myth of the conversion of Britain to Christianity. In the romance, Joseph collected the Blood of Christ on the Cross in the *escuele*, or dish, used at the Last Supper. He was put in prison for forty-three years by the Jews, but fed by manna from the Grail. Freed by the Roman Emperor Vespasian, he was baptised and sailed as a missionary from the Holy Land with his wife and virgin son on the Ship of Solomon. The sacred dish was enshrined in a precious ark.

Reaching the port of Sarras in the south of France, then governed by Saracens, Joseph converted the infidel rulers. An initiate of the mysteries of the Grail within the ark, he was consecrated by Christ himself as the first bishop of western Europe. Briefly a sinner, he was pierced in the thigh by the lance of an angel, foretelling the fate of the Fisher King. But his piety cured his wound without the need of the intervention of a Knight of the Round Table.

From Sarras, Joseph proceeded on his mission to Britain. The Grail worked its wonders; it was now the symbol of Christ's miracle, multiplying the loaves and fishes to feed thousands of the faithful. Alain, the nephew of Joseph and twelfth son of his brother-in-law Bron, had caught the original fish and became the first Fisher King, building the castle of Corbenic to house the Grail and wait for the coming of Galahad, here born by divine intervention to the aged Joseph and his wife as Galaad, so similar to the Gilead of the Bible.

The Grail of the *History* was not a chalice, but a dish or platter of plenty. Britain was said to be converted to the Greek rite directly from Jerusalem and Constantinople, as was happening from Ireland in the time of King Arthur, who was held to have as an ancestor the Empress Helena, the discoverer of the True Cross in Jerusalem. The Gospel according to St John had put the stamp of the New Testament on Nicodemus, Joseph of Arimathea, the Bread of Life and the Holy Blood. Seeming almost a Gnostic, Jesus declared to Nicodemus, 'a ruler of the Jews', in those texts:

And as Moses lifted up the serpent in the wilderness, even so must the Son of Man be lifted up:

That whosoever believeth may in Him have eternal life.

For God so loved the world, that He gave his only begotten Son . . .

Jesus it was, Who told the Jews of Himself as the bountiful Grail:

I am the bread of life. Your fathers did eat the manna in the wilderness, and they died.

This is the bread which cometh down out of heaven, that a man may eat thereof, and not die . . .

Verily, verily, I say unto you. Except ye eat the flesh of the Son of Man and drink His Blood, ye have not life in yourselves.

Moreover, Jesus chose Judas in his fatal betrayal of his Master by giving him the sop at the Last Supper and by telling him, 'That thou doest, do quickly', and so creating the Siege Perilous that would kill the unworthy at the Round Table:

It was Joseph of Arimathea and Nicodemus who prepared Christ for his tomb.

So they took the body of Jesus and bound it in linen cloths with the spices, as the custom of the Jews is to bury.

Now in the place where he was crucified there was a garden; and in the garden a new tomb wherein was never man yet laid.

And it was the risen Christ who stood on the shore of Lake Tiberias and watched the disciples as they fished:

Jesus therefore saith unto them, Children, have ye aught to eat? They answered Him, No.

And he said unto them, Cast the net on the right side of the boat, and ye shall find. They cast, therefore, and now they were not able to draw it for the multitude of fishes . . .

So when they got out upon the land, they see a fire of coals there, and fish laid thereon, and bread . . .

Jesus saith unto them, Come and break your fast. And none of the disciples durst inquire of Him, Who art Thou? Knowing that it was the Lord.

Such passages from the Gospel according to St John were used by the author of *The History of the Grail* to give further authenticity to his claim

King David in the waves worships God with his cosmic Tau cross.
(Burdett Psalter, c. 1285)

that his text was copied from a book actually written by Jesus. That the Gospel was Gnostic and heretical as well as Catholic and orthodox did not trouble an inspired writer, who used of his knights the dangerous word *perfecti*, the name of the leaders of the Cathars. The author was already mixing the pagan and the Christian elements in Robert de Boron's version of *Joseph of Arimathea*.

The *Lancelot* prose cycle became famous for its amalgam of myth and faith. Some hundred manuscripts still survive. In the words of a leading French critic, the series was 'the best propagator of the conception which represented chivalry as an ideal of moral nobility, far removed from the reality in the brutal society of the Middle Ages'. As on the hilt of Roland's sword, the Holy Cross stood above the bloody blade.

Beside this legendary *History* appeared *The Quest of the Holy Grail*. Probably written by a white monk of the Cistercians, the inspired manuscript was acclaimed by another member of that Order, Cesarius of Heisterbach, who found the subject more stimulating than the Good Book. It told a tale of the Abbot Gevardur who, faced with a dozen sleepy monks, awoke them with another

A unique illustration of the Arthurian knights Bors and Galahad witnessing the Gnostic double nature of Christ, flesh and spirit, arising from the Grail. (The Quest of the Holy Grail, *Le Mans* manuscript, c. 13th century)

version of 'In the beginning was the Word': 'Listen, brothers, listen! I have something new and wonderful to tell you. Once upon a time was a King. His name was Arthur . . .'

The Order of the white monks was always associated with the Knights Templars. Galahad was now preferred to Perceval as the man without sin, who could find the Grail. Significantly, he had to prove his descent from King Solomon to take up the mystic sword of David which would achieve his quest – the Templars were the Knights of the Temple of Solomon in Jerusalem. As Emma Jung wrote in *The Grail Legend*, 'In the *Quest*, many motifs, such as the legend of Solomon, which stem from Oriental fables are to be found side by side with Celtic motifs.'

The Grail itself was a dish of plenty when it came to King Arthur's court at Whitsuntide. There the Round Table of the universe of the knights was said to be the third most important table in the world, the first being the square table of the Last Supper, the second the square Grail table of Joseph of Arimathea. There was a clap of thunder and a brilliant ray of light, as if all were illuminated 'by the grace of the Holy Ghost'. The Grail then appeared, covered with white samite, floating free. 'The hall was filled with a pleasant fragrance, as though all the spices of the earth were spilled there. When the Grail went round the table, each person was served with the food he desired.'

The Grail appeared at Arthur's court for the first time since it had dispensed manna from heaven to the Israelites and the Paschal Lamb at the Last Supper, only because Galahad, the son of Lancelot by the daughter of the Fisher King and the descendant of King David and Joseph, had sat in the Siege Perilous at the Round Table, the Judas seat which tipped any imperfect knight into hell. He had also pulled the sword from the floating stone in the nearby river to prove his saintliness. After hearing Mass, the twelve best knights,

matching the apostles, left on the Quest for the Grail. The first stop of Galahad himself was an abbey of white monks, where he earned by jousting a sacred shield bearing a red cross traced from the blood of Joseph – the sign of the Templars, who were the mailed fist of the Cistercians.

The Grail next appeared to Galahad's father Lancelot, who was too sinful to receive its grace because of his love for Queen Guinevere. Looking through an iron grille into an ancient chapel, he saw a silver table covered by a silken altar-cloth, lit by the six-branched silver candlestick that signified the six days of the Creation. In a waking dream, he saw the table, the candlestick and the Grail issue from the chapel to where a wounded knight lay beneath a stone cross. The knight was healed and took Lancelot's arms, the holy objects returned to the chapel, while Lancelot himself never stirred, either from exhaustion or from the weight of sin. A heavenly voice then reproached him for daring to approach the Grail when he was 'harder than stone, more bitter than wood, more barren and bare than the fig tree'.

Perceval then rode to the chapel of his aunt, who was once called the Queen of the Waste Land. He learned more of his family history, including the bringing of the Grail to Britain. The other knights on the Quest, particularly Gawain and Bors, went through their trials and temptations in a sort of chivalric *Pilgrim's Progress*. But while Bors was justifying himself by his works like a Protestant before his time, Galahad was justifying himself by his faith. The pair of them, together with Perceval, reached the Ship of Solomon, so rich in biblical allusions to the Ark of Noah and the Ark of the Temple with its tabernacle of the Holy of Holies. On board they found a bed like that of Ulysses, hewn from a living tree representing the Tree of Life in the Garden of Eden. Stained by the blood of Abel, killed by his brother Cain, the bed contained the True Cross. Its three posts were a natural white, red and emerald green, the colours of alchemy comprehended by Solomon, who was 'wise with the knowledge that would be grasped by human understanding; he knew the powers of every precious stone, the virtues of all herbs, and had a more perfect knowledge of the course of the firmament and of the stars than any except for God Himself'.

On the bed lay the Sword of King David made by Solomon, with a stone pommel combining all the colours found on earth, each with its own virtue in magic and science. The hilt of the sword had two ribs, one made from the salamander or Serpent of Wisdom, the other from a Euphrates fish, which induced forgetfulness and purpose. Celtic and Gnostic in shape, it was like the sword of Arthur in the early Welsh poem, *Dream of Rhonabwy*, with twin serpents inscribed upon its hilt in gold. When drawn, 'two flames of fire burst out of the jaws of the two serpents and so wonderful was the sword, it was hard for anyone to gaze at it'. The Ship of Solomon had been launched by a man descending from heaven, who blessed it with water sprinkled from a silver pail and told its builder that the last knight of his line would lie on the bed and be told about him. Galahad took up the Sword of David and lay on his forefather's bed.

Later, Lancelot replaced Galahad on the Ship of Solomon to search for the Grail Castle on the sea. Finding a fortress guarded by two lions, he came to a chamber so bright that all the candles on earth might be burning there. He observed the Holy Vessel, now covered with red samite, on its silver table. Angels swung silver censers or held candlesticks and crosses. An old man raised the host to a Trinity of three men. One of them was given to him in the place of the wafer, and he staggered under the weight of the divine body. Lancelot went to his aid, but he was struck down. As he was recovering in the sea castle, the Grail appeared at table to feed all with their desires. Although Lancelot might not reach the Holy Vessel, he could benefit from its bounty.

Five years later, Galahad, Perceval and Bors reached the Castle of Corbenic of the maimed Fisher King. There Galahad put together the two pieces of the broken sword, which had wounded Joseph of Arimathea in the thighs. Then a man from heaven in ecclesiastical robes, carried on a throne by four angels, appeared as Joseph, the first Christian bishop consecrated by the Lord God in

Sarras, the heavenly city in France from where the Grail had been carried on to Britain.

Joseph was set down beside the Holy Vessel on its silver table near the Fisher King. The four angels now bore candles, a cloth of red samite and the bleeding Holy Lance. The candles were placed on the table, the red cloth was laid beside the Grail, while the drops of blood from the raised Lance fell into the sacred cup, which was then covered with the cloth. In the vision of the knights, Joseph performed the miracle of transubstantiation, in which a burning child replaced the host, before disappearing. Then the bleeding naked Christ appeared from the Holy Vessel and gave the sacrament from it to the kneeling knights, who found the blessed food 'so honied and delectable it was as if the essence of all sweetness was housed within their bodies'. And the vision of Jesus identified the Grail:

> It is the platter in which Christ partook of the Paschal Lamb with His disciples. It is the platter which has shown itself agreeable to those whom I have found My faithful servants, they whose sight has ever stricken the faithless. And because it has shown itself agreeable to all My people, it is called most properly the Holy Grail.

The vision of Christ commanded Galahad to remove the sacred dish from the British Castle of Corbenic to the heavenly city of Sarras. Yet first he must heal the wound of the Fisher King with drops of blood from the Holy Lance. Once the King was healed, the Waste Land turned green, and he entered a monastery of the white monks. So the Cistercians rejoined the story of the Quest, while the Arthurian knights of the red cross of the Templars were compared by the spirit of Jesus to the apostles. 'For as they ate with Me at the Last Supper, even so did you eat with Me now at the table of the Holy Grail.'

Bors, Perceval and Galahad now returned to the Ship of Solomon, where they found the Grail resting on its silver table on the bed of the Tree of Life and the Cross. After a voyage, Galahad carried the great weight of the table into Sarras, where the knights were imprisoned until Galahad was chosen as king. He had made an ark of gold and precious stones, a huge reliquary to house the Grail on its silver table. In the Holy Vessel, he perceived 'the source of great deeds and the cause of all prowess [and] mysteries that surpass all other mysteries'. Praying before it with Bors and Perceval, he saw Joseph of Arimathea, who released his spirit from His Body to reach heaven.

A great marvel followed immediately on Galahad's death. The two remaining companions saw quite plainly a Hand come down from Heaven, but not the body it belonged to. It proceeded straight to the Holy Vessel and took both it and the Lance, and carried them up to heaven, to the end that no man since has ever dared to say he saw the Holy Grail.

Many distinguished French critics saw *The Quest of the Holy Grail* as a Christian allegory, imbued with the mysticism of St Bernard's doctrine of grace and spiritual union with God. Although the Grail was never described, it represented the dish at the Last Supper, the vessel in which Joseph of Arimathea caught the Blood of Jesus on the Cross, and the chalice at the Eucharist. It was the grace and bounty of God. And while it might appear and be given to all, only the pure in heart could receive it. Yet in *The Quest of the Holy Grail*, Celtic and heretic doctrines survived. Knights might see the Holy Vessel during their trials and tribulations without the benefit of the Church. And as one superior authority on the Christian emphasis of the Quest admitted:

> At the very heart of the Grail legend, there lies a grave ambivalence in that the relics of the Last Supper and the Passion are made to appear responsible for the malefic enchantments and perils afflicting King Arthur's kingdom, while the sacred lance and the miraculous sword of King David, the 'sword of the spirit', appear at times in the light of weapons of vengeance and Nemesis. Underlying the Christian symbolism, there flows a primitive current that occasionally threatens to perturb the smooth and limpid surface of the stream.

EIGHT

THE KNIGHTS OF THE GRAIL

Take the sign of the Cross. At once you will have indulgence for all the sins which you confess with a contrite heart. It does not cost you much to buy, and if you wear it with humility, you will find that it is the Kingdom of Heaven.

St Bernard of Clairvaux, 1095

Although incomplete, Perceval had invented the bardic quest for the Grail. Yet St Bernard, the son of a nobleman from Burgundy, created the real Knights of the Grail. With his brothers and friends in the early 12th century, he built a monastery at Cîteaux and an abbey at Clairvaux, which would become the spiritual beacons of the Europe of the crusades. The genius of Bernard was to put together the Church with chivalry. To defend his Cistercian Order of white monks, he had sanctified the Order of the Knights of the Temple of Solomon, with their black-and-white banner, *Le Beauséant* of light and dark, and the red Cross of Galahad on their shield.

The Cistercian monks and the Knights Templars were always to be linked by place and sympathy, but not by history. For when the Templars were proscribed as heretics and lost their thousands of commanderies, the white monks kept their distance and their monasteries. Bernard himself was always a disciple of Rome. He could not foresee the consequences of his diplomacy with the Vatican in securing papal blessing for the armoured guardians of pilgrims visiting the holy places in Jerusalem, where the Templars had their base.

In 1146, St Bernard preached the Second Crusade to King Louis of France and many nobles at Vézelay. His fervency and tongue of quicksilver, praising the remission of grievous crimes for all who took up the Cross, provoked a gale of acceptance. His hearers cried out for the favours of

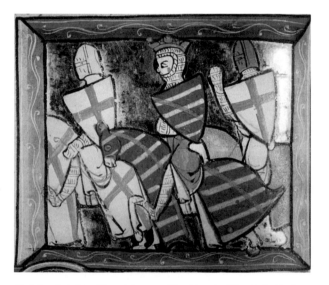

Christian knights ride out to war. (The Quest of the Holy Grail, Le Mans manuscript, c. 13th century)

Christ. Before too long, all the prepared red strips of cloth were finished. St Bernard had to give up his red robe to be cut into pieces for those who would go east. His helpers became tailors and stitched on the pledges of the holy pilgrimage to the faithful. An orgy of commitment promised another holy war. After preaching later to the people of France, Bernard was able to write to the Pope: 'The Crusaders have multiplied to infinity. Villages and towns are now deserted. You will scarcely find one man for every seven women.'

St Bernard's sermons were almost impossible for a Christian knight to resist. The promise of absolution was paramount. In his letter to the English, he emphasised his message:

> What are you doing, you mighty men of valour? What are you doing, you servants of the cross? Will you throw to the dogs that which is most holy? Will you cast pearls before swine? O mighty soldier, O man of war, you now have a cause for which you can fight without endangering your soul; a cause in which to win is glorious and for which to die is but gain . . .

This was a sermon to knights in search of the Grail, if the finding of the Grail also dealt with the defence of Jerusalem. St Bernard was not preaching a personal quest for the divine, but the remission of the sins of the crusaders through the Church of Rome, which also wished to assert its authority over the warlords of Europe. The refrain of a popular crusading song offered the same benefit:

> He who leaves with Louis
>   Need not worry about Hell.
> His soul will go to Paradise
>   With Our Lord's angels as well.

Furthermore, St Bernard persuaded the Pope to consecrate the future Knights of the Grail, the Templars, founded in Jerusalem in 1118 by Hugh de Payens and eight companions from Champagne and Provence. Their duty was to guard the pilgrims to the Holy Land, where they were masons as well as monks with a sword. Their strongholds and chapels would become models for many Grail castles, while their service to God would make them examples to all chivalry before they were condemned as traitors to orthodoxy. In his day, Bernard of Clairvaux compared them to the early saints and pilgrims:

> They come and go at a sign from their commander; they wear the clothes which he gives them, seeking neither other garments nor other food. They are wary of all excess in food or clothing, desiring only what is needed. They live all together, without women or children. . . . Insolent words, vain acts, immoderate laughter, complaints and murmurs, when they are perceived, do not go unpunished. . . . They crop their hair close because the Gospels tell them it is a shame for a man to tend his hair. They are never seen combed and rarely washed, their beards are matted, they reek of dust and bear the stains of the heat and their harness.

This way of life was modelled on the chaste and questing Knights of the Round Table as well as on the early Christian saints. Here the standards of chivalry met the ordinances of the Church. But these directives could not bridge the deepening chasm between Templar wisdom and the Holy See. The knights of that Order were a permanent standing army in Palestine, a few hundred horsemen holding the Holy City and a broken necklace of castles across the waste.

They were particularly influenced by the rival Isma'ili warrior sect of the Assassins, who held fortresses and territories in the mountains near the Caspian Sea and in Syria. Their founder and first Grand Master, Hassan Ibn al-Sabbah, was a poet and a scientist and the inventor of modern terrorism – the *fedayeen* are the descendants of his fanatical killers for the faith. Marco Polo on his travels described the stronghold and garden of delights of this Old Man of the Mountains, where he trained his political murderers. With the tales of the returning crusaders, this account would provide some of the material for the medieval stories of a paradise on earth and a Grail Castle of the Fisher King.

The material link between the Grail romances and the crusaders was also forged by the Cistercians. Their mutual theme of 'Onward, Christian Soldiers', was a blessed invention. When St Bernard created the Knights Templars as the armed fist of the Church in order to defend his Cistercians in their monasteries, set often so close to the military commanderies, he did not forget that a trade in weapons might benefit both Holy Orders. The industrial technology of the white monks matched their agricultural expertise. To their fired pottery kilns, they added water-powered trip-hammers over the forges at the abbey of

Above: The crusaders assault Al-Mahdiya, an Islamic sea-fortress in north Africa.

Overleaf: The maps of Matthew Paris of the Kingdom of Jerusalem and the stronghold of Acre. *(British Library, London)*

Fontenay. Clairvaux itself was situated in the heart of the best deposits of iron ore in France. Before 1330, the monks already owned a dozen factories, which produced iron ingots for sale to armourers. They were the leading iron and steel producers in the Champagne region, where the troubadours flourished.

The use of water power was the Cistercian contribution to an industrial revolution in the weapons trade. Powered by rivers and burns, stamping mills were built to break up the iron ore, while water-driven bellows could produce a draught that raised the temperature of the furnaces to 1,500 degrees Centigrade. This heat made the furnaces produce molten iron, ready for casting. In the 14th century, the first blast furnace was already in operation, although the blacksmith with his forge was still the usual metalworker.

The Knights Templars were known as those 'of the trowel and the sword'. In Palestine, they were totally dependent for their weapons and castle-building upon Semitic and Arabic craftsmen. The laymen of the military Orders were recruited from local skilled workers. And at the time, the Damascene blade was superior to the Frankish broadsword. After their expulsion from the Holy Land, the Templars would have taken their armourers with them, as the Roman Legions once had. These craftsmen would become known as

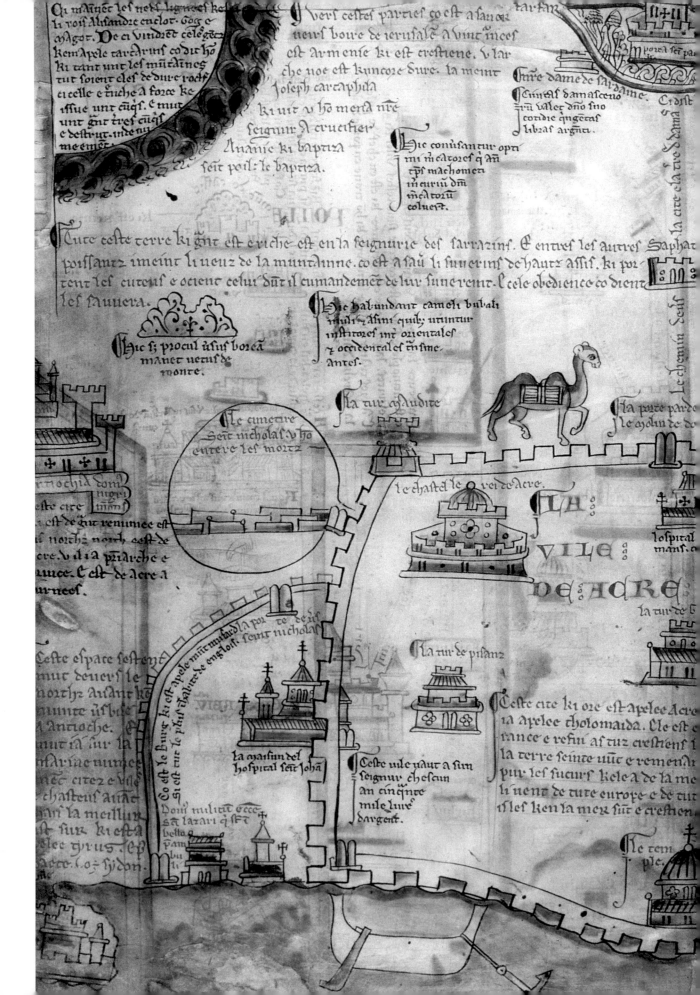

Romanies or Egyptians or gypsies. They were accustomed to a vagrant life with a cart and a forge, camp followers at the back of an army. Without them, the military could not sustain a campaign. Those who remained in the Near East were recruited by the Seljuk Turks, and so they became the first makers of cannon in North Africa. These heavy weapons were used by the Frankish crusaders against the Moors in the assault in the 14th century on Al-Mahdiya, a stronghold on the sea. The makers of weapons worked for those who employed them.

In his account of 1804 of the medieval Masons, William Preston asserted that they were superintended by the grand Master of the Knights Templars in building their Temple in Fleet Street. 'Masonry continued under the patronage of this Order' until the reign of King John, when Peter de Colechurch became Grand Master. He began the rebuilding of London Bridge with stone; he was succeeded in his office by Peter de Rupibus with Geoffrey Fitzpeter, the chief surveyor of the King's works, acting as his deputy. Even after the condemnation of the military Order, 'under the auspices of these two artists, Masonry flourished in England during the remainder of this and the following reign'.

The loss of the Holy City to Saladin in 1187 had put an end to the main purpose of the Knights Templars, who were the protectors of pilgrims to the Christian holy places, now in Muslim hands. Although they were to survive for another 120 years as a military Order, they had to find a new role. They fell back to the sea and built fortresses there, preparing for another crusade to take back Jerusalem. More and more, the Templars became merchants, bankers and administrators of their estates rather than seekers after the divine.

Their fate was foreshadowed by a nearer crusade, now directed by Rome against its brother Christians in France. The victims – the *cathari*, or pure ones – were called heretics, as the Templars were to be in their turn. Since their foundation by Hugh de Payens, the Templars had been closely connected with the Court of Champagne, Provence and the Langue d'Oc. The patrons of the culture of the south of France, certainly the richest and most civilised in Europe in the 12th century, supported the crusades and often died while serving upon them. But the kings of France coveted these independent principalities, and the popes distrusted the increasing power of the Cathar priests, called *perfecti*, who wanted to reform the faith by preaching a personal contact with the Light of God.

Both the Cathars and the Templars were influenced by Manichean, Sufi and Islamic doctrines, as well as by early Christianity and the Kabbalah. They believed the flesh was corrupt and life was an ascension to the spiritual, rather like the Quest for the Grail. For the Cathars were convinced that Lucifer, or the Devil, had brought about the creation of man. Plato, in the *Gorgias*, was right when he quoted Euripides: 'Who knows, if life be death, and if death be life?' Also right was the Grail King in the romance *Diû Krône*: 'We only seem to be alive, in reality we are dead.'

In that German text, the Grail was a casket containing a piece of bread, a third of which was presented to the Grail King. Beside it was a beaker, holding three drops of the Holy Blood. Through the mystical feast, known as the *manisola*, and the *consolamentum*, the chaste kiss of reception into the faith, the *perfecti* took their initiates into the path of the Spirit. This religion was certainly more pure and personal than Catholicism at the time, for an individual was made responsible for his or her own soul by an ascetic way of life. Cathar influences were evident in the Quest for the Grail and in the early crusading zeal to reach the holy city of Jerusalem. The Albigensian Crusade was turned into a tragedy against a source of the previous assaults on the East. A chronicler of the period even claimed to have foretold the disaster. William of Tudela considered himself an expert in the art of geomancy, and he wrote that 'he knew that fire and devastation would lay the whole region waste, that the rich citizens would lose all the wealth they had stored up, and the knights would flee, sad and defeated, into exile in other lands, all because of the insane belief held in that country'.

St Bernard himself incited this perversion of a holy war. He considered the people of the south of

An episode from the Albigensian Crusade. An attack on a Cathar castle, with naked celebrants of a heretical rite. A drawing of a bas-relief in the Church of St-Nazaire at Carcassonne.

France to be little better than heathens. White and black monks preached the conversion of Provence to the orthodox faith. They denounced the direct contact with God, so attractive to the south of France with its wandering knights and minstrels. The concept of the quest for self-perfection through trial, hope and fear was thought an oriental and mystic heresy, even if its philosophy had wide popular appeal in the Grail romances and the poems and love songs of the troubadours. The ruthless and ambitious Simon de Montfort was given the task of suppressing the heresy by fire and slaughter. When he was finally killed at the siege of Toulouse by a stone on his head, a Cathar poet wrote an ironical vindication of this crusade:

If, to kill men and splatter their blood,
To lose their souls and connive in murder,
To believe in perverse advice, to light up burnings,
To destroy the barons and dishonour their rank,
To seize lands and support Arrogance,
To swell evil and suppress the good,
To massacre women and kill their children,
Or if, for all that, a man may,
In this world, so conquer Jesus Christ,
Then that one has the right to the crown
And to shine in glory in the sky.

The lands and cities of the Langue d'Oc were as thoroughly ravaged as the Waste Land of the Fisher King. Predictably, Montségur, one of the last Cathar castles to hold out, was held to be the Grail Castle, where spiritual food and life were available to the *perfecti*. The Catholic besiegers called it the 'Synagogue of Satan', the term that the Cathars used for the Church of Rome. There may have

The expulsion of the Cathars in 1209, after the fall of Carcassonne. *(14th-century French manuscript)*

been a form of Mithraic worship at a temple of the sun at Montségur, which was the heart of the heresy. A chalice and other treasures used at the *manisola* were said to have been smuggled out of the stronghold by four refugees before its fall and to be buried still – a material Grail – in the caves near that fortress or at Usson. Although some of the Templars joined in the Albigensian Crusade, most of the Cathar knights who escaped the slaughter were to be received into the military Order of the Temple of Solomon, which itself was permeated with oriental influences.

The Grail epics were always an irritant to the Catholic Church, which was prepared to require the massacre of Christians seeking a direct approach to the divine Word and Light. In both *Perceval* and the later *Parzival* of Wolfram von Eschenbach, the way to the Grail was suggested by a holy lay hermit, as well as a hideous sorceress. Such a revelation might be reached in a castle, not in a chapel. The priests of Rome had little to do with the transmission of the grace of God to humanity through a jewelled cup or a dove of the Holy Spirit.

The premier romances of the Grail diminished the role of the Church as the mediator between heaven and earth. Even if the Knights of the Grail went to Mass regularly and the Holy Spirit came to them at Camelot during the feast of Pentecost, their trials along the many ways to the Castle of the Fisher King made them able to act and endure by the grace of God. By their deeds, not by the Latin of the Vulgate, they were chosen to view the divine.

Once the quest for the Grail had been described by Chrétien de Troyes, many actual Grails were identified within the Christian faith. Although that sacred vessel had ancient and pagan sources, it was declared to lie within the bowls, dishes, weapons and instruments that the Gospels associated with the Last Supper and the Crucifixion. Anything that was believed to have contained or touched the Blood of Jesus Christ was considered to be a kind of Grail.

In the ecstatic confusion of the real and the visionary that was the inspiration of the crusades and the early Middle Ages, sacred relics were venerated and became the advertisements of the

Map of Jerusalem. *(Travel book of Arculf, c. 700)*

Church of the Holy Sepulchre. *(Book of Bernhardt von Breytenbach, 1486)*

abbeys and cathedrals, which were spreading the worship of God across Europe. If the ceremony of the Mass changed bread and wine into the Body and Blood of the Son of God, his actual image, drops from his veins, or evidence of his martyrdom in Jerusalem were the literal proofs of a dominant faith. Holy relics were the medieval verdict of history on the Bible. What was believed, had taken place.

The most precious Grails of the 12th century were the Holy Lance and the Holy Shroud, the Holy Veil given to St Veronica, the True Cross, the Crown of Thorns and the cup of Joseph of Arimathea. Pieces and replicas of all of these were surrounded by jewelled reliquaries of precious metal. As early as the 6th century, Antonius Placentinus had reported that the Holy Lance and the Chalice of the Last Supper were on show in the Church of Sion and the Basilica of the Holy

Sepulchre. The pilgrim Arculf, who travelled a century later from the British Isles to Palestine, described the sights of the Holy City. In a chapel, he saw a vessel, said to be from the Last Supper. 'The chalice is silver, has the measure of a Gallic pint, and has two handles on either side.' He also saw the Holy Lance in the porch of Constantine's Basilica. Although these vanished with the Arab conquest of Palestine, pieces of the True Cross emerged again in Byzantium, or Constantinople, along with the Crown of Thorns, the Holy Shroud and the Holy Veil, ransomed from the Muslims at the siege of Edessa and returned to Greek Christian ceremonies.

After the capture of Jerusalem at the end of the First Crusade, two more Grails were recognised. One of them, described by Albert of Aix, was the golden urn hanging from the centre of the Dome of the Rock, the marvellous Muslim shrine mistaken by Christian pilgrims for the Temple of Solomon. That precious vessel was believed to hold manna from heaven and the Holy Blood of Christ. And there was the True Cross, recovered from the Orthodox Syrians in 1099, a golden and jewelled reliquary containing a little of the wood from the torture of Jesus. The rest of the Holy Cross had been taken to Constantinople, but this relic was carried into battle by the crusading knights until it was lost to Saladin at his victory at the Horns of Hattin. It was either sold to the Byzantine emperor by Saladin's brother and successor, or it disappeared in the Islamic wars after the capture of the Kingdom of Jerusalem.

Three years before the Fourth Crusade seized Constantinople in 1204, the Treasurer of the Pharos Chapel, Nicolas Mesarites, warned the enemies of the Byzantine emperor not to attack the place: 'In this chapel, Christ rises again, and the Shroud with the burial linens is the clear proof.... They still smell of myrrh and are indestructible since they once enshrouded the dead body, anointed and naked, of the Almighty after His Passion.' But a crusader, Robert de Clari, saw the Holy Shroud in the Church of Saint Mary Blachernae. Here 'was kept the Shroud in which Our Lord has been wrapped, which stood up straight every Good Friday, so that the features of Our Lord could be plainly seen there.'

After Jerusalem, Constantinople was considered Christendom's second repository of holy relics. Along with the golden *capsula* containing the veil of St Veronica, and the jewelled holder of the Holy Shroud, there were a host of others. Mesarites stopped a mob seeking the blessed relics by telling them of three other instruments of the Passion, which he also held in the palace. The first was 'the holy Crown of Thorns, which remained intact

This engraving shows some of the most venerated relics, which were in their reliquaries in the Sainte Chapelle in Paris: (a) the Crown of Thorns; (b) the swaddling clothes of Christ; (c) the relics of the Passion – Christ's bonds, the sponge at the cross, the reed and a phial of Christ's blood; (d) a fragment of the True Cross; (e) the point of the Holy Lance; (f) a flask of the Blessed Virgin's milk; (g) Moses' rod; (h) the crown of John the Baptist's skull.

Crusaders take Constantinople, 1204.

because it took on incorruptibility from touching the sacred head of Jesus'. The second was the last 'Holy Nail preserved just as it was when it penetrated the most holy and merciful Flesh'. The third was the *flagellum*, the whip with the thongs that still bore the blood of Christ. These five remains of the Passion were among the holy treasures of Constantinople, which remained for the looting.

There were many other sacred valuables. The German Albrecht's *Later Titurel* told of a costly dish, which was a copy of the Holy Server: it was so richly decorated and flawless in its holiness that it was said to be 'the true grâl'. As early as the 4th century, the bodies of Sts Andrew, Luke and Timothy had been disinterred for reburial in the Sancta Sophia. Most of these relics were now plundered by the Venetians and the crusaders. By a long and elaborate process of international bribes, saintly King Louis the Ninth of France arranged for the Byzantine Crown of Thorns in its Grail casket to be redeemed from Venice and enshrined in Paris within the miracle of the building of the Sainte Chapelle. Even when the Treasury of the Basilica of San Marco was gutted by fire in 1231, the most holy of the looted remains were providentially spared by the flames – the wood of the True Cross, the flask of the Blood of Jesus

Christ, and the head of St John the Baptist. Fire forged faith; it did not destroy it. Until the French Revolution scattered the relics in the Sainte Chapelle, these were venerated for their profusion.

When Robert de Clari found his most precious relic – the Holy Shroud or Veil – in Constantinople, he added a description of another Grail. For the image of Christ was on a cloth imbued with the Water and Blood of Jesus, soaked with the fluids from his Body. In the Church of St Mary, the cloth with his features was contained in a rich vessel 'of gold hanging in the middle of the chapel by heavy silver chains'. To the Knights Templars, that container of His Blood and the image of His Head signified a Grail, for the Holy Shroud most probably came into their possession after the sack of Constantinople.

When the Grand Master of the Order, Jacques de Molay, was to be executed in 1314, he was burned alive with another Templar, Geoffrey de Charny, Preceptor of Normandy. One generation later, another Geoffrey de Charny emerged as the possessor of the Shroud, for which he built a shrine at Liray near Troyes in Champagne. This was apt, given that Chrétien de Troyes had written the first story of the Grail. The Shroud's new guardian, however, was killed at the Battle of Poitiers, where he lost the sacred Oriflamme of St Denis to the English victors.

The mania for parading and viewing evidence of the Crucifixion and the bones of the saints was

Crusader forces in Jerusalem.

وَكَادَ يَرْعَزِعُ الْجَمَالُ لَا الشَّمَرُ وَاسْدَ

مَا الْحَجِّ سَبِيلٌ تَاوِيَّاوَاذْلَاجَا وَلَاعَنَّاسِ الْجَمَالَاوَاحَدَلَاجَا

Muslim Turcopole cavalry.

part of a faith that believed in the resurrection of the body. More than a pagan cult of the dead hero, orthodox Christianity continued to venerate the flesh as the home of the Holy Spirit. St Augustine himself had complained of travelling salesmen dressed as monks who sold pieces of martyrs; but he had praised the carrying of the remains of St Stephen to Tibilis, where these worked miracles.

Although this traffic was outlawed, ambitious abbots and bishops went on buying sacred remains and housing them in precious boxes to attract contributions from massed congregations. Pope Gregory the Great had refused to donate the head of St Paul to the Byzantine Empress Constantina, yet his condemnation of cutting up the bodies of the martyrs and distributing them for profit was ineffective.

So many relics of Christ found their way to the West that miracles were needed to explain the host of them. Paulinus declared that the True Cross at Jerusalem renewed itself, however many slivers were cut from it. As a profound study of medieval faith and fable found, the belief in

> the power and fragments of the cross to multiply themselves was constant in the Middle Ages, and was compared to that of the body of Christ in the Eucharist. The nails of the cross had the same power of reproducing themselves, though many nails perhaps contained only filings of the originals. The crown of thorns, spear, sponge, and reed, the seamless coat, the pillar to which the Lord was bound, the stone of the sepulchre, earth from that or from the Holy Land, even our Lord's footprints, were known from the 4th century.

There were dozens of authenticated examples of napkins with the sweat of Jesus, of boards from the Bethlehem manger, and of the Holy Coat that the Empress Helena was said to have given originally to Trèves. Christ's tooth and even the foreskin from his circumcision were encased in gold and glazed with gems.

These lesser Grails of Europe multiplied in His name. In his abbey, Angilbert described parts of the True Cross and the manger, the sandals and vestments of Jesus, the vinegar sponge of the Crucifixion and water from the Jordan river, a hair from the beard of St Peter and breast milk from the Virgin Mary. There were two attested heads of John the Baptist and three bodies of Mary Magdalene. Of the 800 monasteries and 10,000 churches in Germany in the 12th century, many claimed to possess more than 500 sacred objects. As in the stories of this or that Grail among many and of 'the Grail', all remains of the suffering of Christ and of the saints were held to retain the grace of God and to give out the Light of the Spirit. They could perform miracles and were talismans against danger.

The power of sacred relics was unique to medieval Christianity. It was based on the articles of the faith. At the Last Supper, Jesus had broken bread and given it to His disciples, saying that it was His Body. He had offered them wine, saying that it was His Blood. At the ceremony of Communion, the faithful literally believed that the consecrated bread and wine were changed into the Body and Blood of Christ, the Saviour.

Christians also believed that their own bodies would be resurrected at the Second Coming. No such corporeal faith lay in the Jewish or Muslim religions. But it allowed the Christians of the Middle Ages to become obsessed with bones and vials of blood and objects that were said to derive from the tombs of the saints and martyrs. These even sanctified the weapons of war. In Roland's lament at his death for his blade, Durandal, he recalled the sacred treasures in his sword:

> Ah, Durandal, you are holy and fair
> Many are the relics in your gilded hilt:
> Saint Peter's tooth, some of Saint Basil's blood,
> Hairs from the head of lordly Saint Denis.
> Part of a robe that blessed Mary wore.
> It would be wrong for infidels to hold you:
> To wield you is for Christian men alone.

What Arthur had been to the history of the kings of Britain, Charlemagne was to a Europe that did not yet know its name. He had formed the Holy Roman Empire, recalling the majesty of the past and the holy city on the Tiber that preached a united Christendom. He had built his own new Jerusalem at Aachen, with its sacred octagonal chapel where later emperors would be crowned, and he had filled it with holy relics. The Treasury of the Dom still houses many reliquaries; three of the Bohemian ones show through rock crystal some holy things: the belt of the Virgin Mary, the belt of Jesus and the rope used to whip Him. A great pilgrimage still takes place every seven years around the Virgin's dress that she wore at His birth, His swaddling clothes and loincloth, and the shroud of John the Baptist. The thigh bone of Charlemagne himself is displayed in a triple-spired reliquary,

The 6th-century octagonal Baptistery in Ravenna, which influenced Charlemagne's imperial chapel of the Dom in Aachen.

along with a piece of a nail driven through the feet of Christ, a splinter of the True Cross and a fragment of the Crown of Thorns. Most striking is a horn, said to be Charlemagne's, but dating from the 10th century; it is made from an elephant's tusk and serves as a reminder of the Roman cornucopia; also of Roland's last bugle call at Roncesvalles before his death.

The octagonal marble chapel of the emperor in the Dom is the fount of the Matter of France. Influenced by the Baptisteries at Byzantine Ravenna and the original Church of the Holy Sepulchre in Jerusalem, the mosaics and marble patterns predict the symbols of the Grail legend. Over the entrance, a mosaic displays the Heavenly Jerusalem, surrounded within its circular walls by

An octagonal cross and cosmic symbol from the Dom, Aachen.

four men in white robes, pouring from Greek jars the four sacred rivers of Eden. The Temple of Solomon with its two pillars and quartet of arches looks classical, but is surmounted by a cross, while below are curtains hiding the Ark and a hanging lamp. Beside the windows are chalice patterns made of coloured marble; over a door is an eight-pointed cross with a round stone or cosmos dropping from it. Yet most prophetic is the mosaic over the golden altar, which shows the Holy Spirit as a dove, descending with rays of fire, some in the shape of the Cross, and holding in its beak the Word of God to lay on the empty throne of Charlemagne. This allegory of the divine emperor bringing revelation to his people, as Melchizedek and King David did in Israel, is confirmed by a Latin inscription declaring that God gave Charlemagne the right to build his Temple because he ruled so well.

The chapel and Treasury at Aachen were to become the inspiration for the architecture and the collection of holy relics across all Europe. Although Charlemagne's empire at his death was split into three parts, and these into many more duchies and countries, the mystery of that blessed *imperium* continued to haunt the imagination of the medieval troubadours, particularly the legend of Roland and his end. Versions of *The Song of Roland*, indeed, were being sung at the time of the First Crusade, and gave the best contemporary insight into the barbaric, fearful and proud temperament of the European knight. Recalling a defeat by Charlemagne in his campaign against the Ummayads in Spain, the destruction of his rearguard in a Basque ambush at Roncesvalles was translated into a heroic slaughter of the Muslim hordes and the sacrifice of a hero and martyr through betrayal.

This legendary epic was shot through with the silk and blood of the period. It was a declaration of a holy war against Islam, in which chivalry was restricted to the knights on both sides, while there was no mercy for the rest of humanity. Those who died in Charlemagne's cause would enter the gates of paradise, as the sanguinary Archbishop Turpin promised. 'Infidels are wrong and Christians are in the right,' proclaimed Count Roland. 'I will set no bad example.' Killing a few hundred infidels with Durandal – which could split rock like the Shamir that built the Temple of Solomon, and King Arthur's Excalibur – Roland thought a good example, even though he condemned himself and his 20,000 men to death by refusing to summon help from Charlemagne with his horn. The sacred relics in the hilt of Durandal made it more murderous, while the count's arrogance and the butchery of the enemy turned strategic folly into sacred romance.

The Song of Roland presaged the disaster that would befall the later Christian Kingdom of

The dying Roland with his horn and holy relics in the hilt of his sword Durandal is taken to heaven from Roncesvalles by the Hand of God, bearing a Grail. *(13th-century Spanish illustration)*

Jerusalem, which was born in the confused ideal of a crusade, and condemned by the pride and treachery of the actual rulers of the expeditionary force that was to occupy Palestine. In *The Song of Roland*, the Franks were the Chosen People of God, and their enemies were doomed to hell or the sword, unless they accepted conversion. When Charlemagne took Córdoba and razed its walls, the poet considered it a matter of course that 'all infidels in the city had been slain/Or else converted to the Christian faith'. The Holy Roman Emperor himself held court in the great garden or paradise there, created by the Moorish king, 'the foe of God, who served Muhammad and to Apollyon prayed'. The massacre of the unbelievers who resisted a forced conversion to Christianity, was advocated as a habitual strategy in the counter-attack of Europe on Islam. To die in such a holy war would be to enter the heavenly gates with warrior angels as a guide. When Count Roland prayed with his dying words for remission of his sins, he offered up to God the mailed glove on his right fist, and St Gabriel took it from his hand. And so he died:

> To him God sent angels and Cherubim
> Along with Saint Michael of the Peril;
> And with them came down Saint Gabriel
> To carry the Count's soul up to paradise.

The master of the School of Charlemagne, the British monk Alcuin, might advise the emperor that it was better to copy the example of the saints than to carry around their bones. Yet with the prevailing mania for relics, his counsel went unheeded, certainly in the case of Roland and Durandal. And after the crusades and the fall of Constantinople, multitudes of sanctified things – blood and bones, wood and linen, hair and nails – were brought back from the Near East to become the blessed treasures of the West. The success of the story of the Grail invested these precious pieces with even more mystery and veneration. And yet, however infinitely the Light of God might manifest itself to pilgrims everywhere through religious things, the Knights of the Round Table only sought one source of the Grail in the medieval romances, even with so many circumstances set as snares about their questings.

NINE

THE PRODIGAL GRAIL

> The scholars who have offered the three chief solutions for the problem of the Grail have been able to make out an excellent case. The Grail as Celtic talisman, as fertility symbol, as Christian relic – each conception is supported by masses of detailed evidence. The judicious scholar is driven to admit that the Grail has signified many things to many men at many times.
>
> Roger Sherman Loomis, *Celtic Myth and Arthurian Romance*, 1993

 n the Middle Ages faith mixed with fact. Miracles were not confined to the time of Christ. They were still frequent happenings when holy relics were found. St Louis of France said that miracles were only necessary for those who did not believe. Bishop Hugh of Lincoln declared that those who took the Eucharist daily did not need to pursue signs and wonders. Yet the people of that age needed present proofs to confirm their creed. For these were written in the Old Testament as well as the New. When Moses led the Israelites out of Egypt, he overcame their doubts by setting up the Brazen Serpent of healing, and by reducing the Golden Calf to powder. Elijah called down fire from the Lord to challenge the pagan priests. And although Jesus refused to perform miracles to prove that he was the Son of God, he relented by feeding the 5,000, as the Grail would, and by changing water into wine at the feast of Cana.

Actually, one of the reasons for the spread of the Grail romances was a papal edict through a Lateran Council. In 1215, Innocent the Third withheld the communion cup from the laity. The dogma of transubstantiation was confirmed. Only the priest might eat and drink the Body and Blood of Christ before the congregation. This ban increased the power of the Church, which now stood between the supplicant and salvation. Yet equally, it added to the appeal of a legend, which told of the personal approach to God directly through a life of trial.

The Church rides on its four-headed Horse of the Apocalypse, catching in a Grail the blood of Christ released by St Longinus with his spear. *(12th-century Crucifixion in Herrade de Landsberg, Hortus deliciarum)*

Jesus changes water into wine at the wedding in Cana.
(From the chair of Maximian, Museum of the Archbishop's Palace, Ravenna)

When the Grail was also described as a Christian symbol from the Last Supper, the heresy that the religious institution from Rome had less significance in reaching the divine was most attractive.

The doctrine of transubstantiation was a late addition to the Catholic Church. One of its first appearances was in the 6th-century Coptic *Book of the Resurrection*, which told of the Apostles celebrating the sacrament after the Ascension of Christ. The mystical text stated: 'His body was upon the table, which they were all gathered around. And they divided it. They saw the blood of Jesus pouring out as living blood into the cup.' Such visions were also described by Gerald of Wales, when he wrote of the conversion of some

of the heretic Paterini to the true faith. In Ferrara, they saw the host changed into a Holy Lamb or pieces of flesh and blood.

In the ninth book of the *Dialogus Miraculorum* of Caesarius of Heisterbach, many witnesses spoke of the wafer taking the shape of Christ, or the wine changing into blood. Sometimes the host became a crucified Child, whose blood flowed into the chalice. In the different Grail romances, all of these miraculous visions were variously given to Perceval, Galahad and Gawain, who once saw the Grail as flesh 'with a king crowned, nailed on a Cross, and a spear fast in his side'. These sightings derived from the popular religious culture of the period.

Other Grail stories were told in medieval terms. That Holy Vessel was given the power of selecting good from evil, the sheep from the goats, the blessed from the sinners. Dissolute priests often found the communion cup empty, while a dove flew off with the wafer. Before he was burned in 1290, a Jew of Billittes was denounced for blasphemy. The accusation declared that he had stabbed a consecrated host and nailed it to a wall:

> Blood was shed from it. He cast it into the fire: it flew round the room. Mad with rage, he fixed it on a stake and flogged it. He tried in vain to cut it in pieces. Again he fixed it to the wall and stabbed it, and a river of blood flowed from it. Finally he threw it into a cauldron of boiling water, which became bloody. The Host rose in the air, and the Jew saw Christ on the Cross.

Such metaphors as the bloody cauldron seemed to have their genesis in the Celtic chivalric romances about the Grail. Certainly, Caesarius of Heisterbach affirmed that a knight took the sacrament before a joust to safeguard himself from wounds. When he had won, he declared to his opponent that he had only eaten the host that day. The reply was, 'If you had eaten the Devil, I would have overcome you.' Albigensian heretics, who were walking on water, were said to have drowned when the consecrated wafer was cast into the river. And when the Italian founder of the Apostolici was burned in 1300, he put out the fire by calling on the help of the fallen angel Asmodeus, only to have it rekindled by the bringing of the host.

In the bloody romance of the *Perlesvaus*, the Grail was said to appear to King Arthur at the ceremony of the Mass 'in five different forms that none ought to tell'. The reason was that the Catholic Church had now reserved to the priests the mysteries of the sacrament. Only those elected by God should speak of them. 'King Arthur beheld all the changes; the last of them was a change into a chalice.' This communion cup was not his to receive. It was withheld by the Church because of his regal sins. Yet the Grail was not always so constrained. It remained accessible to any perfect knight, who might reach it by his own endeavours.

The Knights Templars did believe that they had a direct approach to the divine without the benefit of the Catholic Church, which they appeared to serve. This claim was their worst heresy, although they were charged with many others. They shared this spiritual arrogance with their Islamic counterparts, the Sufis. To some, that name came from the Arabic for wool; for others, it derived from *Sophia* or Wisdom, dear to the Gnostics. Like the troubadours, the Sufis wrote poems of mystical love in the style of the Song of Solomon. Their cup of wine was a transcendent chalice, which might be broken at death.

The Sufis – like the Isma'ilis, the Templars and the Cathars – divided their initiates into classes: the Masters, the Prophets and the Saints. The Masters were the everlasting priesthood standing between the human and the divine; the Prophets were the teachers and messengers of the will of God; while the Saints reached the Heavenly Light through their good life on earth. The Templars had their Masters, too, and the Cathars their *perfecti*, with grades beneath them. The point of all these mystical Orders and sects was clear. Total enlightenment was only granted by God to the elect.

The Prophet Muhammad himself was subject to ecstatic visions. He was given some of the text of the Koran in his dreams after visits from the Angel Gabriel, who brought him the command of God.

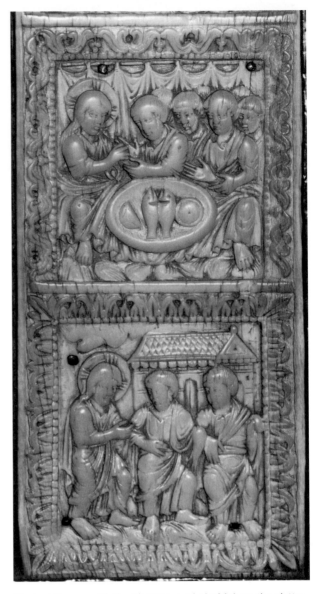

The Last Supper, with the Christian symbol of fish on the platter of the Grail. *(Museum of the Archbishop's Palace, Ravenna)*

'He came to me,' said the apostle of God, 'while I was asleep, with a coverlet of brocade whereon was some writing, and said, "Read!" I said, "What shall I read?" He pressed me with it so tightly that I thought it was death; then he let me go and said, "Read!" I said, "What shall I read?" He pressed me with it again so that I thought it was death; then he let me go and said, "Read!" I said, "What shall I read?" He pressed me with it the third time so that I thought it was death and said, "Read!" I said, "What then shall I read?" – and this I said only to deliver myself from him, lest he should do the same to me again. He said:

"Read in the name of the Lord who created,
Who created men of blood coagulated.
Read! Thy Lord is the most beneficent,
Who taught by the pen,
Taught that which they knew not unto men."

So I read it, and he departed from me. And I awoke from my sleep, and it was as though the words were written on my heart.'

Such were the trances in which the Knights of the Round Table saw the Grail turn into flesh. Such was the vision that the Prophet Muhammad had of the green goblet, when he ascended into the seventh heaven from the Dome of the Rock in Jerusalem. Such was the Prophet's decision, when he decided to retain the pagan Ka'aba in Mecca as the holy cornerstone of Islam. As the Koranic verse testified: 'Glory be to Him who made His servant go by night from the sacred Temple to the farther Temple whose surroundings We have blessed, that We might show him some of Our signs.'

The Sufis also felt, along with the Gnostics, a personal sense of identity with God, which put them at odds with their orthodox churches. They likened their mystical experiences to the Prophet Muhammad's *mi'raj* or vision of the divine. Their Otherworld, however, was not that of the Celts or the Arthurian Grail Castle. It was not a heaven or a hell, but rather an area in the cosmos, where the individual soul met the One Maker of the universe. The Prophet Muhammad had spoken in the Koran of the ninety-nine names of God. But for the Sufis, there were infinite names of God, each appropriate to the seeker after his identity. As with the Quest for the Grail, it revealed itself in the form appropriate to each searcher after its truth.

The Sufis also stressed self-knowledge as the only way of progress towards the knowledge of God. This was the lesson of Bernard of Clairvaux, the founder of the Cistercian monks and the supporter of the Knights Templars. It was echoed also in the character of Perceval in the first Grail romance by Chrétien de Troyes. St Bernard even dared to write his *Advice to a Pope* on this theme:

What does it profit you if you gain the whole world and lose one person – yourself? Even if you were a wise man, your wisdom would lack something if it did not benefit you. How much would it lack? Everything, I feel. Although you know every mystery, the width of the earth, the height of the heavens, the depth of the sea, if you do not know yourself, you are like a building without a foundation; you raise not a structure but ruins. . . . You should consider what you are, who you are, and what sort of man you are: what you are in nature, who you are in person, and what sort of man you are in character. What you are, for example, is man. Who you are: Pope and Supreme Pontiff. What sort of man: kind, gentle, and so forth.

In the original Grail tale, Perceval did not understand his own name, let alone his nature. Even when he was told what he was called, he did not know whether his name was the true one. Ignorance of the death of his mother at his departure, and of himself, made him fail his test at the Grail Castle. St Bernard had condemned not knowing oneself as the source of pride and sin. To be unaware was not good enough:

Do you suppose it availed the first man, or was it allowed that he did not sin willingly, because he pleaded with his wife, that is, the weakness of the flesh, in defence? Or will the stoners of the first martyrs, because they had stopped their ears, be excusable through ignorance? . . . For God knows what you do not know, and He is the one who judges you.

Self-knowledge and self-control might allow the Sufi or the Knight Templar to achieve the ecstatic vision of the One Creator, whose sign was the Grail. Perceval might have achieved that as Parzival would in his German story, for Chrétien de Troyes left his original masterpiece incomplete. He did describe the Grail as golden and jewelled, but blazing with brilliant light, *tant sainte chose*, or such a sacred thing. It was more than the Christian chalice, it was the giver of spiritual life, which by its qualities had also nourished for twelve years the body of the maimed Fisher King. It was the Holy

Light, which blazed from the stone Grail in *Parzival*, the Shining Wisdom of the One that united Sufi and Gnostic and Knight Templar in the vision of the wholeness of the universe.

This was not the heresy for which the Templars would be condemned. They were brought down by the original sins of Perceval: arrogance and ignorance of themselves within the ways of the world. With the loss of their function as the defenders of pilgrims and the Temple of Solomon in Jerusalem, they had become money brokers and guardians of treasure rather than the Grail. They owned some 9,000 manors across Europe, all of which were free of taxes, and they provided security for the storage and transport of bullion.

The treasury of the King of France was normally kept in the vaults of the Temple in Paris; the King himself took refuge there when threatened by mobs. The only cash drafts that were readily redeemable were issued by the Templars. They became the bankers of the Levant, and later of most of the courts of Europe. When King Louis the Seventh accepted a large loan from the Order, he noted that the money must be repaid quickly, 'lest their House be defamed and destroyed'. Even the Muslims banked with the Templars, in case the fortunes of war should force them to ally themselves with the Christians. Though usury was forbidden in the Middle Ages, the Templars added to the money they stored or transported by paying back an agreed sum less than the original amount, while a debtor returned more than his debt. The Paris Temple became the centre of the world's money market.

The Templars were so proud that they became the judges of monarchs in the way that the Grail judged sinners. 'So long as you do exercise justice,' the Master of the Temple declared to Henry the Third of England, 'you will reign, but if you infringe it, you will cease to be King.' The implication was that he might be deposed by the military Order.

Pride, or *superbia*, was considered the worst of sins in the Middle Ages. To this, the Templars added secret rituals and diplomacy, which aggravated the envy and hatred of them by the princes and the people. They were seen both as the poor knights of Christendom and as rich conspirators against the state and public welfare. When King Philip the Fourth of France imprisoned more than 600 of the 3,000 Templars in the country in 1307, according to Inquisition records, their interrogation and torture produced confessions that corroborated medieval superstitions, but were the result of applying force and pain. They were not the evidence of truth.

Although the initiation rights of the Templars were secret, there was a Rule of the Temple. Their hidden regulations were to provide the key to their destruction, although they could hardly have existed as a proud and efficient military caste without special ceremonies to distinguish them from other orders such as the Knights Hospitallers of St John and the Teutonic Knights. The investitures were secret, being held under cover of darkness in a guarded chapter house. The Rule was clandestine, in so far as it was known in its entirety to only the highest officers of the Temple. There are copies that describe the constitution of the order, and the duties and ceremonies of each rank. But because of the element of secrecy, and because the original manuscript of the Rule has not survived, opponents of the Templars have always postulated the existence of a separate and secret Rule that would endorse blasphemy and sexual licence.

An unbiased account of their initiation ritual gave the following details. The Master of the Temple asked the assembled knights three times, if there was any objection to a particular novice's admission to the order. The novice himself was shown 'the great hardships of the House, and the commandments of charity that existed'. He was also asked if he was betrothed or had a wife, debts or hidden disease, other vows or other Master. If the novice answered these questions satisfactorily, he knelt in front of the Master and asked to become 'the serf and slave of the House'. The Master replied that many things were required of him and that the Templars' beautiful horses and costume were no more than the 'outer shell' of their life, as was the armour of the knights in the

Grail Quest. The self-control and service taught by St Bernard was their duty.

> You do not know the hard commandments that are within; because it is a hard thing for you, who are master of yourself, to make yourself the serf of another. For you will scarcely ever do what you want: if you wish to be on this side of the sea, you will be sent to the other side; or if you wish to be in Acre, you will be sent to the land of Tripoli or Antioch or Armenia, or you will be sent to Apulia or Sicily or Lombardy or France or Burgundy or England or to many other lands where we have Houses and possessions. If you wish to sleep, you will be made to stay awake; and if you sometimes wish to stay awake, you will be ordered to go and rest in your bed.

Guiot de Provins, the contemporary monk and poet, who belonged to holy Orders and condemned his own time as 'vile and filthy', testified to the Templars' integrity, praising them above all other religious orders. He found them dedicated unto death, ascetic knights, whom his shrinking flesh could admire and refuse to join.

> Better far be cowardly and alive,
> Than dead, the most famous of them all.
> The Order of the Templars, I know well,
> Is beautiful and excellent and sure –
> But keeping healthy keeps me from war.

Guiot from Provence was the most likely source of the *Parzival* of Wolfram von Eschenbach, who certainly shared his opinion of the worthiness of the Knights Templars, whom he would make the Keepers of the Grail. After their destruction, many would join another military order familiar to Wolfram, the Teutonic Knights, then carving out an empire towards Russia. Their new headquarters was in the stronghold of Marienburg in Prussia. Their opportunity lay on the Eastern Marches, and they did not wish to share in the fate of the

Pope Urban the Second consecrates the altar at Cluny in 1095. *(12th-century French manuscript)*

Right: The Knights Templars are arrested and imprisoned, 1307. **Below:** The Knights are burned at the stake.

Templars in France. They would be protected in Germany as military agents of the states and the bishops on a crusade to dominate and convert the pagan Lithuanians.

With its twelve bailiwicks in the Holy Roman Empire stretching from Alsace to Austria and Saxony, and its Baltic conquests as far as Livonia, the Order was a temporal power. The inhabitants were converted to Christianity by the sword and the efficient administration of the knights from their fortresses. As the English philosopher and cleric Roger Bacon observed, the brothers of the Teutonic Order, who laboured for the conversion of the heathens, wanted to reduce them to serfdom. Resistance to the Christian Knights was against 'oppression, not the arguments of a superior religion'.

Particularly significant in the German military Order was its cult of the Virgin Mary. Her Office was said daily, while a golden 20ft-tall mosaic of her was inlaid on the church of the great Castle of the Knights at Marienburg. This was a development in northern Europe from the oriental beliefs of the Templars, although their Rule also declared Our Lady to be the beginning and the end of their religion. Her supreme symbol as Queen of Heaven was the foliate rose, the rose of the centre of the world. She was also the living Grail, for she contained and gave birth to the Body and Blood of her Son.

A drawing of the centre of the painted vault of the chapel of the Templar Commandery at Monsaunès near Toulouse.

with a sacred purpose is a Grail, an emblem of one of its properties. For it may be present as manna or ambrosia, as blinding light or the Holy Spirit, as bounty or baptism, as the sacrifice of captives or of Jesus Christ, as a heavenly stone or a severed head, as a jewelled chalice or a bleeding lance, as a platter or a book, as a fish or a dove with the host in its beak. Many are the forms of the Grail. After all, the search for its discovery is a personal quest. If that holy presence is sensed, it may appear in a different vision to each seeker. Any sign of it is equally valid to a tracker after a truth.

Yet the markers along the way are enigmatic. They are not as clear as the indications on all the roads that lead to Rome. They are variable and often insubstantial. Rather as the Stations of the Cross can only be symbols of the Passion, so the pointers to the Grail may only suggest a path to a beatific vision of its manifestation. Each finder discovers a unique insight into the divine.

This is not deconstruction. The viewer does not create a picture of the Grail, any more than a reader understands the texts of the holy books better than the God who made the Word. The Grail shines to those who are worthy to receive it after long trials of the body and the soul. In the Grail romances, it came to King Arthur and the Knights of the Round Table in a series of altered states, or not at all. The point was that its changing presence was only possible, given the experiences and mistakes of those on the Quest. Divine grace granted a view of the Grail as a reward for the long journey towards perfection. Each sight of it was suited to the individual struggle towards it.

To travel towards the Grail was to take one of the multitudinous and mysterious ways of Creation. Through the control of the body and the refining of the spirit, an understanding of self might be followed by a revelation of the divine. To attain the ever-changing Grail was to search deep within, and so reach out to a personal path to God.

A discerning proof of the Templars, as the guardians of the Grail, was painted on the principal Commandery of the county of Comminges and Couserans, founded in 1156 at Monsaunès near Toulouse, on the pilgrim way to Compostela. The Romanesque chapel in stone and brick, a great rectangle ended by a choir in a semicircle, houses the confirmation of the Templars as the keepers of the Grail and the Holy Spirit. On the vault is painted a red octagonal cross *pattée*, which supports a chalice bowl ornamented by the flower with six petals of the builders and masons of the *compagnonnages* of Maitre Jacques, and by the entwined worms or serpents of Gnostic wisdom. Arrowheads as plumblines and stars with the sun and the moon, triangles and pyramids, and an encompassing cosmic bowl, argue for greater mysteries within this medieval military Order.

In one sense, every cup or bowl or reliquary

TEN

CELTIC GRAILS

Hear ye the history of the most holy vessel that is called the Grail, in which the precious blood of Jesus was received on the day that He was put on the Cross.

The Perlesvaus

Before the writing of *Perceval*, the lost Arthur's connection with Glastonbury and the Grail was suggested as early as 1130 by the Welsh Caradoc of Llancarfon in his *Life of Saint Gildas*, said to be a contemporary of the legendary king, whose wife Guinevere was kidnapped by Melvas, the ruler of the summer West Country. Secure in his castle surrounded by marshland, Melvas refused to return his hostage, until Gildas advised him to give her up or risk the wrath of God. With his queen restored, Arthur granted lands to the abbey of Glastonbury, and he and Melvas swore nevermore to violate that most sacred place.

The following Celtic romance of the *Perlesvaus* was 'obsessed with blood, murder, decapitation, dead bodies, and their mutilation'. In the terms of modern psychology, the hero Perlesvaus was a sadist, who harked back to pagan Celtic rituals of human sacrifice. The medieval fixation on sacred relics and treasure was also stressed. The Crown of Thorns was mounted on a golden and bejewelled base, the sword that beheaded John the Baptist bled at noon every day, a stained rag from the Passion was sealed in the boss of the protective silver shield of Joseph of Arimathea. Although Perlesvaus became the ruler of the Grail Castle, he divided the blessed reliquaries among some neighbouring hermits. Then he sailed away on a ship with a red Templar Cross on its white sail, and he vanished, as though he had never been. 'From that time forth, no earthly man knew what had become of him.'

In this work, the Knights Templars were described as the keepers of the Grail, which was defined as the vessel that caught Christ's blood, collected by Joseph of Arimathea. There was no peace or compromise with Muslim chivalry or faith in the *Perlesvaus*. Its unknown French author claimed that it was based on a Latin script by a monk of Glastonbury, and so served as propaganda for King Arthur's burial there. Yet its detailed accounts of weapons, armour and military strategy, as well as its praise of crusading Knights of the Grail protecting their sacred secret in their mantles embroidered with red crosses, suggested that the writer was a sympathiser of the Templar military Order.

The Grail was said to be the Eucharistic chalice of the Last Supper; but that was only its final and fifth form, as seen by King Arthur after attending a sacrament given by hermits. The bleeding lance was also the Holy Lance of Longinus, which pierced Christ's side on the Cross and was rediscovered by the crusaders at Antioch. Also visible was the bloody sword that had cut off the head of St John the Baptist, revered by the monastic cavalry. And the Grail Castle was put into transcendental terms, filled with sweet scents and aromatic spices, under the names of Eden and the Castle of Joy and the Castle of Souls, while the river around the walls came from the Earthly Paradise. And all who died within were assured of reaching bliss in heaven.

There was a strong Celtic influence in the legends of the Grail, particularly about an Otherworld to which the dying heroes went — Arthur to Avalon, Bran to the Blessed Isles of the West rather than to Munsalvaesche or Mount of

Salvation, on which the Grail Castle was built. All the marvels of that keep of the Fisher King were further to be found in the fortress of the divine Lug, which had held the treasures of the Celtic gods, including a bleeding lance, a Spear of Destiny, a bottomless drinking vessel, a cauldron that could feed an army, an unconquerable sword, and a stone fallen from heaven as in *Parzival* – a Stone of King David or Scone, on which the Irish and Scots kings were crowned, until the English took it away to Westminster Abbey for their coronations of the rulers of Great Britain.

Joseph of Arimathea was declared the author of the Welsh romance through the voice of an angel. The text mentioned both him and St Longinus, who honoured the body of Christ, burying it in the Holy Sepulchre with the Holy Lance which had pierced His side, and the Grail used by Joseph to drain His Blood. Descended from King David, Joseph was held to be the progenitor of the Grail lineage, until the time of King Arthur. Perlesvaus, the perfect knight, had failed to ask the right question of the Fisher King, allowing Arthur's kingdom to be changed into a Waste Land.

The ruler had become slothful; his best knights had left the Round Table. To redeem himself, Arthur went to St Austin's chapel in Wales, where he saw a vision of Christ as Child and Redeemer. Returning to his court at Cardeuil, he met the sister of Perlesvaus, who healed him of a wound with blood from the severed head of a Black Knight. She told him of her brother's youth in Wales, where he had lost his inheritance to the Lord of the Moors. She reproached Arthur for bearing the name of so evil a king; she did not know that he had begun to reform.

Holding court at Penzance, Arthur was drinking from his golden cup when three maidens entered the hall. They were surrounded by scents and covered with jewels; but the first was bald. She had lost her hair because of the failure of Perlesvaus at the Grail Castle, but she brought the shield of Joseph for him – azure and silver with a red cross.

Left: In the Celtic romance *Arthur of Little Britain*, severed heads litter the waters of the Porte Noire of the castle.

Above: The crucified Christ on the Templar Cross on the shield of the Blood of Joseph of Arimathea. (The Quest for the Holy Grail, *Le Mans manuscript*)

Again, with the Celtic stress on severed heads and gory relics, she carried with her in a cart, drawn by three harts, the heads of 150 knights sealed in caskets of gold, silver and lead. Leaving the court, the maidens met Gawain, who took up the Quest. After various adventures, he asked a hermit how to attain the Grail.

'Sir,' Gawain said, 'by what way can a man reach this castle?'

'Sir,' the hermit said, 'none may teach you except for the Will of God. And would you reach it?'

'Sir,' Gawain said, 'it is my great desire.'

Seeking the Grail Castle, Gawain found himself in meadows near a forest. High walls and battlements enclosed the great halls of Camelot; its dead lord Alain was descended from Joseph of Arimathea. His widow was beset by the Lord of the Moors, whom Gawain defeated in combat, so freeing her stronghold. Riding through further trials to the Land of the Fisher King, Gawain reached the Grail Castle, but he was refused entrance until he returned with a sacred Templar relic, the sword that had beheaded St John the Baptist. 'If you bring that sword,' a priest told Gawain, 'you may freely come into the castle, and everywhere in the realm of the Fisher King, you will be made most welcome.'

Gawain won the relic from the cannibal Gurguran, who ruled Scotland and was now converted to Christianity – a folk memory of the first Irish missions to the pagan Picts. Now the knight was conducted by angels and rode over the perilous bridges into the Grail Castle; they were flaming with the fire of the Holy Ghost, and the keep was ablaze with brightness. He gave the biblical sword to the maimed Fisher King, who was reclining on an ivory bed before a cross of gold, containing a piece of the True Cross.

Then Gawain met with a group of initiates, who had a red cross on their breasts, and two Masters. After a feast with twelve of the knights he repeated the mistake of Perlesvaus in failing to ask the right question of the diseased Fisher King. He was struck dumb by the sight of the Grail and the three drops of blood falling from the Holy Lance, held in the hands of two maidens. He was not the perfect knight. He could not heal the royal wounds. Yet he had a vision of two angels bearing golden candlesticks and of the Grail as flesh 'with a king crowned, nailed on a Cross, and a spear fast in his side'.

Lancelot now took up the Quest. The brutality of the period intruded on his mission. Martyrdom was presented to Lancelot in the guise of mutilation. He sat with the lady of a castle:

The first course was brought in by knights in chains who had their noses cut off. The second by knights in chains who had their eyes put out, so that squires led them. The third course was brought in by knights with one hand and chained. After that, other knights with one foot brought in the fourth course. And with the fifth course came tall and fair knights, each with a naked sword used to cut off their heads, now given to the lady.

Lancelot disliked such a sacrifice and refused to be the lord of the castle. He was accused of loving Queen Guinevere too much, and so set off after the Grail, which he could never reach because of his mortal sin. Arriving at the Castle of the Fisher King, he was richly fed at an ivory table with the other knights, from vessels of gold and silver, but the Grail did not appear. He was not worthy of it.

Perlesvaus again took up the Quest, carrying the shield of azure and silver with the red cross of Joseph of Arimathea. A curious encounter with another red cross in the forest left him watching a white hart torn apart by hounds. A knight and a maiden appeared, collected the bloody pieces in golden vessels and kissed the cross. When Perlesvaus kissed it, he smelled all the scents of paradise. Two priests then came on the scene and sent him away. They kissed and whipped the cross with a rod, then they wept. When Perlesvaus protested, one of the priests told him that it was no concern of his what they did. The mystery of their Christian act or heresy was their secret alone.

Ignoring the treacherous killing of the son of King Arthur, Perlesvaus rode to his mother's aid at Camelot. He met his sister, who told him of the death of the Fisher King and the disappearance of the Grail. His castle had been seized by the King of Chastel Mortel, who upheld the Old Laws and not the New Testament. Meanwhile, the Lord of the Moors had again taken Camelot. On delivering his mother's castle from Islam, Perlesvaus proved himself the pagan Celtic knight rather than the crusader. His killing of the Muslim chief and his warriors was exactly the scene of ritual slaughter depicted on the ancient Gunderstrup Cauldron of Nordic sacrifices:

'Our Lord God commanded in both the Old Law and the New,' Perlesvaus said, 'that justice should be done to mass-killers and traitors, and justice will be done upon you so that His Law is not transgressed.' He had a great vat made ready in the middle of the court, and ordered the eleven Moorish captive knights to be brought out. He had their heads severed into the vat with all the blood drained from their bodies, then he had the flesh taken out so there was only the blood in the vat. After that, he disarmed the Lord of the Moors and took him before the vessel filled with blood. Perlesvaus had the Lord's hands and feet bound fast, and after that he said, 'You were never satisfied with the blood of the knights of my lady mother, now I will satisfy you with the blood of your own knights.' So he had the Lord of the Moors hanged by the feet in the vat with his head in the blood as far as his shoulders, until he was drowned and quenched. After that, Perlesvaus had all the twelve bodies and heads dumped in an ancient burial pit beside an old chapel in the forest, while the vat of blood was cast into the river, so that the waters were all red.

If any act in the Grail romances identified the Holy Vessel with the Celtic sacrificial cauldron of death and rebirth, it was this bloodiness of the perfect knight Perlesvaus on the way to Camelot in the rescue of his family from the evil deeds of the Muslims. While the vat of slaughter was not identified with the Grail, it was a necessary rite of passage for Perlesvaus to achieve the Grail, which was finally to be seen by King Arthur in five different forms. Destroying the Castle of Copper, where metal men made by alchemy worshipped a brazen bull, Perlesvaus reached the land of his Quest, riding on a white mule and carrying the shield with the red cross. He crossed more bridges of peril, forcing the King of Chastel Mortel – the Cain of his brother, the good Fisher King – to commit suicide from fear.

Now Perlesvaus saw, in the castle chapel, the Grail appear again, and also the bleeding Holy Lance, the sword that had beheaded St John the Baptist, and many other holy relics. These now included the Holy Shroud, obtained by his sister, and the body of his ancestor Joseph of Arimathea. 'For Our Lord God much loved the place.' Perlesvaus buried the Fisher King in a tabernacle loaded with precious stones, illuminated by a divine light that did not come from candles. The New Law or Testament was preached, and Perlesvaus killed those who did not follow it. 'The evil belief was done away in her kingdom, and all were assured again in the New Law by the courage of the Good Knight.'

King Arthur was now summoned back from Cardeuil to the Quest by an angelic voice and two suns in the sky. His son's head, smelling of sweet spices, was brought back to him in a casket. Rebellion was brewing in Brittany from his seneschal, Kay, and Brian of the Isles. Passing through Tintagel on his mission, Arthur heard of the death of Queen Guinevere from grief at the loss of their son, and of an invasion by Brian of the Isles. Lancelot left him to bury the Queen and repel the attack, while Arthur pursued his vow. Reaching the Grail Castle and the river from the Earthly Paradise and the Valley of Plenty, Arthur had a vision of what he desired to see:

The Grail appeared at the ceremony of the Mass, in five different forms that none ought to tell. For the secret things of the sacrament should not be told openly, except by him given by God to tell them. King Arthur beheld all the changes; the last of them was a change into a chalice.

The Holy Spirit with the divine sun-disc comes down at Pentecost to St Mary Magdalene and the twelve Apostles, St Peter with the key, another with a crusading sword. *(Burdett Psalter)*

In none of the Grail romances were there appearances that so confirmed its infinite metamorphoses. It appeared in many shapes; it altered its substance and its essence; it was all things to all knights, yet it gave all that was needed – divine food, drink and grace. The hermit, who had held the Mass, found a writ under the host, which declared that 'Our Lord God would that His Body be sacrificed in such a vessel, and that this should be set on record.' And he told Arthur that the bell that he carried was one of three cast by Solomon for the Saviour, Mary Magdalene and the Saints, and sent by Pope Gregory the Great to Britain. So Arthur was to institute in his realm the chalice and the peal of bells to announce the celebration of the Mass.

Civil war broke out in the kingdom of Arthur, who even wrongly imprisoned Lancelot for treachery. Perlesvaus was carried over the sea to the Castle of the Four Horns, where he found a company of white monks with a red cross on their breasts. They led him to a glass casket, entombing an armed knight. They washed at a great gold basin and dined gloriously. Perlesvaus was given a white shield and was directed to a Plenteous Island to redeem the knights' heads sealed in the gold, silver and lead caskets in the cart of the maidens, as well as the heads of the local king and queen. He took back all the severed heads and was given a golden cup of healing for his chivalry and pains.

Finally, Perlesvaus returned to the Grail Castle, where he found his widowed mother and his sister, who led with him a religious life there until their deaths. A voice from heaven told him that the Holy Grail would no longer manifest itself. He must take it elsewhere. He distributed the holy relics to the churches and abbeys of Britain, where they remained as evidence of the Grail. He himself waited for the coming of the blessed Templar ship with its white sail and red cross. The bodies of his mother and the Fisher King were buried in the richest coffins of gold and silver that had ever been seen. And Perlesvaus departed on the Ship of Solomon to another world, taking with him the body of Joseph of Arimathea, while the Grail Castle fell into slow ruin.

Here ends the story of the most Holy Grail. Joseph placed it on record and gives the blessing of Our Lord to all who hear and honour it. The Latin text which inspired the Romance was taken in the Isle of Avalon, in a holy house of religion that stands at the head of the Adventurous Moors, where King Arthur and Queen Guinevere lie, according to the witness of the religious good men there.

So the author of the *Perlesvaus* ended his book, giving the credit to his patron, Jen de Nesle, who had served on the Fourth Crusade that took Constantinople rather than Jerusalem. Certainly, he was a propagandist of the white monks at Glastonbury as well as of the Templars, who had almost certainly come into possession of two 'Grails' at the fall of Constantinople: the jewelled vessels containing the Holy Shroud and the Holy Veil of St Veronica. And yet the *Perlesvaus* was more significant for its Celtic relish in severed heads like those of the divine Bran, and in sacrificial cauldrons of blood, while the Grail itself was translated into mystical as well as actual shapes. This was a sanguinary Christianity, well suited to the chivalry and slaughter of the crusades.

Another Welsh tale of the Grail in the collection of ancient Celtic texts, the *Mabinogion*, named the hero as Peredur, a popular name in Celtic literature. A Peredur with steel arms was slain with his companions at the Battle of Cattraeth at the beginning of the 6th century. In his *History* and *Vita Merlini*, Geoffrey of Monmouth recorded two kings called Peredur and a Knight of the Round Table of the same name. The *Dream of Rhonabwy* dealt with a Peredur of the Long Lance, while *pryderi*, or 'anxiety', was the attribute given to the mythological princes of Dyved, who ruled in South Wales, one of the possible realms of King Arthur.

The romance of *Peredur* may even have antedated the *Perceval* of Chrétien de Troyes. They were both written at much the same time and probably from the same sources. Certainly, its primitive content referred to a Welsh knight as the heir of King Arthur, with a kingdom extending from Scotland and the north of England to the

West Country and Wales proper. The motive of Peredur was revenge on the killers of his father and his six or eleven brothers. He was summoned by his uncle Arthur to Caerleon in order that he might become the last king of the Grail Castle. At the stronghold of a second uncle, he passed the test of the sword, cutting an iron column in two with his blade. Then a horrific Grail procession took place. Two youths entered the hall carrying 'a spear of huge size, and three streams of blood running along it from the socket to the floor'. All who were there cried out in grief. And then 'two maidens came in holding a great salver between them, with a man's head on the platter bathed in blood'.

This version of the Grail procession was a Celtic blood ritual, referring to the sacred head of Bran, as well as a gory reminder of the death of St John the Baptist. Later in the story, Peredur heard of the truth of the spear and the platter. The head was that of Peredur's cousin, who had been killed by the Caerloyw Witches, and Peredur must avenge him. Yet in a Grail romance, it also symbolised the Holy Lance of St Longinus and the Holy Vessel of the Last Supper and the Crucifixion. This startling confusion between pagan and Christian was paralleled in the *Perlesvaus*, when a maiden brought to the hero in an ivory vessel his cousin's remains, along with all the other severed heads of the knights of that text.

More Celtic mysteries were revealed when Peredur went to the court of the Witches to improve his military skills; a tradition of women warriors that stretched back as far as the Amazons. He then fell into an ecstatic trance before a hermit's cell, a necessary preliminary for so many knights on the Quest for the Grail. He looked out at dawn on a fall of fresh snow. A female hawk was feasting on the bloody body of a wild duck. Disturbed by the stamping of Peredur's horse, it flew off, to be replaced by a carrion raven. The combination of red spots, black feathers and white snow reminded the demented knight of his beloved Blanchefleur, with her crimson cheeks, raven curls and alabaster skin. Madly, Peredur struck dozens of Arthur's knights to the ground, before his uncle restored him to his senses.

Peredur's adventures became more mythical. He had to kill a Black Worm with a magical stone in its tail, a reference to the Druid totem and the Philosopher's Stone of alchemy. Peredur then dealt with a monster named Addanc, which lived under a dark lake and killed other knights with its stone spear. Eventually he reached Constantinople, as the crusaders would. There he became the husband of a beautiful empress, whose foremother Helena was meant to be a progenitor of King Arthur. She gave him a prehistoric stone talisman with magical powers, similar to the Stone of Scone, the Grail in *Parzival* or the sapphire pendant of Charlemagne. And Peredur became the sire of the Swan Knight Lohengrin in this genealogy of the Fisher Kings. Returning to the Grail Castle, he was initiated as its ruler, becoming celibate until his death. His last act of vengeance was to kill his mentors, the Witches, with the help of King Arthur. For they had maimed the previous Fisher King as well as severing the head of his cousin, which had appeared on the bloody platter of the Grail.

This most Celtic of romances stressed the roots of the legends of the Grail in Welsh mythology. A leading scholar identified six prototypes: the pearl-rimmed cauldron of the Head of Annwn; the Cauldron of Britain always guarded by Manawyd; a similar cauldron of Bran; the Cup of Truth of Manannan; the Cup of Sovereignty in the palace of Lug; and the Cauldron of Blathnat. All these sacred vessels shared characteristics with the Grail and its many properties. They could heal wounds and madness with sweet spices. They could provide endless supplies of food and drink in the manner of the cornucopia of the classical age. As was said of the unearthly palace of Labraid in the Irish poem of the *Sickbed of Cuchulinn*:

> There is a vat there with joyous mead,
> Which is distributed to the household.
> It continues ever – enduring is the custom –
> So that it is always constantly full.

Another shared property of the Celtic and Christian Grails was their refusal to sustain the unworthy. In Robert de Boron's *Joseph*, when the

Blessed Jew from Arimathea fed the multitude with the Grail, one part of the crowd was filled with sweetness and its heart's desire, while the other part felt nothing. The Cup of Truth of Manannan shattered if three lies were told, and combined its pieces if three truths were said. And in the Cauldron of Britain, the meat of a coward would never boil, while the meat of a hero was instantly cooked.

An interpretation of the Grail Castle of Corbenic equated it with the Greek and Celtic horn of plenty. In Old French, it was *li Chastel del Cor Benit*, or the Castle of the Blessed Horn, the name of one of the Cathar fortresses. In the *Livre de Caradoc*, a horn that tested the virtue of the drinker was described as ivory, studded with precious stones, and *beneis* or blessed. This ancient version of a Grail of plenty, allied with the fiery and bleeding spear of Lug, and with the trial of the Good Knight in welding together his broken sword as in the Sword of Gurgulan, were all reminders of the Celtic origins of the legend.

The mysteries of the Holy Vessels confirmed their Gnostic antecedents. Only Master Blinis could reveal them in the *Elucidation* that preceded *The History of the Grail*. In the *Continuation* by Gautier de Doulens, the maiden on the white mule said that these were matters too sacred for anybody not in the holy life to tell. Robert de Boron declared in his *Joseph* that he did not dare to describe his story, unless he had the great book in which were written the secrets called the Grail. And in the *Didot Perceval*, the Voice of God said to Bron: 'Our Lord commands you to teach to Perceval those secret words which he taught Joseph in prison, when he delivered the Grail to you.'

Peredur and the *Perlesvaus* drew from a similar tradition and material, yet they did not correspond except in the guiding myth of the Grail. Both were probably inspired by the Irish *Baile in Scáil*, an account of Conn's visit to the palace of the god Lug, who appeared as a pale horseman. Conn arrived to find a princess on a crystal throne, who gave him magic food and wine from a golden drinking cup. With each draught, Lug named the descendants of Conn, who would reign in Tara.

The palace and the figures disappeared, leaving Conn with two Grails in the shape of a golden vessel and silver vat.

Conn's posterity and power were confirmed in the Irish myth, while Peredur and Perlesvaus failed in their first attempts to replace the Fisher King at the Grail Castle. When Peredur saw the maiden bearing the Grail platter, he did not realise that she was the empress, whom he would later marry and so achieve power and his inheritance. And in *Peredur*, unlike in the *Perlesvaus*, the author was conscious that the Welsh peoples were being invaded and conquered by the Normans, who had taken over England. The huge and bleeding spear that preceded this platter was a symbol of a wasted Wales with its wounds and sufferings. His hero had to inspire his countrymen to resistance, before he could rule again in the Celtic castle of the Grail.

The Fisher King himself was usually called Bron after the Celtic god Bran, and his characteristics were confused remarkably with those of the legendary Joseph of Arimathea in the romances of the Quest. The head of Bran was kept alive by spiritual food, as was Joseph in prison. Both had access to magic vessels that dispensed life. Bran, indeed, was also wounded in the leg by a poisoned lance, and was connected with the sea, a fisher of men; so was Joseph with his miracles. And as a leading Welsh commentator on *Peredur* has pronounced, the melting pot between Celtic and Christian sources in the tales of the Arthurian knights brewed a hotchpotch of sources:

The story of the Grail is the story of a symbol which is transferred from one religion to another, retaining most of its original significance. The Celtic god who possessed the marvellous vessel was the god of the sun, lord of the Otherworld, creator of mankind. The maiden who carried the cup and 'married' the hero was Sovereignty, the goddess who represented the kingdom. The union between hero and goddess symbolised the possession of his kingdom by the

God sits on his throne with the cosmic orb of the Tau Cross, signifying the Trinity. *(Burdett Psalter)*

hero. In the sovereignty tales the hero is given food, and in the Grail castle the events occur during, or shortly after a meal.

The symbolism was easily fused with already existing Christian symbolism. The ceremony is still connected with food and drink of a kind easily recognized by men, but endowed with ritual significance. The Last Supper was a meal on which was based the sacrament of Holy Communion. . . . The Grail's power to produce food may be traced to the marvellous vessels possessed by the gods and Otherworld beings in Celtic mythology. The power to move of itself comes from the same source. Both characteristics were easily adapted to the demands of Christianity by attributing them to the power of God.

ELEVEN

WHAT AND WHERE WERE THE GRAILS?

Heaven is as near to us in Britain as in Palestine.

St Jerome

The abbeys and cathedrals of Europe competed with each other to attract pilgrims through their holy relics. The source of these sacred remains was Palestine, which the Byzantine Emperor Constantine the Great and his mother Helena had made into the goal of Christian faith. As Gibbon wrote of the empress, 'she united the credulity of old age with the warm feelings of a recent conversion'. At the age of seventy-nine, she was taken by Bishop Macarios around the sites of the Passion. The three crosses of Jesus and the two thieves were discovered, marked by Pilate's board identifying the King of the Jews and the four nails driven into his Body. One of these nails calmed a storm in the Adriatic, another became the bit in the mouth of the emperor's warhorse. Most importantly, the Church of the Holy Sepulchre, with its great rotunda, was built over the tomb of Christ, as later the Dome of the Rock would be built over the stepping-stone of the Prophet Muhammad to heaven.

As Dante recognised, the three great places for Christian pilgrimages in the Middle Ages were Jerusalem in the Holy Land, Compostela in the north-west of Spain, and Rome. Yet Jerusalem was the superior attraction, for it was held to be the Heavenly City, the centre of the earth and even the gateway to paradise. The pilgrim guide to the city, the *Breviarus* of the 6th century, claimed that the

sacred relics there included the True Cross, the Holy Lance, the Crown of Thorns, the column of Christ's flagellation, the stones from the stoning of St Stephen and two later symbols of the Grail – the horn with the divine oil that had anointed David as King of Israel, and the platter of blood that had held the severed head of St John the Baptist.

With the success of the First Crusade – which had fortunately rediscovered the missing Holy Lance at Antioch – and the establishment of the Kingdom of Jerusalem for ninety years, pilgrims could now travel there in relative safety. And they could see and even touch the containers of the Blood and Body of Christ, His tomb and the

Crusaders playing dice in the Church of the Holy Sepulchre, Jerusalem.

stained remains of His execution. Although the crusaders brought back many fragments of the holy relics to be housed in little Grails all across Europe, enough remained in the Church of the Holy Sepulchre to attract many of the faithful, even after Saladin had recaptured Jerusalem for the Muslim faith.

William Wey, a fellow of the Royal College of Eton, travelled once to Compostela and twice to Jerusalem in the middle of the 15th century, and he left a charming doggerel about the treasures in the Holy City. He had his doubts, particularly over the authenticity of the bloodstains of Christ on the pillar where He was flogged, and the lamp over His sepulchre, which was put out at His death and reappeared at His Resurrection. Wey also feared that the stone, on which the Body of Christ had been laid, was taken away to Constantinople, while the Saviour's footprints preserved on the hard rock seemed to be carved by hand. Yet even so, he was overwhelmed by the sacred relics 'within the temple of Jerusalem':

> The first place within the door
> Is Our Lord's holy sepulchre.
> The next that is without failing,
> Is a chapel of Our Lady where friars do sing.
> There was Our Lady in her prayer
> When Christ was risen from His sepulchre,
> And He full lowly, when He come thither,
> Said unto her, Hail, holy Mother.
> And in that same chapel is
> Of the pillar a great piece
> That Christ Jesus was bound unto,
> When Pilate Him beat, and wrought Him woe.
> There is in that place a stone also
> That a dead man by the cross was raised from.
> Without the chapel door,
> Right in the chapel floor,
> There is a stone, round and plain
> Where Jesus as a gardener met with Magdalene.
> In that stone by Christ was made
> An hold wherein He put his spade.
> By yonder, as pilgrims gone,
> They find two holes in a stone:
> In those holes Christ's legs were put,

> And with chains fast knit,
> There is by a vault within,
> Which is called Christ's prison.
>
> Next to that in our procession
> Is a place of great devotion.
> There at the dice knights gan play
> Who should bear Christ's tunic away.
> Beyond there is a pillar also,
> Upon which Christ sat naked through;
> Where the knights, to His scorn,
> Set on His head a crown of thorn.
> Beyond is a chapel, it is right low,
> Twenty paces down as men it know;
> In that chapel under the ground
> There was the holy cross found,
> There is full remission in that place
> To all men that thither go for grace . . .

These blessed objects were only some of the evidence of the Passion available in Palestine. Many had been transported away by the Byzantines and the crusaders. With the cult of relics, which were held to work fashionable miracles, a lucrative trade lay in small pieces of the remains of the Crucifixion and the Saints. The custom of cutting up the remnants of martyrs and distributing them to new churches and abbeys that bore their sacred names spread from east to west. As Theodoret observed as early as the 5th century:

> No single tomb covers a martyr's body. Cities and villages, having divided the bodies among themselves, entitle them preservers of their souls and healers, and honour them as guardians of their city and protectors. They employ them as intercessors and obtain divine gifts through them. Though the whole body be divided, the grace is undivided, and the smallest relic has equal power with the whole body of the martyr.

This illumination of the three Magi offering their gifts to the infant Jesus comes from a Book of Hours, use of Paris, late 14th century.

Each remnant of the Passion was housed in a reliquary, resplendent with jewels, gold and silver. And other symbols of the Last Supper, particularly the chalice, had become parts of love feasts in early Christianity. In his *Confessions*, St Augustine had denounced the practice of drinking wine from decorated cups in memory of holy men. Many examples of these vessels, incised with the heads of St Peter and St Paul and resembling Celtic sacrificial bowls, have been excavated near Rome, merely a continuation of the pagan practice of pouring libations to the gods and celebrating the dead. St Jerome also reproached a friend who asked him to a feast, with the words, 'We must celebrate the birthday of Peter rather with exaltation of spirit than with abundance of food.' Yet when a broken crystal chalice placed on the altar of St Lawrence was miraculously restored as whole, Gregory of Tours reported that the Bishop of Milan had to institute new feasts for the saint to satisfy public demand.

With the sack of Constantinople and the loss of Jerusalem, the attention of Western pilgrims turned to those points near the coasts of the Atlantic and the Mediterranean, where the first saints and missionaries were said to have landed, bringing the gospel with them from the Holy Land. The foremost of these places was Santiago de Compostela in the north of Spain, followed by St Maximin in the south of France and Fécamp in Normandy. These were the ports of the legendary conversion of mainland Europe. One account of St James held that he had landed in Galicia and preached the gospel before returning to Jerusalem, where he was beheaded by the Romans. Another declared that His Body had arrived in a marble ship, had chased away a devilish snake set on him by a witch, Queen Lupa, and was finally buried in Santiago de Compostela by a knight covered in scallop shells, the badge of pilgrims to the renowned shrine and cathedral.

Certainly, St James became the patriotic symbol of the small kingdom of the Asturias and of the Spanish crusades against the Moors. He is shown on the tympanum of his cathedral at Santiago, riding a white horse and killing the infidels at the Battle of Clavijo, after a mysterious reappearance. On the eve of the fall of Coimbra, he was said to have appeared to a doubting Greek bishop in a dream while dressed as a crusader in white, saying, 'God has made me a soldier and a contestant and set me to fight for the Christians against the Saracens and to gain the victory for them.'

On his visit to Compostela, William Wey discovered more than the patron saint's remains, confirmed by Beatus's celebrated *Commentaries on the Apocalypse*. There was the tunic of Jesus, remnants of Sts Paul, Stephen and Sylvester, and the incorruptible body of Zebedee the fisherman, the father of St James, who was also the nephew of the Virgin Mary and the cousin of Christ. Treasures, indeed, that made the journey worthwhile. The image above the Tree of Jesse in the Portico de la Gloria of St James, who had curbed the infidel and driven the pagan from Spain, was even more inspiring than St George of the Near East and England, or St Andrew of Scotland. And the miracles of healing at his shrine were attested in a sermon attributed to Pope Calixtus the Second:

> From the time it was begun until today, that church displays the glory of the miracles of Saint James. For the sick are restored to health, the blind receive their sight, many tongues that were dumb are loosed, the deaf hear again, the lame are given the strength to walk, demoniacs are set free, and what is even more, the prayers of the faithful are heard, their vows are fulfilled, and the chains of their sins are unloosed.

Although the capital of the empire of Charlemagne at Aachen still houses many blessed relics, those not seized by Napoleon have mainly been transferred to Vienna. The Hofburg there now holds the Imperial Crown, the Holy Lance or Spear of Destiny, the Gothic Sceptre and Charlemagne's Gospel Book, as well as a large Roman agate dish once thought to be the Grail, along with a narwhal horn, the cornucopia of the ancients. In the Sacred Treasury is St Stephen's purse of the 11th century, a reliquary containing one of the nails from the Passion, and a monstrance holding a fragment of the True Cross. Still in the Dom at Aachen is a golden casket of Charlemagne, which used to contain some of the Holy Blood.

The Dom at Cologne was also a magnet for the reverent. It possessed the embroidered skulls of the three Magi, who had brought their bountiful caskets of riches, frankincense and myrrh to the cradle of the infant Christ at Bethlehem. The Empress Helena had found these relics, too, in the Holy Land, and they had been transported by way of Constantinople and Milan to their final resting place; the donor and thief of the relics was said to be the alchemist Albertus Magnus, rumoured to possess a talking head, in the manner of the Celtic god Bran; this preserved skull acted as an oracle. However that might be, the remains of the Eastern Wise Men were held in a shrine created by Nicholas of Verdun, which had sculptures of their gifts to Jesus, of his baptism in Jordan and of his Second Coming.

For pilgrims to Italy, the Santa Casa on the hillside at Loretto was the house in Nazareth where Christ was born, miraculously wafted there from Palestine by flights of angels. This spot was believed to be the fact of the mystery of the Incarnation, particularly when the crusaders were driven from the Holy Land. Its presence out-shone the venerable relics in other Italian cities − except Turin, which held the Holy Shroud, pressed from the naked body of Christ taken from the Cross.

Rome itself had always been ambiguous towards the symbols of the Grail, tasting in them flavours of heresy. Outside St Peter's and the Vatican, there are two churches particularly

This carved skull, wearing a Templar cross, is still used in the ceremonies of a Scottish preceptory.

significant in this Quest. The medieval chapel of St John at the Latin Gate was replaced by an octagonal Renaissance church. Its paintings show the saint drinking from a Gnostic chalice containing the serpent; also escaping from a cauldron of boiling oil to write his *Book of Revelation*. And at St Lawrence Without the Walls, frescos picture the holy man giving the Grail to the Spanish legionary, who would carry it on its journey to end in Valencia.

Within the Vatican, Fra Angelico depicted Pope Sixtus the Second bestowing the Grail on St Lawrence. And there is a statue of St Longinus in St Peter's, while a yellow jasper chalice in St John in Lateran − possibly the cup of the Last Supper − is held to have been brought by St Jerome from Jerusalem. Yet the most holy relics are kept hidden in the four huge pentagonal hollow piers, designed by Michelangelo himself, which bear the weight of the soaring dome of St Peter's. Always chary of putting too much faith in relics that work miracles, let alone actual objects from the Passion, the papacy has varied its policy of concealing and showing its blessed treasures over the centuries.

As well as the remains of its name saint, St Peter's holds the Holy Veil of St Veronica, probably acquired after the Fourth Crusade. It also claims the iron tip of the Holy Lance, although this relic is like the hydra with many heads, one of them in Vienna. And to the skull of St Andrew, also reputed to be in Scotland, Pope Urban the Eighth added a large piece of the True Cross, which was transferred from the Church of Santa Croce in Gerusalemme. These sacred remnants are still housed within the labyrinthine piers, if they were not dispersed in 1527 at the sack of Rome.

St Veronica with the Holy Veil.

From time to time, the relics of St Peter's – particularly the Veil of St Veronica, at Epiphany and Easter – have been disclosed. The cloth was a form of a Grail, granting absolution to those who saw it and adored 'the very mystery of this likeness', in the words of Pope Innocent the Third. Dante even recognised the urge of the Christian faithful to view this revelation in the 'Paradiso' of his *Divine Comedy*. He compared the sight of the Veil to St Bernard's wish for grace from the Virgin Mary, the Queen of Heaven:

> As he who perhaps comes from Croatia
> To look upon our Veronica
> And still desires it despite her fame,
> But says in thought, as long as He is shown:
> 'My Lord Jesus Christ, the true God –
> Was this way Your appearance made?'

However creditable the provenance of a holy relic, it could only be a symbol, also a sign pointing towards a personal vision of God. Without that perception of grace, nobody could reach the divine, whatever the arrow pointing to the Virgin Mary or to the Almighty. Moreover, the Middle Ages were renowned for mass belief – the Children's Crusade was the worst example of common credulity. Crowds and congregations wished to see miracles performed, and acts of healing often happened at shrines and reliquaries through faith, hallucination or hypnotism. The example lay, after all, in the New Testament. St Lazarus, raised from the dead, was a popular icon in the south of France. Curing the sick, making the deaf hear, the blind see, the dumb speak and the lame walk, casting out demons and evil spirits, these were expected in medieval as well as biblical times.

More popular even than the Grail romances were the *Lives of the Saints*. These were stories of a quest for spiritual rather than knightly adventures, for jousts against demons and battles against the Devil, as engaging as those of Arthur and Charlemagne. And beatific vision was the insight of the holy men, whose long fasts persuaded them that they were being fed by manna, as if from a Grail. St Cuthbert and St Columba were often visited by angels in their dreams, as well as nourished by their faith. Furthermore, experiences of the soul leaving the body were widespread among the elect. These might occur in the form of a rising dove, a flight of cherubim or even an ascending globe of fire, as St Benedict reported on the death of Germanus. The Grail was so portrayed, and in such ways did the Knights of the Round Table also envision its form in its many guises.

In the ecstasy of prayer, some saints were seen to levitate or appear in two places simultaneously. St Columba had gifts of second sight and prophecy, a Christian Merlin from the Arthurian legends. Describing his gift, he said, 'There are some, though few of them, who have been granted divine grace, so that they can see clearly and distinctly at one moment as under a sunray the whole circuit of the world surrounded by the ocean and the sky. The inner part of their mind is miraculously enlarged.' This was the same as the blinding vision of the Grail, the moment of communion with the One Maker of the cosmos. As Pope Gregory also said of St Benedict: 'He saw the whole world because, by the supernatural light of the Creator, the soul is enlarged, and being suffused with the light of God, it is inwardly exalted above itself. Looking down, it sees what it could not understand as a small matter.'

For the Church, beatific vision and a personal contact with heaven through ecstatic prayer was illumination for a saint, but heresy for an Arthurian knight or a rebel against the authority of Rome. Experiences of the godhead must remain within the pale of orthodoxy. Although revelation was admitted through dreams as well as through fasting and prayer, these apparitions might be demoniac as well as divine.

The dreams of the Otherworld that occurred to the saints, often presented themselves in Jewish, Greek or Celtic forms, as in the stories about the Grail Castle. Their culmination was in *The Divine Comedy* of Dante, partly devised from his inspiration about the nature of the inferno, purgatory and paradise, partly from his invocation of the current European myths of the hereafter outside the Bible.

Some of the dreams recorded about the saints might have been sources of Grail romances. Roger of Wendover declared that in 1206 St Julian ordered Turchill of Tunsted to prepare for a journey. While he was asleep, the saint took his spirit from His Body and served as a guide through hell and heaven, as Virgil served Dante. Evading demons and tortures, Turchill saw Celtic and alchemic cauldrons in four courts, some burning with fire, others filled with snow and ice, and still more holding boiling sulphur or black salt water. Souls were purged in these vessels of regeneration before passing on to the golden temple on the Mount of Joy, where they ate copious and delicious food from the nearby Earthly Paradise.

Opposing pictures of purgatory and paradise were the perceptions preached by the medieval Church. These images possessed the Christian mind, entering into reveries and dreams. They also provided the real power of the Church of Rome on earth. Excommunication did not only consign the soul to hell; it also denied the sinner his feudal and property rights until he was absolved. Suspects might be accused of witchcraft as well as heresy. Unorthodoxy could be proof of interior demons.

Emperors and apostate kings had crusades preached against them as if they were infidels. As well as the miracles of healing at the shrines of the saints and the Holy Blood, the spectacles of aristocratic repentance at the great cathedrals were the dramatic masterpieces of the age. Dressed in a shift, flogged for misdeeds, those of the high-born who offended Rome – such as the Holy Roman Emperor and Raymond the Seventh, the Count of Toulouse – might have to journey on to Canossa or to Notre-Dame in Paris to submit to the Church, abjure heresy and show that the decree of Rome was more powerful than the crown and the sword.

Relics, miracles and public penitence might impress the masses, but the abuse of these presentations and redemptions would lead to the great split within the Christian Church and the destruction of its general images. Miracles were too easily made, indulgences were widely sold, forgiveness for sins came with bequests rather than penitence. There was a schism in the papacy, with rival claimants in Avignon as well as in Rome. The popes began to recruit their own troops to defend their possessions in Italy. Military funds were needed, not to send another crusade to the Near East, but to defend Tuscany and Umbria, ruled by the Vatican. The coins, paid for tokens or parchments of absolution, debased the treasures of the faith.

In early medieval times, it did not matter whether the Holy Blood or the bones of the saints were genuine. Popular belief supplied the origins, and to the theologians, such signs and wonders were only symbols on the way to God through the goodwill of the Church. Yet with the waning of the Middle Ages, rebel and purifying creeds would act as the Knights of the Grail had done in the romances. By trial and self-discipline, they would attack corruption and licence, seeking their own salvation in the refinement of their vision of heaven.

— TWELVE —

THE GRAIL OF GERMANY

Then Kyot my master read the tale Flegitanis told,
And he searched in old books of Latin for the name of the people,
Who God accounted worthy of keeping the wonderful Grail,
Who were true and pure in their acts and in their humble hearts.

Wolfram von Eschenbach, *Parzival*, 12th century

After the fall of the Roman Empire and the advent of orthodoxy to the Byzantine Church, three Persian sages had developed alchemy and astrology. The greatest of these was the Sufi, Jábir ibn-Hayyán, who was the court scientist to Haroun al-Raschid, the contemporary and correspondent of Charlemagne. Practically, he prepared red oxide of mercury, silver nitrate and white arsenic, while experimenting with many salts and elixirs. Magically, he related numbers and letters to earth, air, fire and water, thus producing alchemic texts for the conversion of dross into gold, both in the crucible and the human spirit. Called Geber by the Latin alchemists, he was followed by other instructors, Rhazes and Avicenna, in his researches.

Rhazes attempted to classify drugs and chemical compounds, and to group them as animal, vegetable and mineral; he also used, as his instruments, retorts and alembics and glass flasks. He was followed by Avicenna in

A miniature of Wolfram von Eschenbach, the author of *Parzifal*, a romance of the Grail.

discovering new chemicals and medicines, but his pupil disagreed that alchemy could produce gold. All the processes might achieve were to redden white metals, so they looked like gold, or whiten red metals, so they resembled silver.

Through the supreme Arab academies of Córdoba and Toledo, the mysteries of alchemy would reach the Grail romancers. In his *Parzival*, Wolfram von Eschenbach would even claim that the source of his plot was a Jewish philosopher from Moorish Spain. For had not a pupil of Zosimos, the Alexandrian Morienos, declared to an early Arabian alchemist and poet, Prince Khalid,

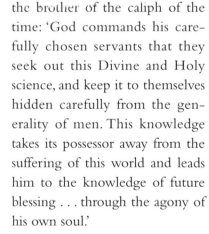

the brother of the caliph of the time: 'God commands his carefully chosen servants that they seek out this Divine and Holy science, and keep it to themselves hidden carefully from the generality of men. This knowledge takes its possessor away from the suffering of this world and leads him to the knowledge of future blessing . . . through the agony of his own soul.'

In all countries, alchemy was held to possess three elements, the *Alkahest* or universal solvent; the *Lapis*, or stone or powder of transmutation; and the *Elixir*, or the healing power of being. In *Parzival*, these three properties would be combined as a Trinity within the Grail, defined as *lapis elixir*, a stone fallen from heaven, bearing the secret of eternal life. In alchemy, much concerned with the fusion of the metals, the lead of the body would be converted into the silver of

The sun's heat raises or lowers the vapours in Philo of Byzantium, *Philosophia Moysaica*, reproduced by Robert Fludd, *Utrisque Cosmi . . . Historia*, 1617.

A healing alchemical still. *(Robert Fludd, Medicina Catholica, 1629–31)*

the soul to dissolve into the gold of the spirit. The hermetic system united all nature by combining in a moral code, the mineral, the animal and the vegetable. Metals resembled organisms. Even Moses was held to be the first adept, because he reduced the Golden Calf to powder, before the Ten Commandments were inscribed on stone. Gerbert of Auvergne, who became the millennial Pope Sylvester the Second, had studied the planets and the stars and their effects on human courses at Córdoba; in Florence, an astrolabe, probably belonging to him, is still preserved.

With such a mystical background, *Parzival* was also beholden to other previous messengers. If the Celtic bards dwelt on a Grail of blood and sacrifice, and the French troubadours elected a Grail of bounty and love, the German poets of the time preferred a Grail of chivalry and of stone. The Arthurian romances passed over to the Hohenstaufen renaissance in Germany with the works of Hartmann von Aue. Almost as obscure as the other authors of the Round Table, he was probably a knight himself in imperial service, from the canton of Zurich in Switzerland. In the last two decades of the 12th century, he wrote epics in verse, including an *Erec* and an *Iwein*, adapted from Chrétien de Troyes and the Welsh *Owein* in the *Mabinogion*.

For von Aue, such Arthurian adventures concentrated more on his contemporary society of

serving knights than on any search for the divine. He praised chivalry as a social and moral duty. His heroes were limited in their use of force by a code, not by the intervention of grace or angels. Both of his German successors in Arthurian romances, the rivals Wolfram von Eschenbach and Gottfried von Strassburg, praised his genius: 'How he adorns his stories inside and out with words and wisdom!' Whoever could appreciate fine language had to grant von Aue 'the crown and the laurels'.

Gottfried von Strassburg could not extend such admiration to the greatest of his fellow poets, Wolfram von Eschenbach. His own *Tristan* was a polished piece in praise of courtly love, but in the middle of his work he denounced the author of *Parzival* as 'the friend of the hare', fanciful and inclined to alchemy and nonsense. He totally misunderstood Wolfram's subtlety and fervency in pursuing the secrets of the Grail. For Gottfried, that quest from Camelot for the source of divine plenty and grace was merely the consuming passion found by Tristan and Isolde in the Cave of Lovers – no hermit's retreat with a bare altar.

Their high feast was Love, who gilded all their joys; she brought them King Arthur's Round Table as homage and all its company a thousand times a day. What better food could they have for body or soul? Man was there with Woman, Woman there with Man. What else should they be needing? They had what they were meant to have, they had reached the goal of their desire.

This praise of ecstasy in human want was secondary to the author of *Parzival*. Like Hartmann von Aue, Wolfram was probably a poor and unfree knight in imperial service, from Upper Franconia in Bavaria. He reached the court of the Landgrave Hermann of Thuringia, who had also welcomed the great *Minnesinger* Walther von der Vogelweide. A claim to illiteracy – 'I haven't a letter to my name' – may well have been proof of his sense of irony. If he said that he could neither read nor write, in company with so many of the troubadours, yet he knew in depth much of contemporary German and French literature, as well as oriental tales.

In giving the source of his *Parzival*, Wolfram von Eschenbach claimed that Chrétien de Troyes had wronged the tale, which actually derived from a Provençal cleric named Kyot, probably Guiot de Provins, a supporter of the Knights Templars, who visited Mayence in 1184, when the Holy Roman Emperor Frederick Barbarossa conferred knighthood on his sons at Pentecost. Another claimant was the *joglar* and troubadour and historian of the Albigensian Crusade, William of Tudela in Navarre,

a practitioner of geomancy as well as poetry and song. In his native Aragonese dialect, Kyot was said to mean *Guillot* or *Guillem*, little William. Wolfram stated that Kyot came from Dôlêt, translated as Tudela, which produced the best shields, helmets and spears of the time from Catalan smelting works and forges, as well as being a source of Arabic learning from neighbouring Saragossa, which bubbled with hermetic doctrines.

Wolfram was clear on the alchemic sources for his tale. He stated that every wise man would like to know the authority for the messages in his story. The well-known master Kyot had found it 'set down in heathen writing, the first source of this adventure'. Wolfram continued to declare an ancient inspiration:

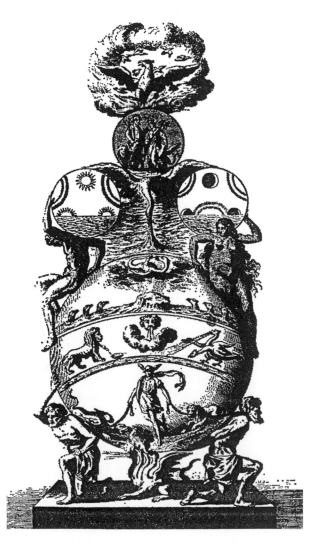

An illustration of the Great Work by Libavius, 1660.

Hear now age-old tales
as if they were new,
that they may teach you to speak true.
Plato foretold it in his day,
and Sibyl, the prophetess, too.
They told us long years ago,
with neither fault nor error,
that redemption would surely come to us
for the greatest guilty fear.

In the 4th century, Lacantius, known as the Christian Cicero, had equated Hermes Trismegistus with wisdom. He had instructed Plato, and later he interpreted the prophecies at Delphi of the Sibyl. A version of the *Corpus hermeticum* informed Wolfram's myth of the Grail and its wondrous nature.

The ancient Grail was the symbolic vessel of the Krater. In the fourth *Treatise* of the doctrine, Hermes said that God 'filled a great Krater with intellect, and sent it down to earth'. A herald – identified in Gnostic teachings as Jesus or Mary Magdalene – delivered this speech to all the world. 'Dip yourself in this Krater, you who are able; you who believe that you will ascend to Him who sent this Krater down; you who know for what purpose you have been born.' Those who heard the message were baptised in their divine understanding, and so became perfect. 'Such is the science of the intellect, which provides an abundant possession of things divine and the comprehension of God, for the Krater is divine.'

Thus for Wolfram, the Krater was the antecedent of the Grail, round which a brotherhood of *perfecti* or *templiese* could gather in a holy place. In the *Pistis Sophia*, the soul on its way to the hereafter was given two bowls by Hermes for his refreshment; one brought wisdom, the other forgetfulness. And so Wolfram's Flegitanis saw the name of the Grail in the constellations. 'A host left it on Earth and then flew away over the stars.' That stone had 'always been in the care of those God called to this task and to whom He sent His angel.' The carrier of immortal life, the Gnostic Krater preceded a waiting for a Resurrection. 'Such power does the stone give a man that flesh and bones are at once made young again. The stone is also called the Grail.'

Wolfram claimed that Flegitanis was a Jewish astrologer from Moorish Toledo, who was versed in Arabic astrology.

And the heathen Flegitanis could read in the high
heavens
How the stars roll on their course, how they circle
the silent sky,
And the time when the wandering ends, and the
life and the fate of men
He read in the stars, and he saw strange secrets ...

The name of Flegitanis may have derived from the Arabic *felekthâni* – in Latin *sphaera altera* or 'alternate spheres' – an astronomical work, said to have been written by the famous philosopher Thabit ben Qarah. In *Parzival*, however, the reported Flegitanis watched the heavens and discerned the mystery of the Grail, which was written in a cluster of stars. Angels had left it on earth to be guarded by the best of the knights, as *Parzival* would relate. It was identified as a green stone fallen from heaven after the battle of Lucifer with the Trinity. Furthermore, it had close affinities with the source of the sacred Islamic black stone at the centre of Mecca, a meteorite also believed to have fallen from heaven and to be a means of communication of God.

The Koran stated that the stone was given by the Angel Gabriel at the time of the building of the cubic shrine, the Ka'aba, where it was kept. The Muslim commentator, Ibn Malik, also told of a vision of the Prophet Muhammad, in which he ascended to the skies and saw a green goblet 'of such penetrating brightness that all the seven heavens are illuminated by it ...'. A voice declared, 'O Muhammad, the All Highest God has created this goblet for Your enlightenment.' Both divine stone and cup remain important in Islamic belief.

For 1,300 years, pilgrims on the *hajj* to Mecca have been directed to enter the Ka'aba and kiss the black meteorite, embedded in the wall. Once it was stolen by a Shi'ite sect, but it was ransomed and returned. Religious traditions associated the sacred stone with Adam and with Abraham, as well as with Allah, stating that an angel brought it to earth to record the deeds of the faithful, to be examined on the Day of Judgement.

Worn smooth by tens of millions of lips, this heavenly blessing was the sole object from the pagan temple kept by the Prophet Muhammad when he converted the idolatrous shrine at Mecca into an Islamic temple. Apparently, a flash of lightning persuaded the Prophet to retain this Muslim Grail. As the poet Ikbal Ali Shah wrote, the Ka'aba was the heart of the body of the world:

> And the stone that you call the Black Stone was itself a ball of dazzling light. In ages past, the Prophet said, it shone like the crescent moon, until at last the shadows, falling from the sinful hearts of those who gazed on it, turned its surface black. And since this amber gem, that came to earth from Paradise with the Holy Spirit, has received such impressions upon itself, what should be the impressions which our hearts receive? Indeed, whoever shall touch it, being pure of conscience, is like him who has shaken hands with God.

In *Parzival*, Wolfram von Eschenbach went as far as giving his perfect Christian knight a piebald half-brother, Feirefiz, born in the Levant. The subtext of the long romance was, indeed, the reconciliation of Christians and Muslims, and their respect for one another, also the change of the nature of the Grail to a stone fallen from heaven as at Mecca. *Parzival* began by defining lack of faith as dark and the Christian soul as white.

> As one sees the magpie's feathers, which are both
> > black and white,
> Yet one may win no blessing . . .

Eschenbach also stressed the hidden significance of his text: 'I tell my story like the bowstring and not like the bow. The string is here a figure of speech. Now *you* think that the bow is fast, but faster is the arrow sped by the string.'

In *Parzival*, Gamuret Angevin, a knight from the crusading French family of Fulke of Anjou, which produced the kings of Jerusalem, took up service with the Muslim Baruch of Baghdad. Dressed in his surcoat 'green as the emerald vase', Gamuret defended a black Muslim queen's city, defeating Scots, Norse and French crusaders. He then married the queen, returned to Europe and left her with their son Feirefiz, striped like a humbug, 'dark and light, black and white . . . as a magpie the hue of his face and a hair'. Feirefiz grew up to become a supreme knight, whose surcoat of precious stones, asbestos shield and cloak of salamander could defeat the knights of fire. Back in Europe, Gamuret married Queen Herzeloyde and then returned to fight for the Baruch at Alexandria, where he was treacherously killed because the blood of a he-goat was poured onto his diamond helmet, which made it soft as a sponge and vulnerable to a spearthrust. Other crusaders serving their Muslim rulers buried the Angevin knight under an emerald cross presented by the Baruch, while Parzival was born to Gamuret's abandoned queen.

As in the romance by Chrétien de Troyes, Parzival began his career in chivalry as a fool, a rapist and a robber. So when the Fisher King, with his incurable wound, whose 'life was but dying', directed him to the Grail Castle, he was tongue-tied at the wonders that he saw. A squire carried the bleeding Holy Lance through the great hall in front of the assembled knights of the Holy Grail, while the Grail Queen bore the Grail stone on a cushion of green silk:

> Root and blossom of Paradise garden, that thing
> > that men call 'The Grail',
> The crown of all earthly wishes, fair fullness that
> > never shall fail.

Unknown to Parzival, the Grail Queen was his aunt. She laid the Grail on a pillar of jacinth, and its horn of plenty nourished all the knights and maidens in the castle.

> It was the Grail that fed them, who before the
> > Grail did stand.
> For the food and drink each was desiring, each
> > might stretch out his hand . . .

Food warm or cold, or dishes that known or
                      unknown can be,
Food wild or tame – Such riches you never on
                      earth shall find . . .
For the Grail was the crown of blessing, the
                      bounty of the earth's delight.

Parzival was given a mystical sword, its hilt carved from a ruby. But he did not question the mystery of the bleeding lance, the abundant Grail or the incurable wound of the Fisher King. Simpleton that he was, he woke in the morning in a deserted castle and rode away to King Arthur's camp, where he was blamed by the sorceress Cundrie for not asking the Fisher King the question that would heal him. He was even told that his Muslim half-brother Feirefiz would marry the Grail Princess on Munsalvaesche, the Mount of Salvation.

Parzival left again on the Quest for the Grail and killed a knight who was defending the Grail Castle. He was bitter against God, who had made a fool of him. But he met a hermit, Trevrizent, who had a green shrine or reliquary, and who revealed to him the origin of the Grail and the nature of its later defenders.

Here *Parzival* specifically identified the Knights of the Grail as *templeise*, wearing white surcoats with red crosses as the Templars did. In the dialects of Provence and Catalonia, the Templars were known as *templés*, a likely source for Wolfram's use of the term. These religious knights had many contacts with their Muslim equivalents, the Sufis, and some of their secret practices – particularly a belief in selfless obedience and purity – derived from oriental mysticism. The German romance preached religious toleration between Christianity and Islam, especially when a crusader might rule over a Muslim land or a Muslim over Christian believers.

When Parzival finally asked the Fisher King the right

A Templar Knight, from an early French history of the military order.

question and healed him, and himself became the Grail King, Feirefiz was baptised from a ruby font standing on a round pillar of jasper: this was filled with holy water by the Grail. Feirefiz now married the princess of the castle, who would give birth to the Christian African emperor Prester John. The black-and-white colour of his skin could now be seen as the Templar battle-flag, *Beauséant*. At his baptism, these words appeared carved on the Grail, a prophecy of the fate of Lohengrin, the son of Parzival:

The Templar whom God to a strange folk should
                      send as head,
Must ban all word or question of his country or
                      home or race,
If his subjects want their rights from him and
                      would in his sight find grace.
They must not ask his origin, for he must leave
                      them straightaway.

This concept of semi-divine rule on earth by a companionship of mysterious monastic Knights Templars confirmed the links between the concept of the Grail, the crusades and the military orders, which were influenced by Islam because of a mutual respect bred by long diplomacy and frequent wars over the Holy Land and Jerusalem.

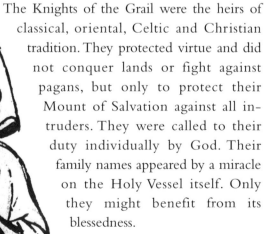

The Knights of the Grail were the heirs of classical, oriental, Celtic and Christian tradition. They protected virtue and did not conquer lands or fight against pagans, but only to protect their Mount of Salvation against all intruders. They were called to their duty individually by God. Their family names appeared by a miracle on the Holy Vessel itself. Only they might benefit from its blessedness.

Parzival had begun his Quest as a search for his mother, only later turning to the discovery of the Grail. The mystery of the relationship between the sacred stone and divine intelligence and the Christian Trinity was not made clear until the conclusion of the saga. Then the Hand of God intervened, once Parzival had directly healed the Fisher King Anfortas and so had become the Lord of the Grail. For both him and Feirefiz, the holy stone was only made manifest when each of them was ready to receive its blessings. To the Muslim knight, the Grail was the sign that he had truly converted to Christianity. Yet that conversion was his responsibility, not because of the intervention of the Grail. In a sense, the triple nature of the holy stone was made clear. After the trials of learning through the material world of experience and encounters with messengers from heaven, the essence of the Grail or Grailness or the Holy Ghost was revealed.

Most significantly, Wolfram von Eschenbach wrote of the Knights of the Grail as the possessors of eternal youth:

> By a stone they live,
> And that stone is both pure and precious – Its
> name you have never heard?
> Men call it Lapis Exilis –
>
> If you daily look at that stone
> (If a man you are, or a maiden) for a hundred
> years,
> If you look on its power, your hair will not grow
> grey, your face appears
> The same as when you first saw it, your flesh and
> your bone will not fail
> But young you will live for ever – And this stone
> all men call the Grail.

Wolfram von Eschenbach developed this description of the Grail as a stone taken down from heaven by angels, who then returned on high because of the sins of mankind. On Good Friday, a dove flew down with the white host to lay on the stone – the Body and Blood of Christ.

> The stone from the Host receives all good that on
> earth may be
> Of food or drink, which the earth bears as the
> bounty of Paradise.

> All things in wood or water and all that fly
> beneath the skies.

This fallen stone, which was all fruitfulness and gave eternal life, was also called *lapis exilis* by the alchemist Arnold of Villanova. He identified it as the Philosopher's Stone, not as the Grail. It was not made from green emerald, but was unremarkable in appearance. Such a correspondence made commentators look for alchemy in *Parzival* and presume that the author meant *lapis elixir*, the life-giving or Philosopher's Stone.

Certainly Wolfram von Eschenbach was influenced by oriental and Cathar beliefs. The Jewish philosopher Flegetanis, whom he declared to be the discoverer of the Grail and of the bloodline of King Solomon, was thought to be Thabit, who lived in Baghdad at the end of the 9th century and translated Greek texts into Arabic from the legendary emerald tablet of Hermes Trismegistus, the semi-mythical founder of alchemy. Moreover, Wolfram's authority, Kyot or Guiot de Provins, was said to have lived in Jerusalem and at the court of Frederick Barbarossa, as well as being an initiate of the Templar mysteries, including their association with the Gnostics and the Assassins, the Islamic sect founded by the Old Man of the Mountains, almost as important in Eastern myth as King Solomon.

Moreover, the Templars were believed to be the guardians of both the Grail and the Temple of Solomon. Perhaps it was significant that Solomon's Temple stood upon a rock, *lapis*, at the centre of the world, and it contained the Ark of the Covenant, the fount of the Christian faith. The cornerstone 'which the builders refused' in the Psalms was another symbol of Christ. And it was also upon this *lapis* or rock that the Christian Church was founded.

In the Book of Revelation of St John the Divine, the Holy Spirit as a stone and a green gem, or fire and crystal, was also emphasised. As the holy man saw in his vision:

> Straightaway I was in the Spirit: and, behold, there
> was a throne set in heaven, and one sitting upon the

throne. And he that sat was to look upon like a jasper stone and a sardius; and there was a rainbow round the throne, like an emerald to look upon. . . . There were seven lamps of fire burning before the throne, which are the seven Spirits of God. And before the throne there was a sea of glass like unto crystal . . .

The visions of the legendary Knights of the Grail of *Parzival* also depicted the Holy Vessel as a sacred stone, which derived from the Philosopher's Stone that, in its turn, harked back to the Orphic mysteries of ancient Greece. The celebrants believed that the sun was hatched from a primal egg, floating upon a cosmic ocean. The solar presence reproduced himself three times in his rising, his noonday and his setting. The world itself was born of an egg, destroyed by fire or deluge, and then reborn in another Creation. And love itself was the legacy of the original egg through Venus, the morning and the evening star.

In nature, the snake-stone was also a progenitor. Said to be found in a serpent's brain as well as in the nest for its young, Pliny declared that the talisman was a rainbow ball and a Druid badge, formed by the envenomed spittle of twining adders or vipers. Confused with the fossils of small ammonites, the curled stone was given Gnostic properties, when the Serpent became an ambiguous reptile of Evil and Good. In the Garden of Eden, the Snake was the Devil; yet Moses set up a Brazen Serpent as a healing agent against a poisoned bite. The Ophites and other sects worshipped the snake as a messenger of wisdom from heaven to earth. Its product, the

The Brazen Serpent on the Tau Cross.
(Woodcut, 1699)

Above: The alchemical serpents of wisdom and the cosmos.
(Biedermann, Materia Prima, Graz, 1673)

Right: A Scottish Knights Templars' Teaching Board, 18th century, Scotland.

egg, became confused with the meteorite, fallen from the sky, and so a symbol of transmutation. In all, the serpent on the Tau Cross became an emblem of the hidden connection between human and godly intelligence.

Indeed, the priests of the cult of Mithras gave the novice a white pebble of regeneration. From such sources derived the Philosopher's Stone, sought by the alchemists. This fusion of sulphur, mercury and mineral salts had as many shapes as visions of the Grail. To Raymond Lully, it was a *carbunculus*; to Paracelsus, a form of ruby, floppy and transparent; to other alchemists, a red or white, black or blue, yellow or green powder. A poem attributed to Basilius Valentinus described its nature:

A stone is found which is esteeméd vile,
From which is drawn a fire volatile,
Whereof our noble Stone its selfe is made,
Composed of white and red that ne'er will fade,

It's called a Stone and yet is no Stone;
And in that Stone Dame Nature works alone,
The Fountain that from thence did sometimes
                                    flow,
His fixéd Father drownéd hath also . . .

By Vulcan's art, but first it's thus indeed
The Father from the Spirit must proceed;
Body, Soul, Spirit are in two contained,
The total art may well from them be gained.

It comes from one and is one only thing,
The volatile and fixt, together bring.
It is two and three, and yet only one,
If this you do not conceive you get none.

This fabled object shared the properties of the
Grail. It was an elixir of a long life, as was the
Fountain of Youth. It cured diseases and wounds,

A sacred groundplan. From the
notebooks of the French architect
Villard de Honnecourt, c. 1250.

while encouraging wisdom and understanding. Its
material claim of processing lead into gold was an
allegory of refining the spirit from the flesh. More
materially, Arnaldus de Villa Nova wrote that the
Stone could increase its own weight a hundred
times over during a conversion into bullion, while
even Roger Bacon declared that the ratio was a
100,000:1 in the scales of turning dross into
treasure.

Moreover, a blessed stone was seen as the
foundation of the Christian faith. Bishop William
Durand de Mende made this clear in his manual of
the 13th century for understanding the symbolic
significance of cathedrals and churches. Repeating
from the words of Christ, 'I will liken him unto a
wise man, which built his house upon a rock', the
bishop or the priest who had permission to
conduct the ceremony should sprinkle holy water
to chase from that place ghosts and demons. Then
he should put on the foundations the first stone, on
which would have been engraved the sign of the
Cross. Onyx should adorn the sanctuary, while the
church should be the replica of the human body of
Christ, facing to the east.

As for the chalices in the church, Bishop de
Mende admitted that they were first carved from
simple wood, then made of glass, but at the
Council of Reims, Pope Urban had said that the
ceremony of the Mass must use vessels of gold or
silver; brass might serve in poor churches.

> The chalice must not then be of glass, because of its
> fragility and the danger of spilling the Blood of
> Christ, nor of wood, because it is porous and like a
> sponge, and absorbs the Blood of Our Lord, nor of
> tin or copper, because the force of the poison
> produced by these metals provokes bile and vomiting.

Quoting from the Bible that many chalices were
made in gold, the Bishop declared that we should
offer the Lord what was most precious to us to
vanquish our avarice, even if he preferred plain
holders of his Body and Blood.

Another source for *Parzival* was a legendary treasure of Solomon, which was taken to Rome after
the fall of Jerusalem, then seized by the Visigoths.

When Muslim armies captured Toledo, they asked after Solomon's Table, which was meant to be able to feed all who sat down to eat, and to be made from a gigantic emerald, the sacred green stone of the alchemists. The table was said to be hidden away in a Grail Castle in the mountains of Spain.

Moreover, Charlemagne was said to have copied the Table of Solomon by having the universe made as three circles in jewels and precious metals, then set on legs of gold as another version of King Arthur's Round Table, for himself and twelve knights. The Koran itself referred to a table brought down from heaven by Jesus to feed him and the Apostles, but this divine gift disappeared again because of the sins of mankind.

Significantly, in *Parzival*, when the oriental sorceress Cundrie came to the court of King Arthur, she listed seven planets by their Arabic names. She was not referring to the cosmic disc of silk spread on the grass as a knightly tablecloth; but she was conferring a blessing on Parzival, prophesying that he would become the Fisher King

and the father of the perfect Swan Knight Lohengrin, who would be his heir. He was fated to succeed by the courses of the heavens, although when he would be asked about his origins, he would have to abandon his family and retire into the obscurity of his arrival.

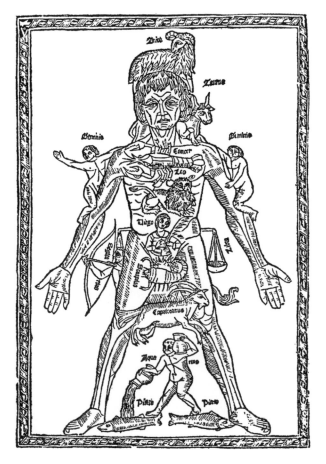

Listen, Parzival! The highest planet Zwal [Saturn]
And swift Almustri [Jupiter], Almaret [Mars] and
    bright Samsi [the Sun],
They declare your fortune. The fifth is called
    Alligufir [Venus],
And the sixth Alkiter [Mercury], and the nearest
    one Alkamer [the Moon].
I do not speak as in a dream. These are the stayers
    in the firmament.
Their whirling speed controls their opposing
    paths.
Care is gone now. All the circuit of these stars
    encompasses,
All they illuminate is in your reach to be attained
    and won.

Above: The sun. *(Woodcut, 1489)*

Left: Astrological figure showing the signs of the zodiac and the parts of the body they govern. *(Epilogo en Medicina y Cirurgia, 1495)*

There had been little oriental alchemy in the *Perlesvaus*, which also named the crusading Templars as the keepers of the Grail. But they were hardly given Muslim blood brothers, as Parzival was Feirefiz. They were presented as brutal killers against pagan Islam. The Grail was the chalice of Christ's Blood, not a mystic stone that might also signify *vas Hermetis* or the Philosopher's Stone of the alchemists, capable of transmuting all to spiritual harmony. Cruder and uncompromising, the Celtic texts lacked the sympathetic synthesis of the mysticism of the Near East, which was the history of the Grail as given in *Parzival*, according to the hermit Trevrizent, who made the hero repent and reach for his goal at last.

Another source of the Grail in *Parzival* was most likely a version of the *Alexanderlied*. In this Latin book of the exploits of the Greek conqueror, Alexander went to the Earthly Paradise, which some poets declared was, or was nearby, the Grail Castle. He was presented with a stone that gave youth to the old. This *lapis exilis* was like a human eye, but brilliant and rare in its colours. An ancient Jew told Alexander that it would tip the scales, heavier than any sack of gold, yet a feather would weigh more if any dirt stained the holy stone. While human greed was insatiable, even the eye of the conqueror would be stopped by dust. 'This stone came before you, master of the world. It warns you and rebukes you. This small talisman restrains you from desire and base ambition.'

So Alexander was deterred from making the whole earth into his empire. This tale of the stone from paradise was an admirable metaphor for Wolfram's version of the Grail. It was also the fountain of life, restoring youth to the aged. Although Wolfram wrote that his stone was given its powers by a dove descending from heaven on Good Friday with a bountiful wafer in its beak, its provenance was Greek and Jewish and Islamic mythology and belief. The host brought by the Holy Spirit was the moss on the pagan rock.

While he was composing his *Parzival*, Wolfram was living in the forest castle of Wildenberc, probably near Amorbach in the Odenwald. In describing the Grail Castle of Munsalvaesche, he correctly put together the Mount of Salvation with the Wild Mountain, derived as much from the Latin *silvaticus* or 'wooded' as from *salvationis* or 'redemption'. The Grail itself was kept in a temple, allowing its keepers to be called *templeise* or Templars. Uniquely, the bleeding spear that was lamented by the Knights of the Grail had a poisoned head, occasionally thrust into the stinking wound of King Anfortas to relieve his pain with another one, if the planets stood against him.

The pair of silver knives in the Grail procession had been made by the mystic smith Trebuchet to cut off the hard ice round the tip of the piercing and healing spear. They may be connected with the knives used by Nicodemus to scrape off the dried blood of Christ. These were discarded when Anfortas was cured of the sinful sore in his genitals and Parzival himself became the Grail King, with his relation Repanse de Schoye, as the goddess of plenty, bearing the Grail. Lay people performed all the ceremonies of the Grail, and a priest was only brought into Munsalvaesche to baptise the pagan Feirefiz – even then, the font was filled with holy water by the power of the Grail, which was the direct grace of God brought to the elect without the intervention of the Catholic Church.

Moreover, the Grail was given the power of restoring youth. After his recovery, Anfortas was declared to look more beautiful than Parzival himself. The mythical phoenix, which rose reborn from the flames and the ashes, was uniquely associated by Wolfram with the Grail, suggesting its powers of resurrection before the millennium. The comparison also recalled the Fourth of the Twelve Keys of the alchemist Basilius Valentinus:

> When ashes and sand are thoroughly baked for just the right amount of time, the master makes a glass out of them which henceforth will always resist the fire and resembles in colour a transparent stone and can no longer be recognised as ash. To the ignorant that is a great mysterious art, but not to the wise, for

A copy of the Tassilo chalice, 8th century.

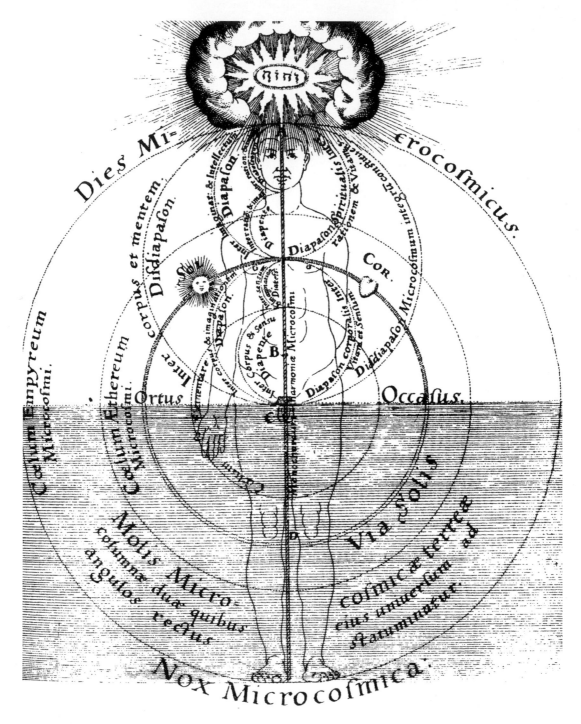

by knowledge and repeated experience it becomes a handicraft . . . At the Last Judgement the world will be judged by fire – fire that has been created by the Master out of nothing – the world must again become ashes through fire; out of these ashes will the Phoenix at last bring forth again her young.

Wolfram gave his holy stone the further power of creating a paradise on earth around Munsalvaesche

and granting a life approaching the eternal to its dedicated servants. In this way, the Wild or Wooded Mountain became the true one of salvation, and the Waste Land was turned into a Garden of Eden.

Parzival made the Knights of the Grail a higher order than those of the Round Table. While they might move from the court of King Arthur to Munsalvaesche, nobody could join the elect without being named on the Grail, the judge of his

Left: 'The *Spiritus Mundi*, the limpid spirit, is represented here by a string. It extends from God to the Earth, and participates in both extremes. On it are marked the stages of the soul's descent into the body, and its re-ascent after death.' *(Robert Fludd, Utrisque Cosmi . . . Historia, 1617)*

knightly service. The military orders of the crusades, particularly the Templars and the Teutonic Knights, inspired Wolfram into grading such cavaliers dedicated to God above the run of the *Ritter* in imperial service. Yet their duty was mortal combat. Parzival could not conceive of any way of finding the Grail without jousting, if necessary to the death. He was, indeed, only saved from killing his half-brother Feirefiz by the breaking of his sword through the will of God. As he told Trevrizent:

> If one can win fame in this world and paradise
> In the next, through the use of shield and lance,
> Then knightly fighting was my only wish.
> I fought where I could find a combat.
> So I have acquired some fame. If God is wise in
> > battle,
> He ought to summon me there [to the Grail
> > Castle]
> So they will know me: I will turn down no fight.

Knightly devotion and loyalty, or *triuwe*, to a feudal lord was linked to devotion to the Lord God Almighty. Parzival began his adventures hardly knowing the difference, but Trevrizent instructed him to be true without wavering, 'since God himself is devotion'. In return for the love of Christ, the knight should serve his representatives on earth, the good rulers and the holy men, as well as save priests and women.

Four levels of existence in the works of Wolfram were complemented by four of time. There was the romantic world of King Arthur in the past. There were the real exploits of the House of Anjou exemplified by Gamuret, the father of Parzival, in Europe and the Near East. There were the adventures of Gawain, who rode between legend and fact, and served Wolfram as a vehicle to extol

and gently mock the ideals of contemporary German chivalry. A higher dimension called everyone upon the Quest for the Grail.

Politically, Wolfram was urging an ordered and disciplined succession to the Grail Castle of the Holy Roman Empire, the octagonal palace chapel of Charlemagne within Aachen Cathedral where his heirs were crowned. Spiritually, he demanded that the high standards of the crusading knights of the military Orders be followed by all the imperial servants of Germany. Only through such a mystic sense of duty could a holy reign be reached.

For his next epic, Wolfram turned back to the legend of Charlemagne in defence of the Holy Roman Empire. Shortly before his death, the Landgrave of Thuringia gave Wolfram a French romance, *Aliscans*, about William of Orange, the first cousin of the emperor, a great warrior who ended as a Benedictine monk and saint near Montpellier. *Willehalm* was a paean of praise to the virtues of holy soldiers in the military Orders. Wolfram combined *Aliscans* with the *Chanson de Roland* and the old German *Rolandslied* to commemorate Charlemagne's defeat at Roncesvalles with his successful conquest of north-eastern Spain, in which the historical William played a large part by a cavalry manoeuvre in the capture of Barcelona. He was eventually canonised as St William of Aquitaine.

The enemy was Islam; yet with his respect for Muslim chivalry, Wolfram did not make monsters of the foe. Their leader was King Terramer, a pagan said to worship Mahmet, Apolle, Tervagant and Kahun. His sin was to try and take the crown of the Holy Roman Empire. Rome itself was named nine times in the text, but not as the central city of Christendom, only in relation to Charlemagne at Aachen, where the imperial power lay. Wolfram's inspiration was probably his new patron, the young Landgrave Ludwig, a saintly crusader who had married another saint, the Hungarian Princess Elisabeth. On Ludwig's death from the plague while helping the Emperor Frederick the Second on a punitive expedition to the Holy Land, Elisabeth put on a Franciscan habit and devoted the rest of her life to the poor and sick. She was canonised shortly after her death, and would be resurrected in *Willehalm* as Countess Giburc, a 'holy lady'.

The opening of Wolfram's epic was devoutly Christian, with an invocation to the power of God over all things, even the elements important to the Gnostics and the alchemists:

> In Thy hand runs the swiftness of the seven stars so they sustain the sky. Air, water, fire, and earth dwell wholly within Thy grandeur. At Thy command stand all things, wild and tame, that live. Moreover, Thy divine might has delimited bright day and dark night and differentiated them by the course of the sun. Never shall be, never was Thy equal. The virtues of all stones, the odours of all herbs, Thou knowest utterly. Thy Spirit has substantiated style and content of true writing, and my mind takes note of Thee mightily. Of all that is written in books I have remained unskilled; I am learned in no wise but in having skill with which insight endows me.

Apparently Wolfram had been stung by the attack on the heretical parts of *Parzival*, which he now excused as his lack of skill, while stressing the supremacy of the Christian God over all. Indeed, he soon mentioned *Parzival*, to say that it had been praised by many people, but many also 'found fault with it and adorned their narrative better'. In *Willehalm*, he would state his own and others' complaints 'that men and women of loyal nature have made since Jesus for baptism's sake was plunged into Jordan'. He would now produce a matchless and worthy story, told with dignity and truth, so silencing the critics of his honour as a German knight.

Although *Willehalm* was not a Grail romance, it did deal with the Holy Lance and characters from *Parzival*. The hero's nephew Vivianz asked for the wafer of the Eucharist as he lay dying, with the words, 'Yet give me His Body, Whose Incarnation died of the blind man's spear when Godhead survived.' In the *Aliscans*, Rainouart, another hero, had prayed during a lull in a battle, 'By the lance

The Grail casket of Charlemagne. *(German National Museum, Nuremberg)*

Thou was wounded deep. Longinus did that, who had good reward, for where he saw not before, (that by faith it might be known), Thy Blood did pour down upon his hands, and when he touched his eyes, he had illumination.'

Wolfram was drawing deeply on the legend of the Holy Lance, which would be confused in Germany with the pagan Spear of Destiny. Fortunately discovered on the First Crusade by Peter the Hermit, the weapon had boosted morale and was later lost with the fall of the Kingdom of Jerusalem, although fragments of the shaft continued to be venerated in various sacred relics. To buttress his claim to be the Holy Roman Emperor, Charlemagne claimed to have received the spear-point from Byzantium; the Emperor Constantine had found it in Palestine. Two iron winged flanges were added to the metal tip as a symbol of the European priest-ruler, now anointed by a weapon from the Passion. In the 11th century, a silver sheath was added to the Holy Lance, while three centuries on, the Emperor Charles the Fourth built a golden chapel in Prague for the head of the sacred spear; its blade now included a nail from the True Cross and was held in a golden scabbard.

When pilgrimage became big business in the Late Middle Ages, the merchants of Nuremberg brought the relic for exhibition. It was placed in a coffer ornamented with silver and hung on ropes from a chapel ceiling, with two choirboys sleeping beneath in order to frighten away thieves. With the coming of the Reformation and the Thirty Years' War, it would be hidden for three centuries, until Napoleon would decide that he wanted to prove that he was founding a new domain of Charlemagne. After his abdication in 1806, however, the last Holy Roman Emperor would take the treasure to Vienna, and there it would remain until Hitler would seize it in 1938 with his invasion of the remnants of the Habsburg Empire.

Thereafter, the Holy Lance would be confused with the pagan Spear of Destiny of the Nordic God Wotan, and it would become a symbol of the Nazi ceremonies, again held in Nuremberg. At the end of the Second World War, it would be returned to Vienna by the United States armed forces, then be tested by modern XRF technology, which would pronounce the blade to be a forgery from the 8th century, the time of Charlemagne. Indeed, only the inserted Holy Nail might date from the time of Christ. And so faith in a sacred weapon had inspired the warriors of Christianity and French Liberty and Fascism in their conquests of other peoples. Their advances had followed that blade.

After the Holy Lance, another abiding heritage of the Grail legend in Germany derived from the fragments of Wolfram's *Titurel*, later completed by another poet, Albrecht, under his predecessor's name as *Jüngerer Titurel*, 'The Young Titurel'. The theme of *Titurel* had been self-control, or the leash, which kept the knight or the dog on the true quest. Titurel had given the crown of the Grail Castle to his last surviving son, Frimutel, who was

soon to die. His abdication was mourned by the Templars, 'whom he had often saved from many a difficult situation when he was defending the Grail with his own hand and with their aid'.

Wolfram had stressed again the importance of kinship and inheritance, particularly to the succession of the Holy Roman Empire. But his message was the leash on the hound, long and adorned with a green Arabian band and precious stones, emeralds, rubies, diamonds, chrysolites and garnets, held by Schionatulander, who had been on a crusade with Gamuret:

> Let me tell you what else he laid hold of along with the hound: he must experience unflinchingly grief lined with toil and great striving for combat. The hound's leash was indeed for him the source of joyless times.

The young Schionatulander must die while jousting in defence of the lands of Parzival. Inevitably, the love that he felt for the maiden Sigune was turned into a trail of blood that led him to his death. Yet in the *Jüngerer Titurel* of Albrecht, the leash became a guide on the Quest for the Grail. Its pursuit would lead the hero to the Mount of Salvation. It also had messages written upon it, but they praised the code of the holy knight more than the desire for the divine.

In Albrecht's long story, the Grail Castle was a version of the Heavenly Jerusalem. Many stanzas praised its construction. On the top of its columns flew angels. Its altars were of sapphire beneath velvet canopies. The doves that brought the host of the Grail in *Parzival* were sculptures. God was the source of all the architecture. The dome of the castle was the cosmos and set towards the east. An astronomical clock charted the movements of the heavens. In the small temple in the centre, there was an organ with singing birds, a sculpture of the Last Judgement, bells, gargoyles and all the paraphernalia of Gothic cathedrals.

Believing in unbelief, Albrecht transmitted his Grail Castle to India, a magic realm where it could hardly be visited, although the Gnostic gospels had led St Thomas there. This fanciful Temple of

Solomon would not have convinced even a credulous medieval audience. Yet Albrecht's tale followed Wolfram's *Parzival*, and the Grail was changed from a cornucopia of bounty to the bond of a way of life shared by an elect. The goal of Schionatulander was perfect Christian knighthood, not the vision of God's grace. He proved himself the best of the knights of King Arthur, but not a holy seeker. The leash only brought joy to its possessor, while the Grail brought plenty and release from suffering.

The leash was always material, hardly spiritual. When Sigune read the messages upon it at the court of King Arthur, they were a sermon on knighthood. God and priests should be served; widows and orphans should be protected. Human traits were preferable to those of animals. A sense of shame, generosity and courage were the leading virtues. A Christian and knightly morality replaced the perilous quest for revelation. After the hero's final crusade to the East, he put the flashing leash on his helmet in his last Western combat, where he was destroyed with his talisman. For it was only the emblem of a German hero, never the search for the spirit of God.

The Grail itself for Albrecht enhanced that of Wolfram. In his temple within the jewelled Grail Castle, a floating stone was the centre of the world. It represented Alexander's oracle at Siwa, the Stone of Destiny of the Celts, the meteoric Ka'aba at Mecca, and the step into heaven of the Prophet under the Dome of the Rock in Jerusalem. Yet Albrecht also took that version of the Grail into alchemy. He wrote that the Grail was a crystal, a compound of fire and water. These two of the four humours of medieval chemistry were capable of birth and resurrection. In that stone was the secret of life.

THIRTEEN

THE WANING OF THE GRAIL

In the Middle Ages the choice lay, in principle, only between God and the world, between contempt or eager acceptance, at the peril of one's soul, of all that makes up the beauty and the charm of earthly life. All terrestrial beauty bore the stain of sin.

J. Huizinga, *The Waning of the Middle Ages*, 1924

In the classic work by Huizinga, *The Waning of the Middle Ages*, the nobility was clearly shown as acting out a vision and a dream. The feudal courts saw themselves as Knights of the Round Table and so were elevated towards the sublime. Yet there were rules in that passionate and violent age, 'always vacillating between tearful piety and frigid cruelty, between respect and insolence, between despondency and wantonness'. One of these formalities was a curious reduction of the Grail procession. At the ceremony of the Mass, where the congregation could not take communion from a chalice reserved for the priest, a disc of silver, ivory or wood called the Pax was passed around for everyone to kiss after the Agnus Dei. This communal observance was the nearest material symbol on offer to the laity of the approach to the divine.

The spirit of the Middle Ages wanted to lay out each conception in mosaic. A holy thought should become an image, while reaching for God might be seen as a sign along the way. There was a danger in confusing the spiritual with the temporal, the bones of the Saints with the examples of their lives. Even secular tournaments with jousting knights were called 'a great indulgence conferred by arms', as if pardon came with victory.

As in any crusade, an absolution for sins was the incentive for holy war. Although the Church of Rome knew that images were merely for the illiterate, these were not condemned. They were the seen and spelling lessons towards the Word of God. And religious extravagance was tolerated, as long as it did not lead to radical change. Beatific visions of Christ were admitted, if they remained within the teachings of the Church.

Extreme and material visions of the Saviour were included. 'A man feels quite deluged in the blood of Christ and faints. All the red and warm blood of the Five Wounds flowed through the mouth of Saint Henry Suso into his heart. Catherine of Siena drunk from the wound in His side.' Such ecstatic enlightenments were still considered Christian revelations. Jean Berthélemy, indeed, was literal and cannibal in describing the Eucharist in *Le Livre de crainte amoureuse*:

You will eat Him roasted at the fire, well baked, not at all overdone or burnt. For just as the Easter lamb was properly baked and roasted between two fires of wood or of charcoal, so was gentle Jesus on Good Friday placed on the spit of the worthy cross, and tied between the two fires of His very fearful death and passion, and of the very ardent charity and love which He felt for our souls and our salvation. He was, as it were, roasted and slowly baked to save us.

A certain voluptuousness and paganism had always been a part of the *chansons* of the troubadours. Religious music was used for love poetry. And the most popular of all the lays, the *Roman de la rose*, mixed carnal love with the Passion of Christ quite shamelessly. In the opulence of the courts before the Renaissance, even the ascetic quest for the Grail would become a luxurious voyage. In tapestry and royal theatre,

Left: The Virgin with the Child in the rose garden. *(15th century, Strasbourg)*

Above: *The Glorious Life of Christ*, an Arras tapestry, made for the Cathedral of San Salvador in Saragossa.

chivalry would appear as a drama of gilt and circumstance.

There were nine cult heroes in the romances and images of the Late Middle Ages. Three were leaders from the Bible: Joshua, King David and Judas Maccabeus; three were from classical times: Hector, Alexander the Great and Julius Caesar; and three were historical Christian warriors: King Arthur, Charlemagne and Godfrey de Bouillon. These were particularly celebrated on the tapestries from Arras and Tournai, commissioned by the nobles of Burgundy. In a curious fantasy of history, all wore contemporary costumes dripping with silks and brocades, spiked with lances and long-toed pointed boots. Weapons, ships, musical instruments and tools were also of the time, as were legends and alchemy.

In one Flemish tapestry of the 15th century, presently in the Palazzo Doria in Rome, the young Alexander was flown up to heaven through the spheres of air and fire on a winged chariot, blessed by God the Father. This was a sacred adventure before the Greek conqueror would acquire dominion over nature and the earth. In the tapestries about Christ, display trampled over purity. Particularly sumptuous was *The Adoration of the Magi*, woven in Brussels of gold and silver silk thread, and presently in the cathedral at Sens. A naked baby Jesus sits on his mother's damask robe. There is no manger, but a carved throne. The Magi wear regal oriental costumes and bear wrought and jewelled caskets, gifts of infinite bounty.

Even the agonies of the Passion are described as part of *The Glorious Life of Christ*, an Arras work for the cathedral of San Salvador in Saragossa. His entry into Jerusalem is a triumph. His crucifixion is a stylised tableau with the traditional symbols of the Grail, the Holy Lance of St Longinus and the sponge of vinegar taken from the cup and held up to him. In addition, a curious scene of the three Holy Marys shows them placing two golden Grails of spices on the broken tomb, while an angel announces to them that Christ is already risen. One gilded cup has the stone fallen from heaven by dropping into it, pointed out by the Virgin Mary, whose growing cult was a strange paradox in the laxity of that age.

The crusades were depicted in dramas and pageants. At the French court of Charles the Fifth, the fall of Jerusalem in the First Crusade was redone in 1378 for the Holy Roman Emperor. Fifteen tapestries on Godfrey de Bouillon decorated Pleshey Castle, while Henry the Third of England commissioned wall-paintings on the same theme. And William Caxton not only printed the Bible and Malory's *Morte D'Arthur*, but also an English translation of the romance *Godfrey de Bouillon or the Siege and Conquest of Jerusalem*. However decadent the contemporary action, crusading retained its popular appeal.

Although the Church condemned tournaments, the nobility revelled in them, the expression of ideal chivalry. As concepts of the Grail and the crusades became more lavish, so extravagant military orders arose to replace the Hospitallers, the Templars and the Teutonic Knights. In instituting and financing the Order of the Golden Fleece, the dukes of Burgundy gilded the rough virtues of the ascetic knights of the Holy Land. Instead of protecting pilgrims to the sites of the Passion, tHis Body of elect aristocrats attended rituals and had love affairs. Holy wars were hardly their concern. Status and entertainment were replacing swords and engagement. Betterment was becoming the enemy of the good.

Penance and savagery had always underlaid the Quest for the Grail and for Jerusalem. This purpose was now encrusted by ornament and boast rather than rigour and vow. As in the other classic work by Huizinga, *Homo Ludens*, war was being reduced to play. The Grail romances had changed the holy combat and the joust unto death into fables, and the Burgundian court altered the chivalric quest into an orgiastic entertainment.

The process would culminate in Tudor times at the extravagant Field of the Cloth of Gold. Cannon had already arrived to end the era of the armoured knight. England and France had fought a Hundred Years War, when women saints were burned alive and chivalry was the mask of brutality. This fantastic tournament was a necessary charade for Henry the Eighth of England to persuade himself that the old noble values still survived into a mechanical age, when the gun was already mightier than the blade. Yet it was already the travesty as well as the tapestry of peace. The Order of the Garter was worth no more than the Golden Fleece. Ceremonial was the memorial of a fierce faith lost.

The luxury that tainted the purity of the Quest for the Grail slowly suffocated the impulse for the crusades. At Lille in Burgundy in 1454, the year after the fall of Constantinople to the Turks, Duke Philip the Good gave a banquet for the Feast of the Pheasant. On the neck of the drugged bird, Philip swore to join a crusade to the East with one other ruler. Two hundred nobles vowed to accompany him. Yet they did not reach the Holy Land. The victory against the advancing Turks under Sultan Mehmed the First was achieved by thousands of Hungarian believers, but not by their rulers, who seemed to have lost stomach for the fight against the infidel in filling their own bellies.

The intention to leave on crusade remained among the kings of Europe, but the conquest of lands nearer their borders usually intervened. After his capture of Paris, the dying Henry the Fifth of England interrupted the priest reciting the penitential psalms to declare that if his life was spared, he would leave to rebuild the walls of Jerusalem. His pledge was too late and too antique. The real problem no longer lay in retaking the Holy City, but in repulsing the Muslim assault on central Europe. As the later Pope Pius the Second put it in a letter to Nicholas the Fifth: 'Now Muhammad reigns among us. Now the Turk hangs over our very heads. The Black Sea is closed to us, the Don has become inaccessible. Now the Vlachs must obey the Turk. Next his sword will reach the Hungarians, and then the Germans.'

The last great crusade towards the Levant had ended in the total disaster at Nicopolis in 1396, when the previous Duke of Burgundy, Philip the Bold, had subsidised thousands of French and other European knights to join King Sigismund of Hungary's efforts to drive the Turks back to the Black Sea. The land war had turned into a defensive operation. The advance of Islam would have to be stopped finally by the walls of Vienna. In the north of Europe, the crusades against the pagan Slavs by the Teutonic Knights were being defeated by the rising power of Poland. Only in Spain did the *reconquista* gradually move from the northern mountains to the southern beaches, and then on to a naval war against the Ottoman admirals and the fleets of Barbary.

The dimming of the light of the crusades lay in turning them into papal wars that were financed by the corrupt sale of indulgences. After the Albigensian suppression, the papacy stressed the policy that the enemy had to be defeated at home before he could be attacked abroad. When Gregory the Ninth wrote to King Louis of Hungary, he assured him that the tyrant Visconti had to be deposed in Italy to prepare for a holy war against the Turks. Pius the Second repeated the same message, stating that battles against Ferrante of Naples and Sigismondo of Rimini were the same as attacking the Turks. The vows of crusaders who had elected to sail to the Near East were commuted to service in Lombardy. And while donations were collected for the recapture of Jerusalem, these assigned tenths in the coffers of St Peter's paid for besieging cities in Tuscany or Sicily.

The failure of many of the crusades against fellow Christians, who were declared to be heretics, appeared to point the finger of God at the motive behind their calling. Heaven seemed to be signalling its disapproval. This was particularly true of the five crusades against the Hussites in Bohemia, which heralded the rise of Protestantism in Europe. Jan Hus himself said that these fiascos were witnesses of the internal corruption of the Church, a theme taken up by the reformers of the Renaissance.

The conquest of the infidel in the Near East had already been translated to the subjugation of the pagan Slavs and Lithuanians on the Prussian borders. The Teutonic Knights had taken over the mission of the Templars, leaving the seaborne Hospitallers to hold Rhodes and, with its fall, Malta against Islam. From their headquarters in Marienburg, the Teutonic Knights had become more representative of German national expansion than of a Christian crusade.

From the 14th century onwards, foreigners were excluded. 'The Order is a German Order,' the

Right: The Virgin Mary and Child with donor and St Mary Magdalene holding a Grail in front of an early medieval garden. *(11th-century oil painting on wood, Museum of Religious and Mosan Art, Liège, France)*

Left: The Grand Master of the Knights Hospitallers of St John prays before St John the Baptist holding the Paschal Lamb with banner on a green Grail platter. From the Burdett Psalter, *c*. 1285. This psalter was the only surviving treasure of the military Orders, taken from Acre as it fell to the Muslims in 1287 and the Kingdom of Jerusalem was lost for ever, despite later crusades

Grand Master wrote, 'in which nobody who is not German, but only Germans, healthy and trained people, who are in all respects born to the shield, are included by custom.' The imperial knights, the Ritter and the Reisen of *Parzival*, were becoming provincial rather than international, and yet their Order took them back to the immortal days of King Arthur and the Grail. Their Table of Honour was described in 1375 by Jean de Chastlemorand:

The Grand Master, seeing that this Reise had been honourably completed, on the day of Candlemas feasted the knighthood that were with him and highly; and for the honour of the day, after Mass in his castle at Marienburg he had spread the Table of Honour, as it was his will that there should be seated at it twelve knights of the several kingdoms . . . and they were served, for the high dignity of the day, as was their due. And thanks be to God to those twelve they explained this Order of the Table and how it came to be established. And then one of the knights

of that religion gave to each of them a shoulder badge, on which it was written in letters of gold '*Honneur vainc tout!*'. And the next day the knights took their leave of the Grand Master, and returned each to his own country.

Yet this Order, which retained the traditions of Camelot, was doomed by the nationalism it encouraged. The Poles were becoming powerful. Heretical Hussite ideas, which opposed the Catholic hierarchy and demanded direct access to God, were spreading from Bohemia. Marienburg was defended in the early 15th century, but it was lost in 1457, surrendered by paid mercenaries. Poland, rather than the Holy Roman Empire or the Church of Rome, became the sovereign of the Order. The crusade to the East in the north of Europe was over.

In literature as in art, the versions of the Grail were only a series of descriptions or images. They were milestones on the way of the pilgrim towards

The Church was mocked for its guzzling monks and friars.

the vision of God. But the official signs and blessings of the Church, the relics of the Passion and of the Saints, the sale of indulgences and the pardon for sins, were becoming incredible and discredited. In the amazing and popular *Travels* of Sir John Mandeville, completed in 1356, pilgrimage was taken to the limits of fable. The author displayed both the belief and the scepticism of his age in visiting the sacred remains, scattered among the abbeys and the cathedrals.

At the Church of the Holy Sepulchre in Jerusalem, Mandeville wrote that 'in this temple was Charlemagne when the angel brought him the prepuce of Our Lord Jesus Christ of His circumcision. And after King Charles let bring it to Paris to his chapel, and after that he let bring it to Poitiers and after that to Chartres.' As for the head of St John the Baptist, the back of the skull was in Constantinople, the jaws in Genoa and the chin at Rome. 'And some men say that the head of Saint John is at Amiens in Picardy, and other men say that it is the head of Saint John the Bishop. I wot never, but God knoweth. But in what wise that men worship it the blessed Saint John holdeth him apaid.'

That was the point of faith. However true the provenance of the relic, the belief of the pilgrim in the Messiah or saint from whom it was meant to come, transformed the object into the search for revelation. The trials of the voyage were the Quest for a Grail of sorts, even if the history of the sight seen was dubious. In so far as the worshipper of the fragment of the head of the Baptist believed in

his holiness, the saint would repay him for his sincerity. As it was, Mandeville praised the simple Christianity in the land of the African Prester John, the son of Feirefiz in the *Parzival* of Wolfram von Eschenbach. There the people were said to sing the Mass as the Apostles had, 'as Our Lord taught them [in] a good faith natural'.

This hankering for the simplicity of a reformed religion was transformed by Mandeville into a travesty of the Eucharist, which he set in the Isle of Rybothe or Tibet. He seemed to mock its pope and its carnivorous ritual. At the death of the father, the son cut off his head and fed His Body to the birds – angels of God in the Tibetan liturgy. The brains were served to friends of the family, the skull used as a memorial vessel. 'And that cup the son shall keep to drink of all his lifetime in remembrance of the father.' This echo of the words of Christ, 'Do this in remembrance of me', was heretical in the extreme, a curious questioning of the doctrine of transubstantiation by bringing up the rites of the Zoroastrians, whose descendants still expose the bodies of the dead to be eaten by vultures in open burial towers.

Chaucer certainly had read his Mandeville before he composed *The Canterbury Tales*. The first comic epic in the English language was written 200 years after the murder of St Thomas à Becket. Pilgrimages to his tomb were even more popular than to Our Lady of Walsingham. To the Church, of course, such piety was bliss, for it hallowed the triumph of religion over the secular state. In the *Tales*, the first pilgrim, the Knight, was praised as a crusader, 'late y-come from his viage'. His son the Squire had only been on a false crusade, the recent pillage of Flanders. The Wife of Bath had been three times to Jerusalem and to other shrines, without doing her character much good, although she found a homily on her travels:

And eek I pray Jhesu shorte their lives
That will not be governed by their wives.

But the profiteers from the Christian faith and the pilgrimage were mocked and run down, the Summoner and the Pardoner, the Monk and the Friar, although the Prioress and the Second Nun were allowed their virtue and their anti-Semitism, as the crusaders were. Corruption in religion, particularly the sale of the faith, was endemic, as the Pardoner confessed:

> I wol nat do no labour with myne handes . . .
> Nay, I wol drynke licour of the vyne
> And have a joly wenche in every toun.

Such effrontery led to the inescapable reaction. When the great Dutch humanist Erasmus visited Canterbury in the company of his learned friends Dean Colet and Sir Thomas More, he thought of Christ comparing the scribes and the Pharisees to whited sepulchres that were outwardly beautiful, but inwardly full of dead men's bones and of all uncleanness. He demanded:

> What would Jesus say could he see the Virgin's milk exhibited for money, with as much honour paid to it as to the consecrated body of Christ; the miraculous oil; the portions of the True Cross, enough if they were collected to freight a large ship? Here we have the hood of Saint Francis, there Our Lady's petticoat or Saint Anne's comb, or Saint Thomas of Canterbury's shoes; not presented as innocent aids to religion, but as the substance of religion itself – and all through the avarice of priests and the hypocrisy of monks playing on the credulity of the people. Even bishops play their parts in these fantastic shows, and approve and dwell on them in their rescripts.

Walsingham in Norfolk was called the English Loretto, because it held in its wooden chapel a reproduction of the Sancta Casa. The primitive shrine was blessed when the crusaders brought there the milk from the breasts of the Virgin Mary. Erasmus also visited the sacred place, and he was impressed by the contrast between its simplicity and the riches deposited there. The sea winds blew through the bare boards. Worshippers were admitted into the unfinished church by a narrow door on each side. The chapel had little light, and only from wax candles that had an agreeable odour. Yet 'if you looked inwards, you would say it was the mansion of the gods, it glitters so with jewels, gold and silver.'

That was the contrast of pilgrimage. The more holy the place, the more it was overloaded with precious memorials. The truth lay between the essence and the encrustation. Outside Walsingham, there were two holy wells of miraculous healing rather like the ancient wishing wells in Ireland. The pilgrims knelt on the forestones, dipped their hands in the sacred flow of water and requested their heart's desire. This act did not mean that they would achieve their demands. When Ogygius questioned the custodian of the sanctuary at Walsingham, he found the building of the roof, the thatch and the crossbeams rather too new. He was then shown a decayed bearskin and the reliquary of the Mother of Jesus. 'So being persuaded, and excusing our stupidity, we turned to the heavenly milk of the Blessed Virgin.'

Such enquiry would turn into heresy. The German reformer Martin Luther, for instance, in 1510 went on a pilgrimage to Rome. His purpose was to expose the sale of indulgences. Paradoxically, he sought to put justification by faith before the good works performed by pilgrims visiting sites of uncertain reputation. John Calvin of Geneva would go much further. To him, pilgrimage was a useless action. The direct approach to God through one's own faith was the best way to the Creator. There were no symbols or images needed on the path to him. These representations should be destroyed as Moses had destroyed the idols and the Calf of Gold. Personal vision was the road to the divine.

When Henry the Eighth broke with the Church of Rome over the divorce and execution of his various wives, he loosed iconoclasm on his holy places, as the Byzantine emperors had done before. Statues of the Virgin were burned in London; a movable image of Christ at Boxley Road in Kent was broken into pieces. At Walsingham, two of the clerics were hanged, drawn and quartered, and the shrine itself was

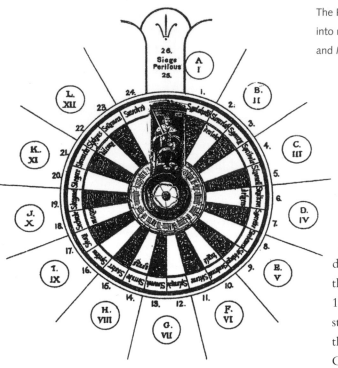

The Round Table of King Arthur at Winchester was converted into mysticism. *(Hargrave Jennings,* The Rosicrucians: Their Rites and Mysteries, *1907)*

desecrated. Before he died in the Tower of London, Philip Howard, Earl of Arundel, wrote in an epitaph:

> Owles do shrieke wher the sweetest hymnes
>   Lately were sunge;
> Toades and serpentes holde their dennes
>   Wher the palmers did thronge.
>
> Weepe, weepe, O Walsingham,
>   Whose dayes are nightes,
> Blessings turned to blasphemies,
>   Holy deedes to despites.
>
> Sinne is wher our Ladie sate,
>   Heaven is turned to hell,
> Sathan sittes wher Our Lord did swaye,
>   Walsingham, oh farewell.

Even at the ending of the mass veneration of bodily and blessed objects, tradition and fanaticism kept them alive. As Huizinga pointed out, the deep faith of the Middle Ages was never afraid of disillusionment or profanation through handling holy things coarsely:

The spirit of the 15th century did not differ much from that of the Umbrian peasants, who, about the year 1000, wished to kill Saint Romuald, the hermit, in order to make sure of his precious bones; or of the monks of Fossanuova, who, after Saint Thomas Aquinas had died in their monastery, in their fear of losing the relic, did not shrink from decapitating, boiling and preserving the body. During the lying in state of Saint Elisabeth of Hungary, in 1231, a crowd of worshippers came and cut or tore strips of the linen enveloping her face; they cut off the hair, the nails, even the nipples. In 1392, King Charles VI of France, on the occasion of a solemn feast, was seen to distribute ribs of his ancestor, Saint Louis; to Pierre d'Aily and to his uncles Berry and Burgundy, he gave entire ribs; to the prelate one bone to divide between them, which they proceeded to do after the meal.

With the Reformation, Europe would be split between the Protestant north and the Catholic south. As with any radical change, extremes tipped the balance, and art was lost to Puritanism. The Swiss reformer Zwingli declared that the Eucharist was an idol. Material or carnal things such as icons or relics could not hold within them the transcendence of God. In Scotland, France and the Netherlands, images were smashed and churches were desecrated. The adoration of relics and elaborate ceremonies was seen as worship of the Devil.

The religious revolutionaries were the heirs to the medieval heresies and the personal quest for the Grail of divine revelation. The Brethren of the Free Spirit were the catalysts between the dissident Cathars of Provence, the Taborites of Bohemia and the German Anabaptists of the Renaissance. They believed that every created thing was divine. A person who truly searched for the Creator should look into himself, where he already was. On death, the speck or spark of God was reabsorbed into the essence of the everlasting. Throughout eternity, man was God and in God. There was no need of a priest or Church on earth to mediate in the salvation of a soul. Each had to seek out and find God, who already occupied the body of all beings.

To the doctrine of the divine within every living thing was added the myth of Eden. Humankind would return to the state of Adam and Eve in the Garden of Paradise – where there was no property or poverty or oppression – after the destruction of Orthodoxy, the victory of the Antichrist and the reign of Jesus for 1,000 years. The adepts of the Free Spirit would enjoy that state of paradise now and should rule the elect, chosen from other believers. They could recall the Golden Age, which Jean de Meun had hymned in his popular *Roman de la rose*, or the Grail Castle of the romances. Such visions and egalitarian dreams had been behind the Peasants' Revolt in England, where the preacher John Ball had asked his famous question:

> When Adam delved and Eve span,
> Who was then a gentleman?

God's law meant that all authority should be overthrown and all goods held in common. Such doctrines inspired the extremists among the Hussites, after their victory in Bohemia. These Taborites believed in an Apocalypse, in which only

Above: The Church, however, was protected by militant knights on crusade.

Below: The Garden of Eden became a dream of a lost paradise and not an article of faith in the Renaissance work by Bergomensis, *Summa de todas las cronicas del mundo*, 1510.

their towns would be spared, while the rest of the world was condemned. And from them broke off a more fanatical sect, the Adamites, who supported a holy war against the rest of humanity. They saw themselves as the angel with the fiery sword at the gates of Eden. They burned and massacred the inhabitants of all the neighbouring villages, until the Taborite commander was forced to exterminate his own zealots, for fear that their message would subvert the whole of human society.

The Reformation opposed pilgrimages to holy places and the veneration of relics such as the True Cross. These stimuli to the crusading movement, however, did not prevent the Protestants from using religious zeal to mount their own crusades. Luther, indeed, supported the extermination of the Anabaptists in their fanatical paradise in Münster, and the rebellious peasants. To him, the Pope was the Antichrist, and Catholics and Muslims were both heretics in alliance with Satan, who should be pursued by war.

As for the Jews, Luther anticipated their mass conversion, then turned on them in fury in his Wittenberg pamphlet, *On the Jews and their Lies*, the first popular work of anti-Semitism. He wanted all synagogues burned, prayer forbidden, Jewish homes razed, and forced labour inflicted on the people of that faith. He was instrumental in driving the Jews from Saxony and many German cities. Faced with Protestant persecution, the Jews looked for protection to the Catholic bishops and the Holy Roman Emperor, whose pogroms were inter-mittent. And grouping themselves in ghettos became the Jewish way of survival in the European city, beginning in Venice and spreading north and east, a forced segregation, which would make their bunched communities even more vulnerable.

The Reformation split Scandinavia, north Germany, Holland and Britain from southern Catholic Europe, and initiated centuries of strife by land and sea, in which national interest could hardly be distinguished from religious differences. For the Counter-Reformation proved as sanguinary and savage as the excesses of the Reformers against priests and nuns. The stake was now the fate, not of St Joan of Arc, but of the Protestant martyrs described by Foxe, and captured sailors of the Elizabethan navy. The Inquisition was not used only against the Muslims and the Jews, but also against the breakaway Christian factions – now identified with the conspiracies of the Devil.

As the Reformation incited the Counter-Reformation, so the fanaticism of the Protestants had its revenge. In 1544, the Council of Trent allied the removal of religious discord with a fresh crusade against the infidel. And for the next 100 years, until the end of the Thirty Years War in Middle Europe and the English Civil War, elements of the crusading ideology would surface in the propaganda of the conflict of the faiths. Notably, the year after the great Christian sea victory at Lepanto, the French religious wars began with the Massacre of St Bartholomew's Day, when the Catholics turned on their fellow Huguenot citizens with the ferocity shown by the crusaders when they first took Jerusalem, or by the slaughter of the Moorish knights in the *Perlesvaus*. The merciless-ness, maiming and torture used by the French spiritual rivals towards those of another faith were as dreadful and inexcusable as in the crusade against the Cathars – a national self-mutilation in the name of nothing very much, but an excess of terror.

The crusading imagery was more credible in terms of imperial ambition. When the Spanish Armada left in 1588 to conquer England, red crosses billowed on its vaunting sails, and the mission was blessed as if against the Turks at Lepanto. Its disaster was seen by the King of Spain as a divine judgement on his crown. And in effect, it was a perversion of his faith. For the way to London was hardly towards another Jerusalem. Indeed, a survivor of Lepanto would write the first modern novel of genius, *Don Quixote*, which would mock the ideals of chivalry, translating them into the visions of an aged knight, tilting at windmills. What Godfrey de Bouillon had inspired, Cervantes would prick, although the crusades in Spain had created the nation.

FOURTEEN

THE ROAD TO COMPOSTELA

All Mankind is of one Author, and is in one volume; when one Man dies, one Chapter is not torn out of the book, but translated into a better language; and every Chapter must be so translated; God employs several translators; some pieces are translated by age, some by sickness, some by war, some by justice; but God's hand is in every translation; and his hand shall bind up all our scattered leaves again, for that library where every book shall lie open to one another.

John Donne, *Devotions*, 17th century

At Vézelay, St Bernard had preached the Second Crusade, after founding the Cistercian Order of white monks and having the Knights Templars of the octagonal red cross blessed at the synod of 1128 at Troyes, the original city of the Grail romances. Their function was the protection of pilgrims to the holy places, not only to Palestine, but also to Santiago de Compostela in Spain, where so many prospective crusaders found themselves fighting the Moors, before they managed the passage towards Jerusalem. Although the Benedictines from Cluny had already established the Knights of Saint John as the protectors of the sacred way, the Templars were also needed in the holy war in Spain. The bones of the repentant St Mary Magdalene brought pilgrims to Vézelay; the arms of the Hospitallers and the Templars took them through the town from the coronation place of the kings of France at Reims to the Cathedral of St James at Compostela.

As far as the French border, a way lay through Autun, Neuvy St-Sepulchre, Charroux, Civray, Aulnay, and Saintes to the pass at Roncesvalles, where Roland had died. At each of these places,

The reliquary of Mary Magdalene at Vézelay.

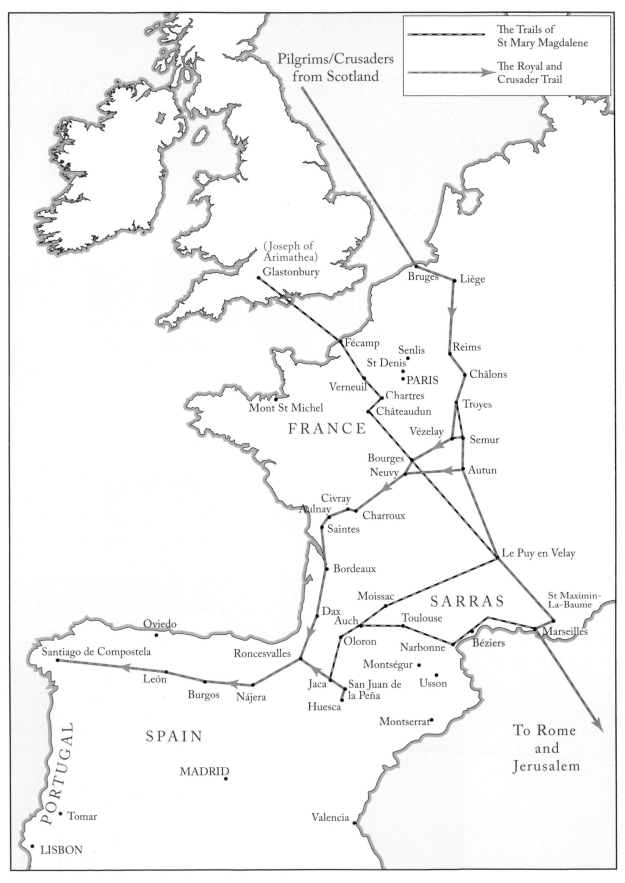

The Grail in Spain and France.

they can still be seen on the tympanum of the cathedral with their shoulder bags, sporting crosses and scallop shells. On one capital of the Flight into Egypt, the child Christ is shown on his mother's lap as she rides on a donkey led by St Joseph. Uniquely, the Blessed Virgin holds a globe in the palm of her hand, while Jesus puts his fingers on this stone cosmos. But such an indication of the quest for the divine is only a signpost on the path to Neuvy St-Sepulchre, where the Blood of Christ is still kept, and on to Charroux and Civray, where two of the earlier depictions of the Grail in France remain to this day.

At Neuvy, the Abbé may demonstrate the two drops out of the three of the Holy Blood, which survived the French Revolution. These were

Left: The font of blessings and rebirth at Neuvy St-Sepulchre.

Below: The tower of the abbey at Charroux.

there remained symbols of the Grail. Odo of Cluny particularly connected the ancient myth of the Holy Vessel to the womb and the sin of Eve. For had not Christ first appeared to the Magdalene after the Crucifixion in his healing garden as the doctor of her soul? Odo's hymn for his fellow monks celebrated her story:

> After the scandal of her frail flesh
> From a cauldron she made a cup afresh
>   Into a vase of glory, she altered
>   The vessel whose worth she had bartered.
> To her Doctor she ran, spent and sick,
> Bearing her vase so aromatic.
>   All the illnesses she had endured
>   By the word of the Doctor so were cured.

Pilgrims on the crusading trail from Vézelay to the north of Spain passed through Autun, where

Above: Two doves drink from a chalice at the base of the Charroux tower.

Below: The reliquary of the Holy Blood at Neuvy St-Sepulchre.

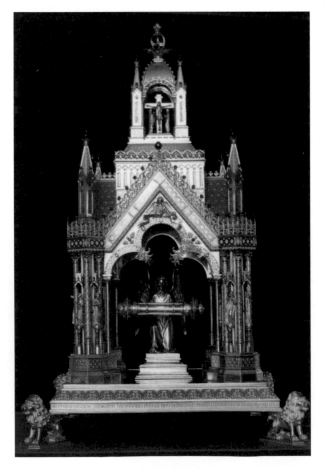

presented to the basilica by Cardinal Odon of Châteauroux, after he had acquired them in the 13th century in Palestine. They are kept within a phial inside a modern reliquary: a kneeling golden angel carries the precious burden. Yet another form of a Grail is always on show in St Joseph's chapel, which is set beside the ten pillars that support the high dome of the round structure, modelled on the Church of the Holy Sepulchre in Jerusalem. There is an immense stone urn with a copper cover surmounted by the Cross – a true font of blessing and rebirth.

Further along the way to Compostela, the pilgrims arrived at the wonder of the abbey of Charroux. Its supreme surviving tower on its soaring octagonal arches derived from Charlemagne's chapel at Aachen, more exact a replica of the Church of the Holy Sepulchre than at Neuvy. Most remarkably, one stone carving has been left out of the museum within the abbey ruins, where the other statues may be found, including one of the Foolish Virgins squandering the riches of nature by turning her pitcher upside down.

Secluded in there, three jewelled reliquaries may also be seen, one of which housed another piece of the St Vertu presented by Charlemagne. To the west of the crypt of the round tower, however, an incised relief of the 11th century has been placed so that the rays of the morning sun illuminate it. Among fronds of lilies, two doves are drinking from a chalice. If there is one supreme time and place of Grail pilgrimage in France, it is sunrise at the tower of Charroux.

Among the seventy-five relics that made the abbey of Charroux such a magnet in the Middle Ages, were a piece of the True Cross, a version of the Holy Face of Lucca, and the St Vertu, now kept in the cathedral at Poitiers. The name of this last remnant of the body of Christ was a euphemism. The Pope called it the Holy Prepuce, actually the foreskin of Christ taken from him at his circumcision. The original benefactor of the abbey, Charlemagne, might well have wished to own a part of the virility of God as a symbol of his own blessed power and virtue, and as the sire of a race of sanctified rulers in the manner of King David of Israel.

Romanesque portico of the Church of St Nicholas at Civray. Crusading knights with crosses on their shields are shown treading down devils and pagans on this stage of the route to Santiago de Compostela.

Before Charlemagne took the little remnant of sacred skin from the Church of St Mary in Aachen to present it to Charroux, it had a strange provenance. It was reputedly given to him by an angelic boy in a vision during the saying of Mass in the Church of the Holy Sepulchre in Jerusalem. There he saw the right Hand of God descend, as can be seen on the portico of the cathedral of St Peter at Saintes, also on the route to Compostela. The Almighty placed a small thing on the communion chalice, the St Vertu, capable of curing and restoring to life. In point of fact, Charlemagne never visited the Holy City in his life.

Seven miles to the west of Charroux, carved Templar knights continue to guard pilgrims above the entrance doors to the painted church of

St Nicholas at Civray. Standing on the rim of a half-moon, their nailed feet tread down the devils and pagans that threaten the faithful, while protecting Christ ruling in heaven below them. Inside, there is a rare fresco of the 12th century; a holy man reaches out towards an altar bearing two candles and a chalice. An angel holding the scroll of the Word of the Lord flies down, bringing grace. This is the only mural of the period on the route to Compostela showing the Grail.

Aulnay to the south-west is the best-preserved of all the stopping-places along that pilgrim road. On its west portico, crusading knights recline, guarding the Paschal Lamb on its round platter. On another tympanum, St Peter is shown as crucified upside down. He is seen as a descending figure of the divine, his two torturers hammering the nails into his feet and standing above him on the arms of the cross – a theme that could be interpreted as a revolt from the authority of Rome, even though it was traditional.

Further to the south towards Bordeaux, at Saintes, there is an architrave of slaughter above the entrance to the cathedral of St Peter. Primitive men butcher each other above two Templar symbols, the Lamb of God carrying the Cross, and the Hand of God, pointing down with two fingers curled back from a sunburst, the supposed vision of Charlemagne in Jerusalem. In the Middle Ages, Saintes was as famous as Hailes as being a sanctuary of the Holy Blood; but, as in England, the remembrance of the faith lost has long gone.

The pilgrims on their path through France towards Spain had other goals. Although the rusty sword stuck in the rock at the Rocamadur was not the Durandal of Roland any more than it was the sword of King Arthur in the stone, yet the Black Virgin there was as celebrated as the one in Montserrat in Catalonia. The pilgrimage to her shrine up the steep steps on bleeding knees was for the guilty almost as purging as the journey to Compostela or Vézelay, where also the penitents threw off their chains in front of the bones of the Magdalene. Throughout the south of France and northern Spain, the cults of the Black Virgin and the Magdalene were often confused in the desperate need of the sinner to be shriven.

First, the pilgrims had to cross over many rivers on the way by some of the few bridges over their torrents. At Cahors, the Valentré Bridge with its three towers, said to be the Faustian gift of the Devil, resisted the English during the Hundred Years War and Henry of Navarre in the religious wars. At the bridge over the Tarn at Moissac, further south, the abbey and church of St Peter has a masterpiece of the Vision of the Apocalypse according to St John over its doorway. Also there, as at Auch, is a fine life-size carving of the late 16th century, the putting of Christ's Body into the Tomb. Ignoring the Gospels, the Virgin Mary has joined the scene with the other women. The Magdalene holds up her sacred vessel, overshadowed at the feet of Jesus, as she was to be by the Mother of Christ.

At Orthez, modern pilgrims may still cross over the famous fortified bridge with its central tower, spanning the road. The ongoing trail to Compostela leads through Sauveterre, where the Church of St Andrew has the most charming small Romanesque façade within the fortified town. At the foot of the Pyrenees, there is the long winding climb to Roncesvalles beginning at St Jean-Pied-de-Port, where medieval pilgrims used to arrive by riverboat. But at the scene of Roland's defeat by the pagan Basques, not the Moorish infidels, only a small 15th-century church of Santiago shows itself, together with a wayside cross. In place of the old monastery that was so hospitable to pilgrims there are modern blocks for teaching prayer; also hostels. Within them is encased the Gothic chapterhouse of the founder King of Navarre: he still lies there with his Queen. Roland, incidentally, is said to be buried at the pilgrim Atlantic port of Blaye, in the estuary of the Gironde opposite Bordeaux. His body may lie beside the two surviving towers of the triangular Château des Rudel; its famous son, the minstrel Jaufré, died in the arms of his love, Melissende of Tripoli, after falling sick in the Mediterranean, crossing to her crusading domain in Syria.

The two Grail trails of France which cross at Vézelay – the ways of the crusaders and the Magdalene – also meet at the approaches to Spain. For she was an inspiration to the holy warriors against the Moors, who must have found the Christian faith of the little enemy mountain towns overwhelming. Every cluster of houses, tenaciously clinging to a rock or slope, boasts a church or an abbey or even a cathedral.

The Muslims may have built a spate of mosques in the south of Spain, but they were confronted by so many spires in the Pyrenees that their attack would have seemed to be blocked by a stockade of stones, even if these were not as terrifying as the thickets of impaled victims that met their eyes when they invaded the Transylvania of King Vlad the Impaler. To the modern traveller, the evidence of that long-gone holy war still bristles against the sky. And the cults that crossed at Vézelay – the sword borne by the knights against the infidel, along with the Grail of grace carried by the Magdalene – can still be found together on the borderland of the struggle between the Cross and the Crescent.

In Provence, the legend was that Mary Magdalene had landed with Joseph of Arimathea at Les-Saintes-Maries-de-la-Mer, near Marseilles. The Gnostics had adored the Magdalene as the favourite disciple of Jesus. Her history was told in *The Golden Legend*, the most popular medieval version of the *Lives of the Saints*. She and her brother Lazarus and her sister Martha were said to have owned castles and lands near and in Jerusalem. One home was a tower at Magdala on the Sea of Galilee; another at Bethany. She was engaged to John, the other beloved disciple; but when Jesus changed the water into wine at Cana, John left with him and Mary became promiscuous before being redeemed by Jesus, who also brought back her brother Lazarus from the dead.

The cult of the Magdalene also spread due west along the Mediterranean coast to St Maximin-La-Baume, where a fresco is painted of her in the nude, somewhat covered by her long red hair, and bearing a Grail and the Cross. At Béziers, there is a large church dedicated to her with an octagonal tower constructed by the apse. Viscount Trescard was murdered in the holy building, and at the massacre of the population of the city in 1209 during the Albigensian Crusade, the worst slaughter took place in this sanctuary where the Cathars had fled, seeking a vain mercy. The grim words of Arnald-Almaric, the Abbot of Citeau, to the vengeful crusaders against the heretics still resound: 'Kill them all: God will look after His own.' During the French Revolution, the church was turned into a workshop for making bayonets, but now the only sign of war on its outer wall is a crusading knight within a large medallion, while a gigantic scallop shell design reminds the pilgrim today of the holy way to Spain.

The Church had always been militant about the crusades, for these were inspired by the Church. In the 9th century, the blessed Pope Leo the Fourth exhorted the Franks to follow the example of Charlemagne in his attacks on the Islamic invaders of Spain. 'Have no fear, and be mindful of your fathers. Whatever the number of enemies, these warriors were always victorious . . . God will not close the gates of Heaven against him who dies in such a battle.' And the great Cistercian white friar, St Bernard of Clairvaux, absolved his creation, the Knights Templars, of any bloodthirstiness:

> They can fight the battles of the Lord and can be of a surety the soldiers of Christ. Let them kill the enemy or die; they need to have no fear! To embrace death for Christ or to cause His enemies to submit to it is naught but glory – it is no crime! Moreover, it is not without reason that the soldier of Christ carries a sword; it is for the chastisement of the wicked and for the glory of the good. And we must recognize in him the avenger, who is in the service of Christ, and the liberator of the Christian people.

And as for wounded knights, they looked to Mary Magdalene for their example and redeemer. Before he took Jerusalem, Godfrey de Bouillon fell, pierced in liver and lung, outside the walls of Antioch. His plea was 'Most Glorious Father, the beautiful Mary Magdalene came to Thee in the house of Simon and there shed so copiously the

Right: Mary Magdalene carries a Grail at the taking up of the body of Jesus Christ. This carving comes from the church built in the midst of the arched mosque preserved at Córdoba in Spain.

Left: Mary Magdalene with a Grail in a fresco in St Maximin-La-Baume.

tears from her heart that she washed Thy feet with them, and then anointed them with spikenard. She did wisely, and was rewarded, for she received from Thee pardon for all her sins. If this be true, O Lord, and if it be that we believe it, preserve my body from prison and from death.'

Dante wrote in the 'Paradiso' about the massacre of the heretics at Marseilles by its Bishop Folco, who had been a troubadour and a Franciscan monk. Now, by his zeal, 'with blood was made the harbour warm'. And in Narbonne, the old Bishop's Palace still has a Magdalene tower and chapel, now converted into an archaeological museum. A faded fresco of the Deposition from the Cross has almost expunged the saint, while two clearer angels swing their censers on chains above her. At Albi, there are a pair of Magdalenes carrying her vase, almost lost among the exuberant Renaissance portals. But at Carcassonne and Perpignan, there are no traces of her. Below the Langue d'Oc, the land of the Catalans honoured the Black Virgin in another tongue.

Just so do modern times endeavour to wipe clean the ancient cult of the Magdalene, the St Mary of the Middle Ages with her 150 shrines.

Why was this done? The medieval Church was at its most successful in making Christians feel guilty. Its control over barbaric passions lay in the necessity of expiation only granted by the priest. And much repentance was demanded in that cruel and plundering age. For the warlords and the knights, whose greed made them into considerable sinners according to the Bible, the Magdalene was their perfect forgiveness – a stained woman, blessed by Christ himself. In a strange way, she became associated with Queen Guinevere in the Arthurian cult: both erring ladies needed pardon, as so many others did.

Yet in later ages of materialism and psychiatry, guilt would be at a discount and pardon would become merely a confession from a couch. The Vatican would think that purity was a better message, particularly for women; Hail Marys should be repeated for transgressions, rather than walking with bleeding feet along rocky paths. Jung himself, one of the fathers of analysis, would study alchemy and the Grail in order to find out the wellsprings of those legends in the human psyche. In the course of this progress, the cults of the Magdalene and the Grail were to be lost or mistaken.

St Lawrence with his gridiron. *(Unknown artist, 15th century, Strasbourg)*

With the waning of the Grail at the end of the Middle Ages, the Magdalene was gradually taken over by the Virgin Mary or Our Lady, although the Gospel of St John never put her at the Tomb. The three Marys there were a later invention. Yet churches were renamed; the Gospels and the Golden Legends were forgotten. The Mother of Jesus was shown superseding the Magdalene at the foot of the Cross; also washing his wounds there and taking care of his Body at the opening of the Tomb. By the 19th century, she was dominating the Magdalene at most of the second Mary's sites in France, such as Meaux, where the windows of the Lady Chapel even show the Virgin at the feast of Cana and with the disciples at Pentecost. The attraction of the repentant sinner, who brought the Grail to Sarras, was replaced by the vision of the purity of Our Lady. So the sinful woman, already

forgiven by Christ, was remade without spot or stain.

The small northern kingdoms of the Asturias, Navarre, Aragon and León with Castile were the front line of the crusades against the Islamic incursion into southern Europe. Their fierce belief was their morale and left little room for heresy and the individual search for God. They thought that they held in various places the true Grail, presented by the Pope to St Lawrence. Their adventures as knights were real against the Moors, not performed in a legendary quest for grace. They achieved their benediction on the field of battle with the aid of St James and the military Orders, who helped the Knights of Santiago defend the pilgrim way to Compostela. Their religion was a defence of the faith and an aggressive assertion of its power through war.

In the 3rd century, St Lawrence had been the devoted pupil of Pope Sixtus the Second in Rome and had assisted his master during the Mass. Sixtus was martyred by the Emperor Valerian during a persecution of the Christians. Lawrence asked the Pope why he was going to his death without his teacher, who had raised the host with him before the congregation. Sixtus answered that Lawrence would also die within three days, but after doing great deeds for the Church.

The Roman Emperor then pressed Lawrence to surrender the holy relics of the faith. One of them, the legend declared, was the cup that Christ had used at the Last Supper. Lawrence would not give it up to the Romans. As he stood before the judge of the court, he pointed to the crowd of the poor, declaring that they were the true goods of the Church. He was then put on the hot gridiron and burned slowly to death. 'See the one side is roasted enough,' he was alleged to have said. 'Turn me on the other side and eat.' He delivered the sacred cup to two Spanish legionaries to take to his parents at Lloret above Barcelona, from where it was transferred to the converted Visigothic rulers of Huesca in Aragon, the first of many resting places near the Pyrenees.

The oldest of the Romanesque cathedrals in Spain was at Jaca, the first capital of Lower Aragon and the key to the Somfort Pass. Its carvings reflected the influence of the south of France and swayed the minds of the masons working on other cathedrals all the way west. The remnants of its carvings are playful and do not bring up the Grail, although the St Lawrence vessel was held there for some time.

From the early frontier city of Gerona in Catalonia, however, come two of the more remarkable examples of the Grail, created during the time of the Spanish Crusades. In a manuscript in the Cathedral Treasury, the Sophia or Wisdom carries the Grail on the back of a beast from the Book of Revelation towards the Tree of Jesse and Life. In another brilliant altarpiece with five panels, Christ is seen riding on a donkey into Jerusalem and then washing the feet of his disciples. The centrepiece shows the Last Supper; he holds up a golden cup, while the ball of the cosmos drops within; on the cloth are crusts of bread and a flayed whole Paschal Lamb, with the disciples drinking his Blood from wine glasses and a decanter. The

The Sophia or Wisdom carrying the Grail on a beast from the Book of Revelation towards the Tree of Life. (Treasury, Gerona Cathedral)

These five scenes from the life of Christ come from an altarpiece of the School of Gerona in Catalonia, *c.* 1370–1400. The central panel (right) shows the persistence of the Gnostic heresy. The cosmos drops as a stone into the Grail, held by Jesus, while the flayed Paschal Lamb lies on a platter before him. *(Private collection, Weiss Gallery, London)*

final two scenes show the Agony in the Garden, with the kneeling Christ praying to an angel bearing a censer and the Cross, and then his taking by mailed Roman soldiers.

At the cathedral of Huesca, the Gothic tympanum stresses particularly the legend of that Holy Chalice, as it was kept there as well as in Jaca. On one side of the crowned Virgin Mary holding the infant Christ, the three Magi bear gifts to him, yet on the other side the risen Christ appears by a Tree of Life to the kneeling Magdalene, the bringer of the Grail to Sarras. Above, two angels sprinkle grace from their usual hanging lamps or censers.

Buried in the monastery of San Pedro el Viejo of the 11th century in Huesca is King Alfonso the First of Aragon, named the Battler. He was also given the name of Anfortius or Anfortas, the Grail King, in his crusade to begin the *reconquista*. He became a Templar in 1130 and bequeathed a third of the whole kingdom of Aragon to that military Order. The archives of the crown of Aragon confirmed the legend of the gift of the Grail by the Pope to St Lawrence; it was held in Huesca until the loss of the city to the Arabs after the defeat in 711 of Jerez de la Frontera. Hidden in a series of caves in the Pyrenees, it eventually reached San Juan de la Peña for its safe keeping.

From necessity, the cathedrals and monasteries of northern Spain were built as fortresses as well as houses of God. The approaches to San Juan de la Peña are through gorges and forests. Its thick walls, constructed from the siege knowledge of the Templars, back onto a cliff and a cavern with a trickling pool, which would become the inspiration for the descent of Don Quixote into the Cave of Montesinos. Within this massive structure is a delicate cloister with capitals showing some of the mysteries of the New Testament, particularly a graphic pouring of water from a pitcher into bowls to be turned into wine at the feast of Cana; also a fish on the dish at the Last Supper.

Altarpiece, School of Gerona, Catalonia, c. 1370–1400, shown in its entirety (see page 165).

On the way to Santiago, other castellated monasteries defend the route: Javier and Leyre, where the Magdalene can again be seen on the tympanum, kneeling at the foot of the Cross with the Virgin Mary and two other women behind her. And at Sangüesa, the Church of Santa Maria la Real defends the pilgrim bridge, with three women saints by the entrance door overlooking the passing of the faithful.

Among this dour and defensive architecture, nothing is more surprising than the delicate Santa Maria de Eunate, on the pilgrim road towards Puente de la Reina, where a perfect pediment bridge still takes voyagers across the river. Near a Templar commandery, the small Eunate church was built in the sacred octagonal shape of the military Order; the eight sides of the arches of the cloister enclose the eight walls of the church with its little curved apse. Standing isolated, yet surrounded by sheep grazing on brown grass, this holy place is the most contemplative on the blessed road.

The Sanchos, the kings of Nájera, expanded their realms to Pamplona, and eventually to León and Castile, creating a northern Spanish kingdom stretching from the Atlantic to Catalonia. Led by his falcon chasing a partridge into a cave, the young King Sancho the Third discovered at the end of the cavern a painted statue of the Virgin

Mary with a lamp burning before her and the two birds at peace. Kneeling down, the King asked her protection, then rode out to win a victory against Islam at Calahorra. With part of his spoils, he began the building of the Monastery of Santa Maria la Real, which remains a marvel on the road to Compostela. Its Cloister of the Knights, containing a Garden of Paradise, a carved and painted choir, the royal pantheon of tombs, and the sacred cave where the image of the Virgin was found, is still a testament to the faith along this way to salvation.

Along the track at León, there is a Grail in the museum to rival the St Lawrence example, which ended in the cathedral at Valencia. Similar to those that the Abbot Suger collected for St-Denis near Paris, the Chalice of Urraca, who was the daughter of King Ferdinand the First, is a Roman sardonyx cup and dish united by gold mounts adorned with pearls and gems, which form a Christian liturgical chalice. In the city, the south transept portal of the Basilica of San Isodoro shows the deposition of the Christ from the Cross, with Nicodemus using the pincers to take out His nails, Joseph of Arimathea receiving His Body, and Mary Magdalene kissing the wound on His hand. At the side, the Magdalene appears again with the Virgin Mary and Mary, the mother of James, to watch astonished as an angel opens the empty Tomb. Furthermore, two angels lift the dead Jesus heavily towards heaven in a muscular Ascension.

On the pilgrim path lies the Atlantic port of Oviedo; its kings of the Asturias fought the *reconquista.* They claimed to possess the Spanish Ark of the Covenant, the *Arca Santa*, which included the Holy Blood, a part of the Holy Shroud, the milk of the Virgin Mary and hairs from the scalp of the Magdalene. The wooden chest was said to have originated in Jerusalem, finding its way somehow to Toledo and then to Oviedo, where its arrival by sea was guarded by a wolf. Once shown to El Cid, the Roland of his nation, it was later covered with a silver lid which depicted St Longinus piercing the side of Christ to receive His Blood. A portion of this, miraculously re-created in a silver chalice and paten, was donated by the sovereigns of all Spain, Ferdinand and Isabella, to the mountain villagers of O Cebreiro, who still believe that their home was the legendary Sarras, where Galahad arrived on his Ship of Solomon with the Holy Grail.

Although the cathedral of St James is entered through the Doorway of Glory, the extraordinary Goldsmith's Doorway of the 11th century terminates the quest for the grace of God in the north of Spain. One scene upon it demonstrates Adam and Eve driven from the Garden of Eden by the angel with the fiery sword – surely a forecast of righteous war putting human frailty to flight. A second scene depicts Christ pardoning the woman taken in adultery. She may well represent the Magdalene. With their ferocious judgements, the crusades of the north of Spain never forgave human weakness, as Christ himself did. Yet in the search for grace, the Knights of the Round Table did not win the vision of God by their combats or their swords, but by their repentance.

At the Mediterranean end of the Pyrenees, Catalonia also played its part in repelling the Moors, as Charlemagne had done. Its religious shrine was the massif of Montserrat, where strange jagged pinnacles pierce the sky in an unearthly austerity. Richard Wagner was so impressed by its appearance and its name – another version of the Mount of Salvation – that he set his Grail Castle in his opera *Parsifal* on the site of the monastery there. Its Black Virgin, La Moreneta, is revered as the patron saint of the Catalans; although the French army destroyed the original priory, the

Entrance to the monastery of San Juan de la Peña, where the St Lawrence Grail was hidden before a crusade took it to Valencia.

Grail Cloister in Gerona Cathedral.

Above: The bridge on the pilgrim road in the direction of Puente de la Reina.

Opposite, top: The castle of Javier, Navarre, birthplace of St Francis Xavier, on the pilgrim route to Santiago de Compostela.

Opposite, bottom: The lion fountain of the 14th century in the Alcázar in the kingdom of Grenada.

polychrome wood statue was saved. The caves of the original hermits are gouged into the white cliffs, including the one where shepherds were said miraculously to have found the Black Virgin, as Sancho the Third found his in Nájera in another cavern. There is no record of how the two Virgins reached their rock niches. In matters of faith, a fierce belief is enough to establish a truth or win a holy war as well as a seat in heaven.

The *reconquista* of Spain from Islam by the Christian north began before the crusading movement, but was mightily helped by it. The idea of a continual holy war promoted by the papacy, the Frankish knights and the Cluniac monks provided spirit and recruits for the cause. Many crusaders passed through the Iberian peninsula on their way to Palestine and never reached their goal, fighting their Muslim adversaries on the way and remaining to occupy the hard-won lands.

The Templars and the Hospitallers were originally welcomed as ascetic warriors against the Moors, but these military Orders were largely replaced by home-grown varieties. For the emphasis of the primary Orders was still on the Holy Land. Spain was a place to stop off, not to defend. The Knights of Calatrava took over those abandoned frontiers from the Templars. They were originally Cistercian monks, who put on the sword. By the 13th century, they had become the effective standing army of the kingdom of Castile. They wore black armour and a white surcoat with a red cross fleury, its leaves bent back until they formed the M of the Virgin Mary.

The other leading Spanish Order was the Knights of Santiago, formed to protect the pilgrims on their way to pray at the shrine of St James at Compostela. Their duty, according to the Archbishop of Toledo, was the sword of defence. 'The sword reddens with the blood of Arabs, and faith burns bright with the love of their mind.' Their rule was adopted from the Templars, but they were not a monastic order. Uniquely, they were allowed to marry and have families and personal possessions, although these were surrendered to the Order on the death of each knight. They transcended the borders of Spain, reaching France, Italy, Hungary, Palestine, and especially Portugal, which would form its own knights of service, the Orders of Évora and Aviz, and later the extraordinary Knights of Christ, created from the ranks of the fleeing Templars.

The frontier war with Islam in Spain led to a continuous crusade. A class of popular knights emerged, any Christian who had enough money to buy weapons and a horse. They were known as *caballeros villanos*, and these medieval cowboys often reached a noble status by their deeds, as the rustic Perceval did in the first Grail romance. A successful mounted warrior could aspire to high estate. The Spanish frontier was an early version of the American one, with the Moors playing the role of the people, who were miscalled the Indians. It produced the virtues of an independent raiding society, which built communities and cities behind its forays and its new castles. Particularly important in the Christian north was the port city of Valencia in Aragon, where the only material Grail blessed by the papacy was to come to rest.

The conquest of the interior of Spain in the 13th century, which effectively excluded the Muslims to the kingdom of Granada in the south, was a crusade, a looting expedition and a migration helped by ethnic clearance. 'Waves of friars, contemplatives, military monks, canons, parish priests, and nuns, transported like a numerous garrison into this borderland, gave tangible shape to the Christian self-image, making it a living thing.' The Word of Christ was imprinted upon the land through its new settlers, although tolerance was ordered by a royal edict. 'We decree that Moors shall live among the Christians in the same way that . . . Jews shall do, by observing their own law and not insulting ours.'

The crusading impulse in Spain and Portugal led to the spread of Arthurian literature there. As early as 1170, King Alfonso the Eighth of Castile married Eleanor of England, whose father and mother, Henry the Second and Eleanor of Poitou, were strong supporters of the troubadours and the Grail stories. Soon Arturus was used as a Christian name in Salamanca, while the fabulous history of Britain and the Battle of Camlann began to appear in state records. As the lance was the devastating weapon of the Spanish knights in their charges against the cavalry of Islam, it was soon given a holy point of vengeance as well as healing. In the *Demanda di San Graal, la lanza vengadora* was worshipped as it projected from a golden vessel or hovered above that Grail. Many traditions of the Arthurian romances and ballads were copied: those concerning Lancelot would influence Cervantes. But the great Spanish epic of chivalry was *Amadís*, which imitated the legend of Lancelot without acknowledgement. And in the Catalan tale of *Tirant lo Blanc*, the characters praised the Round Table and described the murals of the palace at Constantinople, covered with scenes from the Quest for the Grail, as were the walls of the castles of Aragon and Castile in tapestries.

If the Pope was the preacher of holy war against the infidel, the Arthurian romance was the theatre. Its scenes of fantasy and devotion inspired crusaders into acts of extraordinary heroism. This everlasting crusade against the Moors went further in Portugal. By the middle of the 13th century, King Sancho the Second had conquered Islam as far as the Algarve. His shock troops were the military Orders, Franks and Germans as well as his own knights. As Robert the Bruce did in Scotland, the Portuguese Crown incorporated the refugee Templars on their downfall into the Knights of Christ. For that small country was the first since the Normans to imagine a Mediterranean empire, an extraordinary ambition that would grow into a global reality.

At Castro Marim and Tomar, the Knights of Christ took over the Grail architecture of the Templars. The sacred octagon of the central choir at Tomar was surrounded by a polygon with sixteen sides. The design was based on the Mosque of Omar and the Dome of the Rock, mistaken for the Temple of Solomon, and on the Church of the Holy Sepulchre and the Aachen chapel of Charlemagne. Frescos including Templar crosses covered the vault. The eight-sided shape was repeated in Spain, particularly at the Church of Vera Cruz near Segovia, where a similar structure housed a piece of the True Cross, brought back by the Templars from Jerusalem.

Moreover, the Grail of Spain, the *Santo caliz*, was already in its final home. When Valencia was taken from the Moors in 1399, the St Lawrence Grail cup from Rome was carried there for the coronation ceremonies of the conquering Don Martin. It has remained in the cathedral, a simple agate carving the size of a sliced orange. It is set on a seashell base on a silver pedestal with four legs. Its handles and goldwork contain two emeralds and twenty-six pearls. An Arabic inscription on its base praises Allah, 'the Merciful One', perhaps a reference to the cup found by the Prophet in the seventh heaven. As the stained-glass windows in Rome still show, this chalice was the only Grail recognised by the Catholic Church, usually so opposed to the doctrine of the individual approach to God.

Another legend took the Grail to Toledo, where its literary origin was discovered by Wolfram von Eschenbach in *Parzival*, also Cervantes in the visions of Don Quixote. The story went that the Roman Emperor Titus, on his sack of Jerusalem, removed the objects of the Passion to Rome, and these fell into the hands of Alaric the Visigoth when he in his turn, in 410, sacked the city of Rome. The cup and platter of the Last Supper were transferred to another cavern beneath Toledo by its last Visigoth rulers. They foresaw the future victory of the Arabs in the Iberian peninsula. The myth of Toledo still asserts that the mysteries of the Temple of Solomon and of the Passion, the Ark of the Covenant, the emerald Table of Solomon and

the cup from the Crucifixion, were buried somewhere at the frontier fortress during the crusades against Islam. Certainly at the Tavera Palace there, a visitor is told to view the Virgin Mary's footprint on a holy stone, perhaps fallen from heaven.

A special contribution from Spain to the Quest for the Grail were the intense religious experiences, when the mystic saints took the Holy Vessel from Jesus himself. In the words of St Gertrude of Helfetha:

> On one occasion, when I assisted at a Mass at which I was to communicate, I perceived that You were present, by an admirable condescension, and that You did use this likeness to instruct me, by appearing as if parched with thirst, and desiring that I should give You to drink. And while I was so troubled and could not even force a tear from my eyes, I beheld You presenting me with a golden cup with Your own Hand. When I took it, my heart immediately melted into a torrent of fervent tears.

St Theresa of Avila continued these beatific visions of a holy chalice and a jewelled Grail Castle into the 16th century, before Cervantes in *Don Quixote* struck them down.

The struggle against Islam was continuing outside Spain. Even before the final conquest of the outpost kingdom of Granada, ports were being seized in North Africa. But they were unprofitable. For exploration was becoming far more interesting than assault on the infidel. The fleets of Europe would reduce the Mediterranean from being the cauldron of world trade into a begging-bowl held out to the Atlantic and Pacific Oceans. The colonisation of the Americas by the Spanish and the Portuguese would be followed by ships and settlers from France, England and Holland. The process would be repeated across Africa, India and the islands of Asia. The bullion of Mexico and Peru and the spice trade of Zanzibar and Java now flowed across the great oceans, with some of the wealth siphoned into the Mediterranean, which had previously served as the exchange and mart of the overland gold, silver, silk, herb and spice routes.

Like a slower Puck, the European sea powers cast their girdle round the earth in eighty years or so, and strangled their founding sea within the noose of the far-flung rigging of their voyages. According to the eminent historian Braudel:

The opening of the Atlantic destroyed the age-old privilege of the Levant, which for a time had been the sole repository of the riches of the Indies. From that point on, every day saw a widening of the gap between the standard of living of the West, which was going through a revolution in technical and economic progress, and the eastern world of low-cost living.

As the caravel and the carrack took the place of the caravan, and as the ocean superseded the desert, so the commercial centres of the Near East became less attractive for the new imperialist nations of western Europe. There was more profit to be had in the slave trade of Africa than of Circassia, and even more opportunity to convert the multitudinous infidels in the Gold Coast and Dahomey than in Beirut or Tripoli. The Levant was no longer the *souk*, where Asia bargained with Europe. Its commercial and industrial importance was in decline. The New World of the Americas and the spice islands of Asia attracted the greed and the desire of the fading knights of the Old World. Although they still had to find a truce line with Islam in the Mediterranean and central Europe, their cornucopia lay in their voyages across the Atlantic and Pacific Oceans.

Miguel de Cervantes fought at the Battle of Lepanto, the great Christian victory of a Holy League against Islam. The son of a wandering chemist and surgeon, he lost the use of his left hand in that victory, and was wounded twice in the chest. His scars of battle were enhanced by five years of slavery beneath the Moors, before he was ransomed from Barbary pirates. Altogether, he knew well the triumphs and illusions of the finale of the crusades, the reach between the promise and the hard cold cell.

Certain episodes in *Don Quixote* recalled the medieval preoccupations with another world. The Don and his squire Sancho encountered Death riding on a cart with a human face, an angel with painted wings, an emperor and a Cupid and an armoured knight with a feathered hat. They represented the strolling play of *The Parliament of Death*. 'Being a demon,' the leader of the troupe said, 'I am capable of anything.' Although an imp with bladders frightened Quixote's horse Rocinante so that he was thrown to the ground, Sancho persuaded his master not to contest Death and fallen angels and emperors, even in show. There was not a real knight among them.

In another adventure, Quixote fought a joust with a Knight of the Mirrors, wearing an alchemical costume of green, white and yellow feathers. For once, he won the passage of arms, only to have his victory taken away by sorcery. 'Learn what magic can do,' he declared to Sancho, 'and how great is the power of wizards and enchanters.' For he saw in his fallen foe the face of his old bachelor friend from his home town. And so Cervantes poked fun not only at the *danse macabre* of medieval melancholy, but also at the legends of Merlin, alchemy and magic which still persisted in his age.

These questionings came to their apogee, when Don Quixote was lowered into the Cave of Montesinos, where marvels were said to happen. He was guided there by a student of works of chivalry, whose job was to compose books for the printers, all of them of great use and most entertaining. He had done *The Book of Liveries* and a book of inventions, based on Vigilius Polydorus. Quixote was hoisted into the underworld and returned after three days and nights in a coma of beatific visions. On awakening, he declared that he had seen the Elysian Fields and a Grail Castle with walls of crystal. From it emerged the robed wizard Montesinos, who swore that he was held under a spell by the French enchanter Merlin.

Quixote then told of the speaking corpse of Charlemagne's nephew, who died at Roncesvalles and was laid out on a slab. His salted heart, like that of the Bruce or the Douglas in Scottish history, was carried in a Grail procession by black-robed women with white turbans. Other guests in the

nnum et .iiii. animalib' dicis sic uo
cem thonitrui. Veni et uide. Et ec
ce equus albus. et qui sedebat sup
eum : habens arcum . et data e ei
corona et exiit unicens ut uinca̅:
Et cum aperuiss; sigillum sedm : au
diui sedm animal dicis. Veni et
uide. Et exiit alius equus roseus : ⁊
sedenti sup eum : datu ei tollere
pacem de tra : et ut inuice se occi
derent . et datus e ei gladius mag
nus. Et cum aperuiss; tercium sigillu :
audiui tercium animal dicis. Veni
et uide. Et ecce equus niger : et qui
sedebat sup eum habebat in ma
nu sua stateram . Et audiui uocem
de medio .iiii. animaliu dicentiu.
Bilibris tritici denario . Et tres bi
libres ordei denario. Vinu et oleu:
ne leseris. Et cu aperuiss; quartu sigil
lum : audiui qrtu animal dicens.
Veni et uide. Et ecce equus pallidus
et qui sedebat sup eum : nn erat il
li mors. Et inferni sequebat eum ⁊
data e ei potestas sup qrtam par
te tre et interfice gladio. fame et mor
te ⁊ bestiis tre . finit ystoriam.
Incipit explanatio in libro .iiii.
sup̅ signe illione. Explanatio d'equo
Callo

The crusades in Spain were led by the cross and the sword. *(From a 14th-century Catalan manuscript)*

castle included Queen Guinevere and her maid, who poured the wine for Lancelot 'when from Britain he came'. Sancho laughed at the Don's testimony, but here Cervantes mixed credibility with fantasy as Wolfram von Eschenbach had in *Parzival*. He claimed that the original history of Quixote was actually written by a certain Spanish Arabic Jew, Cid Hamete Benengali; so Flegitanis of Toledo was claimed as the original author of the German masterwork.

Cervantes made Hamete evaluate in notes on his text the worth of the vision in the Cave of Montesinos, declaring that he could not believe in everything that had happened there to the valiant Don Quixote. Until now, all the adventures were possible. But the one in the cavern was beyond reason. Yet Quixote could not lie. Therefore, the wise reader must decide for himself. However, it was reported that Quixote retracted his vision on his deathbed, confessing that he had invented the Arthurian pieces, because of what he had read in other romances.

Here Cervantes appeared to invent the modern novel of deconstruction. He would not declare that he did not believe in the legends of chivalry. He would only write that a fictitious scribe doubted them and that the invented Don Quixote had denied at his dying a particular adventure. The reader had to decide on the text himself.

In two final references in *Don Quixote*, Cervantes had his knight and squire Sancho reach the River Ebro, which looked like liquid crystal. The Don was reminded of the Cave of Montesinos, although Sancho considered the visions there to be lies. Even so, an enchanted bark floated downstream, like a Ship of Solomon. Knight and squire boarded it to meet a company of millers. Quixote declared the water mills to be a fortress where knights or princesses were held captive, and he brandished his sword, but fortunately the boat capsized in the river race and the Don and Sancho were rescued by the millers' poles.

Later, Quixote encountered the bronze speaking head from the Grail legends. It was set on a jasper table and said to be cast by an enchanter, Escotillo.

When the Don asked the head whether the happenings in the Cave of Montesinos were a dream, it replied, 'There is much to be said on both sides.' The head was revealed to be mechanical and broken up by orders from the Inquisition, 'the sentinels of our faith'.

When previously attacked by a canon of the Church for believing in the chivalric romances such as *Amadís*, Quixote said that his questioner, not he, was bewitched. To try and persuade anybody that Amadís and the other knights had never lived was the same as saying that the sun did not shine, ice was not cold and the earth did not bear fruit. If all the romances were lies, 'there was no Hector nor Achilles nor Trojan War nor Twelve Peers of France nor King Arthur of England, who still goes about in the shape of a raven and is expected to reappear in his kingdom at any time'.

Here Quixote did speak of the truth of the Quest for the Holy Grail, which he called *Grial*, and the love of Guinevere and Lancelot. He then described another vision of a Grail Castle, in which he was the Knight of the Lake. Plunging into a seething cauldron of water, he found himself again in Elysian Fields of paradise in front of a jewelled castle made of diamonds, rubies, pearls, gold and emeralds. There beautiful maidens bathed and fed him and told him they were held under a magic spell, until a knight would release them. This perception, Quixote said, made him a better man, brave, polite, generous, courteous and bold. If the Arthurian legends were the stuff of dreams, they became actual in the change of character of their believers.

This was another way of saying that the romantic search for the divine was still a valid way to God, a moral journey in its own right. Even

Don Quixote prays before Sancho Panza lowers him into the Cave of Montesinos; a Grail princess is offered the heart of her beloved dead knight; the maiden in the Grail procession, carrying an embalmed human heart in a fine linen cloth; Don Quixote addresses Merlin and the Grail maiden in the Cave of Montesinos. (*Vignettes by Tony Johannot from* L'ingénieux Hidalgo Don Quichotte de la Manche, *Paris, 1837*)

if the knight on his quest in Spain in the 17th century was out of date and a figure of fun, his trials were real enough, as were his sufferings, and these purified his spirit. When illusions became deeds, they made a better man.

These arguments could not survive the final verdict of Cervantes, when he killed off his glorious character. The deluded knight was received back into the Christian faith. Chivalry and the crusades were finished, although not the inward quest for the divine.

Death came at last for Don Quixote, after he had received all the sacraments and once more, with many forceful arguments, had expressed his abomin-ation of books of chivalry. The notary who was present remarked that in none of those books had he read of any knight dying in his own bed so peacefully and in so Christian a manner. And so, among the tears and laments of all who were there, he gave up the ghost. That is to say, he died.

The enduring popularity of the work made Don Quixote live for ever. Cervantes's mockery of actual pilgrimages on earth concentrated the quest for revelation on the interior journey towards the soul. The Cave of Montesinos would become the examination of self-despair and dream. The voyage would lie through the individual brain and bowels towards redemption.

FIFTEEN

THE GRAIL IN ITALY

The present heroism is bound to become grotesque, the strongest faith is bound to become madness, when the ways leading to the transcendental home have become impassable.

Georg Lukács

The earliest carving of the Grail in Italy is on the tomb of Archbishop Theodorus at Sant' Appollinare-in-Classe, near Ravenna, but no longer on the sea. This mysterious relief of the 6th century combined Greek and oriental Christianity and cosmogony. On either flank, a dove sits on a plant with two flowers of four petals each, representing the Gospels. In the middle, a stone supporting the crescent moon drops into a wrought bowl. Within the cup of the moon is the base of the eight-pointed cross, while the dove of the Holy Spirit plunges down with the point of its beak into the top of the crucifix. This Trinity of symbols of the Holy Spirit blesses bowl, stone, moon and cross, the main signs of the religious faiths of the Near East.

The Byzantines translated the horn of plenty and the pagan gifts of the gods into Christian symbols of the Grail, the gift of the Holy Spirit. Ravenna abounds in the early signs of the Holy Vessel. Dating from the 5th century, their style and content would influence all Europe. The key two mosaics are those of a gold chalice with handles put on a white tablecloth in front of Melchizedek,

A Grail carving on the sarcophagus of Archbishop Theodorus at Sant'Appollinare-in-Classe, Ravenna.

the ancient king and priest, while Abel offers to him and God the first fruits, a sacrificial white lamb. On the cloth are a pair of round loaves in the shape of sun-discs and a paten, two misaligned squares making up an octagon within a circle, the sacred building shape of the Baptisteries at Ravenna, which both have exquisite and naturalistic mosaics of Jesus being baptised in Jordan with the Holy Spirit as a dove descending on him.

Opposite the mosaic at Sant' Appollinare-in-Classe stands the bearded Emperor Constantine the Fourth granting privileges to his bishop's minion, while holding a bowl. The first Emperor Constantine had turned Byzantium to Christ: he and his heirs were the rulers of state and Church: that was the message of the Melchizedek mosaics, as the statues of that Old Testament priest and sovereign were for the Merovingian and early Capetian kings of France, who placed him in the cathedrals of Reims and Chartres. They did not have to claim a fictitious bloodline from Jesus and Mary Magdalene to prove their sacred role, for that would have been blasphemy of the worst kind. Like the Emperor

Constantine, they felt that their heredity was blessed by God. Even King Arthur was given in the Grail romances a descent from Constantine's mother Helena; so was the Grail King Anfortas, as were Peredur and Lohengrin. To be of the blood royal was to have a divine right, whatever the Church might deny.

This was no message for the later popes of Rome, who not only fought against the Greek rite and eventually sent out their crusaders to take Constantinople, but also were in perpetual conflict with the German Holy Roman Emperors, who often claimed to be supreme in religion as well as in politics. But no potentate went on his knees to Canossa to seek papal forgiveness in Byzantine

Ravenna. The churches were for the glory of the imperial family. The second mosaic of Melchizedek is in San Vitale, a huge octagonal church consecrated in 547 by the great Archbishop Maximian along with Sant' Appollinare-in-Classe. The Empress Theodora, dripping with pearls, is shown as a priestess holding a golden chalice studded with gems in front of her court; the three Magi are embroidered on her robe and appear time and again in mosaic and marble, thrusting their generosity at Christ as the Byzantines did. Theodora faces her husband, the Emperor Justinian, who holds a large gold paten, instead of Archbishop Maximian, whose ivory throne and last resting place remain an encyclopaedia of early signs

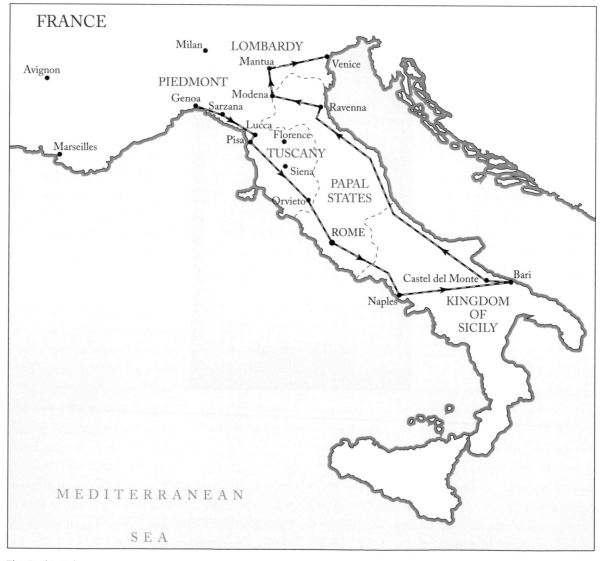

The Grail in Italy.

Section of the earth, showing hell, purgatory and the passage by which the poets ascend. *(Alighieri Dante, Divine Comedy, early 14th century)*

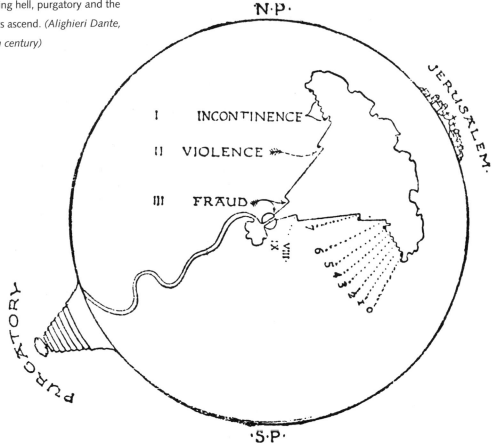

of the Holy Vessel. There are two doves drinking from a flowing Grail on his sarcophagus, and on his ivory throne we see the feast at Cana, with much water flowing from huge pots into wine; the miracle of the loaves and the fishes occurs with many scones and one fish-head; four Evangelists surround the Virgin Mary, and two of them bear a dish, one with little loaves and one with the Lamb.

In the moving fresco of the 14th century at Santa Chiara, three Christian angels use cups to catch the Blood from Christ's wounds, as on the reliquary at Fécamp in Normandy. Other mosaics in Ravenna show female saints in a procession, confirming the theory that the women in the Grail ceremony in the Castle of the Fisher King may derive from a Greek ritual. St Lawrence also appears at Galla Placidia, advancing towards the burning gridiron, bearing the Holy Writ and a golden cross, although not the Holy Vessel given to him by the Pope and sent on to Spain.

The emphasis at Ravenna on the Gospel of St John puts only the Magdalene with Mary the mother of James at the Tomb of Christ in Sant' Appollinare Nuovo; the later intrusion of the Virgin Mary into the scene is a Renaissance phenomenon. Other Byzantine symbols of the Grail may be found in the city of the Italian sea-power, responsible for the sacking of Constantinople on the Fourth Crusade, in the courtyards of the great Piazza of San Marco in Venice. These cosmic carvings were brought back from the eastern Mediterranean by a decree of the Doges, which required Venetian ships to use ancient stone works as ballast on their voyage home.

The legend of St Lawrence had sanctified the carrying of the Grail to Spain. The later opposition of the papacy to its message, which was the independent search for God, could not diminish the popularity of the Arthurian romances. In the 'Inferno' of Dante's *Divine Comedy*, indeed, the Matter of Britain led to the downfall of Paolo de Rimini with his sister-in-law Francesca:

MELCHISEDECISCMVETVS SCRIBVRADE

One day we read in pastime how in thrall
Lord Lancelot was to love, who loved the Queen.
We were alone – we thought no harm at all.

As we read on, our eyes met now and then,
Our cheeks were changing both from red to pale,
But just one moment overcame us, when

We read the smile, wanted by lips that could not
                                              have me,
Such a smile, by such a lover kissed away.
He who may never more try now to leave me.

Trembling all over, kissed my mouth. I say,
The book the writer, he did pander me
Like Gallehault, we read no more that day.

In this passage, Dante revealed how he was
beholden to the Breton and Provençal
troubadours. Their verses spoke of Gallehault as the
go-between, serving Lancelot and Guinevere,
while Dante himself in the 'Purgatorio' praised
Arnaut Daniel for being 'peerless in all verses of
love and stories of romance'. That minstrel and
poet spoke Occitan and was called *il miglior fabbro
del parlar materno*, 'the better workman in the
mother tongue'. Before the writing of *Perceval*,
Celtic myth had reached Italy with its symbolism
of sacred regeneration.

Yet even if forbidden love consigned sinners to
hell, the warrior saints making up the shape of a
shining celestial cross were praised in the 'Paradiso',
as they were on the tapestries of Flanders: Joshua
and Judas Maccabeus, Charlemagne and Roland, or
Orlando and Willehalm, or Guigelmo and Godfrey
de Bouillon. Holy war was still the path to
salvation, however much the Church of Rome was
misusing the finance and the direction of its
crusades.

Priest and king, Melchizedek at the altar of sacrifice with an
ancient Chalice and two loaves as sun-discs. He is attended by
Abel and Abraham. *(6th-century mosaic, Sant'Appollinare-in-
Classe, Ravenna)*

Furthermore, the troubadours kept alive the myth of the never-dying hero. As with Charlemagne, the legend that King Arthur would return was prevalent in Italy and later in Tudor England. The eldest son of King Henry the Seventh would have been King Arthur the First or Second had he not died young and lost his bride and his throne to his younger brother Henry, who would be crowned the Eighth of that name. In his *Otia imperialia*, Gervase of Tilbury confused the wounded British monarch with the Grail King; Arthur was found reclining on a couch in the crater of Mount Etna. And in Guillem de Torroella's Catalan and French tale, *La Faula*, the poet claimed to have travelled to Morgan le Fay's island, where Arthur was nourished annually by the Grail until the day of his homecoming.

By the beginning of the 16th century, Erasmus noted that people had completely turned against buying forgiveness for their sins through indulgences. They said that this was nothing but commerce. 'The justification changed all the time. At one moment it was war against the Turks, then the military needs of the Pope, then the Jubilee.' There was no limit or end to the haggling. Princes took a part of the proceeds, as did officials, commissioners, deans and preachers. 'Some were given money to talk, others to keep silence.'

The money that reached Rome was being used for the wrong causes. It was being raised under false pretences. Erasmus, in his *Consultatio*, was clear about these errors:

Every time that this farce has been acted out by the popes, the result has been ridiculous. Either nothing

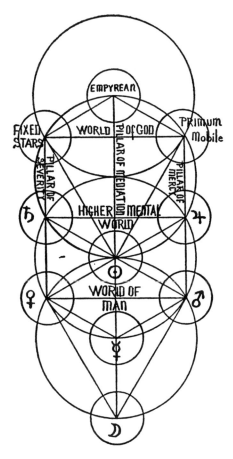

The cabbalistic Tree of Life. Its Three Worlds probably influenced Dante.

came of it, or the cause actually deteriorated. The money, people say, stays stuck to the hands of the popes, cardinals, monks, dukes, and princes. Instead of the wages, the ordinary soldier is given licence to pillage. So many times we have heard the announcement of a crusade, of the recovery of the Holy Land; so many times we have seen the red cross surmounted on the papal tiara, and the red chest; so many times we have attended solemn gatherings and heard of lavish promises, splendid deeds, the most sweeping expectations. And yet the only winner has been money.

A contemporary tale spoke of Cesare Borgia losing 100,000 ducats at cards, the sum raised from granting absolution for offerings given towards a crusade. 'There go the sins of the Germans,' he said.

Although the cardinals advising Pope Leo the Tenth in 1517 still believed that many would 'gladly purchase eternal life for a small price', if they saw others fighting for God in earnest, the French replied that nothing would now come of any attempt to sell absolution. People had been deceived so often that calling for a crusade was now seen as a clever trick to extract their money. Even the faith in wonder-working relics was diminishing; these lesser Grails of the Holy Blood or bones of the Saints were being replaced in the knightly romances by talismans and magic stones.

Yet while the Reformation grew in power and questioning, Rome remained the spiritual centre of the Christian faith and the focus of European pilgrimage. Although holy relics were widespread across Europe, the papal city held the choicest of them. This was recognised by a Netherlands romance of the 14th century, in which the hero,

Seghelijn of Jerusalem, became emperor and pope and transferred all the sacred objects of the East, including the True Cross, from the city of the death of Jesus to the Curia and the Tiber. The most precious of these relics were to be housed in the gigantic hollow piers of St Peter's itself.

Yet while these pillars were still incomplete, Pope Clement the Seventh reaped the dragon's teeth sown by the sale of pardons. The Holy Roman Emperor Charles the Fifth attacked Rome in 1527 with an army of levies, many of them Lutherans determined to destroy all Catholic symbols of the search for divine grace. While the Pope and the Curia defended the Castel Sant' Angelo, the Swiss Guard was decimated trying to defend His Holiness. The patients in the papal hospice were thrown into the Tiber, while nuns were sold to brothels. As for the holy relics, a letter to the Duchess of Urbino claimed that they were all scattered. 'The Veronica was stolen. It was passed from hand to hand in all the taverns of Rome without a word of protest. A German stuck onto a pike the lance point that pierced Jesus' side, and ran mockingly through the Borgo.'

A second letter, from Cardinal Salviati to the papal envoy in Madrid, confirmed the profanation, so similar to the sack of Constantinople on the Fourth Crusade and by the Turkish Sultan. The great chapel of St Peter and Pope Sixtus was burned, as was the Holy Veil of St Veronica. The heads of the Apostles were stolen, the Sacrament thrown in the mud, the reliquaries ground underfoot. 'I shudder to contemplate this, for Christians are doing what even the Turks never did.'

A contemporary Lutheran soldier confirmed the looting of chalices, monstrances and precious religious ornaments; but he denied the finding of the Veronica. His testimony was corroborated by the Roman Marcello Alberini in his I Ricordi. The Veronica, the heads of St Andrew, St Peter and St Paul, and 'the miraculous effigy of the Saviour in the Sancta Sanctorum' were not desecrated in the sack of the Holy City.

Certainly, these relics were on public display soon afterwards, especially the Holy Lance and the Veronica, which the Grail scribe Robert de Boron declared had cured the Emperor Vespasian of leprosy, before he went to Jerusalem to rescue Joseph of Arimathea from prison. Even the sceptic French essayist Montaigne referred to the fervour and grief of the crowds, who saw the Veil and the Lance in procession. Whether they survived the emperor's pillage of Rome hardly mattered. They were held to have done so. They retained their credibility and inspired mass worship. They were still as fundamental in the display of Catholic piety as the symbols of the Passion were in the Grail processions of the medieval romances.

This was true in the rival city states of Italy. The Procession in Piazza San Marco by Gentile Bellini, now hanging in the Academia in Venice, showed the sacred relics of Christ, seized from Constantinople, now carried under a canopy in a precious Grail casket attended by scores of monks and dignitaries. The Holy Face of Lucca, said to have been created by Nicodemus, was displayed secure in an octagonal chapel of green, white and gold from the early 12th century, the dukes of Normandy and St Catherine of Siena were pilgrims there. In his 'Purgatorio', Dante was told by the demons above the lake of boiling pitch that not even the Santo Volto could save the Luccan sinners from their fate. The actual bones of Nicodemus were given to the Pisans for their help in the First Crusade and remain in his marble tomb in the duomo of the Italian city. In spite of the sack of Rome, traces of the Passion and the jewelled reliquaries built to house them were still venerated across the land.

No actual bowl is a Grail; but if it has a sacred meaning or use, it recalls that Holy Vessel. In Christianity, there are many representations of the Grail, other than the cup used in the Mass. These are religious versions of the pagan cauldron of birth and regeneration, as the font was the symbol of receiving the passport to paradise. In the spectacular carved marble vase of the font at San Frediano in Lucca, or the huge urn of Neuvy St-Sepulchre, where the Holy Blood is also housed, the full significance of baptism may be understood. This is confirmed by the numerous

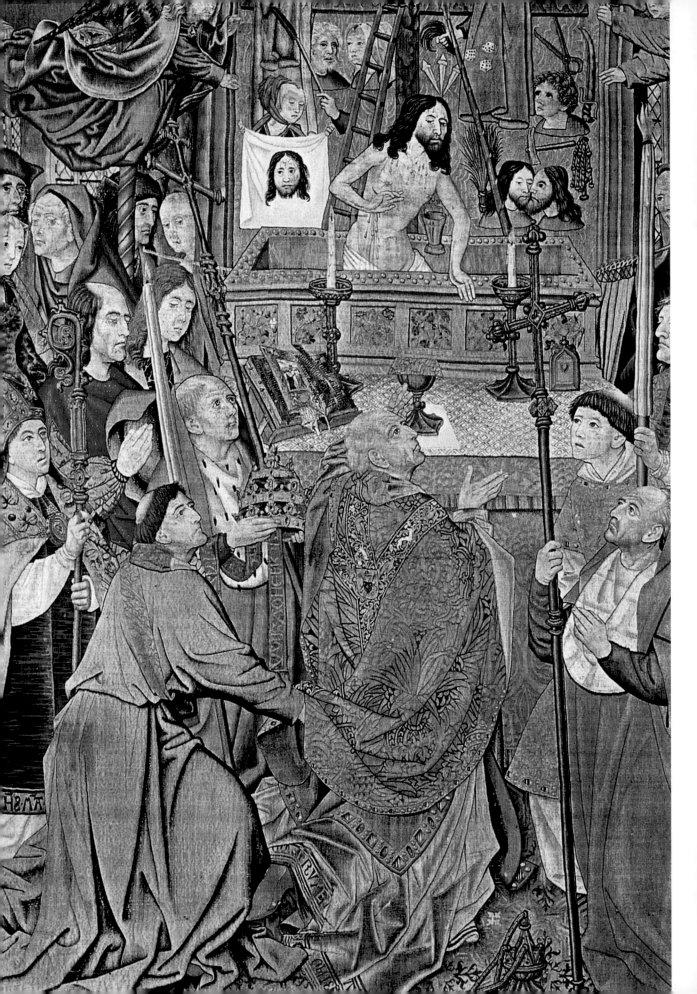

Left: St Gregory the Great celebrates the Eucharist in the Church of the Holy Cross of Jerusalem in Rome. Christ, surrounded by the instruments of the Passion, including the Holy Lance and the Veil and Grail, appears above the altar. (The Passion, *tapestry, Brussels, c. 1500*)

Above: An angel on horseback bears the Grail in this charming fresco. *(Santa Chiara in Ravenna)*

reliefs in the cathedrals of Europe, which showed Christ's blessing in a rock pool in the River Jordan by St John the Baptist, whose severed head on a platter became another representation of the Grail.

In Dante's *Inferno* and in the many hells depicted within the churches of Europe, the damned are stewed alive in vast vats and pots, tormented by devils. As with the Cauldron of Annwn, they demonstrate the judgement of life. Human beings pass into oblivion and reduction through eternal pain, or into resurrection. For as at Chartres and Bourges, female saints can be discerned in barrels, being baptised into the faith, or being broiled. Either a blessing or a torture, the vat of water was a means of change.

The only time that the sinful King Arthur, carved on the architrave of the duomo in Modena, was permitted to view the Grail in the romance of *Perlesvaus*, he saw it in five different forms. These were not described. They could only be understood by those who knew the mysteries of the sacrament. The Christian equivalents of the Grail were the reliquary for the remains of the Passion, or the Communion dish for His Body, or the chalice for His Blood. The Renaissance chapel of the Sancto Sacramento in the duomo at Lucca has the effigy of a rotunda above an altarpiece of the Lamb of God, holding the cross in front of a sunburst. The rotunda contains a silver-gilt Grail medallion with a flared top. Two phials of the Holy Blood, said to have been found behind the Holy Face when it landed on a magic airborne craft in the mouth of the River Magra, are housed behind that metal plaque.

At Bocca di Magra, the Carmelite Fathers still claim that their replica of the Holy Face is the true one, for it contains below the nape of the effigy's neck two niches for phials. Yet as far back as Dante, Lucca was believed to have the original *Santo Volto* and the two bottles of his Passion. The claim of the Basilica of Santa Maria up the Magra river to possess the Precious Blood appears to be a recent assertion. The shrine is worth a visit, however, for the Renaissance relief beside the tabernacle of the supposed Blood of Christ. On its pale marble are carved many of the Grail symbols, such as the spear

of St Longinus; they include two of the rarer ones: the Hand of God offering the Bitter Cup to the kneeling Jesus in the Garden of Gethsemane, and the Presentation in the Temple, where the child Jesus is received by an elder over the Ark, which is lit by a sacred lamp surmounted by the dove of the Holy Spirit in a burst of six rays.

Further to the south, a miraculous appearance of the Blessed Blood led to the building of perhaps the most magnificent duomo in all Italy. In 1263, a Bohemian priest called Peter of Prague was a Doubting Thomas, who had reservations about the bread and wine of the sacrament changing into the Body and Blood of Christ. After a pilgrimage to Rome to pray at the tomb of St Peter, he stayed at Bolsena on its mountain lake in order to celebrate Mass in the grotto tomb of St Christina. As he held the host above the chalice towards the congregation, it turned into the Holy Body and Blood, as it had in the visions of some of the Knights of the Round Table.

Traces of the actual blood that fell on the stones below the altar are preserved above the altar of the Miraculous Eucharist in the Basilica of St Christina at Bolsena; beside them is carved an eight-pointed cross. The footprints of the saint are kept on a floating rock, which also came to ground in the city. At her feast day, at the vespers of St James on the pilgrimage route to Compostela, dancing women still break four crystal vessels full of perfume, similar to those used by Mary Magdalene to wash the feet of Christ.

The chalice cloth imbued with those blessed bloodstains is housed in the special Chapel of the Corporal in the duomo at Orvieto. A doorway was built in the cathedral to carry in the precious linen; a sculpture over it commemorated the occasion. Pope Urban the Fourth decreed the celebration of Corpus Christi in honour of the miracle, as well as commanding the building of the duomo. St Thomas Aquinas was with him at Orvieto during these blessed times and wrote hymns for the new feast day. The sacred cloth is housed in the most superb reliquary in the region. Its twelve panels of silver gilt and blue enamel display episodes from the Life of Christ and Peter of Prague's transformation of the spiritual into the actual at Bolsena – perhaps too direct an approach to the divine substance for the Church not to include it in its ceremonies. Indeed, the stunned anguish on the faces of the Risen in the fresco by Signorelli in the Capella Nuovo still shows the great difficulties of a religious faith that insists on the link between the flesh and the soul, even in resurrection.

Yet the duomo in Orvieto is less a place of the Grail than is the Church of San Lorenzo de Arari. This simple Romanesque building holds two remarkable frescos of the 14th century. One recounts the life of St Lawrence, read in four episodes right to left, as in Hebrew. The first panel shows him healing the sick, although Christ as a boy bears a Grail, no larger than a round purse or stone, for the holy man. The second panel depicts his condemnation, the third his burning on the gridiron, the fourth his rescue from purgatory of the sinners who believed in his message of redemption. An even more remarkable fresco of the Virgin and Child recalls the Grail symbol as a giver of divine life. Mary is feeding the infant Christ openly with her right breast, while her aurora is made of the leaves of the Tree of Life, and two angels hover above with a heavenly crown.

In three of the Arthurian romances, the *Quest*, the *Perlesvaus* and the *Morte D'Arthur*, the Mass of Our Lady, the Mother of God, was heard at the ceremonies of the Grail. Through her womb, an inverted bowl, the Virgin Mary gave birth in blood to Jesus; through her breast, as in the fresco in Orvieto, she gave milk to the Son of God. In the medieval text the *Litany of Loretto*, she was described as three vessels, spiritual and honourable and singular in devotion. In the little rose window at Reims, she has further attributes: the Ark of the Covenant, the Morning Star and the mystic rose, the palm and the olive tree, the sun and the moon, the exalted cedar and the stainless lily, the refuge of sinners and the doorway to heaven, the golden house and the ivory tower of David, the royal crown and the throne of wisdom, the Holy City and the faithful dove.

As well as containing within her flesh the Body and Blood of the infant Christ, the Virgin Mary gave out delight and nourishment to all: she was sanctity and security, wisdom and justice, refuge and prophecy. Her symbol was the rose with five petals, sacred particularly to the Knights Templars, who were also virgins dedicated to the protection of the Cross. And in the medieval *Minnelieder*, the songs often compared the Virgin Mary to the Grail. At San Lorenzo de Arari, signs of the Holy Vessel may be seen as a gift from God, as a scale of judgement, and as female food for the spirit. With the eternal inventiveness of Italy, the patterns of the Grail there confirmed its infinite varieties, as if the importance of its message – the individual quest for God – were being disguised from the Catholic Church.

The material Grail of Italy – the *Sacro Catino*, or Holy Cup – is in Genoa. William of Tyre, who was a historian of the early crusades, wrote that the Genoese, the ferrymen to the Holy Land, were given the cup in 1101 in Jerusalem to honour their services after the capture of Caesarea. Yet as the city cathedral was dedicated to St Lawrence, who can still be seen roasting on his gridiron above the main door of the duomo, other traditions made the *Sacro Catino* come from Spain, where it was sent by the martyr, to remain by repute in Valencia. The Genoese claimed that the sacred trophy was part of the booty of Almeria, which they helped to take from the Moors in the 12th century; alternatively, a tribute from the fall of Tortosa. Whatever its origin, the *Sacro Catino* was so venerated in the Middle Ages that it was guarded by twelve knights, modelled on the disciples and the dozen Peers of the Round Table of Charlemagne. At the end of the next century, Jacopo da Voragine, the author of *The Golden Legend*, authenticated the *Sacro Catino*, which the English called the *Sangraal* in their books.

The Holy Cup was thought to be carved from a huge emerald, as was the tablet of the alchemist Hermes Trismegistus. When Napoleon conquered Genoa, he had it taken back to Paris for analysis. Broken there, it was discovered to be made from Roman glass of the time of Jesus Christ. One piece of the sacred vessel was kept in France, the others returned to be repaired. Presently on display in the

Procession of female martyrs, bearing crowns. *(Sant'Apollinare Nuovo, Ravenna)*

city museum with the relics of St Lawrence and the supposed ashes and head of St John the Baptist, the six-sided goblet with a gold rim is placed on a wrought-iron tripod. Its bowl is shallow, opaque and dark green, a memorial of how the Near East sent to Europe the mystic concept of the personal search for God, even at the time of the assault from the West.

The literature of the Grail had depended upon the courts and principalities that paid the troubadours to sing it and the monks to write it down. This remained true, as the Middle Ages were moulded into the Renaissance, in providing the new words and symbols of the personal search for the divine. The visitors of today may still read and see what was commissioned then. Riven by the

wars between its city states as well as the ambitions of the French and the Habsburgs of Spain and Germany, Italy became the cornucopia of grants to artists for the glory of rulers and governments, as well as God.

The supreme patron of Florence, Cosimo de' Medici, was a banker. Through international finance, he endowed and influenced the arts on a scale that surpassed even Maecenas. He was the first magnate in business to sponsor the culture of his time, and though his collections were mainly of classical antiquities, he commissioned works from

Cloisters of the Cistercian abbey of Fossanova, Italy.

leading contemporary artists. He bought paintings by Masaccio, Fra Angelico, Uccello, Donatello and Giotto. He gave generously to the family church of the Medici, Brunelleschi's San Lorenzo, the saint who had transmitted the Grail to Spain. He supported libraries, monasteries, convents and foundling hospitals.

In acquiring power in his native city from the *Signoria*, he always showed a studied modesty. He rode a mule in an effort to hide his wealth. Only his successors, such as Lorenzo the Magnificent, displayed the luxury of the Burgundians. In 1533,

indeed, when the daughter of the Holy Roman Emperor Charles the Fifth married a Medici, the garden courtyard of the palace in Florence was transformed into an Earthly Paradise, a symbolic Garden of Eden.

As well as building for his patron the circular roof of heaven on the duomo in Florence, Brunelleschi manufactured a mechanised paradise in the monastery of San Felice-in-Piazza. Writing his *Lives of the Artists*, Vasari could not contain his admiration:

Imagine a heaven full of moving figures and an infinity of lights that go on and off like lightning! Brunelleschi suspended a huge half-globe from the beams of the roof. This was like a barber's bowl, edge down, made of thin planking. Within the outer edge of the rim were fixed brackets exactly the size of children's feet. Two feet above each there was an iron fastening to secure a twelve-year-old child so that he could not fall even though he wanted to. About the rim were spaced twelve children clothed as angels with gilded wings and wearing wigs of gold thread. They took hands and waved their arms, and so appeared to be dancing while the basin was turning about. . . .

In the centre of this bouquet of angels was a copper mandorla, which came down, moving softly, to the stage. A boy of fifteen dressed as an angel then stepped from the mandorla and approached the Virgin and made his announcement. Then the entire pageant was drawn up in order. There was, besides all this, a figure of God the Father in a choir of angels fixed near the convex side of the basin. It did truly represent paradise.

This spectacle of the bounty of heaven, with half-globes and mandorlas appearing as divine givers, was similar to the Burgundian practice of translating mystic quest to lavish entertainment. Cosimo de' Medici turned the lethal jousts of the Arthurian knights into an egoistical civic show, held in the square of Santa Croce of the Holy Cross. At the tournaments, each armoured warrior on his charger was preceded by a squire with a symbolic banner: the painter Verocchio painted one for Cosimo himself. The Duke wore a red and white surcoat; also a plume of gold filigree set with diamonds and rubies in his black velvet cap, before it was substituted for a helmet with three blue feathers. In the centre of his shield with the three gold lilies of France, the protector of Florence, shone the huge family diamond. Cosimo won the tournament while the other knights fell off their horses, rather as the Emperor Nero had won the Olympic Games for both his lyre-playing and his chariot-racing. 'I was not a very vigorous warrior,' Cosimo admitted with aristocratic modesty, 'nor did I hit hard.'

He did confirm that life in an Italian city-state was insecure for the wealthy without control of the government. It was equally insecure for the artists, whom he chose to patronise. Two years after Cosimo's death, the raging Dominican monk Savanarola tried to destroy the religious as well as the secular beauty developed by the Medicis: he even persuaded Lorenzo di Credi to slash his own pictures in his studio. In a Bonfire of the Vanities, relics, books, ornaments and works of art were consumed. A furnace of puritanism scorched Florence, until the mob turned against the new rigour and its preacher. In 1498, Savanarola was hanged from a gibbet and roasted on flames below. 'Prophet!' the crowd shouted. 'Now is the time for a miracle.' There was none.

Such a violent reaction from the long tradition of religious art had its history. The Byzantine Emperor Leo the Isaurian had been an iconoclast, who had burned artists and the library of Constantinople, in which he shut scribes and attendants. The reforming monks of the Middle Ages were equally no friends of images. St Francis of Assisi wanted no painting in the churches of his order – 'no wall in honour of Saint Poverty and Saint Humility'. Pope Nicholas the Fifth looted the Colosseum for lime; 2,000 cartloads of statues and marble from the Roman monument were rendered down in the ovens. The Counter-Reformation would imitate the puritanism of Luther and ban the nude from religious frescos. Michelangelo's figures in the *Last Judgement* in the Sistine Chapel would have their private parts covered with draperies. In Venice, Veronese would be hauled before the Inquisition, accused of heresy and forced to paint out some figures in a religious picture. Art now had to be correct in faith.

North of the Alps, the reaction against the symbols of Christianity was even more extreme. The Protestant mobs turned against religious art and all images, as if they were Vandals or Vikings. 'Nothing has survived,' Erasmus wrote, 'neither in the cloisters nor on the portals, nor in the convents. The pictures were covered with white-wash; what could burn was thrown on the bonfire, the rest was smashed. Neither monetary nor artistic value was any protection.' Erasmus himself moved to Freiburg under the personal protection of the Catholic Archduke of Austria: Protestantism threatened to turn Switzerland and Germany into a wasteland of the arts. The Renaissance humanism represented by Erasmus was usurped by the Reformation of Luther, who despised the classical values of his contemporary.

Although in the north of Europe, the patronage of culture became the province of wealthy merchants, guilds and bankers, the Catholic princes still kept their power. Artists saw no wrong in working for contradictory camps or feuding financiers. Lucas Cranach could be the court painter for the electors of Saxony and the designer of great guns for Duke Henry the Pious, yet still be the godfather of Luther's first son as well as the illustrator of his Reformation pamphlets.

The commercial Fugger family in Augsburg were the Medici of the north, making Holbein's birthplace a Renaissance city on the far side of the Alps. Yet all the while, religious subjects were

The octagonal Castel del Monte, built by the Holy Roman Emperor Frederick the Second, near Bari, Italy.

becoming less popular. The medieval craftsman, linked with the patron in the common service of God, was developing into the Renaissance artist, who found that competition for his skills bred inspiration and income. Mutual labour in praise of the divine was being fragmented into various named works at a price.

Benvenuto Cellini, perhaps the finest sculptor in precious metals of his age, served the Pope as a gunner at the Castel Sant' Angelo during the sack of Rome. He melted down many of the sacred reliquaries in the papal treasure, so that these could be spirited away as ingots. He kept the leavings for himself, to create statues for the enemy of Rome, the King of France. He had no sense of piety or dedication to heaven. His extraordinary autobiography was hardly a spiritual journey towards a personal glimpse of the divine, rather the search of the Renaissance artist for the highest bidder.

In the art of the Italian Renaissance, the symbols of the Grail became more rare, perhaps because they were heretical. The Magdalene appeared in her red dress in Piero della Francesca's fresco of St Mary in the cathedral of Arezzo. Her crimson robe was repeated by Botticelli in his *Mary at the Foot of the Cross*, while her long red hair, wiping the wound on the nailed feet of Jesus, was shown by Giotto in his *Crucifixion* in the Scrovegni Chapel at Padua. There, three flying angels catch Christ's Blood in small Grails, while St Longinus smears the fluid from his lance point onto his blind eyes. And in the *Lamentation* there, the Magdalene cradles the wounds on the feet of Christ.

In the Assisi chapel dedicated to the saint, she shows her love of Christ the gardener, as he moves off with his spade. Further episodes of her legend are painted, including the scene after her death, in which angels transport her body to be buried by St Maximin; she is covered only with her long hair and kneels transfigured in an orange shell. She became a cult to the Flagellants and the Penitent Orders, particularly at Borgo San Sepolcro and Bergamo. And she inspired women mystics, such as Margery Kempe, who saw her in a vision at the Church of the Holy Sepulchre in Jerusalem, and Catherine of Siena, who followed the 'sweet and loving' Magdalene, who never left the Cross and 'became drunk and bathed in the blood of the Son of God', some of which passed into her Grail.

If anyone built a medieval Mount of Salvation, he was the Holy Roman Emperor, Frederick the Second. His esoteric wisdom created an octagonal Grail Castle with eight surrounding octagonal towers at Castel del Monte above Bari. Designed like the Temple at Jerusalem and the Ka'aba at Mecca to be an axis of the world, the Castel was once said to have had at its central point another octagonal bowl, carved from a single stone and holding the Holy Blood. Built with the vigour and lack of ornament of the Cistercians, that holy Order was particularly favoured by Frederick, who died, according to Matthew Paris, wearing its white habit. While the sacred octagonal shape might derive from Byzantine Ravenna and Charlemagne's chapel at Aachen, its triangular alignment with Frederick's other castles and cities near Bari was a tribute to his interest in astronomy and mathematics, which could make the Castel, as at Montségur, into almost a temple of the sun.

On a crusade that had more to do with diplomacy than fighting, Frederick had himself crowned King of Jerusalem, asserting his divine right as strongly as Melchizedek. The preamble to his *Constitutions of Melfi* stated that he had been elevated by God 'beyond hope of man to the pinnacle of the Roman Empire and to the sole distinction of the other kingdoms at the right hand of the divine power'. No wonder that the Pope declared crusades against him in Italy. He thought himself almost immortal, and the verse that praised his virtues and magnificence on his tomb ended by declaring, like the legend of Alexander and Charlemagne, 'Then Frederick, who lies here, is not dead.'

Although Italy had produced no outstanding Arthurian romances, the conversion of their style to Renaissance taste by Boiardo and Ariosto was a triumph. A large library had been accumulated by the dukes of Ferrara of the House of Este, and there the two poets were loosed among the themes of the Matters of Britain and France. For Boiardo, tales of Arthur were more interesting than those of Charlemagne, because fighting for love was better than for a crusade. As he declared in his masterpiece, *L'Orlando innamorato*:

> Britain in its glory and its grandeur
> Was known for love and fighting in the fray.
> And so King Arthur there was raised to honour
> And still his name is spread abroad today . . .
> Later King Charles held his high court in France,
> But this was not the same, and nevermore.
> It locked the gate on love and arms and chance.
> Its message and its faith was holy war.

Ariosto made his figure of Roland in *Orlando Furioso* a knight driven to madness by his love of the princess Angelica, the daughter of the Great Khan. He concentrated more on the defence of Europe by Charlemagne against Islam than on the adventures of the Knights of the Round Table. One critic declared that 'as Virgil was the poet of Rome, Ariosto is the poet of Europe'. Certainly, he was so in the waning of the crusades. He wanted to revive the ideals of medieval chivalry, condemning the new artillery that mowed down the armoured cavalry as 'the worst device, in all the years of the inventions of humanity, which was ever imagined by an evil mind'.

Before the sack of Rome, Ariosto saw the Holy Roman Emperor Charles the Fifth as another Charlemagne, the last imperial ruler with the vision to unite Europe in the struggle against the heathen. God had waited for his coming to power so that he might inherit the sovereignty of the New World of discoveries as well as of the Old:

> For, in the wisdom of the Almighty's ways,
> He waits until the world shall be made one
> Beneath an Emperor more just and wise
> Than any who since Augustus shall arise . . .
>
> For valour, whence all other virtues stem,
> God wills not only that this Emperor

> Shall wear upon his brow the diadem
> Which Roman Emperors have worn before.

In the light of this universal need for unity, Ariosto berated other Christian monarchs for warring on each other, not the infidel:

> No longer now defenders of the faith,
> With one another Christian knights contend,
> Destroying in their enmity and wrath
> Those few who still believe; make now an end,
> You Spaniards; Frenchmen, choose another path;
> Switzers and Germans, no more armies send.
> For here the territory you would gain
> Belongs to Christ; His kingdom you profane.
>
> If 'the most Christian' rulers you would be,
> And 'Catholic' desire to be reputed,
> Why do you slay Christ's men? Their property
> Why have you sacked, and their belongings looted?
> Why do you leave in dire captivity
> Jerusalem, by infidels polluted?
> Why do you let the unclean Turk command
> Constantinople and the Holy Land?

Ariosto would be disappointed. The Habsburgs of Spain and Austria would become the main defenders of Christianity in the Mediterranean, while warring on other Christian rulers in Europe. Suffering a breakdown because of his incessant wars against the Muslims and the Protestants, Charles the Fifth would abdicate, instructing his heir Philip how difficult it was to protect an empire stretching from Spain to the Netherlands, and now to the Americas. Foreign aggression and internal revolution would prevent any last crusade against Islam, while it was 'almost impossible to lay down invariable rules, given the instability and uncertainty of human affairs . . . Go to war only when it is forced on you. It exhausts the treasury and causes great misery.'

United Christendom died in the divisions between the nations and the city states. The Quest for the Grail and the grace of God became a personal thing, although their representations in art and literature still fascinated the Renaissance spirit. But these longings were transmuted in *Orlando Furioso* to dreams of bygone chivalry and vain hopes of its revival. Merlin was shown only as a prophet and a sorcerer, pointing the way to the magic garden of Alcina, the sister of the fairy Morgana and King Arthur. Scotland, however, remained the home of Lancelot and still exported its Celtic warriors on prolonged crusades against the Moors:

> For there the cavaliers of Britain roam,
> Valiant in arms, with knights of other lands,
> Some from nearby, and others far from home:
> Norwegian, Frankish and Germanic bands.
> Valour is needed by all those who come,
> For here a knight his death, not glory, stands
> To find; here Tristan, Galahad, Gawain,
> Lancelot, Galasso, Arthur foes have slain.

> And many a brave knight of both the old
> And new Round Table here renown has won,
> As many a monument to many a bold,
> Brave deed, and many trophies have been
>   made known.

Yet Ariosto's chief and melancholy demeaning of blessed legends was his changing of the Quest for the Grail and Eden into an arrival in an enchanted garden with a classical cornucopia.

This was the *reductio ad paradisum*:

> Where everyone in dance or joyful game
> The festive hours employed from early morn;
> Where of sad thoughts no shadow ever came
> To spoil this rosebud life without a thorn.
> There no discomfort was, no cup was empty,
> But endless bounty from the horn of plenty.

SIXTEEN

A TEMPLE OF THE GRAIL

He, whom the silly fiction of the Grail, the lies about Perceval and many other false stories, annoys and fails to please, should prefer The Mirror of History, *for here one finds in particular truth and many wonders, wisdom and beautiful instruction.*

Jacob van Maerlant, *Spiegel Historiae, c.* 1260

he history of the Grail often served as the propaganda of organisations and of nations. In his laboured verses about King Arthur, the contemporary of Malory, John Hardyng, included a Quest for the Holy Grail. The royal father Uther had first constructed the Round Table and the Siege Perilous in memory of the Grail table of Joseph of Arimathea. As in other legends, Galahad achieved the Holy Vessel, and Arthur conquered France before his death and burial at Glastonbury.

Using such a heritage, the Scots chroniclers, such as John Leslie, had the invading Celtic Arthur killed by the Picts and the Scots, while John of Fordun and Hector Boece and William Stewart, whose *The Buik of the Chroniclis of Scotland* was issued at the command of King James the Fifth, claimed that the illegitimate Arthur usurped the Crown from his sister Anna, who was married to the Lord of Lothian. Their sons, Gawain and Mordred, were the true heirs to the throne of Britain; their lawful resistance was merely to claim their birthright and not a matter of treason. Just as English accounts glorified empires won the other side of the Channel, so Scots chroniclers asserted their long rights over the Border lands.

In Lothian, a chapel of the Grail, which is also a Temple of Solomon, remains as a proof in stone

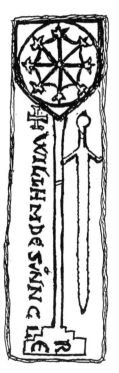

St Clair Templar Grail tombstone at Rosslyn Chapel.

that the Knights Templars served as the guardians of the Holy Vessel. Their many scattered churchyard gravestones confirm their symbolic role. With their proscription in 1314, the French refugee Templars made their way to Scotland, probably with their treasury and the remaining archives from the Paris Temple. One French Masonic tradition declared that the records and wealth – perhaps including the two precious Grails containing the Holy Blood and the Holy Veil from the sack of Constantinople – were taken on nine vessels to the Isle of Mey in the Firth of Forth near the St Clair castle of Rosslyn.

The military Order had been favoured by the Scots monarchy. Their headquarters were based in Lothian at Balantrodach or Temple, near the St Clair castle and early chapel at Rosslyn, and the Cistercian abbeys of Melrose and Newbattle. Since the time of Queen Margaret, that Norman family had been the keepers of the sacred regalia, such as the Black Rood stained with the Holy Blood. When Edinburgh was assaulted by the English armies, the royal treasures were secreted at Rosslyn in the old crypt and vaults.

In the wondrous chapel of the 15th century there, built over a previous one, a tombstone was recently discovered, broken into three pieces in a dank corner. Put together again, the small

Interior of Rosslyn Chapel, Midlothian, Scotland. Fragments of a Templar tombstone were discovered in the Chapel.

Rosslyn Chapel, founded in 1446 by Sir William de St Clair.

memorial demonstrated that the Templars survived their downfall and passed on the mysteries of the Grail. A chalice was carved along the granite slab, which was only 3ft in length. Within the cup at the top was an eight-pointed cypher of the Templars, which referred to the Holy Light within Christ's Blood in the shape of an 'engrailed' octagon with a rose at its centre. It bore the name of the dead man, carved in Lombard lettering: WILLHM DE SINNCLER. The very name of the chapel was said to derive from the Old Scottish ROS-LIN or Rosy Stream or Fall, again suggesting the Blood of Christ. The St Clair knights of the Middle Ages had fought with the 'Engrailed Cross' on their shields; these were also carved on the chapel walls. The base of the Grail or chalice formed the pattern of the steps to the Temple of Solomon.

At Corstorphine near Edinburgh, where the late medieval church-builder, Sir Adam Forrester,

married into the St Clair family, is set a huge Templar stone with a cross fleury inside a circle and a stem leading down to the steps of Calvary and the Temple of Solomon: a crusader sword is etched by its side. By the Priest's Door, another memorial stone is inscribed to a chaplain named Robert Heriot, who died in 1443, with a sole ornament of a chalice or Grail which looks like two triangles set on end, the world as a ball dropping within. It was used as a model for the silver communion cups of later centuries. These are still in use at Corstorphine, emblems of the Grail.

The Sancto Claro heirs were already the keepers of the royal treasure and holy relics in Scotland. Their Latin name connected them with the Holy Light and the Grail. The dating of the sword hilt and the Lombard lettering identified this particular Sir William de St Clair on the Rosslyn stone. He had fought with the excommunicated Templars and with Robert the Bruce at Bannockburn, and had died in 1329, while taking Bruce's heart in a silver casket to be buried at Jerusalem. Surrounded

Melrose Abbey, Scotland, where remains of Templar burial stones depict the steps of Calvary, various crosses and the symbol of the Virgin Mary.

by the Moorish cavalry in Spain, he and Sir James Douglas, together with two other Scottish knights, had flung the casket into the enemy ranks, then they had charged the whole Muslim army and were slaughtered.

Their courage had so earned the respect of their foes that the Heart of Bruce and the relics of the four knights were returned to the sole Scottish survivor, Sir William Keith, who took them back to their native land. The Heart of Bruce was buried at Melrose Abbey, where it has recently been excavated and verified. Douglas's heart is interred at his family chapel, while the bones of William de St Clair were apparently buried at Rosslyn. The remains of the Templars were often placed in the position of the skull over crossed leg bones, an important symbol in their ritual and later Masonic ceremonies. If William de St Clair, as a Master of the Temple, was buried in this fashion, it would explain the small size of his tombstone.

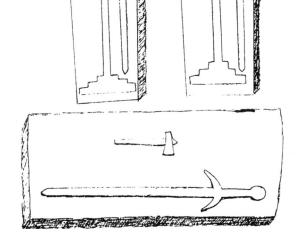

Two Templar grave slabs found at Pentland, near Roslin (now covered up).

Templar gravestones at Westkirk near Culross Abbey, Fife, displaying Masonic symbols.

Other tombstones carved with the Grail and the flowering eight-pointed cross were then discovered, broken in abbey or church cemeteries, the whole length of the Borders into Cumbria. After the Reformation, which destroyed and looted the rich medieval treasures of Scotland, these burial slabs from Templar commanderies were used as building blocks. At Melrose, in the Commendator's House, the design on the gravestone preserved there shows a foliated cross within a chalice. An elongated dirk points down inside the stem of the cup to the base, again depicted as the steps of Calvary and of the Temple of Solomon. Nearby are other fragments from Templar graves, floral crosses contained within a circle or a disc-head and a boss of the five-petalled rose and the symbol of the Virgin Mary. Another boss is carved with clam shells, the emblem of the pilgrimage route to Compostela in Spain.

At the Church of St Mary and St Bega at St Bees in Cumbria, there is more graven evidence. Templar tombs are arranged within the chancel. The grave slab of one of them is surmounted by the round plan of the Holy City of God with its four gates and the inrushing rivers of life, making an octagon of points within a circle, and enclosing a square or tabernacle containing the rose of the Virgin Mary. Below are the mason's tools of the plumbline, the dividers and the spread compasses, sometimes shown in medieval manuscripts in the Hand of God as He measures the world. These carvings are the missing link for those who have long sought to show that the Templars were the guiding forces of the building workers in their pay, later known by the French names of their medieval guilds or *compagnonnages* as the *Enfants de Salomon* and the *Fratres Solomonis*. These masons were associated with the Cistercian white monks, while

Right: Templar tombstones at Bridekirk, Cumbria.

Left: Ruins of the old Templar headquarters in Scotland at Balantrodoch, or Temple, near Rosslyn.

another guild of the *Maître de Saint Jacques* generally toiled for the Benedictines, the black monks.

Moreover, stacked outside nearby Bridekirk Church, a row of six Templar burial stones are ranged, one with shears beside the stem of the Rosy Cross, another with a curved mattock or trowel opposite a crusading sword. These were more proofs of the practical role of the knights in constructing their thousands of castles, chapels and commanderies from the Near East to Scotland. They always tried to build another Temple after the example of Zerubbabel, who was told by the biblical prophet Haggai of the words of the Lord God:

> And I will shake all nations, and the desire of all nations shall come: and I will fill this house with glory, saith the Lord of Hosts.

> The silver is mine, and the gold is mine, saith the Lord of Hosts.

> The glory of this latter house shall be greater than of the former, saith the Lord of Hosts: and in this place will I give peace . . .

In this construction of a Second Temple on the Mount in Jerusalem, there had been strife and discord. As the apocryphal Book of Esdras testified, many attacks made the builders wear a sword while using a trowel. The dream of its foundation would be carved in stone in Rosslyn Chapel beside the 'Apprentice Pillar'. With two other imperial guards, Prince Zerubbabel had interpreted the dream of the Persian ruler Darius.

'Wine is strong,' was the first statement.

'The Emperor is stronger,' was the second statement.

'Women are the strongest,' Zerubbabel declared, 'but above all things, Truth bears the victory.'

So pleased was Darius at this answer that the Prince of Judah was given permission to construct the Second Temple, accompanied by masons and carpenters, whom he paid and fed and put in

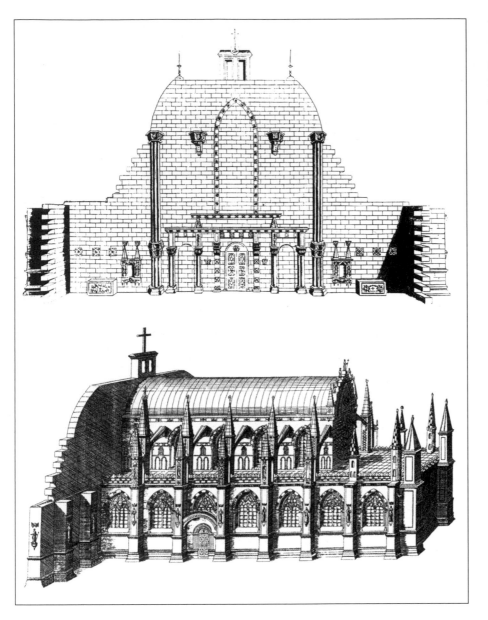

Top: Rosslyn Chapel before 1700, showing the two pillars of the Temple of Solomon, supporting the stone roof.

Below: Rosslyn Chapel before 1700, revealing the ornate carving.

lodges. He also brought a musical tradition with him, as his imitator Earl William St Clair would do in his chapel, for the Prince reached Jerusalem with the notes of 'tabrets and flutes'.

There is little doubt that the architect and designer of the new Rosslyn Chapel, William St Clair, 3rd Earl of Orkney, would try to construct a Third Temple, heralding the coming of the Messiah in Jewish tradition. Herod had already built a further Second Temple, enclosing that of Zerubabbel; but, as the killer of St John the Baptist, the despot could hardly claim his Temple on the Mount to be the forerunner of the coming of the Saviour of mankind.

Earl William knew of the significance of the holy name of St Clair as well as that of St Matthew. This was to be a messianic church and chapel that appealed directly to the divine light. The rough design of the west end of the sacred building would be that of the Temple of Solomon. Two flanking pillars, Joachim and Boaz, would support a carved stone roof. And twenty small Temples of Solomon would be carved within, so that the message might never be lost.

The Knights Templars and the architect of Rosslyn Chapel had long been trying to rebuild that sacred place. The ground plan and façade of this unfinished Collegiate Church of St Matthew

Carvings of the
Passion and of the
Mandylion,
Rosslyn Chapel.

would be a Temple of Solomon, although it was originally intended to become a cruciform cathedral, five times its present size. Its shape was two joined cubes, the design of the original Holy of Holies and sanctuary. The surviving structure was built over an original Benedictine foundation, created at the time of the early crusades. The *compagnonnages* involved in its construction were those associated with the black monks and named after the *Maître de Saint Jacques*, or St John the Baptist, who came to be linked with the martyrdom of the last Templar Grand Master, the condemned Jacques de Molay, who had perished in flames at the stake.

The only surviving illuminated psalter from the fall of Acre and the end of the Kingdom of Jerusalem had been carried off by the Grand Master of the Knights Hospitallers of St John, the fellow military Order to the Templars. The saint was shown holding the Agnus Dei, the Lamb of God, on a green Grail platter, signifying the Blood of Christ. Below him in miniature, a tiny Grand Master knelt in prayer. The Agnus Dei was also carved in Rosslyn Chapel, now bearing on its back a cross with a banner. This symbol was used by Templar high officers as a seal on their rings.

Another frieze at Rosslyn links the Templars to the Grail vessels containing the Holy Blood, which they may have brought to the vaults there from Constantinople. Although headless now, probably due to the fury of the Protestant Reformation, St Veronica holds up her veil, imprinted with the

Mandylion, the true image of the face and beard of Christ. In legend, she wiped off his sweat and wounds during the Passion. Beside her are Templar and Masonic marks on the bearded warrior figure of Pontius Pilate, washing his hands near his guard of armoured knights, carrying battleaxes. This head of Jesus is much the same as on the Holy Shroud of Turin, and its likeness is also painted in the 13th-century presbytery at Temple Combe near Shaftesbury.

An actual carving of a mailed Templar knight with his lance also graces the Rosslyn Chapel. He does not ride alone. Behind his saddle is an angel, carrying the cross of the Church Militant. Traditionally, the knights were said to carry a poor man or a pilgrim on their horses. Such charity was part of their Rule. In fact, as they were usually fighting, their fellow rider was another warrior, an archer or a squire or a man-at-arms. In his celebrated works, the chronicler from St Albans, Matthew Paris, showed two Templar knights riding on a single steed behind their black-and-white standard, an image that also appeared on their minted coins.

More arcane is the carving in the chapel of the horned Moses, an interpretation that the stone mason Michelangelo himself made into a sculpture. These horns referred to the ancient bull cult of Cybele and Mithras, as well as to Leah, the first wife of Jacob: in Hebrew, her name signified 'wild cow' and so an earth mother. Yet the Templars at their trials were often accused of worshipping a Satanic horned head in their heretical rituals, some of which derived from the ancient practices of the Near East. This particular Masonic carving, as that of Michelangelo, also refers to guild practices in the 15th century, when the Lords of Rosslyn regulated the Scottish crafts.

Even more Gnostic and significant in the chapel is the carving of a fallen angel, its hands and body bound by ropes. Traditionally, the work is identified as Lucifer, the carrier of the light of divine intelligence, the castaway from heaven for his rebellion against God. The cult of Sancto Claro and the Templars, whose Masters could even give absolution and communion as did the Cathar 'Perfect Ones', believed in the direct approach of the faithful to the Holy Spirit without the need of papal or royal intervention. This would also be inspiration to the early Masonic guilds and lodges.

The celebrated gashed head of the Apprentice, who was said to have made the pillar in Rosslyn during his master's absence in Rome and so to have been killed in a jealous rage, again points to a revolt against religious authority. While later Masonic lodges associated the wounded bust with the death of Hiram, the builder of the first Temple of Solomon, such a legend also indicated some resistance to state power in the name of secrecy. Certainly, the Freemasons after the Enlightenment would attack kings and churches, while venerating their early martyrs in search of the divine light.

Yet the most telling of the carvings at Rosslyn was that of Melchizedek, one of the highest grades and priestly orders of later Masonry. He was the priest-king of Salem at the time of Abraham, and the ancestor of Jesus Christ through the House of David. He became the symbol for the early Byzantine emperors, who wanted to assert their dominance, not only over their own imperial Greek Church, but also over the See of Rome. Their buildings and images at Ravenna would influence Charlemagne and later German rulers, as well as the French kings, in their assertion of their divine right against the papacy.

Any understanding of the mysteries of Rosslyn Chapel lies in the character and learning of its creator, William, Earl of Orkney, and the European influences of his time. Although he was the designer of his Temple of Solomon and Grail chapel, his masons with their own creative carvings were messengers of the later Lodges of their crafts and guilds. For, as the St Clair chronicler Father Hay attested, Earl William 'caused artificers to be brought from other regions and forraigne kingdoms, and caused dayly to be in abundance of all kinde of workemen present, as masons, carpenters, smiths, barrowmen, and quarriers, with others'.

As a whole, the Collegiate Church of St Matthew resembled the Burgundian churches of the Cistercian Order and the neighbouring abbey at Melrose. As well as ribbed vaults above the altar,

Melrose Abbey. Master builder John Morow inscribed his Masonic epitaph in the abbey's stonework.

the barrel vaulting supported the only stone-carved roof in all of northern Europe. The ornate decorations also appeared to derive from the Church of Rome near Abbeville, the Porch at Louviers in Normandy, and the Savoy Mausoleum in Bresse, where Flemish sculptors worked, some of whom might have progressed to Rosslyn.

Certainly at Melrose Abbey, the contemporary master builder John Morow brought along his *compagnonnages* of European masons. Still carved into the stone there is his Masonic epitaph:

SA YE CVMPAS GAYS EVYN ABOVTE S VA TROVTH AND LAVTE SALL DO BVT DIVTE BE HALDE TO YE HENDE Q° IOHNE MORVO. [As the compass goes evenly about, so truth and loyalty shall do without doubt. Look to the end quoth John Morow.]

Morow also left another inscription declaring that he was in charge of the masons' work in six major Scottish ecclesiastical buildings, and he prayed to 'GOD AND MARI BATHE & SWETE SANCT: IOHNE TO KEPE THIS HALY KYRK FRA SKATHE'. Mary and St John were also venerated by the military Orders as the protectors of holy places from harm. The exuberance of some of the carvings in the ruined chapel at Melrose, poppies and roses and a Moor's head along with devil's masks and Green Men, also suggests the influence of Morow on Rosslyn Chapel with its profusion of stone ornaments. Certainly, the crusading St Clairs and the Cistercians always kept in close touch.

William, Earl of Orkney, continually had need of the best masons and stone-workers of his time. They were trained in sophisticated continental methods of construction and carving, based on sacred geometry. In the extraordinary album of Vilart de Honnecourt, two men wrestling with their feet planted on the ground show the principle of the solid base needed for the circle and

the square, while another couple grasping each other demonstrate the firm foundations of the barrel-vault ceiling, as at Rosslyn. Other models for the foreign lodges were Byzantine and classical architecture, particularly that of the Roman Vitruvius. In his famous picture, Leonardo da Vinci drew 'Vitruvian Man' with eight limbs and a head as a cornerstone within a circle – the principle of sacred architecture, expressed as the Golden Mean of the human frame.

Because of his position and esoteric knowledge, William St Clair served as his own director of works. The family historian Father Hay wrote that the Earl 'caused the draughts to be drawn upon Eastland boards, and made the carpenters to carve them according to the draughts thereon, and then gave them for patterns to the masons, that they might thereby cut the like in stone'. Very good wages were also paid, with the master mason receiving £40 yearly, the other 'free' masons £10

Rosslyn Chapel in its unfinished form.

yearly, and the Earl rewarding by their degree, 'the smiths and the carpenters with others'. The name of that master mason at Rosslyn is unknown, unlike that of John Morow at Melrose.

As well as a Temple of Solomon, the Earl intended to plan his chapel from the ideas suggested by medieval romances. As Lewis Spence wrote, 'Nothing can shake my conviction that Rosslyn was built according to the pattern of the Chapel of the Grail as pictured in Norman romance, and that William St Clair had in his poet's mind a vision of the Chapel Perilous when he set hand to the work.' The many signs of the Knights Templars as the keepers of the Grail in both *The Quest of the Holy Grail* and *Parzival*, are confirmed on the roof at the east end of the chapel. There, a stone dove with a wafer in its beak flies down to a crescent Grail, pouring out the bounty of life on all below in the chapel. Of all the symbols of the Holy Vessel in Europe, this is unique in suggesting a horned moon of Islamic blessing, spilling its riches.

The mystery of the Grail, as well as that of Rosslyn, is augmented by the Prince's or Apprentice Pillar. The barley-sugar and twined column was Byzantine and Near-Eastern in design with a sister at the Templar church at Tomar in Portugal. This inspired creation was as pagan and Masonic as it was Christian. At its base, eight octagonal winged serpents surrounded an apparent stone tree trunk that supported the roof. The concept referred to the Tree of Life, as well as to the Tree of Knowledge of Good and Evil in the Garden of Eden; the winged serpent was not only Lucifer, but also part of the secret wisdom of the Cathars and the Templars. The Apprentice Pillar derived from Gnostic myth in spite of the four strands of stone hemp rope about it, probably a posy to the four Gospels.

There was further symbolism on the Apprentice Pillar. By Rabbinic and Arabic legend, King Solomon built his Temple by means of the Shamir, a fiery Great Worm or Serpent of Wisdom; its touch split and shaped stone. For Deuteronomy in the Old Testament had stated that the Temple should be built without the use of tools made of iron. In Masonic tradition, the martyr Hiram, the architect of the Temple, refused to surrender the secret of the Shamir, which remained one of the Grand Secrets for Freemasons in higher degrees. Eight Great Worms or Shamirs were grouped in a rough octagon round the base of the Pillar. These comprised the number of points and the shape of

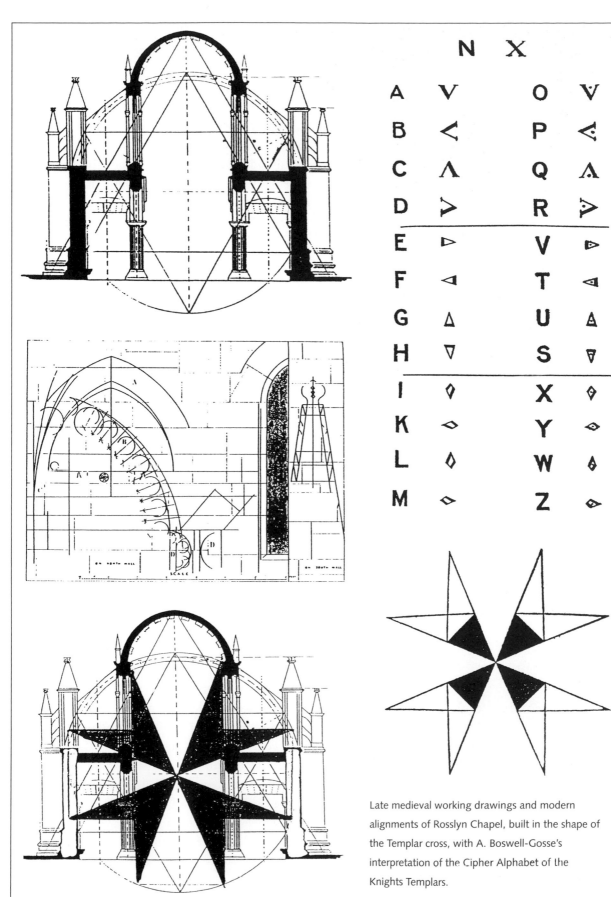

Late medieval working drawings and modern alignments of Rosslyn Chapel, built in the shape of the Templar cross, with A. Boswell-Gosse's interpretation of the Cipher Alphabet of the Knights Templars.

the cross of the Knights of the Order of the Temple of Solomon, who knew of the Shamir when they named the Dome of the Rock as the Temple on its original site in Jerusalem, before its tradition and its symbolism were brought to Scotland.

A similar accretion of Christianity overlaid the carvings in the rest of the chapel. The legend of the murdered Apprentice was probably a Christian cover story for an apocryphal saint and founder of the Order of the Temple of Solomon and of all Masonry with its symbols of the sword and the trowel, the compasses and the maul. And the gash on the stone head may well have been caused by a lead bullet or a pike stroke from one of the Puritan cavalrymen quartered in the chapel and bent on defacing its Catholic figures after the Civil War.

The question was whether Earl William built his Grail chapel because of his wide reading from the best library in Scotland at Rosslyn, or whether, as the keeper of royal and Templar treasures, he stored in the vaults some jewelled reliquaries that had held the Body and Blood of Christ. These would have been the Holy Rood and the precious vessels containing the Holy Shroud and the Holy Veil, seized at the sack of Constantinople. Furthermore, many still believe that the Templars excavated their Stables of Solomon below the Temple Mount in Jerusalem, where they may have found the Ark of the Covenant and the Holy of Holies, secreted there by the ancient priests of Israel.

As Umberto Eco wrote in *The Name of the Rose*, the Templars appear to have to do with everything. Certainly, at Rosslyn, some of their wisdom appears to have passed through Earl William into the architecture of the chapel and, through the Ancient Scottish Rite, on to modern Masonry. A recent discovery in Orkney of a large hanging scroll of the 15th century seemed to locate even the Ark of the Covenant in the vaults of the hallowed place in Lothian. At that time, too, the promise and symbolism of the Grail crossed the oceans.

Above, left: Apprentice Pillar, Rosslyn Chapel.

Left: Rosslyn Chapel's vaulted roof.

SEVENTEEN

MERLIN, MALORY AND THE FAERIE QUEENE

Medieval alchemy prepared the way for the greatest intervention in the divine world order that man has ever attempted: alchemy was the dawn of the scientific age, when the daemon of the scientific spirit compelled the forces of nature to serve man to an extent that had never been known before.

C.G. Jung, *Alchemical Studies*, 1930s

osimo de' Medici, the Duke of Florence, came into possession of the *Corpus Hermeticum* after the fall of Constantinople. He ordered Marsilio Ficino to give up his translation of Plato into Latin and concentrate on these lost works of the legendary philosopher, astrologer and alchemist Hermes Trismegistus, the Merlin of the Orient. Tradition had the *Hermetica* originally inscribed in Greek on an Emerald Tablet in Egypt. They contained elements of Mithraism, Neoplatonism and Stoicism as well as the Gnosis, the understanding of all as one. They declared that man was an image of the sun, which was an image of the cosmos, itself an image of God. As with the Grail Quest, the duty of everyone was the search for the divine:

For it is the height of evil not to know God; but to be capable of knowing God and to wish and hope to know Him, is a road which leads straight to the Good; and it is an easy road to travel. Everywhere God will come to meet you, everywhere He will appear to you, at places and times at which you look not for it.

The idea of the knowledge of God being in everything and every person had been an inspiration in the Arthurian romances, particularly in *Parzival*. In one sense, the trials of the Knights of the Round Table on their way to the Castle of the

Fisher King were the outward description of the inner turmoils of self-discovery. Finally to see the Grail was a vision of the unity of oneself with the universe. The object seen was in the shape of what one's knowledge made one able to perceive. The goal was union with the ultimate Creator.

God makes all things for Himself; and all things are parts of God. And in as much as all things are parts of Him, God is all things. Therefore, in making all things, God makes Himself. And it is impossible that He should ever cease from making; for God Himself can never cease to be.

This figure of sacred geometry is taken from Giordano Bruno, *De triplici minimo et mensura*, Frankfurt, 1591.

This hermetic philosophy deeply influenced such Renaissance scholars as Pico della Mirandola, Ramon Lull and Giordano Bruno. This was an incitement to the alchemists, who saw their scientific experiments with distillation and chemical reactions as an endeavour to combine the material with the spiritual in the knowledge of the wholeness of the world. The Philosopher's Stone, which might turn base metals into gold, was merely a symbol for the transformation of the body into an understanding of the Holy Spirit.

Like the stone fallen from heaven in *Parzival*, or the innumerable blessed relics and chalices in European churches, any earthly sign of wonder was merely a parable of the way to wisdom and the Word of God. Indeed, in the *First Continuation* by Gautier de Doulens, Gawain observed an apparatus similar to the alchemic still. The blood from the Holy Lance flowed down into a holder, then into a silver vessel, from which a golden pipe carried it into another silver vessel. In spite of this process, the Grail King assured Gawain that the lance would bleed until Judgement Day.

Although the Renaissance led to scientific experimentation, it also revived the interest in astrology as well as astronomy, in prophecy along with rational enquiry, and in alchemy as the father of the revelation of the secrets of the cosmos. In his *Ordinal of Alchemy*, Thomas Norton of Bristol wrote that people without a proper training in physics and metaphysics should not try to manufacture gold from an elixir, as he had done; for they would fail. When granting two of the royal physicians his permission to experiment in alchemy, King Henry the Sixth of England noted that if they found the mystical elixir, it would cure diseases and wounds, lengthen life, and serve as an antidote to poisons, as effective as the magic ointment used by Linet to set together the head of the knight hewn into a hundred pieces by Sir Gareth in Malory's *Morte D'Arthur*.

Illustrations from the *Cabala Mineralis* by Rabbi Simeon ben Cantara, *c.* 1650.

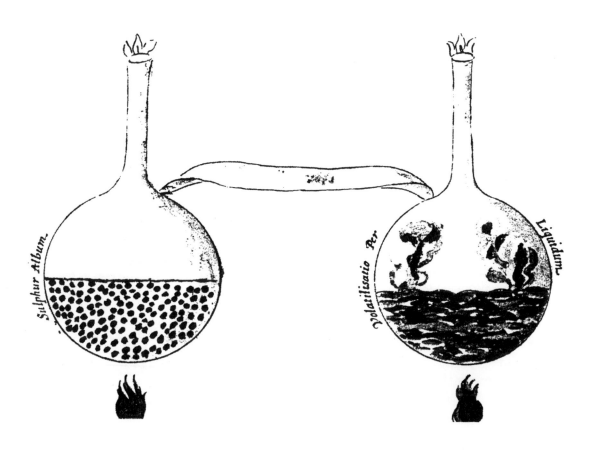

On Consideration of the Fifth Essence by John of Rupescissa was more about distilling alcohol and helpful chemicals than making gold. And even the astrological magic proposed by Ficino in his *On Life* was more of a medical treatise than a star guide to human behaviour, as was the work of Paracelsus. As John Donne slyly noted about alchemical experiments:

> No chemic yet the elixir got,
> But glorifies his pregnant pot,
> If by the way to him befall
> Some odoriferous thing or med'cinal . . .

Isaac Newton himself would be as interested in alchemy as in the law of gravity. Ancient and modern enquiries into the workings of the cosmos were most confused. The discovery that the earth and the planets rotated round the fire of the sun, indeed, had originally been a principle of Hermes Trismegistus on his Emerald Tablet, while the commentary of Ortolanus on that text inferred the principle of condensation: 'Whatever is below is similar to that which is above.'

Most of the alchemists thought of themselves as rigorous researchers, and not necessarily heretics. As early as the 12th-century *Anticlaudianus* of Alan de Lille, alchemy had seemed an allegory for the Christian visionary. The three stages of the process – the blackening and whitening and yellowing – were three mirrors that reduced forms to their original essences and ideas. Later, Sir Walter Ralegh wrote that the art of magic was the art of worshipping God. The Elizabethan sorcerer and experimenter John Dee told the Emperor Rudolph the Second at Prague that he used his Philosopher's Stone and the aid of angels only to intercede with God for the revelation of his Creation. And his contemporary, the influential hermetic philosopher, Robert Fludd, believed that Light and Darkness came from one Divine Essence, and that a heavenly Grail, 'a flashing Spirit of Wisdom, projected its fiery seeds into the womb and matrix of the universal waters, from which all Creation was born'.

Many of the transformations sought by the alchemists had, after all, been done by Moses' rod or Solomon's ring. Miraculous changes had been associated with Christ himself, the Saints and even with the Mass, when the priest changed bread into the Body of Jesus. A popular belief was that if a man saw the consecrated host elevated above the congregation, he would be safe from all harm for the rest of the day. And as late as the 17th century, a weaponsalve was made to cure wounds at a distance by anointing the bloody sword so that the vital spirits of the hurt body would reunite in a sympathetic cure.

The quest for the Philosopher's Stone – the Grail in *Parzival* – gave to certain gems some marvellous properties. King Charles the Fifth of France had a precious stone that helped women in childbirth, as did the Duke of Burgundy. The heliotrope was given the power of making its wearer invisible. *The Book of Stones* by Bishop Marbode of Rennes, written in the late 11th century, ascribed to jewels more power to cure than herbs. The sapphire, for example, cooled the blood, and when it was ground down, it soothed headaches and ulcers.

Gervase of Tilbury brought up Solomon's ring to prove the wonder-working quality of gems. So the Arthurian romances abounded in magic gems and precious talismans as well as in the concept of the stone of bounty fallen from heaven. According to the *Wartburgkrieg*, the Grail was a precious stone that tumbled out of Lucifer's crown when he was thrust from paradise. No alchemical ring had more properties than the one in the *Morte D'Arthur*, given by Dame Lionesse to Sir Gareth at her tournament for the Knights of the Round Table, although it increased her beauty. He would change colours in the wearing of it, as in the process of the crucible and the still. For she said:

> The virtue of my ring is, that is green it will turn to red, and that is red it will turn to likeness of green, and that is blue it will turn to likeness of white, and that is white it will turn to likeness of blue, and so it will do all manner of colours. Also he who bears my ring shall lose no blood.

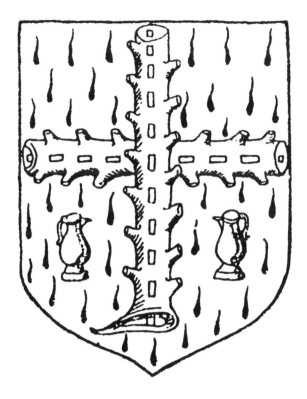

The shield of the bishops of Glastonbury with the two Grails of Joseph of Arimathea catching the blood and sweat of Christ; also the Ragged Cross of the Thorn Tree.

After many successes on the field, Sir Gareth gave up the chameleon ring and reverted to his final true colour of yellow – the gold of the end of the distillation of alchemy. The forerunner of Malory, Chrétien de Troyes, was rare in his discretion in *Yvain*, when the all-protecting ring given to the hero by his wife was never used by him, because he kept on his journey like a later Ulysses and did not return to her.

The three vessels of the alchemical process resembled three forms of the visionary Grail. The crucible purified and refined metal through fire and calcinations, just as the chalice purged sin through the Holy Blood. The retort allowed chemical reactions and the changing of shapes and colours, and corresponded to the magic stone of miracle and spiritual enlightenment. The alembic, or the still, was the process of distillation, in which the essence was separated from the substance. It represented the Grail platter of bounty and nourishment.

Alchemic theories permeated the Arthurian romances. Merlin was the Mercurius of the alchemists, the spirit of the Philosopher's Stone and of the Grail vessel. For in the adventures of the Knights of the Round Table, the material and the

ethereal were mingled. A bloody combat was followed by a magic encounter, ending finally in a prophecy or an ecstasy. And yet the Christian Church was incompatible with both the alchemist and the Knight of the Grail, pursuing an individual vision of the divine and the idea of man's unmediated relation to God. As the psychiatrist Jung would write in his *Alchemical Studies*, in Christ, the Almighty became man by his own will, while the Philosopher's Stone evolved into another bringer of light through human intention and skill.

In the former case, the miracle of man's salvation is accomplished by God; in the latter, the salvation or transfiguration of the universe is brought about by the mind of man. In the one case man confesses 'I under God', in the other he asserts 'God under me'. Man takes the place of the Creator.

When the Welsh Tudors came to power in England, the belief of the people in relics and miracles was still strong. The wonder-working of the *Lives of the Saints* was so popular that a compilation by the Archbishop of Genoa called *The Golden Legend* was translated by Caxton and printed in seven editions before the Reformation, along with Malory's *Morte D'Arthur*. The shrines of the saints at Canterbury, Glastonbury, Lindisfarne, St Albans, Walsingham and Westminster were crowded places of pilgrimage, as was the sanctuary of the Holy Blood at Hailes Abbey in Gloucestershire, where Bishop Latimer declared that the faithful believed 'that the sight of it with their bodily eye doth certify them and putteth them out of doubt that they be in clean life, and in state of salvation without spot of sin'.

The mystery of the Son of God was still the province of the priesthood. The changing of the water and the wine into the Body and Blood of Christ was their sacred alchemy. The accusations of the Lollards in their *Twelve Conclusions* of 1395 had

King Henry the Third
of England carries the
Holy Blood into
Westminster Abbey.
His brother, Richard,
Earl of Cornwall gave
the Holy Blood to
Hailes and to Ashridge
Abbeys. (Matthew
Paris)

King Henry the Third of England carries the Holy Blood into Westminster Abbey. His brother, Richard, Earl of Cornwall gave the Holy Blood to Hailes and to Ashridge Abbeys. (Matthew Paris)

little effect yet: 'Exorcism and hallowings, made in the Church of wine, bread and wax, salt and oil and incense, the stone of the altar, upon vestments, mitre cross, and pilgrims' staves, be the very practice of necromancy rather than of the holy theology.' These early reformers made no headway with their denunciation of saints such as 'the witch of Walsingham'. Indeed, miraculous cures were reported from the grave of the Lollard martyr Richard Wyche, although he had denounced such superstition. And even fifty years after the Reformation had commenced in the reign of Henry the Eighth, a Puritan pamphlet had to admit that 'three parts at least of the people [were] wedded to their old superstition still'.

In romance and belief and other legends, Joseph of Arimathea and the cult of the Magdalene were carried across the Channel to Glastonbury. Outside the abbey there, where King Arthur's bones were held to be buried along with the honest relics of all Britain, a Hospital of St Mary Magdalene was built in the 13th century to house ten poor men or pilgrims. The simple chapel still remains, as sparse as a hermit's cell, pointing the way to the Grail. The medieval chronicler John of Glastonbury associated the neighbouring church at Beckery, dedicated first to the Magdalene and then to St Brigit, with King Arthur. Basing himself on the *Perlesvaus*, declared to be written by a monk of Glastonbury, John proclaimed that Arthur's vision of the Grail happened in the chapel of the Magdalene. There he saw in a vision the miracle of the sacrament, the Virgin Mary offering up the child Jesus to the priest for sacrifice. She then gave to the King a crystal cross, which was preserved among the holy relics of the town. He changed his coat of arms into a green shield with a silver cross, placing Mary and her infant upon it – an image of Christ which the Celtic monk Gildas had declared that Arthur bore at the Battle of Badon. Gildas himself was revered at Glastonbury for writing *The Loss and Conquest of Britain* there, while the abbots adopted Arthur's supposed shield as their own after discovering his remains in the abbey.

As for Joseph of Arimathea, he is still commemorated in Glastonbury as the saint who brought the Holy Vessels from Sarras to Britain. John identified their shapes in an odd alchemic and Gnostic passage, which he ascribed to a prophecy of Melkin the bard, the teacher of Merlin. At Avalon there was a pagan cemetery supervised by thirteen celestial spheres, which was enclosed within the wattle chapel originally founded by St Patrick. 'There Joseph de Marmore, named "of Arimathea", took everlasting sleep . . . with him in the tomb [are] two white and silver vessels, filled with the blood and sweat of the prophet Jesus.' These two cruets, as they are now called, can be seen in the windows of the Church of St John the Baptist at Glastonbury and in All Saints' Church at Langport. In the Church of St John, a recent window showed the bringing of the two cruets by Joseph to Britain, as explicitly as the many windows in France portrayed Joseph and the Magdalene bringing them to Sarras. Joseph can be seen at the Crucifixion, then collecting the Holy Blood from Christ's Body after he was rescued from the Tomb, then sailing to Glastonbury with the two precious containers, and planting his staff on Wearyall Hill, which then sprouted with the flowering thorn symbolising Christ's Crown and Wounds. Actually, the medieval abbey also claimed to possess a part of the Crown of Thorns encased in a splendid reliquary, still preserved in Stanbrook Abbey. A bronze bowl, now in the Taunton Museum in Somerset, lays claim to be a local Grail, as does a sapphire-blue glass dish with eight-petalled star flowers; also the Nanteos olive-wood cup, which, like the Ka'aba stone at Mecca, is worn away by the kisses of the faithful looking for healing and divine guidance.

A portion of the Holy Blood from Charlemagne's Aachen was given to Richard, Earl of Cornwall, who transferred it in a chest to Ashridge and to the Cistercian abbey built by him at Hailes – he also rebuilt Tintagel Castle in memory of King Arthur. His gift of sacred relics to his English abbey became so famous that Chaucer referred to it in The Canterbury Tales:

By Goddes precious herte, and by his nails,
And by the blood of Christ that is of Hailes.

Hailes Abbey was destroyed by Henry the Eighth at the Dissolution of the Monasteries. Only the base to its Shrine of the Holy Blood persists. In the medieval manuscript, Divers Miracles at Hailes, an illustration of the reliquary shows the doors of the six-sided chalice opened by angels to display the liquefying and healing Blood behind its crystal glass panels. Destroyed at the Reformation as a forgery, the Blood remained a reminder of miraculous cures, and in the neighbouring parish church of the 12th century, an octagonal stone font recalls Cistercian simplicity. Ashridge was also pillaged and its glories dispersed. Edmund, the son of Richard of Cornwall, was its founder, while its monks were Bonhommes with connections with the heretical Cathars and the Lollards. Its chief treasurer was presented by the Black Prince after his victory at Poitiers with a great gold and silver table studded with jewels, 'furnished full of precious relics, and in the middle of it a holy cross of the wood of the True Cross'.

For the Puritans and some of the leading ecclesiastics, the Mass was 'nothing better to be esteemed than the verses of the sorcerer or enchanter'. So Bishop Hooper asserted, 'holy words murmured and spoken in secret'. Many followed Martin Luther in condemning the Catholic sacramental system, as he did in The Babylonian Captivity of the Church, declaring that 'the papacy is indeed nothing but the kingdom of Babylon and of the true Anti-Christ'. The Reformation was about a simple approach to God. Ritual and Latin must give way to hymns and sermons in the vernacular. The Word of God must be accessible, the approach to God plain and personal.

Curiously enough, the Quest for the Grail had always emphasised the direct search by each knight for the divine; but the mysteries of that sacred vessel were too subtle for the new Protestants, who rejected transubstantiation. To them, bread and wine were only symbols of the Body and Blood of Christ – as, indeed, were the many markers of the Grail Quest in the Catholic churches of Europe.

When the Puritans came to damn such mysticism as the romances of King Arthur, the propaganda of the state decided to revive them. For the Tudors were Welsh kings, and the Scottish Stuarts would unite the whole island under the name of Britain – the title given to Albion by Geoffrey of Monmouth, when he claimed that King Brutus of Troy had first colonised the giant-ridden white isle of the northern seas.

The seventh book of his *History* consisted of a prophecy spoken to King Vortigern by Merlin in the royal fortress in Snowdonia. Although the references were gnomic and occult, some of them seemed to bear on the future. 'The lion's whelps shall be transformed into sea-fishes' was taken as a reference to the drowning of the royal heir of King Henry the First on the White Ship, while the death of the King in Normandy and the invasion of Ireland by Henry the Second were also foretold. In his early *Roman de Brut*, Wace added to the legend of Merlin, writing of Arthur's death:

Merlin said of Arthur, as I understand it,
That there would be doubt concerning his end:
The prophet spoke truly.

To these reconstructions of the early Welsh bard Myrddin, now named as Merlin, Robert de Boron added a whole history of the magician. His *Merlin* was a sequel to his *Joseph of Arimathea*, an explanation of how the Grail reached Britain from France. A devil and a virgin were the parents of the precocious Merlin, who was given the power of changing shape and knowing the future. He became the royal adviser to Vortigern's successor Pendragon, and then to his younger brother Uther, who also inherited the throne. He had the trilithons of Stonehenge transported from Ireland and established a Round Table at Carduel for fifty knights, based on that of Charlemagne. Later, he created the test of the sword in the stone for Uther's unrecognised son, Arthur, so that he might become the King of Britain.

Two centuries later in the English-speaking world, the *Morte D'Arthur* by Sir Thomas Malory became the supreme source for the legendary king

and the search for the Grail. Written at the end of the civil Wars of the Roses and contemporary with the coming of the printing press, the saga was published in 1485 by William Caxton in the first of many editions, the most popular reading of its age after the Bible. As the publisher wrote at the conclusion of the book, it treated 'of the birth, life, and acts of the said King Arthur, of his noble knights of the Round Table, their marvellous quests and adventures, the achieving of the Sangreal, and in the end the dolorous death and departing out of this world of them all'.

The author was the heir of other Grail romances, written in Latin and French and German, also of the Celtic origins of traditional British history. He took over the character of Merlin as a wise trickster, a guide to the Other-world, a Lucifer and an enchanter. This last medieval Arthurian romance resembled the first, an exercise in propaganda for a new dynasty, recalling King Arthur's conquest of Paris in the manner of Henry the Fifth after Agincourt. In Malory's version, the British king not only defeated with his sword Excalibur a giant and the Roman and Saracen leader, Lucius, but he was actually crowned as emperor by the Pope in the Holy City, which surrendered to him. Curiously, he had the enemy magnates embalmed and buried in chests of lead in the Templar and oriental manner.

The conception of Arthur by Igraine, the Duchess of Cornwall, in the castle of Tintagel began the *Morte D'Arthur*. Merlin disguised Uther Pendragon as her husband the Duke, who was slain on the night of their love, allowing Uther to marry Igraine. Merlin's price was to be responsible for the rearing of Arthur, for Uther had sworn on the Four Evangelists to grant Merlin his desire, if he had his way with Igraine. Her sister Morgan le Fay, however, was put into a nunnery, where she was taught necromancy; she was ever the implacable foe of Arthur and of Merlin, her rival and his adviser.

Passing the test of the sword in the stone, Arthur was only accepted as king after a long civil war, in which Merlin was his armourer, strategist and communications wizard. He procured Excalibur

Woodcut of the *Book of the Grail* presented to the King.
(Malory's Morte D'Arthur, *1516 edn)*

from the Lady of the Lake for Arthur: the magic sword was 'so bright in his enemies' eyes, that it gave light like thirty torches'. He brought reinforcements and placed them in ambush so quickly that the royal knights marvelled 'that man on earth might speed so soon, and come and go'. And Malory claimed a provenance for his accounts of ancient jousts and combats, giving Merlin a master in Northumberland named Blaise, who wrote down 'all the battles that every worthy knight did of Arthur's court'.

In one of his many shapes, Merlin appeared to the British king as a beautiful youth. He predicted Arthur's death, because he had slept unknowingly with his sister and begotten Mordred upon her, in spite of an attempt, like that of Herod, to destroy all male children born on May Day. 'For it is God's will your body will be punished for your foul deeds; but I may well be sorry,' said Merlin, 'for I shall die a shameful death to be put in the earth quick, and you shall die a worshipful death.' He made the father of Arthur's Queen Guinevere institute the Round Table for 150 knights, first in London and then in Camelot, which was identified

as Winchester. Malory confirmed that the royal court was always on the move; he made Arthur lament, 'Alas, yet had I never rest one month since I was crowned king of this land.' And then Merlin fell in love with the water nymph Nimue, who served the Lady of the Lake. She tricked out of the wizard many of his secrets, until she immured him alive under an enchanted rock. So stone finally imprisoned the man of many shapes.

King Arthur found survival difficult without the warnings of Merlin. Morgan le Fay stole from him Excalibur and its healing scabbard of gold and precious stones, so that he was nearly killed by his own wonder-working weapon. And Merlin would have been roasted alive by an alchemic mantle made of precious stones and sent to him by his necromantic sister, if he had not insisted that the messenger wore it first; she 'fell down dead and never more spake word after and burnt to coals'.

The *Morte D'Arthur* shifted from tales of Merlin and his king to the multiple quest of the leading Knights of the Round Table. In one adventure, Lancelot at the Castle Perilous discovered a magic sword by a corpse beneath a hill of silk, and he used it as a woundsalve to cure a sick knight, or as Perceval's bleeding lance healed the Fisher King. So many foreign knights were defeated and sent back to beg for mercy at Camelot that King Arthur could hold an alchemical feast at Pentecost with 50 warriors under a Green Knight, 60 under a Red Knight, 100 under a Blue Knight, and 600 under the metal Sir Ironside. The Black Knight was slain or he would have been there.

Morgan le Fay did have her revenge on King Arthur, by sending him no Grail, but a horn of betrayal. If any woman were false to her husband, she spilt all the drink in it. So Guinevere did, and thus her husband knew of her love for Lancelot. The same happened to Iseult, who had to confess her love for Tristram to her husband, King Mark. She was sentenced to be burned alive, but Tristram saved her. They had originally fallen in love by

The Vision of the Grail at Pentecost. *(13th-century French manuscript)*

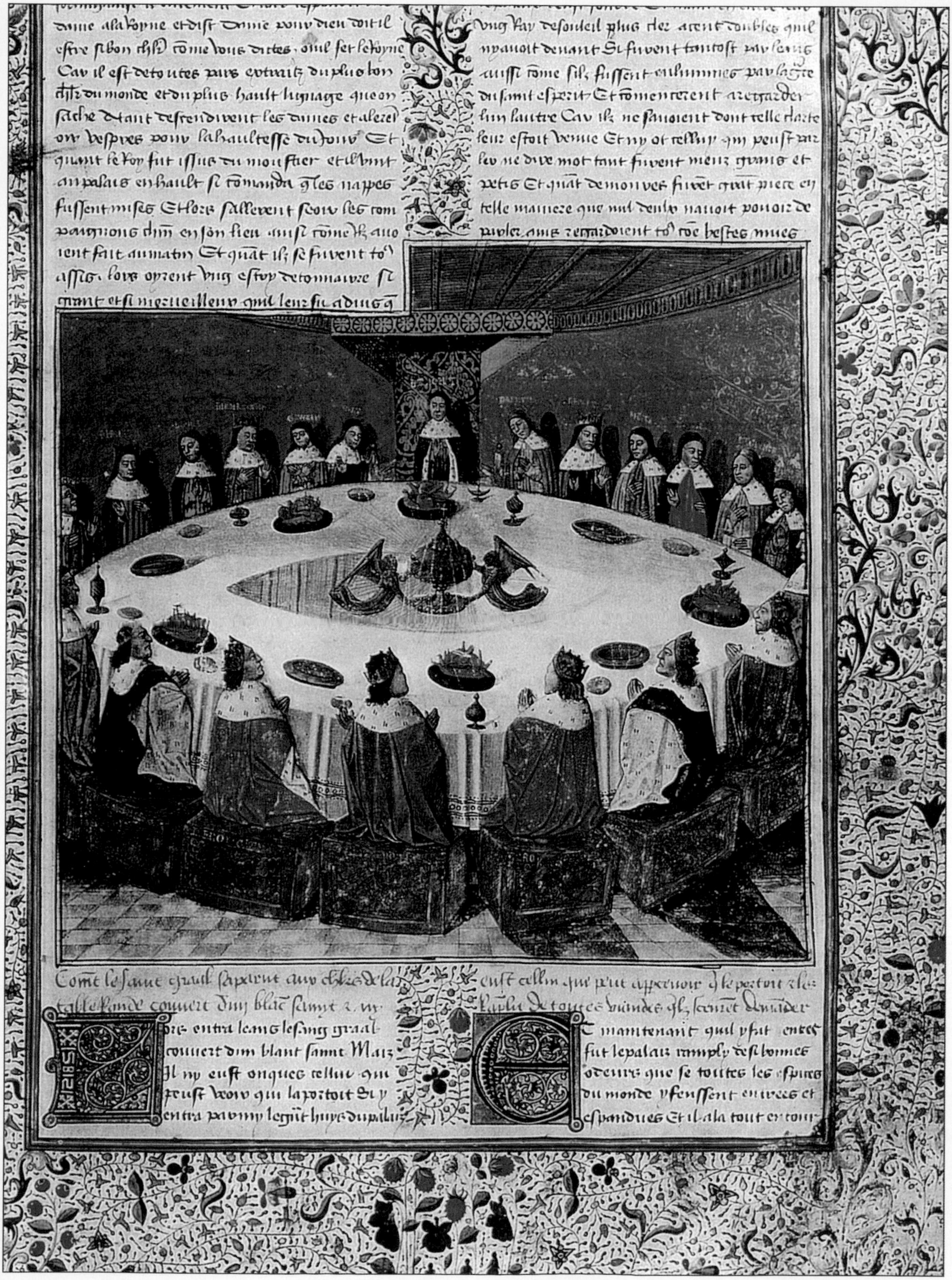

drinking out of a golden flask on their voyage an aphrodisiac meant for her and King Mark: 'they thought never drink that ever they drank to each other was so sweet nor so good'. Later, in his madness in the Forest Perilous, Tristram saved Arthur with the help of the Lady of the Lake, who rode off with a false woman's head on her saddle bow, severed by the King's sword.

Eventually, Tristram was accepted as a Knight of the Round Table, which Merlin had called the cosmos, the whole world represented in the brotherhood at Camelot. The hero of heroes was Sir Lancelot, unable to achieve the Grail because of his adultery with Queen Guinevere. He rescued the Lady Elaine 'naked as a needle [from] a chamber hot as any stew' – a cauldron of rebirth. Then the noble knight slew 'a horrible and friendly dragon', and he met the boiling young woman's father, who introduced himself as King Pelles of a foreign country and cousin to Joseph of Arimathea. At dinner in his Corbenic castle, a dove flew in, a golden censer in its beak, shaking out 'a savour as all the spicery of the world had been there'. On the table was laid every imaginable kind of food and drink. A damsel appeared with a golden vessel held in her two hands. All knelt and prayed. Lancelot asked, 'O Jesu, what may this mean?' The King replied, 'This is the richest thing that any man hath living. And when this thing goeth about, the Round Table shall be broken. . . . This is the Sangreal that ye have here seen.'

This original sight of the Sangreal by Lancelot was different to other visions in the previous Arthurian romances. First seen by the adulterer with Arthur's Queen, it was foretold by the golden flask that bound Iseult and Tristram forever in love. It appeared in two forms: the censer in the dove's beak with its heavenly perfumes; and the vessel born by the Grail maiden. It had the property of providing manna and ambrosia for all. And it stimulated King Pelles into an art of trickery worthy of Merlin. He went to an enchantress, who gave Lancelot some drugged wine that so besotted him that he thought that Elaine, the daughter of Pelles, was his beloved Guinevere. So he fulfilled a prophecy and made Elaine pregnant with Galahad,

whom Pelles knew would deliver his country from danger and would achieve the Sangreal, as Perceval had done in the previous Arthurian romances.

Lancelot rode away, for he could not come closer to the Grail, but Sir Bors followed him to Corbenic, where he saw the infant Galahad in his mother's arms. He wept for joy and prayed. Again the white dove appeared with the golden censer; again the miraculous meal, the sweet smells and the Grail maiden, who said before she disappeared with the Holy Vessel: 'This child is Galahad, who shall sit in the Siege Perilous and achieve the Sangreal, and he shall be much better than ever was his father Sir Lancelot of the Lake.' Sir Bors took confession, although he had little to confess; he was a virgin except for one night with another royal daughter. And so Malory granted him that night some visions of the sacred objects of the Grail Quest and of the future.

A long and great spear of light with a burning point wounded his shoulder. As Bors lay back in pain, he was accosted by a knight, who fought him before being cut down. Then a hail of arrows and crossbow bolts wounded him all over. Next he was attacked by a lion and had to cut off its head. Then a dragon entered with gold letters on its forehead that signified something to do with King Arthur: it fought an old leopard and spat from its mouth 100 small dragons that tore it to pieces – a prophecy of the dissension that would break apart the Round Table.

An old harper now entered with the two adders of wisdom round his neck, and he sang a song of Joseph of Arimathea coming to the foreign country. Bors was told to leave the next day, for he was not worthy of the Grail Castle. Four children appeared with four candles, and another old man with a censer in one hand and the Spear of Vengeance in the other. Four women came to kneel at a silver altar with four pillars. They were joined by a kneeling bishop, but Bors was blinded for a while by a naked silver sword blade hanging over his head. Again he was ordered to depart to Camelot and report the news of Galahad and the Sangreal. Later, Lancelot was tricked for a second time into sleeping with Elaine instead of

Guinevere: he went as mad as Tristram had in the woods when he learned of the deceit.

The Sangreal now appeared as the healing jar of Asclepius, the Greek god of curing. Two of the Knights of the Round Table, Lancelot's brother, Sir Ector, and Sir Perceval nearly killed one another, but they were made well by the 'sweetness and savour' of the bearer of holy balm. As Percival was 'a perfect clean knight . . . he had a glimmering of the vessel and of the maiden that bore it'. Sir Ector pointed out that the damsel in white was carrying part of the Holy Blood of Christ, although no female was allowed to touch the actual Catholic communion chalice. He was referring to the Gnostic belief in a Sophia or a Mary Magdalene as the intercessor between heaven and earth.

Throughout the *Morte D'Arthur*, the Sangreal was given healing powers. It could cure the sick and the wounded, and even the madness of Lancelot when he ran amok, like Nebuchadnezzar, in the wild woods. At another time, Lancelot had a vision of a priest holding the youngest of the three male figures of the Trinity as a Grail between his hands, to show to the people. Fearing the divine load was too heavy to carry, the sinful knight dashed forward to help in the ceremony, only to be struck down by a bolt of fire in his face. For this presumption, he was plunged into a coma for twenty-four nights, before his eventual recovery.

Meanwhile, at Pentecost, the grown Galahad was knighted by King Arthur at the court of Camelot, where the young man sat safely on the Siege Perilous, without plunging down to hell. Later, he drew the sword Excalibur from the stone, and he was told by Queen Guinevere that he was of the Holy Blood: 'Sir Lancelot is come but of the eighth degree from our Lord Jesu Christ, and Sir Galahad is of the ninth degree from our Lord Jesu Christ.' That suppertime, thunder struck all dumb, and the bright sunbeam of the grace of the Holy Ghost dazzled them.

> In the midst of this blast a sunbeam entered clearer by seven times more than ever they saw day, and they were all enlightened of the grace of the Holy Ghost. Then every knight began to behold each other apparently fairer than they ever saw before. There was no knight who might speak one word for a great while, so they looked every man on the other as if they had been dumb. Then covered with white samite, the Holy Grail entered into the hall, but there was no one who might see it, nor who bore it. And good odours fulfilled all the hall, and every knight had such meat and drink as he best loved in this world. And when the Sangreal had been borne through the hall, then the Holy Vessel departed suddenly, but they did not know where it went. Then they all had the breath to speak. And then the king yielded thanks to God, of His good grace which He had sent them.

The coming of this Christian Grail would break up the Round Table. For Malory had lived during the decline of medieval chivalry in the fratricidal Wars of the Roses. All the knights vowed to leave on their individual quests after the vision of God's grace, and King Arthur knew that he had lost the feudal loyalty that had kept Britain together. His warriors were now pledged to God. 'You have bereft me', he told Gawain, 'of the fairest fellowship and the truest of knighthood that ever were seen together in any realm of the world; for when they depart from here I am sure they all shall never meet more in this world. For they shall die many in the quest.' Almost as prophetical as Merlin, Malory was describing how the pursuit of individual excellence and salvation would rend apart the unity of the Catholic faith and feudal ties of obligation. As for the searchers for the Sangreal, they departed with weeping and mourning among rich and poor, and every knight took the way that he liked best.

Galahad was soon given a shield with a cross made with the blood of Joseph of Arimathea after his arrival in Britain. In a vision by a ruined chapel, Lancelot saw a sick knight cured by a floating silver altar with six candlesticks and the Sangreal; but he was too heavy with sin to kiss the Holy Vessel. And Merlin came back into the story in an account given to Perceval by his aunt, the Queen of the Waste Land. She told him that the Welsh wizard had created the Round Table to represent the

world. Those who became knights of it could be heathen as well as Christian. The quest for the Sangreal had broken up this ungodly fellowship, which ignored family and kin.

A vision came to Perceval of the old and wounded Joseph of Arimathea, begging to be cured by the Holy Blood and Body. He was then tricked into lying down with a naked woman, who disappeared into a black cloud after Perceval had seen his drawn sword and its pommel containing a red cross and the sign of the crucifix. He stabbed himself in expiation for his sin and sailed away on the magic Ship of Solomon, which drifted to shore after his use.

So the quests of the knights seeking the Sangreal were recorded. They were made to listen to many sermons, prophecies and Christian allegories; but clearly only three of them would achieve their goal. These were the three wise virgins, Galahad, Perceval and the once-spotted Bors, who would all meet on the magic ship. As in *The Quest of the Holy Grail*, they found on board a bed made from the Tree of Good and Evil in Eden, another magic

sword with a serpent and a fish on its pommel of many colours, and a snakeskin scabbard. King Pelles had been maimed incurably through both of his thighs by the Spear of Vengeance, because he had half-drawn the sword, now identified as the weapon of King David. Only Galahad could cure Pelles and revive the Waste Land of Logres with the touch of the sword, before the three knights might finally seek the apotheosis of the Grail in the Land of Sarras.

Galahad now drew the sword of David, and he used it in the Marches of Scotland to deliver Perceval's sister. Yet by a Celtic custom, she was obliged to fill a dish with her virgin blood in order to cure a sick lady. Then she died, and her body was put on board to be taken to Sarras. The three knights proceeded to Corbenic castle, where they were granted the full vision of the Sangreal, heralded by Joseph of Arimathea, who had been the first Bishop of Christendom in Sarras. 'They saw angels; and two bore candles of wax, and the third a towel, and the fourth a Spear that bled marvellously, so that three drops fell within a box

Galahad sees the Grail procession at Corbenic castle.
(13th-century French manuscript)

the words: 'For thou hast resembled me in two things; in that thou hast seen the marvels of the Sangreal, in that thou hast been a clean maiden, as I have been and am.' Then the soul of Galahad was taken by the angels, and a heavenly Hand came down to clutch the Holy Vessel and the bleeding Spear, which disappeared for ever. From then onwards, there was 'never man so hardy to say that he had seen the Sangreal'.

From this catalyst and confusion of sources, both classical and Christian, Sir Thomas Malory concocted the enduring legend of King Arthur and the Quest for the Grail. And as in *Parzival*, he wrote of the reconciliation of crusader and Saracen. One of the greater Knights of the Round Table was Sir Palomides from Islam, and he rivalled Sir Tristram for the love of the beautiful Queen Iseult; but until he had completed his exploits and slain the Questing Beast, he could not be baptised as a Christian by the Bishop of Carlisle, claimed as the true site of Camelot. He did not become the hereditary Fisher King, as Feirefiz had in *Parzival* after marrying the Grail princess, and after the healing of the maiming of the previous ruler by the bleeding Lance. Indeed, Malory referred to a Queen of the Waste Land, who helped to carry the dead King Arthur to the Isle of Avalon; but he only implied that Logres would grow green once more, when Arthur might come again.

If this was Malory's ending of the search for divine grace, taken to such a large extent from the earlier *Quest of the Holy Grail*, he could not conclude his book. For he had to deal with the death of King Arthur. He defined the legend that still persists: the enduring love of Lancelot for Guinevere, their betrayal to Arthur by Mordred, the siege of the castle of the Joyous Gard by the royal forces, the following civil war abroad, the treason of Mordred and the final battle of Camlann, with the taking of the King's body to the Vale of Avalon. To this requiem of the Grail legend of the Middle Ages, Malory even promised a sequel:

which he held with his other hand.' The sacred Spear was set upright on the Holy Vessel on its silver table. Then Joseph took up a piece of bread, which was transformed into the 'likeness of a child and the visage as red and bright as any fire'. Later, when Joseph had disappeared, the three knights saw a man come out of the Holy Vessel bearing all the signs and wounds of the Passion. He took the Grail and gave Himself through it to the kneeling knights, and He identified it as the dish of the Paschal Lamb at the Last Supper. They must take the Grail back to Sarras; also the blood of the sacred Spear to cure the maimed King of Logres.

So the incurable wounds of King Pelles were healed and he became a white monk, and the three knights sailed to Sarras with the Holy Vessel and the Spear, never to be seen again in Britain. When the ship arrived in the destined port city, the voyagers were imprisoned by its ruler, but they were nourished, as once Pelles was, by the grace of the Sangreal. On the death of the alien king, Galahad was chosen as his successor and was crowned by angels and Joseph of Arimathea with

Yet some men say in many parts of England that King Arthur is not dead, but taken by the will of our Lord Jesus into another place; and men say that he shall come again, and he shall win the Holy Cross. I will not say it shall be so, but rather I will say: here in this world he changed his life. But many men say that there is written upon his tomb this verse: *Hic jacet Arthurus Rex quondam Rex, que futurus.* [Here lies King Arthur, past King, and future.]

Malory's re-creation and definition of the legend of Camelot was a boon for Tudor propaganda. King Henry the Seventh's newborn son – who was born in Winchester, often identified as Camelot – was christened Arthur. The heir of the houses of both Lancaster and York, he would unite Britain as his royal ancestor had done through the Round Table. He might also repeat Arthur's conquests in Europe as far as Rome.

The Faerie Queene by Edmund Spenser was popular in the reign of Queen Victoria. This illustration by Edward Courbauld for the Routledge London edition of 1856 shows Excess offering the golden cup to the knight Guyon. It reflects the contemporary revival and exploitation of the Grail theme.

Merlin's prophecies remained popular. In 1510, Wynkyn de Worde published *A Little Treatise of the Birth and Prophecies of Merlin*, which ran into several editions. Later books claimed that Merlin had predicted the Reformation, while *The Mirror for Magistrates* of 1559 wrote of the Welsh bard as 'learned Merlin whom God gave the spirit to know and utter princes' acts to come'. The astrologer Lilly named his almanac *Merlinus Anglicus*, and by Stuart times, Thomas Heywood's *Life of Merlin* claimed him as a Protestant as well as a prophet. And that he was, in the sense that the Grail Quest was the individual search for grace without benefit of clergy.

In his breach with Rome, Henry the Eighth used the defiance and heresy of the Arthurian legend to justify his institution of an independent Church of England under his authority. Most significantly, a Round Table was created at Winchester in memory of the tables of Arthur and Charlemagne. This piece of furniture represented an allegory of the whole world, which was now open to the domination of the new dynasty, occupied in building the first significant British navy, the force of rebuilding an empire overseas after the loss of France. John Dee and Richard Hakluyt, the chronicler of the voyages of the Elizabethan captains, would use the myth of Arthur's conquests to legitimise expansion abroad. And as Cervantes and Ariosto had sublimated the medieval romances for modern times, so would Edmund Spenser in *The Faerie Queene*.

> Then Merlin thus: Indeed the fates are firm,
> And may not shrink, though all the world do
> > shake.
> Yet ought men's good endeavours them confirm,
> And guide the heavenly causes to their constant
> > term.

America offering her riches to Europe, a severed head at her feet. *(Anonymous illustration from Flanders, c. 1600)*

Spenser tried to follow Ariosto and so become the Virgil of England. To his friend Sir Walter Ralegh, he also confessed the influence of Homer and Tasso. Yet he used the legend of Arthur in a new manner. The quest of the 'Briton prince' was the love of the Faerie Queen. Through this desire, Spenser could lavish praise on Elizabeth the First; as Gloriana, she took the place of the Grail. 'In that Faerie Queene,' he wrote to Ralegh, 'I mean *Glory*, in my general intention, and in my particular I conceive the most excellent and glorious person of our soveraine the Queene, and her kingdom in Faerie Land.' As for Arthur, he was chosen 'as most fit for the excellency of his person, being made famous by many men's former works, and also furthest from the danger of envy, and suspicion of present time'.

יהוה
Dixit et factum est

Spiritus Dñi ferebatur super aquas.

Europe   Africa

Asia   America

COSMOGRAPHIE
in foure Bookes
Contayning the
CHOROGRAPHIE & HISTORIE
of the whole WORLD, and all
the Principall Kingdomes,
Provinces, Seas, and
Isles, Thereof.
By Peter Heylyn
Virgil Aeneid: 1
Quæ regio in terris nostri non plena Laboris?

Europe   Africa

Asia   America

LONDON
Printed for Henry Seile
ouer against St Dunstans
Church in Fleetstreete.
1652.

The frontispiece of Peter Heylyn's *Cosmographie*, 1652.

> The cup to ground did violently cast,
> That all in pieces it was broken found,
> And with the liquor stained all the land.

Tudor propaganda had already identified Arthur as a royal ancestor of Queen Elizabeth, while his ancestor was the Emperor Constantine. A fabulous empire that reached to Rome was re-created to justify Elizabethan ambitions in the Americas. And the long poem was less an imitation of its predecessors than a weapon in the Protestant cause against the Catholic Church. Arthur did wear a bloody cross on his surcoat and shield as a glorious badge to his 'dying Lord'. But on his first adventure after slaying a dragon, he was made to encounter the usual hermit:

> He told of saints and popes, and evermore
> He strew'd an Ave-Mary after and before.

Instead of blessing the knight's sleep, the Catholic priest went to his cell to consult his 'magic books, and arts of sundry kinds'. With these charms, he conjured up devils and nightmares to disturb Arthur's conscience and peace of mind. The holy man was changed into a magician and alchemist in the holy war between England and Spain. He tried to direct Arthur away from the new Grail, the praise of Gloriana, the ruler of his heart and her enchanted realm.

Later in this epic, the cup of bounty that led the questing knights to an earthly paradise was also altered into a savage Puritan reaction. The noble Guyon rode into a Bower of Bliss; his name appeared to derive from the River Gehon in the Garden of Eden, from Gawain and from Guyana, the American Eldorado sought by Ralegh. He met the half-naked lady Excess, who offered him a golden cup of wine:

> Thereof she us'd to give to drink to each,
> Whom passing by she happened to meet;
> It was her guise all strangers goodly so to greet.

> So she to Guyon offered it to taste;
> Who, taking it out of her tender hand,

Spurning the false wine in the cup, Guyon rode on through 'the most dainty paradise', where all pleasures were in plenty, and nobody envied another's happiness. Art and nature had agreed 'through sweet adversity, this garden to adorn with all variety'. In a fountain of silver water, paved with jasper, two nymphs were bathing, almost fairer than the owner, Arcasia, who was then trapped with a young knight, Verdant, under a net. Guyon broke down the paradise and its palace, considering the late medieval world of romance and luxury a wicked delusion.

> Their groves he fell'd; their gardens did deface;
> Their arbours spoil; their cabinets suppress;
> Their banquet-houses burn; their buildings raze;
> And, of the fairest late, now made the foulest place.

This wanton devastation, or destruction of wantonness, was a cruel commentary on what the Elizabethans held against Portugal and Spain in their conquests in the New World. They had destroyed a natural paradise over there. Guyon's worst encounter was with two knights, Pyrochles, or Portugal, and Cymochles, or Spain, directed by Archimago, the Supreme Magus or Pontiff. King Arthur himself rescued Guyon from his terrible combat with these two Paynims, or Pagans, who wanted to despoil him of his gold.

Although wounded with his blood flowing as red as the Rose of Lancaster, Arthur was victorious in honour of the Faerie Queene, whose ancestor Elfin 'all India obey'd, and all that men America now call'. The English magus John Dee had already given Queen Elizabeth a map of the Americas, claiming that King Arthur had colonised it; later the Lord Madoc of Wales, another of the royal ancestors, was said to have reached Florida. On other occasions in the adventures, Arthur was attacked by poisoned arrows, such as the Indians used, and he avoided the foul evil 'that rots the marrow, and consumes the brain', the new strain of syphilis in Europe. So Virginia, or the land of the Faerie Queene, was saved. In his dedication to Elizabeth, Spenser already referred to her as Queene of Virginia as well as France and Ireland.

In a chronicle of the kings of Britain, Spenser exhorted his countrymen to take up the cause of empire for their Gloriana, as the ancient Britons had done for Arthur – and as later Englishmen would do in the name of Queen Victoria. In particular, he wanted them to espouse the cause and dream of Ralegh. He ended a long list of the renowned rivers of the world with the newly found Orinoco, where the warlike Amazons were held to live:

Joy on those warlike women, which so long
Can from all men so rich a kingdom hold!
And shame on you, O men, which boast your strong
And violent hearts, in thoughts less hard and bold.
Yet quail in conquest of that land of gold!
But this to you, O Britons, most pertains,
To whom the right hereof itself hath sold,
The which, for sparing little costs or pains,
Lose so immortal glory, and so endless gains.

So with the discovery of a New World of Nature, apparently inviting its own destruction, the Quest for the Grail would be translated to the search for glory, gold and imperial rule across the Atlantic and Pacific oceans.

EIGHTEEN

VISIONS OF THE IMAGINATION

The world was all before them, where to choose
Their place of rest, and Providence their guide:
They hand in hand with wand'ring steps and slow,
Through Eden took their solitary way.

John Milton, *Paradise Lost* (Adam and Eve)

Nothing is proven about the discovery of the Americas by the Egyptians, the Phoenicians or the Greeks. To admit that pyramids were built in different continents separated by the Atlantic is not to say that their peoples knew one another. Recent discoveries of cocaine and tobacco in Egyptian mummies only infer the later loss of ancient narcotic plants used at the time of the Pharaohs, who were known to achieve ecstasy by dropping lotus on their wine, as well as trying opium and hemp. Platonic accounts of Atlantis have no credible geography. Only the blessed voyage of St Brendan, given the far sea crossings of the Irish evangelical monks after the 7th century, has some shreds and patches of plausibility.

In the *Navigatio*, a Latin work written 300 years later, Brendan was described as spending seven years on a search for a paradise over the western ocean. The voyage was considered a part of the Matter of Britain and the work was translated into most of the European languages, including Provençal. This Celtic *Odyssey* was begun by a monk named Barinthus, who told Brendan of a huge land towards the sunset that contained the early Eden. Sailing away, Brendan and his companions passed a Paradise of Birds, who told him that they were spirits in disguise, neither angels nor devils as in the later legends of Dante and Wolfram von Eschenbach.

Brendan reached a Land of Promise; under an autumn sun, its rich fields and fruits fed the Irish monks for forty days, as the voyagers progressed on foot. Then a Shining One met them to say that God had kept them on their quest for the seven years only to reveal to them the mysteries of the immense ocean; but now that Brendan had reached the frontiers of paradise, his search was over. Like many a Grail knight, he could not achieve his quest. So he returned with his fellows and sailed home.

This Atlantic voyage, recorded before the Vikings actually reached North America, had its believers. Even the great Arab geographer and historian of the 12th century, al-Idrisi, called the land mass to the west of Iceland 'Ireland-the-Great'. The very name 'Brasil', which featured on medieval Venetian maps before the Portuguese reached it, may well derive from Brendan's voyage and the Irish word *breasail*, or 'blessed'. In another fable, the *Voyage of Bran*, an adventurer named Máeldúin visited twenty-nine western islands larger than Ireland, with many more to go. And Richard Hakluyt, wanting to base Elizabethan claims to Virginia on history, claimed that America was reached not only by Hanno from Carthage, but by Britons 'long before Columbus led any Spaniards thither'.

Because of necessary Tudor propaganda, Hakluyt and the astrologer John Dee also emphasised the legend of the voyage across the Atlantic of the

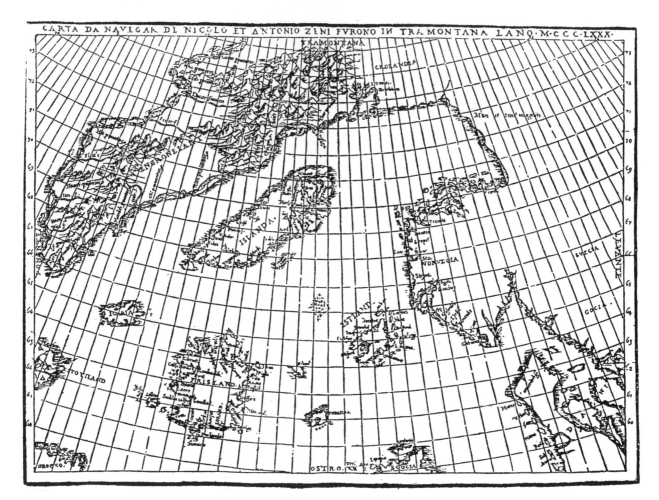

The Zeno map, Venice, 1558.

Welsh prince Madoc. The mythical large island Frisland, which appeared on the Venetian Zeno map and influenced cartographers for 200 years, was claimed as a colony of King Arthur. Madoc, however, was said to have reached North America or the West Indies in the 12th century with a band of national colonists, never to be sighted again. He had existed and became a legend in his own country, the pioneer of Welsh emigrants as far away as Patagonia.

Among the supposed voyagers was Herzog Ernst, the subject of a popular romantic poem in medieval German, its fourth Gotha manuscript probably written by Ulrich von Eschenbach in the late 13th century. Ernst quarrelled with his stepfather, the Holy Roman Emperor, and set off with a companion towards Jerusalem, only to be driven across the ocean by storms. Menaced by sea beasts and monsters, passing like Sinbad the Sailor a coagulated sea and a magnetic mountain, he

reached the Otherworld paradise of the one-eyed Arimaspians, only to steal away in order to defeat the infidels who beset the Holy City. He endowed and prayed at the Church of the Holy Sepulchre as the Teutonic Knights had done, before returning to a reconciliation with his emperor in his native land. Most interesting was the fact that Ernst kept one thing from his Eastern travels: the *weise* or gemstone of the imperial crown, found on a journey along a subterranean river.

Possibly the earliest version of *Herzog Ernst* was an inspiration for the identification in *Parzival* of the Grail as a stone, as was the *Chanson d'Esclarmonde*, in which Charlemagne was the emperor. That medieval poem declared of the hero Huon and his talisman:

A man who keeps such a stone with him
Cannot die in his flesh in a struggle grim,
Nor be brought down in battle or by a charm,
Nor hated by anyone under the sun,
Nor put in prison for any old crime.

The *weise* of *Herzog Ernst*, brought back from the underground water, was turned into the Philosopher's Stone in Ulrich von Eschenbach's version. The hero saw a brilliant stone called a unity, or 'something unique'; there was nothing like it in form or nature anywhere else in the world.

The first European colonists of the New World were the Vikings, who left their traces at L'Anse-aux-Meadows in Newfoundland. They slowly crossed the Atlantic, hopping from Orkney to Iceland, then on to Greenland and Markland, probably Labrador. In the year 1000, Lief the Lucky was held by the sagas to have reached Vinland; grapes do not grow north of Massachusets. For 400 years, a small string of Norse colonies held together a trade in furs, timber, resin and salt fish across the northern ocean, before the last settlements died out in Greenland, as Columbus opened the southern route. Their stories inspired the family of the Holy Light, the Sancto Claros or St Clairs, to undertake a mission of imperial evangelism to the New World.

The refugee Knights Templars wanted to create another paradise and Temple of Solomon beyond the reach of papal authority. Their example was the Teutonic Knights, whose crusade from their headquarters at Marienburg against the pagan Slavs had created an empire on the eastern Baltic Sea. With the accession of Margaret to the thrones of Norway and Sweden and the regency of Denmark, a Commonwealth was created that might engender a trading bloc across the Atlantic. Third in precedence to the Queen was Earl Henry St Clair of Rosslyn, which had housed the fugitive Templars. He was also the Lord of Orkney and the Shetlands, the axis of oceanic trade. When two Venetian captains were shipwrecked there, Earl Henry pressed them into his service. They were the Zeno brothers, whose explorations with their master produced the definitive map of Greenland for the next two centuries; also much later speculation about the truth of their narrative.

Beyond reasonable doubt, in 1398 Earl Henry St Clair set out with a large expedition of soldiers and monks to establish two colonies in the New World: one at Louisburg in Nova Scotia, where a contemporary primitive Venetian ship's cannon has been found; and another at Newport, Rhode Island. The notorious round tower on a hill there, with its eight arches in the manner of the original Church of the Holy Sepulchre and of Charlemagne's chapel at Aachen, could never have served as the colonial windmill that some claim it to be. It was designed as a church and a lighthouse; the fireplace on its first floor, directed through a window towards the bay, still demonstrates that use. Its construction is identical to the base of the round tower at Charroux, which used the same Templar models and now has the two doves drinking from a Grail in its crypt.

The tower at Newport, Rhode Island.

Earl Henry took across the Atlantic the idea of the Grail as the civilising mission of the European knight to pagan countries, as was the mission of Parzival. This ideal would inspire the Portuguese, the Spaniards and even the later British Empire. Although Earl Henry was killed by an English raid shortly after his return to Orkney, and although his two colonies were lost, he set an example for other European nations to follow. The first were the sailors of Portugal, already probing towards the west. The disappearance of the expeditions of the Cortereal brothers argues for another traceless colony. The signature of 'Miguel' on the Dighton Rock, along with a possible Shield of Portugal, suggest an arrival in Massachusetts well before the Pilgrim Fathers.

Portugal was the first founder of the European empires over the oceans. Yet it would lose its independence on a last crusade against the Muslims. Imperial designs were confused with a holy mission. Led by Henry the Navigator and his refugee Templars, the Knights of Christ, a scientific, religious, diplomatic and commercial offensive was launched against Africa, Asia and America. Reinforcements with guns were sent to 'Prester John', the Christian Emperor of Ethiopia. Ships reached Persia, India, the Spice Islands of Indonesia, China and Japan. And Brazil fell into Portuguese hands, although the rest of the Americas went to Spain by papal decree.

The greatest of the Pacific discoverers and empire-builders, Vasco da Gama, was equally fortunate in finding his Virgil, Luis Vaz de Camõens. This epic poet made da Gama's expedition to India a reflection of the voyage of Aeneas to found Rome and its empire under the direction of the classical gods. So he celebrated for ever the global enterprises of Lisbon, which city and port was said to have been built by Ulysses himself.

As Geoffrey of Monmouth had claimed Brutus of Troy as the coloniser of ancient Britain, so Camõens claimed Lusus, the friend of Bacchus, as the father of Portugal, because he discovered the Elysian Fields off the Douro river and thought them too pleasant to leave. Camõens wrote *The Lusiads*, the saga of his nation's mythology,

leading on to its claims to possess new territories around the globe. Ancient history sanctified the Portuguese destiny to spread the true faith all over the world. The Germans and the English were denounced for splitting Christendom, the French for their attacks on the papacy, and Italy for its divisions and vices. Only the people of little Portugal had realised their duty in conquering the lands of the infidel.

> Death you must face wherever he may lead,
>   To spread the Word that brings eternal life.
> You may be few, but Heaven has decreed
>   You shall exalt your faith by valiant strife.

The theme of *The Lusiads* was explicit. This was the story of a regal line that extended the frontiers of faith and empire among the infidels of Africa and Asia. These exploits were greater than those of Ulysses, Aeneas, Alexander and Trajan and their famous victories; even of Orlando in Ariosto's work. The ancient heroes and poets were finished. Another higher courage had appeared. The new King Sebastian would lead his Argonauts and make the whole world tremble more than Julius Caesar or Charlemagne had done. Steering Vasco da Gama's expedition through the wiles of Muslim treachery, instigated by Bacchus, Camõens told stories of the heroic past of Portugal, the tragic love of Inês de Castro, and the twelve who went to England to defend the honour of the ladies of that court.

Defying all the plots of the gods and the infidels, da Gama and his men reached the Island of Love of the sea goddess Tethys and her Nereid nymphs, a paradise of the Otherworld. Gemstones littered the meadows. The sailors trod on emeralds and rubies. Suspended in the air was a marvel of alchemy, a transparent globe showing the motion of the heavens, begun by the Primum Mobile, which started all. The golden belt of the Zodiac was there, and the seven planets, including the Sun and the Moon revolving round the Earth with its centre in Christian Europe, which was so restless that it left the sufferings of dry land for the dangerous seas. Tethys prophesied what Camõens

A History of the Military Orders, including the Knights of Christ, 1771.

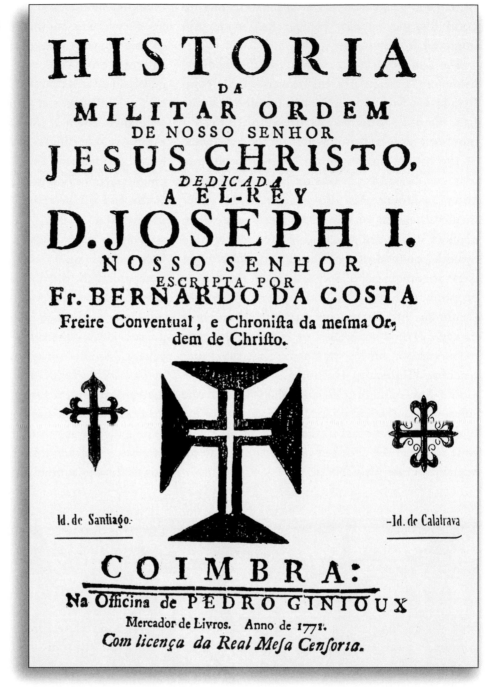

HISTORIA
DA
MILITAR ORDEM
DE NOSSO SENHOR
JESUS CHRISTO,
DEDICADA
A EL-REY
D.JOSEPH I.
NOSSO SENHOR
ESCRIPTA POR
Fr. BERNARDO DA COSTA
Freire Conventual, e Chronifta da mefma Or,
dem de Chrifto.

Id. de Santiago.   -Id. de Calalrava

COIMBRA:
Na Officina de PEDRO GINIOUX
Mercador de Livros.   Anno de 1771.
Com licença da Real Mefa Cenforia.

already knew: that the new regions of the East would fall under Portuguese dominion; also Brazil in the West with its forests of red wood.

The epic poem concluded with another sad invocation to King Sebastian. The work was published six years before his catastrophic crusade against Islam in North Africa, where he and his army of 25,000 were wiped out at Alcácer-Kebir in 1578, leaving Philip the Second of Spain to march unopposed across the frontier and unite the Iberian peninsula and the overseas empires. Camões was already dead in despair; his hopes of a worldwide mission and conquest were spilt on the bloody desert sand. How could he do what he had promised his dead ruler, who had failed to level the fortifications of Morocco? Wanting a sequel to *The Lusiads*, he had decided that he would sing to all mankind of his king, a second

Alexander, who would not even envy Achilles his good fortune, because Homer had made him immortal. It was too late.

The Lusiads included elements of the medieval romances, particularly the travels of Sir John Mandeville, who had approached paradise from the East. He had also found that blessed place to be a mountain, so high that it almost touched the circle of the moon, but its mossy wall had only one entrance, barred by fire so that no mortal could enter. Camões was also influenced by other medieval legends of a material Grail peak where precious metals and stones were scattered. For the Spanish conquest of the New World had brought back so much silver and gold that the whole economy of Europe was transformed. Originally, Columbus had set out on a crusade to discover paradise, as the Portuguese had. He made this clear in his entry in his log on Boxing Day, 1492, after reaching Hispaniola. He hoped to God that he would find enough gold and spices so that the rulers of Spain would undertake the capture of the Holy Land. He wanted all the profits of his enterprise spent on the conquest of Jerusalem, whatever happened in his New World.

In his letter back to Spain, Columbus described his discovery as another Garden of Eden. Among the nightingales, green fields and metal mines, the natives were naked and innocent. 'They are so guileless and generous with all they possess, that no one would believe it who has not seen it.' They even knelt down at the time of the Ave Maria, as the Spaniards did. At the Azores on his voyage home, he declared that the theologians and the philosophers were correct: the Earthly Paradise was at the end of the temperate Orient, and he had discovered it.

If on his later voyages Columbus found that the West Indians could retaliate and that some of them were cannibals, this revelation never dispelled his illusion that he had found another natural heaven on earth, with gold mines to add to bliss. His purpose was to spread the Word of God among the pagans. As his original biographer, Antonio de Herrara, declared, the sending of his mission and the papal donation that gave the Americas, except for Brazil, to Spain was justified. 'Because it was not in prejudice of any man, and because their Catholic Majesties had acquired a just title by temporal power for the promulgation of the Gospel.' Even

The return of the Portuguese explorers to Lisbon. *(Theodor de Bry, 1590)*

the fourth − and last − and failed voyage of
Columbus to the Americas ended with a biblical
prophecy in a letter to his sovereigns:

Detail from the *Carta Atlantica, c. 1525. (Department of Maps
and Plans, Bibliothèque Nationale, Paris)*

the fourth − and last − and failed voyage of
Columbus to the Americas ended with a biblical
prophecy in a letter to his sovereigns:

The Indies are part of the world, so rich, and He
gave them to You as Yours. You gave them to those
who pleased You and He gave You power to do so.
The fetters of the Ocean, bound with such strong
chains, these keys He gave to You. And You were
obeyed in many lands and won such honour and
fame among Christians. What more did He do for
the people of Israel when He led them out of
Egypt?

Just as there had been sacred vessels in the
hanging ornamental bowls of the 6th century at
the time of King Arthur, and in the jewelled

reliquaries of the Holy Blood in the Middle Ages,
so there were in Mexico and Peru, when the
conquistadors reached those American empires.
The colonists were looking for silver and gold.
They found the precious metals in treasuries and
mines. When Cortés and his 400 invaders took the
Aztec state, they sent home to the emperor in
Brussels 'a whole golden sun, a fathom wide, and a
whole silver moon of the same size' and armouries
of gilded weapons, valued at 100,000 gulden. The
artist Albrecht Dürer had never seen anything that
so filled his heart with joy. That these vessels might
have contained the heart and the blood of a

sacrificial victim was in the style of some of the Grail romances.

When Pizarro and his small force ransomed the Inca emperor, the booty was a large room filled with exquisite works in gold and silver, valued at 4½ million ducats. Most of these treasures were melted down. The few that survive argue their quality, as the Celtic bowls do; flasks as golden gourds, chalices of grinning faces, dishes on tripods ornamented with scrolls, skulls and beasts. These works of art had also given offerings of blood and food to the gods of other cultures.

The New World was seen as a cornucopia of riches, a vast wealth. Contemporary drawings show semi-naked Indian women with feathered head-dresses, offering platters dripping with pearls to carracks offshore. 'How much the richest empire in the world', Oviedo wrote, 'is that of the Indies.' Dominion and motive were symbolised as a whole by the frontispiece of a Spanish captain's book of 1599, *Military Occupation and Description of the Indies*. This showed the conquistador Vargas Machuca with one hand on the hilt of his sword and the other on top of a pair of open compasses measuring the span of the globe. The motto was:

> By the compass and the sword
> More and more and more and more.

A signed attribute of the Grail, the gift of eternal youth, was named across the Atlantic Ocean. On the Canary Isles, a pool was discovered below the Tree of Life, which dripped down rainwater from its leaves. There, the naked creatures of this new Eden carried away the balm of eternity in buckets and clay pots. And in Florida, Ponce de Leon claimed to have found a Fountain of Youth. In pursuit of that vision, the aged colonists of modern North America have since taken to the creeks and keys there, in a dreamlike denial of their geriatric woes.

The Puritan colonists to Massachusetts did not emigrate in search of rites or tobacco plantations to be worked by slaves, as in Virginia. They wanted to set up a model society. Its example might serve to reform the abuses of Christendom. 'For we must consider', their governor John Winthrop declared, 'that we shall be as a City upon a Hill, the eyes of all people are upon us.' In America, they would find more of the wisdom, power and truth of God than from their former acquaintance with Him in royal England. Their mission was not dissimilar to that of the Knights of the Round Table, for they sought divine grace at the end of a terrible journey, leaving temptation behind them. As Cotton Mather declared in his work on faith in the New World, 'I write the Wonders of the Christian Religion, flying from the Depravations of Europe, to the American Strand.'

By the irony of history, their search for liberty led them to institute a state of repression. They were cruel to their own dissenters and to the local Indian tribes, almost as bloody as Perceval enforcing the New Law in the place of the Old in the land of Logres. In a sense, the 'errand into the wilderness' of the Pilgrim Fathers was another crusade towards the unknown. Too terrified of the licence they found in the savage country as well as within themselves, they preferred self-restraint to the enlightenment of the free spirit.

They had not fulfilled the mission of *The Pilgrim's Progress*, the achievement of the Celestial City, although it was written by their contem-porary, John Bunyan. He turned the romances of the Grail into Protestant propaganda, but only in allegory, not in fact. Yet paradoxically, *The Pilgrim's Progress* confirmed the hidden message of the Holy Vessel – the direct path of the individual to the Heavenly City – while condemning the previous Catholic signs and pointers on the path. As Bunyan promised in his apology for his work:

> This book will make a traveller of thee,
> If by its counsels thou wilt ruled be:
> It will direct thee to the Holy Land
> If thou wilt its directions understand.

In the author's dream, a ragged pilgrim called Christian set out, as had similarly the Perceval of Chrétien de Troyes, to reach the City of Zion and find salvation for the City of Destruction. In his trials on his way through the Slough of Despond,

Pope, one of the two giants at the end of the Valley of the Shadow of Death. *(Illustration by Frederick Barnard from John Bunyan's* The Pilgrim's Progress, *revised edn, Alexander Strahan, London, 1889)*

he was met by three Shining Ones, who forgave him his sins, changed his clothes, and gave him a pass for the celestial gate. His way lay through the Delectable Mountains, before he encountered the fiend Apollyon. Suddenly armoured, he smote the devil with his two-edged sword, as so often Arthur used Excalibur in the romances.

> Then there came to him a hand with some of the leaves of the Tree of Life; which Christian took, and applied to the wounds that he had received in the battle, and was healed immediately. He also sat down in that place to eat bread, and to drink of the bottle that was given to him a little before.

Surviving the Valley of the Shadow of Death, Christian passed to its end, where lay the blood, bones, ashes and mangled bodies of former pilgrims. The cause of the horror, in Bunyan's words, was two giants, named Pope and Pagan, whose power and tyranny had put so many men cruelly to death:

> I have learnt since, that Pagan has been dead many a day; and, as for the other, though he be yet alive, he is, by reason of age, also of the many shrewd brushes that he met with in his younger days, grown so crazy and stiff in his joints, that he can now do little more than sit in his cave's mouth, grinning at pilgrims as they go by, and biting his nails because he cannot come at them.

Another jibe at the papacy occurred when Christian and Faithful passed through Vanity Fair, where there were British, French, Italian, Spanish and German Rows. Their chief promotion was of the merchandise of Rome, but England and some other nations took a dislike to that. There pilgrims were killed because they only wanted to buy the truth. Christian's companion Faithful died rather as Christ had, before being carried up to heaven.

They therefore brought him out, to do with him according to their law: and first they scourged him, then they buffeted him, then they lanced his flesh with knives; after that they stoned him with stones, then pricked him with their swords, and, last of all, they burned him to ashes at the stake. Thus came Faithful to this end.

Christian carried on, now accompanied by Hopeful. Escaping from Doubting Castle kept by Giant Despair, they reached their goal. At the entrance, they were informed by two more Shining Ones of what they would achieve at the end of their quest.

> There is the Mount Zion, the heavenly Jerusalem, the innumerable company of angels, and the spirits of just men made perfect. You are going now to the Paradise of God, wherein you shall see the Tree of Life, and eat of the never-fading fruits thereof. . . .

Tassacorda   I. of Palma
S. Cruz

I. of Gomera

I. of Ferro

The Paradise Garden in the Canary Islands, 1748.

The pilgrims would receive comfort for their toil and joy for their sorrow. 'You must reap what you have sown, even the fruit of all your prayers, and tears, and sufferings for the king by the way.' And in the Celestial City, they would enjoy perpetual visions of the Holy One. 'For there you shall see Him as He is.'

This was an exact description of the discovery of the Grail. Each knight was rewarded for his trials on his journey by the vision of the grace of God, according to what he had done to reach it. Only the few, such as Perceval or Galahad, would see 'Him as He is'. No Catholic Church stood between the pilgrim or the knight and his search for the divine. It was a personal path towards salvation, which meant abandoning city, home and family. Bunyan mocked any institution that stood between the individual and his pursuit of heaven. The way of a Christian to that bliss lay through his own deeds and sufferings.

Far more subtle than Bunyan, with his Puritan allegories, John Milton long searched for an epic subject worthy of his greater genius. While travelling to Rome as a young man, he met a flatterer called Salzilli, who ranked him above Homer, Virgil and Tasso. Meaning to rival those heroic and epic poets, Milton wrote in a Latin poem, *Manso*, of his aspirations 'if ever I recall in song our native kings, and Arthur waging war even beneath the earth, or if ever I proclaim the great spirit of the heroes of the Round Table . . .'. Returning to England on the eve of the Civil War, he began his *Arthuriad*, but he soon suspended the attempt in order to finish his superb elegy *Lycidas*. To his friend Diodati, he declared that he would still write of 'Igraine pregnant with Arthur by a fatal treachery, of the counterfeit face and arms of Gorlöis, Merlin's wizardry'.

Milton abandoned the project when he began collecting materials for a prose *History of Britain*, which he would never complete. He even doubted the authenticity of Arthur and sneered at the monks and Welsh historians, who had believed songs and romances about the British king rather than the truth. 'He who can accept of legends for a good story may quickly swell a volume with trash.' His reading for these projects went into his stark and ironic *Samson Agonistes*, when his growing blindness was clarifying his inner vision. And the quest for the Grail was transmuted in *Paradise Lost* into the pride of Satan fallen from heaven for daring to challenge God rather than seek his grace. No longer for Milton's muse:

> Wars, hitherto the only argument
> Heroic deem'd; chief mastery to dissect,
> With long and tedious havoc, fabled knights,
> In battles feign'd; the better fortitude
> Of patience and heroic martyrdom
> Unsung; or to describe races and games,
> Or tilting furniture, emblazon'd shields,
> Impresses quaint, caparisons and steeds,
> Bases and tinsel trappings, gorgeous knights
> At joust and tournament; then marshall'd feast
> Served up in hall with sewers and seneschals:
> The skill of artifice or office mean,
> Not that which justly gives heroic name
> To person or to poem.

Because of the Puritan success in the Civil War, Milton even turned against the pilgrims of the Middle Ages, searching for their Heavenly City. They lived in a Paradise of Fools, a Limbo of Vanities, all the hermits and the white, black and grey friars:

> Here Pilgrims roam, that stray'd so far to seek
> In Golgotha Him dead, who lives in Heav'n;
> And they who to be sure of Paradise

> Dying put on the weeds of Dominic,
> Or in Franciscan think to pass disguis'd . . .
> Cowls, Hoods and Habits with their wearers toss'd
> And flutter'd into rags, then relics, Beads,
> Indulgences, Dispenses, Pardons, Bulls,
> The sport of winds. . . .

For Milton, the quest for the Grail was both individual and interior. Turning to his own soul, by his own acts, the pilgrim should travel towards the divine. The public performances of the past, the ritual journeys to Jerusalem, Rome, Vézelay and Compostela, these were the pageants of yesteryear. Now spiritual analysis should provide the clues to the ultimate experience of God. Public shows of faith were worth little. The rigorous examination of one's blind self might point the prickly path forward from one's pride and disobedience to divine will.

This was a reformed faith, but also the dawn of the Age of Reason, when pilgrimages and legends of Arthur and the Grail would be discounted. Few would take the way forward of a Milton or a Bunyan, who sought the truth of the Word of God in verses or parables. As the Apology to *The Pilgrim's Progress* declared:

> Were not God's laws,
> His Gospel laws, in olden time held forth
> By types, shadows, and metaphors? Yet loth
> Will any sober man be to find fault
> With them, lest he be found for to assault
> The highest wisdom. No, he rather stoops,
> And seeks to find out by what pins and loops,
> By calves and sheep, by heifer and by rams,
> By birds and herbs, and by the blood of lambs,
> God speaketh to him; and happy is he
> That finds the light and grace that in them be.

NINETEEN

DESTRUCTION AND
IMPERIAL GRACE

And did the Countenance Divine
Shine forth upon our clouded hills?
And was Jerusalem builded here
Among these dark Satanic Mills?

William Blake, 'Jerusalem', 1804

The building of Pandaemonium, the high Capital of Satan, was a perversion of the Grail. In *Paradise Lost*, the fallen angels no longer sought the grace of God; they mined, forged and moulded base materials in the smithies of hell. Unlike the alchemists, who sought materially and spiritually to transmute lead into gold, Milton's devils debased the Holy Spirit into minerals.

> Mammon led them on,
> Mammon, the least erected Spirit that fell
> From Heaven, for even in Heaven his looks and
> thoughts
> Were always downward bent, admiring more
> The riches of Heaven's pavement, trodden gold,
> Than aught divine or holy else enjoyed
> In vision beatific: by him first
> Men also and by his suggestion taught,
> Ransacked the Centre, and with impious hands
> Rifled the bowels of their mother Earth
> For treasures better hid.

The Industrial Revolution, not the age of chivalry, brought Britain to greatness and empire. Swathes of the peaks, saddles and valleys of the north of England were reduced in the eyes of their visitors to scenes that Dante had viewed in his *Inferno*. The Swan of Lichfield, the poet Anna Seward, lamented that her local Eden was turned from a green idyll into a black hell:

> O, violated COLEBROOK! . . . Their pondr'ous
> engines clang
> Through thy coy dales; while red the countless fires
> With umber'd flames, bicker on all thy hills,
> Darken'ing the summer's sun with columns large
> Of thick, sulphureous smoke, which spread, like palls
> That screen the dead, upon the sylvan robe
> Of thy aspiring rocks; pollute thy dales,
> And stain thy glassy waters.

To travellers, this damaged region was also the forge of a new economy. The full purse or the new job was the goal, no longer the search for the divine or the riches of nature. Riding from Birmingham to Wolverhampton, a distance of 13 miles, John Britton found vats of molten metal rather than cornucopias.

> The country was curious and amusing; though not very pleasing to eyes, ears, or taste; for part of it seemed a sort of pandaemonium on earth – a region of smoke and fire filling the whole area between earth and heaven; amongst which certain figures of human shape – if shape they had – were seen occasionally to glide from one cauldron of curling flame to another. . . . The surface of the earth is covered and loaded with its own entrails, which afford employment and livelihood for thousands of the human race.

The same impression was given to the engineer James Nasmyth, who 'lingered among the blast furnaces, seeing the flood of molten iron run out from time to time. . . . The workmen within seemed to be running about amidst the flames or in a pandaemonium; while around and outside the horizon was a glowing belt of fire, making even the stars look pale and feeble.'

In the works of Joseph Wright of Derby, the best of the industrial painters of the age, can be seen the transformation of a concept of a holy vessel of birth and regeneration, bounty and spirit, into a crucible of gain. In his *The Blacksmith's Shop* of 1771, the figures of the group bend over a fiery bucket, while the smith plunges his ladle into the molten iron, and shadows all around menace their endeavours. Men stoop over the entrance to *An Iron Forge*, as if following the inscription over Dante's *Inferno*: 'Leave all hope, ye that enter here'. Grouped as in a Holy Family, children watch in wonder, as a scientific experiment suffocates a bird in the glass cylinder of an air pump.

A romantic reaction from the Age of Reason and profit would lead to a revival of the cult of the Grail. At the end of the 18th century, the Economic Man of Adam Smith seemed to have extinguished any champion of the Round Table. As the poet Samuel Taylor Coleridge declared in his despair: 'In a few years we shall either be governed by an aristocracy, or, what is still more likely, by a contemptible democratical oligarchy of glib economists, compared to which the worst form of aristocracy would be a blessing.'

The restoration of the Grail would be achieved in spite of Economic Man through a new interest in medieval studies; also through Scottish and German Romanticism, and the coronation of a nostalgic British king, although his nature was rather far from that of Arthur. Macpherson's three epics, translated from fictional Gaelic poetry in *Ossian*, were widely popular; and before his suicide, Chesterton fabricated verses from earlier times. A vogue was beginning again for bardic poems and Gothic romances, as a refuge from the new age of machines. Sir Walter Scott became its advocate and its apologist across the Western world; but its ironic gravedigger was Thomas Love Peacock, in his novel *The Misfortunes of Elphin*. If the Lemuel Gulliver of Swift and Defoe's ultimate survivor Robinson Crusoe had put to rest any transcendental notions such as finding divine cups or extracting sunbeams from cucumbers, Prince Elphin and the bard Taliesin in Peacock's mocking romance put paid to any Arthurian visions.

The first of many poems in *The Misfortunes of Elphin* was called 'The Circling of the Mead Horns' and was taken from an ancient Welsh poem about a Prince Owain, feasting after his victory. For Peacock, the ceremony was farce, merely a prelude to the Lord Seithenyn drinking everybody under the table from his personal golden goblet, while the bard sang:

> Fill the blue horn, the blue buffalo horn:
> Natural is mead in the buffalo horn:
> As the cuckoo in spring, as the lark in the morn,
> So natural is mead in the buffalo horn.

Although deriding the legends, Peacock had read his Welsh history. He stated that the religion of King Arthur's time was Christianity, grafted on to Druidism. He knew of the antagonism of the Celtic clergy to Rome, for they had been converted from Ireland with its Greek rite. His hero Taliesin 'had been with the cherubim at the fall of Lucifer, in Paradise at the fall of man, and with Alexander at the fall of Babylon', the Matter of many of the medieval romances. But for Peacock, 'names are changed more readily than doctrines, and doctrines more readily than ceremonies'.

He was hardly a historian of King Arthur, whom Taliesin went to meet at Caerleon. On the way, the magic minstrel was made drunk again by Seithenyn with the memorable phrase about his drinking cup: 'Horn is well; silver is better; gold is best.' At Arthur's court, however, the Druids were still in charge of the ancient feast called Yule:

> The Druids, at this festival, made, in a capacious cauldron, a mystical brewage of carefully selected ingredients, full of occult virtues, which they kept

from the profane, and which was typical of the new year and of the transmigration of the soul. The profane, in humble imitation, brewed a bowl of spiced ale, or wine, throwing therein roasted crabs; the hissing of which, as they plunged, piping hot, into the liquor, was heard with much unction at midwinter, as typical of the conjunct benignant influences of fire and strong drink. The Saxons called this the Wassail-bowl . . . King Arthur kept his Christmas so merrily that the memory of it passed into a proverb: 'As merry as Christmas in Caerleon'.

So Peacock reduced the Quest for the Grail into a Nordic saturnalia. Avalon, the island of apples afterwards called Glastonbury, was made into a castle of the church militant under King Melvas, the Scourge of the Pelagians, the original British heretics. He had stolen Arthur's wife, but was persuaded to restore the Queen without a fight. The novel ended in a bardic contest rather than a battle or a joust, with Merlin chanting about his apple trees, while Taliesin sang a lay derived from the recent *Mabinogion*, the translations of ancient Welsh literature by Lady Charlotte Guest. This poem, 'The Cauldron of Ceridwen', was named after one of the six legendary Welsh Grails. Taliesin asserted that it had given birth to him, after his mother had made an extraordinary brew:

> She placed the gifted plants to steep
> Within the magic cauldron deep,
> Where they a year and day must boil,
> Till three drops crown the matron's toil.

These were not the three drops of Holy Blood on the Spear of Vengeance, which could heal and regenerate. But they did enable the birth of Taliesin, by his account, in place of his mother's misshapen child. And he was protected from all harm by Ceridwen, who also gave him the gift of prophecy:

> She has for me Time's veil withdrawn:
> The images of things long gone,
> The shadows of the coming days,
> Are present to my visioned gaze.

The truth of Taliesin's song about his coming from the magic cauldron of Wales was not authenticated by Peacock, who washed his hands of his own and ancient inventions. Certainly, Taliesin 'told this story to his contemporaries, and none of them contradicted it. It may, therefore, be presumed that they believed it; as any one who pleases is most heartily welcome to do now.'

The Protestant Grail had already been resurrected by an enigmatic theologian in Tübingen, Johann Valentin Andreae, the probable author of three strange works published in the second decade of the 17th century. The first was the *Fama Fraternitatis . . . The Declaration of the Worthy Order of the Rosy Cross*; the second was the *Confessio Fraternitatis*; and the third, written in German and not Latin, was *Die Chymische Hochzeit . . . The Chemical Wedding of Christian Rosenkreuz*. Borrowing from *Parzival*, Paracelsus, the German mystics and alchemists, the visions of Meister Eckhart and *De Occulta Philosophia* by Heinrich Cornelius Agrippa, the author of these three works claimed that a secret Order of the Rosy Cross had been founded in the 14th century by Christian Rosenkreuz, who had acquired Gnostic wisdom in the Far East. The brothers of the Order had healing powers and possessed the Philosopher's Stone and the elixir of life. Christian Rosenkreuz had also visited a Grail Castle of wonder, where he

The alchemical Grails of the heavens and the earth meet in holy fire in the vision of Maria Prophetissa. *(Maier, Symbola aureae mensae, 1617)*

An alchemical experiment by the Rosicrucian Robert Fludd, *Medicina Catholica*, vol. II, 1629–31.

had witnessed many of the secrets of *Parzival* in an occult setting. The symbolism of the Rosy Cross, the associations of the cult of the Virgin Mary and the Magdalene and the Rose with those of the Passion of Christ, restored the esoteric beliefs of the Knights Templars and the Teutonic Knights. These guardians of the Grail, as Wolfram von Eschenbach had called them, were now revived.

The Teutonic Knights were still in existence. In 1683 they provided a whole regiment to defend Vienna against Muslim assault, and they resisted a later attack on Hungary. Yet they were soon reduced to a core of twenty nobles, who were officers in the German army; these men would play important roles in the Napoleonic Wars. In the

18th century, however, Charles Gotthelf, Baron von Hund and Alten-grotkare, used his Jacobite connections to resurrect the German Order of the Knights Templars. He claimed that he was anointed in Paris by the Young Pretender, Prince Charles Edward Stuart, who was the Sovereign Grand Master of the original refugee Order in Scotland.

By the time of his death, Baron von Hund had recruited twelve reigning German princes to replace the twelve Peers of Charlemagne. These included the Landgraf of Hesse-Darmstadt, the Markgraf of Brandenburg, and the Duke of Brunswick and his three sons. One of these revived Templars, Friedrich Ludwig Werner, produced a poem on the old military order in Cyprus, which defined another version of the Grail:

That which was sought, but never found,
But kept hidden from the world,
So that the world did not burn its fingers . . .
The key that opens the future's iron door,
And all the hidden caverns of the past,
And nature's most occult laboratory.

An old account of the rites and secrets of the Rosicrucians led to a second crucial finding of the most ancient Grail symbol in England, even more illuminating than the relief in the crypt of the tower at Charroux. The cult of the Black Virgin in Europe reached England in the shape of seven black baptismal fonts. The most Gnostic of these is in Winchester Cathedral. Carved about 1150 from black limestone at Tournai in Flanders, the font dates from the middle period of the Kingdom of Jerusalem. After the Second Crusade, Thierry of Alsace, Count of Flanders, had created the Chapel of the Holy Blood at Bruges, not too far from Tournai, while his son and successor Philip had become the last patron of Chrétien de Troyes; he claimed that his first Grail romance, *Perceval*, derived from a book given to him by Count Philip, who was also a crusader and a scholar of Eastern thought. The Winchester font was created from the mysticism of the Levant and the cult of the Holy Blood, which so influenced the maker of the Grail in literature in that same period in Flanders.

On two sides of the black cube was carved the life of St Nicholas. One scene of the blessed man reviving three drowned children also depicted the first North Sea boat with a rudder. The other two façades set out pairs of doves, preening under their wings or picking at a bunch of grapes; also a salamander, emblematic of fire, recalling in the Rosicrucian interpretation a passage from St Matthew's Gospel: 'He shall baptise you with the Holy Ghost and with fire.'

The revelation was the sight of the relief on two of the four corners of the top of the baptismal vessel. On each, as at Charroux, twin doves could be seen drinking from a vase, but now a fiery ragged crucifix rose out of this Grail, with a sun boss in the middle of the flames. These were like the visions of the pure Arthurian knights in the Castle of the Fisher King. The dark colour of the font recalled the sacred meteorite in the Ka'aba at Mecca, while both the dove and the black stone were the Grail symbols in *Parzival*. This mystic cross of fire resembled the flames of the Holy

A fiery cross rises from the Grail on the black font, *c.* 1150, in Winchester Cathedral. Two doves of the Holy Spirit drink from the sacred vessel.

Hermes Trismegistus. (*Senior,* De chemia, *in* Mangetus Bibliotheca chemica curiosa, *1702*)

and white roses were two confirmations of their quest for the Philosopher's Stone, the elixir of life, the perpetual lamp, and the talisman of healing. They interpreted the Arthurian circle as the place where the twenty-six 'Mystic Guards of the Holy Grail' might sit, backed by the Saints in a fusion of the natural and the supernatural, of alchemy and legend and religion, in a common search for the universal.

Rather as the original Templars had been destroyed as a dangerous secret society within the body politic, so the Rosicrucians, the revived military Orders and other Masonic bodies were considered to be threats to the nation state across most of Europe after the French Revolution. Those against Freemasonry saw in the revival of the Templars a long conspiracy that ran forward from the heretic Gnostics through the Essenes, the Assassins and the Cathars to modern times, an enduring subversion against pope and king, a form of revolutionary anarchism.

Various orders of the Rosy Cross were also developed in France, blending cabbalistic and hermetic symbolism with mystic references to the resurrection of the Saviour and His Mother. There were Rosicrucian Societies in Scotland and in England, which culminated in the hermetic Order of the Golden Dawn. With a Chief Adept adopted from the Sufis and the Cathar *perfecti*, the aspirants were given an address that mixed the processes of alchemy with the Passion:

> Buried with that light in a mystical death, rising again in a mystical resurrection, cleansed and purified through Him our Master, O Brother of the Cross and the Rose. Like Him, O Adepts of all ages, have ye toiled. Like Him have ye suffered tribulation, Poverty, torture and death have ye passed through. They have been but their purification of Gold.
>
> In the alembic of thine heart, through the athanor of affliction, seek thou the true stone of the Wise.

Spirit which descended on the disciples at Pentecost, the feast when the Grail occasionally appeared at Camelot in the romances.

Also recognised by the Rosicrucians for its cosmic significance was the Round Table of King Arthur, which is still mounted on the wall of the Great Hall of Winchester Castle. This late-medieval painted circle was influenced by alchemy and the zodiac, as were many of the porticos of Creation over the entrance to French Gothic cathedrals. It was divided into twelve green and twelve white sections, with two for the Siege Perilous. King Arthur was shown ruling from his throne over the mystic red rose – its centre the five petals of the white rose of the Virgin Mary containing a yellow sun. For the Rosicrucians, the black font with its fiery cross and the Round Table with its central red

The true stone of the wise was historically the Philosopher's Stone and the German romantic Grail of bounty and healing. In one of his novels, *The Talisman*, Sir Walter Scott became the heir of Wolfram von Eschenbach. With the scene set in Syria during the Third Crusade, the magic stone was used by Saladin to cure his wounded opponent King Richard the Lionheart, before he sent it as a wedding present to the Prince Royal of Scotland, who, in turn, bequeathed it to Sir Simon of the Lee. This gave a provenance to a known healing stone in the shape of a heart set in a groat and called the Lee Penny.

Walter Scott also involved a 'most holy elixir' of life in the cures of his talisman, which was a meteorite 'composed under certain aspects of the heavens, when the Divine Intelligences are most propitious'. Only to be used by a sage and hermit, the stone was also connected with the Templars. For Saladin worked its powers on the wounded traitor Conrade, Marquis of Montserrat, who was then stabbed and killed by the Grand Master of the Templars, the guardians of the Grail. To some commentators, this meteorite revived the legends of the *shamir*, the Stone of Solomon, and the Gnostic and Zoroastrian Gohar, which rested in its vessel 'like the pearl of the host in the chalice of blood, the globe of the earth in the world-ocean'.

In *Ivanhoe*, his other medieval romance of that period, Scott showed the same appreciation of the Jews as of the Muslims. His villains as well as his heroes were Christians. At her trial, Rebecca was sentenced to death for her medical powers; also for

Anthropos as *anima mundi*, containing the four elements and characterised by the number 10, which represents perfection (1+2+3+4). *(Albertus Magnus, Philosophia naturalis, 1650)*

the employment of drugs, amulets and cabbalistic charms. Ambiguous towards the Templars, Scott made their Grand Master a bigot at Rebecca's trial, condemning her as if she were a second Witch of Endor. Yet her would-be champion was another Templar, Brian de Bois-Guilbert, ordered by his Grand Master to fight against her final champion Ivanhoe. Brian became the victim of his internal conflicts and lost to his foe.

Alchemists at work. *(Mutus liber, 1702)*

However much Scott appreciated the medieval romances of knighthood, he knew their time was long gone. Although he had individually resurrected the feudal, he did not expect it still to rule. Even his paragon, Richard the First, appeared out of date in the 13th century. 'In the lion-hearted king,' Scott declared, 'the brilliant, but useless character, of a knight of romance, was in a great measure realised and revived; and the personal glory which he acquired by his own deeds of arms, was far more dear to his excited imagination; than that which a course of policy and wisdom would have spread around his government.'

Scott had himself been influenced by the bardic writers of Italy and Spain: Dante, Tasso, Ariosto and Cervantes. Explaining the plot of *The Heart of Mid-Lothian*, he wrote that he had followed the digressive *Orlando Furioso*, interleaving the adventures of his people until they met one another again; it was a better method than dropping stitches. He took over characters, acknowledging that his solitary in *The Talisman* was modelled on Tasso's Peter the Hermit. And yet only in his earlier poetry had he taken up the Arthurian Matter of Britain.

Trying to rival Byron's *Childe Harold*, Scott used a modern soldier Arthur to tell stories of a medieval border knight, Sir Roland, and of King Arthur, both of whom were taken to an enchanted castle of St John, full of maidens. The King was seduced for a summer in order to make the sorceress Guendolen pregnant. And his escape rivalled the emblem on the Winchester font, as it was through a cup of liquid fire, offered to him by necromancy rather than the Holy Spirit. Guendolen held up a 'draught which Genii love':

> The courteous Monarch bent him low,
> And, stooping down from saddlebow,
> Lifted the cup, in act to drink,
> A drop escaped the goblet's brink –
> Intense as liquid fire from hell,
> Upon the charger's neck it fell.
> Screaming with agony and fright,
> He bolted twenty feet upright –
> – The peasant still can show the dint,

> – Where his hoof lighted on the flint. –
> From Arthur's hand the goblet flew,
> Scattering a shower of fiery dew,
> That burn'd and blighted where it fell!

The goblet of hellfire was more a Cauldron of Death than a Cup of Life, worse than the golden cup held up by Excess that Guyon broke to pieces in *The Faerie Queene*. Although Scott continued the traditional story of Arthur, ending in the disaster at Camlann, he was reducing the Grail Quest to Nordic folklore and magic tales. The Protestant in him rebelled from the idea of a vessel of divine grace, which to him was more of a superstition than a heavenly vision. His Knights of the Round Table fought their battles and endured their trials for the love of Guendolen's daughter Gyneth and her wealth, not for any revelation of God.

A noble lord, the Earl of Eglington, was so inspired by the novels of Sir Walter Scott and so disgusted by Victorian commerce that in 1838 he held an Arthurian tournament at his Ayrshire castle. There the Knights of the Red Lion jousted in full medieval armour against the Knights of the Burning Tower and of the White Rose, while Eglington himself wore golden mail. Torrential rain and mud spoiled the presentation of the prizes by the Queen of Beauty and her maids of honour, and the tourney was almost washed out. Yet it fired a national interest in medieval history with its creeds and codes. As one critic, Lycion, pointed out, even if the proceedings in Scotland were a sham, the real point about the revival of chivalry was an attitude to life, not a charade in fancy dress.

The popular poet Alfred Tennyson, later ennobled himself, followed the tournament with long poems on Merlin and Lancelot, Percivale and Galahad, and King Arthur and 'The Holy Grail'. In that poem, the monk Ambrosius met the wandering knight Sir Percivale in a Victorian version of the character invented by Chrétien de Troyes. The reason for his solitary quest was this:

> The sweet vision of the Holy Grail
> Drove me from all vainglories, rivalries,
> And earthly heats that spring and sparkle out

Among us in the jousts, while women watch
Who wins, who falls; and waste the spiritual strength
Within us, better offer'd up to Heaven.

The monk asked whether the Grail was a phantom of a cup that came and went. But Percivale identified it as a material thing, the cup from which 'Our Lord drank at the last sad supper with his own'. Joseph of Arimathea had brought it to Glastonbury, where the winter thorn tree blossomed at Christmas. Abiding there for a while, it was taken back to heaven because of evil times. Through fasting and prayer, the sister of Percivale saw 'the Holy Thing' again in a vision, and spoke of it:

And down the long beam stole the Holy Grail,
Rose-red with beatings in it, as if alive,
Till all the white walls of my cell were dyed
With rosy colours leaping on the wall;
And then the music faded, and the Grail
Past, and the beam decay'd, and from the walls,
The rosy quiverings died into the night.

When Galahad, perhaps the son of Lancelot, heard of this vision at Arthur's court, he was transfigured. He wore a sword-belt with the device of the crimson Grail embroidered with a silver ray made from the long yellow hair of Percivale's sister. 'He believed in her belief. Then came a year of miracle.' Galahad sat and survived in Merlin's chair of serpents, the Siege Perilous, which had swallowed up its wizard creator. This act of daring produced the collective vision of the Grail to all the Knights of the Round Table.

And in the blast there smote along the hall
A beam of light seven times more clear than day;
And down the long beam stole the Holy Grail
All over cover'd with a luminous cloud,
And none might see who bare it, and it past.

Many of the knights then swore to leave the sacred mount of soaring Camelot to seek the blessed cup, wherever it had gone from them. King Arthur hated their going, and declared that the Grail hidden within its shining fog was 'a sign to maim this Order which I made'. His knights had won his twelve great battles. How could he fight the forces of evil without them? Meeting mirages and nightmares, Percivale rode out alone. All turned to dust before him, so he thought that if he touched the Grail, it would also crumble into dust. A hermit gave him the sacrament, and Galahad appeared in silver armour, seeing what his fellow knights could not see:

Saw ye no more? I, Galahad, saw the Grail,
The Holy Grail, descend upon the shrine:
I saw the fiery face as of a child
That smote itself into the bread, and went,
And hither am I come; and never yet
Hath what thy sister taught me first to see,
This Holy Thing, fail'd from my side, nor come
Cover'd but moving with me night and day,
Fainter by day, but always in the night
Blood-red, and sliding down the blacken'd marsh
Blood-red, and on the naked mountain top
Blood-red, and in the sleeping mere below
Blood-red. And in the strength of this I rode,
Shattering all evil customs everywhere.

Alfred Tennyson would become the Poet Laureate of the Victorian empire. He was repeating for his expanding nation what Geoffrey of Monmouth had done for the Norman kings and Malory for the Tudor rulers: the equation of seeking dominions overseas with a divine mission. In his quest for the Grail, Galahad was presented as the victor over pagan hordes and realms. He would be crowned finally in a spiritual city, which, like that of St Augustine, would also be represented on earth – in the case of Tennyson by the port city of London. There Queen Victoria, uniquely in Europe, played the ancient role of Melchizedek in Israel; she was the future Empress of India as well as the Queen of Britain; also the religious ruler of the Church of England.

The poem concluded Tennyson's revival of the responsibilities of the global Grail kingdom. Sir Percivale saw Galahad 'far on the great sea in silver-shining armour stormy-clear'. The Holy Vessel hung over his head, shrouded in white

Left: Cover of *The Young Knights of the Empire*, by Robert Baden-Powell.

Right and below: A song *(above)* and a postcard *(below)* from the First World War.

samite or a shining cloud. On a winged boat, Galahad passed to the spiritual city of the Book of Revelation, its spires and gateways made of one great pearl, as the Gohar in the blood-red cosmos. The Grail hung above the knight's head 'redder than any rose', then fell into the floods of heaven, never more to be seen by human eyes. Returning to Camelot, Percivale asked the other questing knights if they had viewed the Grail. Only Lancelot declared that in his insanity he had seen it, fainting in a furnace blast of heat, an ecstatic vision:

> All pall'd in crimson samite, and around
> Great angels, awful shapes, and wings and eyes.
> And but for all my madness and my sin,
> And then my swooning, I had sworn I saw
> That which I saw: but what I saw was veil'd
> And cover'd; and this Quest was not for me.

That was exactly what the bitter King Arthur declared when his surviving knights returned to the misty spires of Camelot. He had not gone on the quest, for he had to guard what he ruled. He could not leave the throne of power, nor indeed should they who had only seen dreams, except for Galahad, now the transfigured ruler of the Grail kingdom of the Otherworld. 'Let visions of the night or of the day,' Arthur said, 'come as they will.' These might be induced by the self or by God. The knights had merely seen what they had seen. Their duty was to defend with him the realms that they had won.

In a sense, Tennyson treated the Quest for the Grail as mass hysteria among the Knights of the Round Table. Only Percivale saw the Holy Vessel and believed he had achieved a sort of revelation. The more important mission and duties suggested by the myth were the service of the British

A picture by Aubrey Beardsley to illustrate Malory's *Morte D'Arthur*, 1485.

Empire. In 1851, at the Great Exhibition, the new technology built the supreme Grail Castle of the industrial age. This Crystal Palace included the machines, cylinders and metal vats that produced the new riches and bounty; but within its walls of iron and glass, trees grew and nature survived among the clanging of the engines. So inspiring was this extraordinary creation that Britain's temporary dominance in the manufacture of goods, rather than the pursuit of the good, was confirmed. The Poet Laureate wrote an ode to be sung at the opening ceremony, emphasising the benefits of the Crystal Palace as a divine cornucopia:

> Uplift a thousand voices full and sweet
>   In this wide hall with earth's invention stored,
>   And praise the invisible universal Lord,
> Who lets once more in peace the nations meet,
>   Where Science, Art, and Labour have outpour'd
> Their myriad horns of plenty at our feet.

Such exhortations on Britain's imperial mission did not endear the Poet Laureate to all of his

friends. The translator of oriental mysticism to the West, the poet Edward Fitzgerald, in his *Omar Khayyám*, hardly enjoyed the *Idylls of the King*, which he bought at Lowestoft. In a letter he declared that Tennyson had gone even further than him into the empyrean:

> The whole myth of Arthur's Round Table Dynasty in Britain presents itself before me with a sort of cloudy, Stonehenge grandeur. I am not sure if the old knights' adventures do not tell upon me better, touched in some lyrical way (like your own 'Lady of Shalott'), than when elaborated into epic form. I never could care for Spenser, Tasso, or even Ariosto, whose epic has a ballad ring about it. But then I never could care much for the old prose romances much either, except Don Quixote. So, as this was always the case with me, I suppose my brain is wanting in this bit of its dissected map.
>
> Anyhow, Alfred, while I feel how pure, noble and holy your work is, and whole phrases, lines and sentences of it will abide with me, and I am sure with men after me . . . I was got back to the substantial rough-spun Nature I knew; and the old brute, invented by you with the solemn humour of Humanity . . . became a more pathetic phenomenon than the knights who revisit the world in your other verse.

Lady Charlotte Guest, the young wife of the self-made master of the Dowlais Ironworks in South Wales, had translated the Celtic legends of King Arthur in the *Mabinogion*. These helped to spread the cult of the resurrected myths into architecture and art. A Gothic revival influenced the style of the reconstructed House of Commons and many cathedral restorations – such as at Ely – while the Pre-Raphaelite painters depicted lush romantic versions of the adventures of the Knights of the Round Table, not seen since the medieval illuminations to the *Roman de la rose*. The artist Edward Burne-Jones wrote to a friend about founding a brotherhood. He should learn

Tennyson's poem on Sir Galahad by heart: 'He is to be the patron of our Order.'

In many sumptuous and sexually disturbing pictures, Burne-Jones, Dante Gabriel Rossetti and William Morris would re-create the loves of Lancelot for Guinevere and Tristram for Iseult. Rossetti dwelt on the Holy Grail as well as on the adulterous lovers, illustrating, for an edition of Tennyson's poems of 1859, 'Sir Galahad at the Ruined Chapel' drinking holy water from a sacred horn cup. Burne-Jones even attended a performance of Wagner's *Parsifal* in the Albert Hall, and was gratified that the German composer had struck the 'Celtic vein' in the Grail legends, as he was trying to do in his art.

The cult of imagery would end at the turn of the century with the perversity of Aubrey Beardsley. His illustrations of Malory's ever-popular *Morte D'Arthur* turned even 'The achieving of the Sangreal' into an ambiguous rite, with Galahad and Perceval as two willowy figures at worship before a hermaphrodite of a winged angel, carrying a spiky vase and veil above the open five petals of the Virgin's rose, a trinity of shoots growing from its stamen.

Queen Victoria even discerned an Arthurian figure in her Prime Minister, Benjamin Disraeli. 'He is full of poetry, romance and chivalry,' she wrote to her daughter. 'When he knelt down to kiss my hand which he took in both of his – he said: "In loving loyalty and faith".' He called Her Majesty 'the Faery' after Spenser's praise of Gloriana and Queen Elizabeth in his *Faerie Queene*. She certainly revelled in her role as the *belle dame* and ideal of Christian civilisation across the globe.

Victoria created knights in her service across her dominions; the numbers of those dubbed with the honour increased sixfold in her reign to some 2,000 baronets. The suppressors of the Indian Mutiny were seen as the paladins and Rolands of their time. 'What knight of the Round Table', asked the historian J.A. Froude, 'beat Havelock and

Sir John Lawrence?' Tennyson, after all, ended the twelve books of his *Idylls of the King* with an ode to his Queen and her faithful subjects across a quarter of the land mass of the earth.

> O loyal to the royal in thyself,
> And loyal to thy land, as this to thee . . .
> Thee and thy Prince! The loyal to their crown
> Are loyal to their own far sons, who love
> Our ocean-empire with her boundless homes
> For ever-broadening England, and her throne
> Is our vast Orient, and one isle
> That knows not her own greatness.

The *Idylls of the King* had concluded after the battle with Mordred, the loss of the realm of Lyonesse and the passing of Arthur to Avalon. Such an end for the Victorian empire was not the prediction of its Poet Laureate, although he did identify his sovereign with her supposed everlasting ancestor:

> He passed to be King among the dead,
> But after healing of his grievous wound
> He comes again.

An engraving of 'Sir Galahad at the Ruined Chapel' by Dante Gabriel Rossetti to illustrate Moxon's *Tennyson*, 1859.

MOTHER O' MINE.   No.

Let the bugles sound the truce of God
To the whole world for ever. — *Summer*

Above and opposite: First World War postcards of knights and angels.

The chivalry and code of honour of those who would be Christian gentlemen and dedicate their lives in the imperial service created a series of petty Camelots in the clubs and officers' messes of Britain, its dominions, its colonies and its garrisons. Belonging to the Masons was an important element in these brotherhoods of service; but military pride was almost more demanding. In his strange poem of 1875, John Addington Symonds, the historian of Renaissance Italy, linked the various Victorian strands of a certain male communion, as if in an Order of the Grail:

O nobler peerage than thou ancient vaunt
Of Arthur or of Roland! Chivalry
Long sought, last found! Knight of the Holy Ghost!
Phalanx Immortal! True Freemasonry!

As Mark Girouard has pointed out in his illuminating book, *The Return to Camelot*, certain military and political leaders used the ancient myths to develop a cult of personality. The imperial and intellectual group named the 'Souls' referred to their leading member, who was to become Prime Minister, as 'King Arthur' Balfour.

Wolseley had his 'ring' in India; Kitchener had his 'cubs' in Egypt and the Sudan; Milner had his 'kindergarten' to help him with the reorganisation of the Transvaal after the Boer War; back in England the kindergarten developed into a closely knit group of imperialists known as the Round Table.

This return to feudal attitudes opposed the making of too much money. Duty was the clarion

call, to be carried out by noble and muscular Christians who modelled themselves on Lancelot, Perceval and Galahad. Even contemporary Americans were not immune to this contagion of antique idealism. Ralph Waldo Emerson wrote four Merlin poems: in one of them, the Harp praised the Wizard who played it:

> But my minstrel knows and tells
> The counsel of the gods,
> Knows of the Holy Book the spells,
> Knows the law of Night and Day
> And the heart of girl and boy,
> The tragic and the gay,
> And what is writ on Table Round
> Of Arthur and his peers.

Meanwhile, the Anglophile Edwin Austen Abbey even played cricket and painted large canvases of the *Quest for the San Graal* for the Boston Public Library. And Camelot would become the name given to the White House in Washington during the presidency of John Fitzgerald Kennedy, although its source would not spring from Tennyson's poems, but from the lyrics of an American musical, as if the troubadours of the Grail had mistakenly crossed the Atlantic Ocean.

Curiously enough, a Congregational minister from Vermont, William Byron Forbush, was the chief influence on Robert Baden-Powell when he formed the Boy Scouts movement; that extraordinary child training scheme would even be feared by the Nazis as a precedent and rival to their Hitler Youth. The American Knights of King Arthur were guided by adult Merlins at Castles and Round Tables. Their sports were changed into quests; their goals were chivalry, courtesy and Christian daring. After his experiences in the Boer War, when he became the hero of the siege of Mafeking, Baden-Powell combined his experiences as a bush reconnaissance expert with the legends of the Grail. The Boy Scouts were brought up between the camp fire and Camelot on a 'Knight's Code' with nine rules, said to date from the reign of King Arthur. These involved self-discipline, honour and helping women and children in distress. The ideal was to bring up Young Knights of the Empire on the model of St George of England and the Round Table.

The First World War removed those trainees out of imperial service and on to the Western Front. To fight there as an officer meant probable death, mutilation or a nasty injury. There was only one cavalry charge by the British, which ended as disastrously as the Charge of the Light Brigade in the Crimea. The slaughter was the massacre of a class that expected to rule. Tennyson had forecast this grand finale of chivalry, when he put this lament into the mouth of the dying King Arthur after his final battle:

> Such a sleep
> They sleep – the men I loved. I think that we
> Shall never more, at any future time,
> Delight our souls with talk of knightly deeds,
> Walking about the gardens and the halls
> Of Camelot, as in the days that were,
> I perish by this people which I made.

TWENTY

ARIAS OF THE GRAIL

And in the middle stands a shining temple,
More valuable than any left on earth.
Inside it, a sacred wonder-working vessel,
Is guarded as the holiest of most worth.
It was – so the purest of the pure
Might keep it safe – brought down by angels.
Once every year, a heavenly dove is sure
To fill it with more power in its walls.
Its name? The Grail. And peace and faith and love
On its close band of knights pour from above.

Richard Wagner, *Lohengrin*, 1845

wo sacred places in the Alps on the Swiss–German border particularly claimed to possess the Holy Blood: the ancient abbeys of Reichenau and Weingarten, now one of the larger baroque churches in Germany. The relic of the Body of Christ and a piece of the True Cross at Reichenau are said to have been given to Charlemagne by the diplomatic Islamic Prefect of Huesca in Spain, after the German emperor's incursion there. The Abbey Treasury also asserts that its split urn from the Near East and the Christian era is a vessel from Cana, in which water was turned into wine. It does not resemble any Greek *amphora* of the period, nor the simple pots of the miracle, as were shown on Archbishop Maximian's ivory throne of the 6th century in Ravenna. Its provenance is held to be a gift from an obscure knight of Charlemagne, while the Holy Blood at Weingarten is said to derive from St Longinus and his spear. Rediscovered twice at Mantua, it also contributed a sacred onyx vessel to Brunswick; there in Italy, indeed, the centurion saint had brought the Blood, which was split three ways in Germany after much argument.

The portion at Weingarten derived from a pious Count Baldwin the Fifth of Flanders in the 11th century. Thousands of Bavarians have appeared for hundreds of years at its procession in its precious reliquary. Further, an engraving and a tradition boast of a piece of earth soaked with his Blood from Calvary; also fragments of the cup of the Last Supper and the bowl of Joseph of Arimathea at the foot of the Cross. As Weingarten was destroyed in the 15th century, these are speculations. Neither the relics there nor those at Reichenau can compete with those of Charlemagne, most of which are now in Vienna or France, other than those still preserved at Aachen, along with a gold enamel and amethyst liturgical pitcher in the treasury of St Maurice Abbey in Switzerland. The history of the Grail in Germany remains the *Parzival* of Wolfram von Eschenbach; the Marienburg and the deeds of the Teutonic Knights; the castles of Ludwig the Second and the operas of Wagner. Hitler's exploitation of these written, sung and constructed legends would be a splendid aberration that would end as a desperate perversion.

Wolfram von Eschenbach had designed the story of Lohengrin to be a sequel to *Parzival*. In the last book of his romance, his hero was reunited with his wife and discovered that he had given her twin sons. Surrounded by his Templar Knights of the

Grail, he appointed one of his sons, Lohengrin, as his successor to be their king on the Mount of Salvation. As a young man, Lohengrin served the Grail as a true knight, and Wolfram was his prophet. He would arrive in the land of Brabant on a boat drawn by a swan, save the heiress Elsa from false accusation, marry her and have children. But in a contradiction to his father Parzival, who did not ask the question of the maimed Fisher King, Lohengrin would return home to become the Grail King. That was if Elsa did not break her word and demand to know his name. She did:

> And her question broke the spell,
> And drove him out unwilling, so shall the story tell.
> His friend the swan found him, a small boat its
>   offering.
> He sailed away and left his sword, his horn and ring.

This tale of the Swan Knight was again ascribed to Guiot de Provins, the minstrel, while the master, Chrétien de Troyes, was accused of not setting it down correctly. 'Thus from the land of Provence,'

Above: King Ludwig the Second's palace of Linderhof.

Below: This 11th-century carving on the exterior of the apse of the Church of Saint-Paul-les-Dax shows St Longinus piercing the side of Christ with his spear, while Joseph of Arimathea collects his blood in a Grail.

Opposite: Neuschwanstein, Bavaria.

The mechanism for lowering the Grail Table to fulfil the orders of King Ludwig the Second of Bavaria.

Wolfram insisted, 'the story was brought to Germany.' It would become a prodigal source, as would the other innovations in *Parzival*. The mysterious oriental Grail stone would be retained as the symbol of the Holy Vessel by the poets of the *Wartburgkrieg* – the inspiration for Richard Wagner's opera *Tannhäuser* – and of the full *Lohengrin* and the *Younger Titurel*. Not until the poet Novalis would the Grail be turned from stone to flower, while Wagner would see it as a cornucopia of excess as well as a Christian chalice.

As the pagan horn of plenty, the Grail was at its crudest in *Tannhäuser*, which was the weakest of Wagner's operas, not only in his concept of the Sacred Vessel, but in his characterisation of the wandering and satanic minstrel on his pilgrimage to Rome – certainly not as complex as his model Wolfram. In fact, Wagner did say that Tannhäuser was a human being, while Wolfram was a poet. The Grail was said to lie on the Hörselberg with Venus, the seductress of the passive Tannhäuser, who

declared, 'I boldly approach the fount of delight.' The Grail was thus the sexual drive of the Goddess of Love, the giver of sensual pleasures, and little more, although Wagner joked in the margins of his first draft of the libretto: 'Study the manuscript, otherwise you won't get to heaven.' At the rival Wartburg of the Landgrave Hermann, where the famous Contest of Song was staged, the heroine Elisabeth only represented spiritual love, although she saved Tannhäuser from the swords of his jealous rivals. This conflict of the flesh and the spirit turned the Grail into a kind of orgy of perversity, hardly a sacrament.

The tragedy of *Tannhäuser* was its effect on Wagner's patron, King Ludwig the Second of Bavaria. The Venusberg became his chief inspiration in the erection of his Grail Castles. Unlike most fantasists, Ludwig had the resources to make his dreams come true. Even a medieval knight who could read the Arthurian romances did not have such royal wealth or self-indulgence. So Ludwig could have his myths made fact, although the dreadful ostentation and bad taste of the 19th century in southern Germany turned these venerations of the fortresses of the Fisher King into gigantic containers for luxury and childishness, the results of the romantic effusions of a lonely boyhood.

The contemporary Bavarian Commission was correct in declaring Ludwig unfit to govern before he finished his last masterwork on the island at the Herrenchiemsee. There, as at Linderhof, he had to have a brute mechanism to lower his golden Grail Table down to the kitchen in order that it might come up with all the fancies of his desires. This iron contraption proved that even industrialisation had forced its way beneath his fairy realm, and Nibelungs of cogs and chains were mining for new riches. If Ludwig's suspicious end by drowning was no repetition of the Lady of the Lake drawing him down like Excalibur under the water, his extravagances still endure, more gilt and replete

The cupola of Venus at Linderhof.

than William Randolph Hearst's Xanadu or Disneyland in California and outside Paris. Curiously enough, Walt Disney would choose Ludwig's castle at Neuschwanstein, the New Stone of the Swan, as his model for the home of the Sleeping Beauty, the princess under the spell of animation.

If Wagner was to ennoble the myths of the Grail in his *Lohengrin* and *Parsifal*, Ludwig dressed up the legends so ornately that they ended in a treasury of vulgarity. The room of the Knight of the Swan in his childhood castle of Hohenschwangau, the living room at Neuschwanstein devoted to Lohengrin and the Grail, the golden shell-boat at Linderhof in which the King used to sit, drawn by a swan as was Lohengrin – how wilful and opulent they appear against the actual chapel of the Swan Knights at Ansbach, the home of the Hohenzollern dynasty. That military order was founded in 1440 by the Elector Frederick the Second of Brandenburg; eleven tombs of the real knights still survive in the rebuilt choir, austere in the style of the Margrave George the Pious, who spread Lutheranism all over the region.

Wolfram von Eschenbach himself, the creator of the original *Parzival*, was born ten miles away and was buried at the town named after him. Under the many-coloured church spire and by the old Commandery of the Teutonic Knights, now the Rathaus and the Alte Vogtei Inn, stands a statue to the poet and knight, donated by the Emperor Maximilian the Second. Four black swans surround its plinth, while Wolfram has his hand on his lyre with its eagle head; also his sword hilt. Dressed in armour, his helmet is crowned by a wreath of laurels. His honour and memory are well preserved in his birthplace, unlike in the gilded dreamlands of the later King of Bavaria.

Ludwig did not approve of Wagner's final conversion to a Christian Grail of redemption in his *Parsifal*, and so he did not attend its first performance. The hill of steps and terraces opposite the Linderhof palace was crowned by a cupola, under which a white marble Venus took a quiver of arrows from Cupid. Lower down, ranks of urns led to two nymphs pouring their pitchers into an everlasting fountain. To Ludwig, love and giving richly were the dominant symbols of the Wagnerian legends. The Herrenchiemsee with its separate Island of Women also stressed the final chaste reclusion of the King, as if he were a Knight of the Grail. There, in external statues, Venus held up an overflowing vase of plenty, while the huge golden royal bed and table were the luxury of delirium.

Having bankrupted his kingdom, Ludwig with his profligacy now helps to pay for the federal state. His fairy castles draw far more prying visitors than even the sick in the Middle Ages, who went to be healed by the Holy Blood and the broken cup of Christ at Weingarten Abbey. Although in his lifetime Ludwig did not appeal to the beggared people of Bavaria, his death has enriched them

mightily. For he was a prophet of the imagination of the masses, which coincided with his own. For a modern pilgrimage, the climb up the slope at Neuschwanstein still compares with a struggle up a Mount of Salvation. As Ludwig wrote to Wagner, 'The place is one of the most lovely that can be dreamed of. It is sacred and inaccessible.' Yet once the lifeless and spectacular kitsch paintings of Germany and Grail myths are reached, nobody can receive any sacred messages in such a bedlam of sightseers and babble of tongues.

Wagner had made dramatic the legend of the Grail at the end of his opera *Lohengrin*, after which he wrote no more music for five years other than some notes for the greatest of his German myths, the *Ring*. The villainess in the libretto, Ortrud, invoked unsuccessfully the pagan Nordic gods Wotan and Freya, but the perfect Swan Knight Lohengrin was so transcendent that his image was preferred by Ludwig the Second in his desire to be king of an Otherworld as well as of Bavaria. Wagner himself thought that he had met a real

Above: King Ludwig's Swanboat from the Venus grotto of Linderhof.

Opposite, top: Hall of Mirrors, Linderhof.

Opposite, bottom: King Ludwig's gardens, Linderhof.

Lohengrin, writing after his first meeting with the glorious young ruler that the encounter was a miracle, 'that precious reward of my genius . . . born for me out of the womb of a queen'. Ludwig replied in kind and with influence: 'Since the power is mine, I will use it to sweeten your life.' His nickname in the composer's circle would be Parsifal, although Wagner's wife Cosima thought that her husband's soul belonged forever to the King, rather than the other way round.

In the opera, indeed, Lohengrin's confrontation with reality led to the first tragedy: his return to his Grail kingdom and the death of Elsa of Brabant. Once his name was known, along with the

King Ludwig the Second in his Swanboat of the Grail in the Grotto of Venus at the Schloss Linderhof.

mundane details of his origins, he had to retreat to the spiritual world, whence he had come. While Tannhäuser saw in the Grail and the Venusberg the fulfilment of human love, Lohengrin looked to the Mount of Salvation as his faith and his destiny. In that year of revolutions, 1848, Wagner himself had caught the radical fervour, when in May the German National Assembly came together at Frankfurt. Having finished the score of *Lohengrin*, he declared that 'the fate of the monarchs will depend upon their conduct'. This was the fate of the Knights of the Grail; by their deeds they attained grace. In the third act of the opera, the King of Brabant and his army were made to shout:

> A German sword for the German land!
> So will the Reich's power take command.

And Lohengrin returned to pledge his sword to the defence of the Grail kingdom.

> He who is chosen to stand and serve the Grail
> Is given by its grace more than mortal force.
> Faced with the power of evil, he'll not fail,
> The sight of it destroys death at its source.

Named and known, Lohengrin had to leave Brabant, which wanted him as its heir. By the magic of art, Wagner found a solution in the swan, which had brought the knight there. The white bird was transformed into Elsa's brother Gottfried, now released from his feathered spell to take his place beside the throne. The white dove of Wolfram von Eschenbach flew down to pick up the chain of the golden shell-boat in its beak and draw Lohengrin back to his Otherworld by the power of the Holy Spirit. Bereft of human love by the will of God, Elsa fell lifeless to the ground.

Certainly in *Lohengrin*, Wagner recognised the mystical thrust of the Grail legend, its strength as a judge between the body and the soul. In his final opera, *Parsifal*, he would see it as the vessel of divine blood and redemption. He translated pagan myth into Christian symbol. The Valhalla of the

Nordic gods became the Temple of the Grail, which also represented the treasure of the Nibelungs, while the Ring of Authority was transformed into the Spear of Destiny and the Holy Lance. Although Wagner's source was Wolfram's medieval poem, he rejected the Grail as an oriental talisman for the chalice of the Eucharist. Using much of Wolfram's plot and many of his characters, he transcended the action in the search for absolution.

The character of the sorceress Kundry led to his supreme transformation. Wagner saw her as 'this fabulous and wild Grail-herald'. She had seduced the Fisher King Anfortas, so tainting the divine blood in him, and allowing him to lose the Holy Lance to the evil magician Klingsor, who transformed it into the pagan Spear of Destiny and so gave Anfortas his incurable wound. Yet she appeared in the first expository act of *Parsifal* with an Arabian balsam that might heal the ever-bleeding sore. While Anfortas despaired with the

Knights of the Grail of any cure for himself and the Waste Land of his kingdom, Klingsor created a false bower of bliss, rather modelled on the Garden of Allah, with Flower Maidens to entice any rescuer who might seize the piercing and healing spear from his domain.

The innocent fool and Nordic hero, Parsifal, entered, killing a passing swan with an arrow. He heard from Kundry that his mother had died of grief at his going. This was the beginning of his repentance and his understanding. He asked the wise hermit Gurnemanz what was the Grail, only to hear that there was no saying; yet if he were the chosen one, the knowledge of it would not escape him.

The next scene at the Grail Castle closely followed Wolfram's *Parzival*. The ailing Anfortas was brought on a litter to watch the veiled shrine of

The Grail Fountain at the Schloss Herrenchiemsee.

Above: The Grail Table at Herrenchiemsee.

Right: The Queen's Bed at Herrenchiemsee.

the Grail carried in front of the waiting brotherhood of its knights, to be placed on an oblong stone table. Anfortas compared Christ's Blood on the Holy Lance to his incurable wound, which was giving him agony because of his sins. The Grail was revealed as a purple crystal goblet, which was illuminated by a brilliant ray of light. With this chalice, Anfortas blessed the pitchers of wine and baskets of bread for the meal of the knights, who sang of changing the Holy Body and Blood into strength and power to fight for the Christian cause. Parsifal remained mute and transfixed, never asking the question that could cure the Grail King.

The second act at Klingsor's magic castle dealt with the efforts of the wizard to entrap Parsifal through Kundry and the Flower Maidens, whom he escaped with ease. And when Kundry gave Parsifal the first kiss of love, he clutched at his heart, thinking that the wound of Anfortas was burning there like a torch. His vision was suddenly concentrated upon the purple Grail. Kundry was overwhelmed. Did her kiss give him the vision of the divine? If he must be a redeemer, let him redeem her or damn her forever. The thwarted Klingsor, who had castrated himself, hurled the phallic Spear at Parsifal, but it hovered above him. He plucked it from the air to describe the sign of the Cross. The castle collapsed, the magic garden of pleasure and corruption became a desert, the flowers withered. Parsifal left with the lethal and curative weapon for the hermit's cell.

There Kundry was waiting for him with Gurnemanz, who enlightened Parsifal on his stupidity and ignorance. Yet he was the chosen redeemer, and Kundry now played the role of the Magdalene, bathing his feet, anointing them from a golden phial kept between her breasts and drying them with her hair. Transformed into another Christ, Parsifal accepted his role and was baptised by Gurnemanz in the nearby sacred spring. He was told that this was Good Friday. Prepared to die in front of his despondent knights, Anfortas was touched on his wound by Parsifal with the head of the Spear, now changed back to the Holy Lance. 'One wound is enough,' he declared. 'The wound

is only healed by the spear that gave it.' The Lance now ran again with the Holy Blood. Parsifal took the purple cup from its shrine and sank to his knees in prayer. The Grail glowed with radiance, the dove of the Spirit descended on the pure knight, and Kundry sank down as Elsa did in *Lohengrin*, forgiven, but dead. The Grail was held over all by its new king.

Although a last work of personal resignation, *Parsifal* was criticised by the philosopher Nietzsche as the relapse of an old man from a bold confrontation with the truth into a weak and sentimental Catholic faith. 'More Liszt than Wagner,' he told a friend, 'the spirit of the Counter-Reformation; it is too Christian and narrow for me.' The novelist Thomas Mann also judged the opera, reckoning that the Christian element was false. The theme of the 'Dresden Amen' with its assurance of redemption was a trick to deceive an audience into believing that the Brotherhood of the Knights of the Grail was not another order of Teutonic or Templar Knights – or early Storm Troopers – ready to lead a racial crusade against evil Eastern forces, as they had done from Marienburg to confront the pagan Slavs, Mongols and Russians. For by now, Wagner had met and read Count Arthur de Gobineau's notorious works on an elite Aryan race.

Yet the facts are that Wagner identified his Grail Castle most probably with Montserrat and the early Spanish Crusades against the Moors, while the inspiration for Klingsor's flower garden derived less from his anti-Semitism than from the enchanted Gothic greenery of the Villa Ruffolo at Ravello, where the precious blood of the alchemist St Pantaleon liquefied each year by some miracle, a testament to the healing power of the Catholic faith.

In his 'Religion and Art', Wagner had already declared: 'Where religion becomes artificial, it remains for art to salvage the essence of it.' The literal belief in the mythical symbol of the Grail had to be re-created by arias in an ideal representation, to recover the profound and hidden truth concealed in the ancient allegory. For him, the noblest heritage of the Christian Church was the soul of its music, which soared out of temple walls, gave life and freedom, and taught 'a new language in which the infinite and the incomprehensible can be perfectly expressed'.

In that desire, the legend of the Grail was the ultimate vehicle for Richard Wagner. Wolfram von Eschenbach had performed a miracle almost as complex as transubstantiation in his masterpiece *Parzival* by blending oriental faiths and Nordic myths into a Christian occurrence. So Wagner transcended the Faustian *Tannhäuser* to reach the Otherworldly *Lohengrin* and an apotheosis in *Parsifal*. There, his anti-Semitism, racialism and crude propaganda for German mastery were transmuted through the genius of his music, which he wanted to 'consist of the elements', into a spiritual drama of the possibility of redemption and the vision of God.

If the rituals of the Knights of the Grail and their fierce chastity seemed to smack of earth ceremonies and even Black Masses, the blessed music, often derived from the liturgy, and the Christian imagery overlaid Wagner's bigotry and contradicted the misuse of his work by the Third Reich. No more than Christ was responsible for the cruelty of the crusades was Wagner guilty of being a cause of German propaganda in the First and Second World Wars. If he was committed to a philosophy, it was Schopenhauer's belief in the primacy of the will. In terms of the Grail, that was its old heresy, that the divine could only be seen by those who deserved by their deeds to see it. God came to those who fought for him. Understanding and compassion were the keys as much as trial and pain. Yet by good acts did Parsifal reach his goal.

In more modern Germany, the great irony was that the Church of St Lawrence in Nuremberg was the centre of the themes of the Grail in the late Middle Ages. Yet the city became the focus of fervent patriotism, Hitler's processions, and, finally, the trial of the Nazi leaders. Nowhere in Europe were the symbols of the Christian Holy Vessel shown in such beautiful profusion. St Lawrence, of course, had been given a Grail by the Pope, but he sent it west to Spain and north to Germany. Lawrence, however, appears twice in his church, carrying the gridiron on his shoulder like an oblong tennis racket. The oriental version of the Grail in Wolfram's *Parzival* is celebrated in the painting over the Krell'scher high altar in the apse, the stone dropping into the chalice and being presented to the Christ child.

One rare unattributed altarpiece of the Risen Christ, created at the waning of the Middle Ages when Catholicism was about to be broken in Middle Germany by the Protestant Reformation, is a parting tribute to the decline of the Grail cult. At the base, there is a carving of the dead Jesus, with three women above his Body, one holding a jar of spices, and Nicodemus and Joseph of Arimathea at his head and feet. In the picture, he appears as Christ the Gardener, holding his spade by a golden Grail bucket with a lid, while the Magdalene kneels alone before him. The medieval closed garden is depicted here as the Garden of Eden; surrounded by a fence, it is all grass except for the two trees from Genesis: the Tree of Life and the Tree of the Knowledge of Good and Evil.

The Church of St Lawrence would be bombed during the Second World War, as if in retribution for the later perversion of its messages. For Hitler would make Nuremberg his place of ceremonies, which in their vast arrangements would surpass even the jousts of King Arthur at Camelot and the rituals of the Fisher King. But the Nazi revival of the Grail myths through the inspiration of Wagner was instituted in order to justify another crusade against the East, equally atheist under Stalin. In that perverted crusade of the two ungodly cults of Fascism and Marxism, each bent on creating a hell on earth miscalled a racial or economic heaven to be, some 50 million human beings would die. Their murders would be at the hands of two dictators who had lost all faith in any divine message, which appeared not to exist outside romantic imaginings.

St Mary Magdalene carries the Grail with the cosmos falling into the cup towards the Christ Child in this medieval painting in the Church of St Lawrence, Nuremberg.

TWENTY-ONE

THE PERVERSION OF THE GRAIL

As I went homeward
At dusk by the shore,
'What is that crimson?'
Said Merlin once more.
'Only the sun,' I said,
'Sinking to rest' –
'Sunset for East,' he said,
'Sunrise for West.'

Alfred Noyes, *The Riddles of Merlin*

he massacres of the First World War were followed by an epidemic of influenza, which killed tens of millions more people in Europe. The coming of peace led to a great disillusionment about the value of fighting. John Maynard Keynes, the chief representative of the British Treasury at the postwar negotiations in Paris, denounced the terms reached at the Treaty of Versailles in a polemic called *The Economic Consequences of the Peace*. It condemned the punitive reparations exacted from Germany and the self-interested land exchanges of the victorious powers. He foresaw that the consequences of the peace would be the financial ruin of Europe and another world war. 'Vengeance', he predicted, 'will not limp.' Nothing would delay a final civil war between the forces of reaction and revolution. In that conflict, the horrors of the late German combat would fade into nothing. It would destroy 'whoever is the victor, the civilisation and the progress of our generation'.

This was to become the prevailing attitude of many of the generation of 1914, who had gone to the trenches so readily and were discomfited by the peace. Their feeling of betrayal by the old men governing them had led to revolutions in Europe,

Memorial to the German war dead, 1914–18. The Church of St John, Ansbach.

Siegfried in the Black Forest.
(From the film Siegfried *by Fritz Lang, 1924)*

suppressed outside Soviet Russia, and to the rise of Fascist movements, particularly in Italy. Extreme solutions advocating social change of the left or of the right promised a catharsis as violent as the recent European conflict, itself welcomed originally by a host of young men as an answer to the political turmoil of the pre-war years. The myth of a lost generation produced in its survivors a revulsion and a determination never to repeat the horrors of the slaughter. Its legacy was a certain pacifism that would abhor self-sacrifice in the name of any cause or modern Quests. Self-fulfilment was a better goal in the face of mass cynicism and disbelief.

For T.S. Eliot, a corrupt London was no Mount of Salvation. Urban civilisation was *The Waste Land* of his Grail lament. He mourned the cracks and falling towers of Jerusalem and Athens, Alexandria and Vienna. As a Fisher King, he hung his rod over a dull canal with a gashouse and an arid plain behind him. Although he mused on his royal heritage, he could not set his lands in order, even with the remembrance of the troubadour Prince of Aquitaine. Paying homage to Ezra Pound, *il miglior fabbro*, and Jessie Weston, whose *From Ritual to Romance* stressed the Grail myths as Christian versions of pagan fertility ceremonies, Eliot emphasised the futility of self-sacrifice in a decadent world. Any chapel of revelation was now full of wind and dry bones. The very April showers were cruel and incapable of generating the dust of the dead. Making love was loveless now without joy or hope of giving birth. The very introduction to *The Waste Land* had the prophetic Sibyl of Cumae answering a question about what she desired. Her reply in Greek was that she wanted to die.

Contemporary Germany, particularly Berlin, gave way to a heady hedonism. These were the years of 'that strange Indian summer – the Weimar Republic', as the English poet Stephen Spender wrote in his preface to his homosexual novel, *The Temple*. 'Germany seemed a paradise where there was no censorship and young Germans enjoyed extraordinary freedom in their lives.' As fugitive American writers such as Scott Fitzgerald and Ernest Hemingway went to France to escape Prohibition, so their English rivals were fleeing repression by going to Germany. 'For them drink; for us, sex,' Spender's friend Christopher Isherwood boasted. He was 'doing what Henry James would have done, if he had the guts. . . . *My* will is to live according to my nature, and to find a place where I can be what I am.'

The Great Depression, which caused a reaction from escapism along with the return home of the intellectual refugees, unleashed in Germany a reversion to barbarism. That was the paradox of Nazism, which aimed to create a new world and a new race by reviving ancient myths and the German spirit. More a dream than a reality, the message preached by Nazi propaganda was of strong and eternal youth with a will to power. The members of the nation could all aspire to being Parsifals and Siegfrieds.

The National Socialist German Workers' Party was a method of carrying out by other means the war experiences of its leader Adolf Hitler in the front line. He wanted another total mobilisation of Germany to avenge the losses of the Treaty of Versailles and to revive the German Empire to the east and the south. The Nazis claimed to be the heirs of that dynamic *Kultur* which had so inspired the First World War. They promised action on the theme of a lost grandeur, to be regained by the 1,000 years of the rule of the Third Reich.

Their great annual September dramas over seven days were promoted at the Grail centre of Nuremberg. There the parades were staged with tens of thousands of uniformed members of the Party. The choreography of the gymnasts and the dancers, evoked by Leni Riefenstahl in *The Triumph of the Will*, almost put to shame the Hollywood extravaganzas of Busby Berkeley. Cathedrals of ice, created by Albert Speer, crowned the massive processions with aerial cones of hundreds of searchlights. Forests of banners recalled the crusades and the imperial Iberian fleets setting off towards the conquest of Asia, Africa and the Americas. All would culminate in a speech by Hitler, high on his podium, the White Knight of the Swastika, as he was so often painted. He called himself the anonymous warrior and the unknown soldier, who had been gassed and decorated three times with Iron Crosses for courage in the front line. Yet his notoriety and power would affect the whole earth.

The imagery of Fascism, in both Germany and Italy, was an aphrodisiac to the masses. Even when the bombing of Berlin by the Allies would cause despondency, Hitler would insist on great shows. 'Theatrical performances are needed,' he said, 'precisely because the morale of the people must be maintained.' His newsreels and those of Mussolini showed interminable ranks of aeroplanes, tanks and guns; also smiling parades of troops and tractors, villagers and harvests and even religious festivals. Instead of Jesus hanging upon the Cross, a bare German youth was draped over the four prongs of the Nazi emblem. Horst Wessel took the place of Christ as the Party martyr in the propaganda of the sacred corpse. The mental pictures of pagan myths and Wagnerian operas, the Nordic themes of godlike battles and intransigent heroes, were evoked in a panoply of nostalgic reverence and imminent action. As Hitler declared, Nazism was a doctrine of conflict.

A streak of perverse mysticism ran through Nazi ideology. After the defeat of the First World War, the mercenary bands of the *Freikorps* had put

The Nibelungs carry their
treasures on a Grail platter.
(*From the film* Siegfried
by Fritz Lang, 1924)

down radical risings in Berlin, Bavaria and Latvia. They saw themselves as new Teutonic Knights, sworn to suppress the heresy of Bolshevism in the east. Their other inspiration was a secret organisation, attributed to Charlemagne, named the *Vehm*, which for many centuries had tyrannised the conquered lands of Saxony with its vigilante tribunals and judgements. The actual inspiration for the Nazi Party was mythical as well as political through the drug-addicted writer Dietrich Eckart, also a leading member of the Thule Society, which sought a pure Nordic homeland. Eckart's talisman was a piece of black meteorite as in the Ka'aba at Mecca, and when he died, he claimed that Adolf Hitler was his successor and would follow his racist and ancestral teachings. Hitler, however, only used paganism as a theatrical device and psychological scalpel into the national subconscious. He left the doctrines of the primitive and the occult to his ringmaster, Alfred Rosenberg, to his deputy, Rudolf Hess, and to his chief of propaganda, Heinrich Himmler. Although a lover of Wagner, Hitler wanted no return to the religion of Odin and Wotan. He wanted a new religion, based on earth ceremonies and blood rituals.

During Hitler's term in prison in 1924 after the Munich uprising, Rosenberg had been the temporary leader of the nascent Nazi Party. Unlike the bible of the movement, Hitler's vainglorious *Mein Kampf*, Rosenberg's book, *The Myth of the Twentieth Century*, was a weird evocation of an Aryan race from a lost Atlantis, which sailed on dragon and swan ships like Lohengrin to found all ancient civilisations, including the Indian one. From there, that master people overran Asia, returning through Iran and the worship of Zoroaster, or the Zarathustra of Nietzsche's Superman.

This noble elite joined the Nordic gods in their struggle for light and life against the forces of darkness, such as the Serpent of the Earth. Rosenberg wanted the suppression of the Bible so that it could be replaced by *Mein Kampf*, for the ultimate Triumph of the Will had arrived in the person of Adolf Hitler. But the later Führer was too politic wholly to discard Christianity, however much he wished to become the Messiah of his New Order. He officially remained a Roman Catholic until his suicide, whatever pagan rituals and sacrifices were enacted in his name.

The Nazis march. *(From* The Triumph of the Will, *by Leni Riefenstahl, 1934)*

Heinrich Himmler enthused about the legends of King Arthur, who had, after all, finally been defeated by the invading Anglo-Saxons when they crossed the Rhine and the Channel. He aimed to re-create the medieval *Ordenstaat* of the Teutonic Knights in Poland and Lithuania, where the Jews and the undesirable Slavs were to be totally exterminated. He encouraged Hitler to see himself as a superior reincarnation of previous Holy Roman Emperors from Charlemagne to the Habsburgs. The coronation regalia of past dynasties was looted from Prague, Reims, Warsaw and Vienna, including the Holy Lance, now confused with the Nordic Spear of Destiny. These sacred signs of power were transported to Nuremberg, the site of the great Nazi processionals, where they might be held to confer on the Führer a mystical and traditional sovereignty over Europe.

The deputy Nazi leader, Rudolf Hess, was particularly affected by the legends of the Grail. He had fallen under the influence of General Karl Haushoffer, who was responsible for two mystic pagan brotherhoods, *Vril* and the Society of the Green Dragon. Rather as in the later *Star Wars* trilogy of films, the secret energy of these groups

was an esoteric 'Force', which had its origins in Lord Edward Bulwer-Lytton's book *The Coming Race*, as well as in Nietzsche's theories of Superman and the Will. Bulwer-Lytton had been the head of the British Colonial Office as well as writing a romance on King Arthur. His biographer was a member of the Scottish Theosophical Society, which was visited by Dr Karl Hans Fuchs of the Nazi Thule Society, an organisation particularly patronised by Hess and Rosenberg with its rituals based on the *Ring* cycle of Wagner and the legends of the Grail.

As that Holy Vessel was said to be concealed within the curious Apprentice Pillar of Rosslyn Chapel near Edinburgh, Fuchs inspected the place in 1930, accompanied by somebody who signed the visitors' book as D. Hamilton. Later, at the Theosophical Society in Edinburgh, Fuchs declared that Hess claimed to have Hamilton blood in his veins and was particularly interested in the 10th Duke, a close friend of Bulwer-Lytton, as well as in the contemporary duke, who graced the Nazi leaders with his presence at the Olympic Games in Berlin. Fuchs added that Hess was known as 'Parsifal' in the inner circles of the Third Reich, and

Left: The Apprentice Pillar in Rosslyn Chapel.

Right: The dove of the Grail descends on angels. (*Gnostic Russian sampler*)

Roman legions. To the mystic philosopher Rudolf Steiner and his follower Walter Johannes Stein, the Externsteine rather than Nuremberg was the centre of the energy and the cult of the Grail in Germany. A medieval rock carving of the 12th century still shows the Descent from the Cross set between the sun and moon, with Nicodemus and Joseph of Arimathea carrying the Body of Christ, while a headless Mary Magdalene holds His head in her hands. Above them, God the Father bears a triple emblem, crowned by the cross of the Teutonic Knights.

At these sacred stones and the monoliths of Sachsenhain, Himmler conducted Mithraic and winter solstice ceremonies of sun worship for some 10,000 members of the SS and the *Ahnenherbe*. And at the triangular castle of Wewelsburg in West-phalia, he developed a monastic college and mausoleum for his secret police. In his great hall stood his oak Round Table, modelled on that of King Arthur; it was placed upon a floor with mosaics of swastikas and the patterns of the zodiac. Thirteen high chairs stood around it for Himmler and his twelve paladins among the *Obergruppen-führers*, who followed his orders with total devotion. In the crypt beneath, a 'Realm of the Dead' had twelve niches and plinths to hold the urns for the ashes of the bones and coats of arms of the chosen SS officers, after their deaths had been purified by fire. If he ever died, Hitler was expected by Himmler to be buried there as well.

The search for the Grail was another task for the *Ahnenherbe*. Hitler's interest in Wagner's *Parsifal* was well known, with its Nordic figure of Christ and its secret male order of Grail knights, modelled on their Teutonic and Templar predecessors. Hitler was painted wearing the silver mail of these literary guardians of the Castle of the Fisher King. And although Hess believed the actual Grail was in Scotland, Otto Rahn, an SS officer, had written a

that he believed Rosslyn was the Grail chapel, 'where the black hand snuffed out the candle'.

The extraordinary flight of Hess in a Messer-schmitt to Scotland during the Second World War may have had something to do with his obsession with the ducal Hamilton family and the cult of the Holy Vessel. Hitler's fury at his defection led to terms in concentration camps for many German Freemasons and astrologers. The Ancestral Heritage Organisation, or *Ahnenherbe*, however, was spared. Some of its fifty departments were connected to the SS secret police, whose head, Himmler, was called 'my Loyola' by Hitler, as though he led a society of lethal Jesuits with his modern techniques of Inquisition.

At Sachsenhain, Himmler imitated Avebury, Carnac and Stonehenge in creating avenues of 4,500 standing stones to commemorate the Saxon victims of Charlemagne, who had them slaughtered before destroying the pagan oak grove and temple at the Irminsul, now reconstructed at the rocky outcrop of the Externsteine, where the German chief Herrmann had once destroyed two

book in 1933 called *The Crusade for the Grail*, which was followed by *The Heart of Lucifer*. He revived the traditions of the Cathar chalice, buried in the nearby caves after the fall of Montségur at the end of the Albigensian Crusade. His version of the Grail was taken from the oriental influences on Wolfram von Eschenbach in his *Parzival*. Rahn believed that Montségur was besieged by the troops of Lucifer, who wanted to recover the emerald that had fallen from Satan's crown at his battle with the angels of heaven. This sacred green stone had been rescued by a white dove and hidden in a black chasm at the fall of the Cathar stronghold.

Rahn used geomancy and sacred geography to locate the places where the Grail of the heretics might be hidden. He spawned a succession of books, overlaying the maps of the mountain peaks of the south of France with triangles and trapezoids to create 'the Hermetic Star of the Templars' or the 'Sacred Rectangle of the Gauls', one of the three 'Grail tables' set upon the earth. In his investigations in the grottos of Lombrives, Bethlehem, l'Ermite, Ornolac and other caverns near the Cathar castles, Rahn became obsessional, declaring that he did not know which was the more marvellous or beautiful. Within them, 'the inscriptions represent a Ship of the Dead which has for a sail the sun, the sun which gives out life and is reborn each winter. . . . Also a tree I saw, "The Tree of Life", drawn in charcoal.'

Rahn declared that the sacred geometry of the walls of Montségur proclaimed that it was a sun temple based on the summer solstice, an interpretation that enthused Himmler with his SS ceremonies. In 1937, he was sent by Rahn a consignment of the objects which had been excavated from the French caves. Without clear proof, writers have claimed that this consignment included the Cathar sacred vessel, which was then placed on one of the plinths in the 'Realm of the Dead' in Wewelsburg Castle. Later happenings did not support such a theory. On his return to Germany, Rahn was probably sent to the concentration camps, along with the other mystics,

after the defection of Hess; certainly, he did not survive the Second World War. And the *Ahnenherbe* sent teams of secret policemen and prehistorians, linguists and archaeologists into Vichy France in order to follow up Rahn's digging around Montségur. This appeared to be a last effort to locate the Holy Vessel as a talisman to prevent the reconquest of France by the Allies on a Second Front and thus alleviate the German crusade into Russia.

The specialists of the *Ahnenherbe* were located in the forest of Basqui at a camp called the Place of the Aurochs. In the grotto of Causson, they discovered some inscribed stones, which were again transported to Germany. Yet whatever was found by Rahn and by this later expedition disappeared in the fall of the Third Reich, which so much resembled the Götterdämmerung of Nordic and Wagnerian legend. If Hitler's bunker in Berlin was hardly the Valhalla of the gods, its destruction with the mass suicide of its inhabitants was as total an ending as any millennial New Order might have desired.

Curiously, the apotheosis of the Grail as the Celtic cauldron of destruction was not in the fire-bombing of Berlin and Dresden, but in the atomic destruction of Hiroshima and Nagasaki, two cities of imperial Japan. A vast incendiary chalice, miscalled a mushroom cloud, intervened as the mythical Nordic world tree Yggdrasil between earth and heaven. Instant and slow dying was its only giving. The ideal of divine bounty and life being distributed by a cup or a dish, a dove or a stone from the sky was undermined into a darker Nordic and biblical past, where the hidden hand of God bestowed retribution and the plague. Out of the classical *krater* or mixing-bowl of Creation had spurted the volcano rather than the seed. Yet the legend of the Grail would not be lost in this immeasurable snuffing-out. Its message – the personal quest for transcendence and the individual vision of the divine – would be revived on the couches of psychiatrists and in the preparations of a New Age.

TWENTY-TWO

BEATIFIC STATES

I saw the best minds of my generation destroyed
by madness, starving hysterical naked,
dragging themselves through the negro streets at
dawn looking for an angry fix
angelhead hipsters burning for the ancient
heavenly connection to the starry
dynamo in the machinery of night. . . .

Allen Ginsberg, 'Howl', 1954

akob Boehme, a mystic of the early 17th century, writing about the conflicts that led him to the insight of the divine, said, 'The Being of all beings is a wrestling power.' He might have been describing the hallucinogenic states of Lancelot and his cousin Yvain, when their dreadful adventures towards the Grail were interrupted by visions of boiling fountains, ravening lions and incinerating fires. They strove towards God, and yet they were denied the final sight of Him because their strife was their unseeing. Unlike the hermits who directed them on their paths to the Castle of the Fisher King, the Knights of Camelot had no knowledge of the spiritual exercises that were the conditions of a final joust with the Holy Ghost. These rules were necessary, if a seeker were to engage beatitude.

Again Jung was the master guide towards a view of the transcendental. To him, prophets and seers were poets as well as mystics. They could glimpse the primordial experience of myths and translate these into our world of forms. They could give a shape to the Grail within 'the strange paradoxes of their vision'. Jung particularly cited the phantasmagoric world of India, the Old Testament and the Apocalypse; also of Dante's *Divine Comedy*, the Otherworld in Goethe's *Faust* and the poetry of William Blake. Such records or archetypes had the power to stimulate the imagination when the

receiver was in an induced trance. 'Formation, transformation,' was Jung's definition. 'Eternal Mind's eternal re-creation.'

The Grail itself in its apparitions was everything to everyone – magic cauldron, cup, dish, stone, or Pentecostal tongues of fire – or wrapped in samite or clouds to hide itself from the unfit. Its shape depended on the state of mind of the viewer after reaching the sight of it. Its original romancers knew of the severe practices endured by hermits and holy people, if they wanted to reach an ecstatic experience by the exclusion of all the world of the senses. St John of the Cross would negate everything except the vision of fiery love, while Jan Van Ruysbroek had to consider sunlight.

Julia of Norwich prayed for the bodily sight of Christ on the Cross and the receipt of His Blood from His three wounds. The price she would pay was a terrible trial by disease. She was granted all her desires. As she lay dying at the age of thirty, a priest held a crucifix before her eyes. In her dark chamber, she beheld a light on the image of the Cross. She could hardly breathe and thought that she was expiring, then suddenly 'all my pain was taken away from me, and I was as whole as ever I was before'. In her hypnotic concentration on the death of Christ, she was restored to her own life and granted her wants, seeing the red blood trickle

Who Are You?, Alexander Calder, 1968, a quest for self.

down His Body from His Crown of Thorns, 'hot and freshly and right plenteously'.

Such mystic perceptions were the essence of the Grail; but they could only be perceived by trial and rigour in the West, and in the East by religious rituals such as the Buddhist tantra. In these, the novices were taught to chant and to concentrate on six syllables signifying six colours – as in alchemy – and six beings. *Aum* was white and denoted the gods. *Ma* was blue and dealt with those who were not gods. *Ni* was yellow and human. *Pad* was green and animal. *Me* was red and subhuman, while *Hum* was black and connected with sinners in the underworld. The repetition of these syllables while meditating upon them resulted in the six transitory realms of being on their passing into the acceptance of the One.

Other mystical traditions had their own series of negations and contemplations, but the aim was the same – the final understanding of and looking at the Creator and the Whole, and reaching the Mount of Salvation. Nicholas of Cusa had to be as foolish as Parzival, when the saint wrote of a loving ascent towards the high wall of paradise, which 'separates Thee from all that can possibly be said or thought of Thee'. Reason failed at the approach. The 'wisdom which is ignorance' must take its place. For a Grail could only be achieved by the pure in heart through the unknown direction of the Hand of God.

This ultimate vision of the divine might be an illusion. 'From my own unforgettable experience,' wrote Martin Buber, 'I know well that there is a state in which the bonds of the personal nature of life seem to have fallen away from us, and we experience an undivided unity. But I do not know – what the soul willingly imagines and indeed is

Right: *Denver*, Alexander Calder, postcard, 1968.

Below: *Flowers*, Alexander Calder, postcard, 1968.

bound to imagine (mine too once did it) – that in this I had attained to a union with the primal being or the godhead. That is an exaggeration no longer permitted to the responsible under-standing.' The short cuts to the experience of the Whole, particularly by drugs rather than penances, did not guarantee the value of the deep insight.

That was especially the way of the American 'Flower Children' of the 1960s, from the Beats to the hippies. They paid for their trips towards a union with the divine with magic mushrooms and other sacerdotal drugs. Timothy Leary was to preach that his League for Spiritual Discovery was a religion. 'The sacraments marijuana and LSD should only be used by initiates and priests of our religion and only used in shrines.' These were the bread and wine, the Holy Body and Blood of his new cult. 'LSD is ecumenical. God is not Christian. He doesn't speak Greek or Latin. When you contact God as we have you realise that His energy and His blueprint were going on long before man worked out these verbal formulas.' The psychedelic revolution was a spiritual revival that would change American culture. Leary's revelation was not original. The genetic code, which he considered to be the main instrument of God, had been telling us the same message for thousands of years. Each of us must search inside the self. That was his primary conclusion. 'Nothing you do outside is important unless you're centred within.'

The use of hallucinogenic drugs to achieve a further reality had already spread from Timothy Leary's pioneering psychological experiments at Harvard, and LSD and marijuana had reached the Beats through Allen Ginsberg and others of the City Lights bookshop congregation. The Californian poets had experimented before Leary: Michael McClure, in *Scratching the Beat Surface*, recalled Francis Crick from Churchill College buying one of the 150 copies of his *Peyote Poem* in

1958 and including two lines from it in his book about discovering DNA and biogenetics, *Of Molecules and Men*:

THIS IS THE POWERFUL KNOWLEDGE,
we smile with it

Just such a radical insight into the secrets of the elixir of life had been a message of the Quest for the Grail. Yet its trials and tests were no part of the new counter-culture, in which each seeker after truth was, in a sense, his or her own work of art. Narcissus rather than Galahad was the ideal of this new generation, which rejected any heritage in favour of instant creation. Among the drug abusers, the Holy Lance became the needle of the hypodermic syringe, and the Crown of Thorns was the tourniquet used to find a vein; all this pain in a quest for a Grail of selfish beatific vision. A dependence on stimulants and a sexual free-for-all pitted this alternative culture against the old moralists and traditions. As the troubadour of the New Age, Allen Ginsberg chanted in 'Howl' that the best minds of his generation were destroyed by madness induced by a narcotic culture.

At the end of the failed revolts against the Vietnam War in 1968, however, the youth rebellion became aware of its own disintegration and coming corruption. Timothy Leary might be declaring in the magazine *Open City* that 'you are a God, act like one', and that if everyone in Manhattan were to 'turn on' and 'tune in', grass would grow on First Avenue, shoeless divinities would dance down the car-less streets, and deer would graze along St Mark's Place. Your body had to become your sacred temple, but you should not 'drop out' until you had 'tuned in' and 'turned on'. Bad trips on drugs were only caused by the failure to 'tune in'. And the reason why? 'When you "tune in", you trigger off energy. Pot flicks on sensory energy. Hashish to somatic energy. LSD to cellular energy. High dose LSD to molecular energy.' Later on in the same issue, *Open City* printed part of Andy Warhol's Velvet Underground and Nico Band, singing 'Heroin':

Heroin . . .
Be the death of me
Heroin . . .
It's my wife . . .
And it's my life . . .
Because a main up to my vein leads to a center in
my head . . .
And then I'm better off than dead.

The psychologists of 'psychedelic therapy' found that their subjects did achieve a central perception. Behind the huge diversity of things in the world of science and the everyday, there was a single reality that appeared to be infinite and eternal. All beings were united in One Being. Any sense of the separate individual was merged in the pervading Spirit. As with those few knights who saw the Grail, the lives of the drug-users who glimpsed the totality of existence were forever changed by that knowledge. Even if chemical substances rather than actual pilgrimages had been their trips, their minds were altered by a perception of the universal.

The privations suffered by the medieval knights and pilgrims had also given them visions. Fatigue and hunger were their hallucinogens. Fasting and sleeping affected their senses and induced sacred fantasies and encounters of a weird kind. Confused by the imbalances caused by hardships along the way, the travellers saw what they saw at the end of their road because of their concentration on their goal and their faith in their illuminations. We do see, indeed, what we believe we see. A mirage is real enough at a distance, unless we choose to examine it too closely.

The Grail was, after all, invisible as the Holy Spirit and the blessing of God. The forms in which it appeared in the beatific states of its followers were the shapes that they were directed to see. In the eyes of the Celts and the Nordic folk, the Grail was the cauldron and the spear; in classical times, the cosmic bowl and the horn of plenty; for the Jews, the Ark and the Tabernacle; for Christians, the chalice and the dish; for Muslims, the Ka'aba with its black stone; for the dissenters, the fire, the serpent and the dove. Yet the Grail was not all things to all men, but only one – a symbol of each person's direct approach to the divine light. Many have sought it, few have found it – or it has found them. In Tennyson's poem, Sir Percivale travelled with the Grail that he was seeking. Under its many aspects, it had sustained his journey towards its final grace. Never did this blood-red 'Holy Thing' fall away from the side of the Arthurian knight, but moved with him all the way to crown him in the spiritual city of his quest.

Some great works on the Grail still emerged from the slaughter and cynicism of the two world wars. David Jones painted a Mass in a blasted chapel with No Man's Land between the trenches depicted as the Waste Land of the Fisher King. *In Parenthesis* and *The Anathemata* showed the Knights of Camelot fighting beside the Tommies. T.H. White published a quartet entitled *The Once and Future King*, in which he traced the old legends from Arthur's education as a boy to his dark ending after the Battle of Camlann. A posthumous sequel, *The Story of Merlyn*, told of the British king's journey to an Otherworld and the divine light.

Charles Williams was one of the Inklings at Oxford grouped around C.S. Lewis and J.R.R. Tolkien, whose works about Narnia and the Hobbit would both be translated into successful screen epics. Williams himself wrote two volumes of bardic poems on Arthurian themes, culminating in a vision of the spiritual intellect, 'the building of Logres and the coming of the land of the Trinity which is called Sarras in maps of the soul'.

As the 20th century declined towards the millennium, the Grail was translated into science fiction, film and musical, to end in derision. Of course, mockery had been a part of the Passion. Jeered as the King of the Jews, Jesus was crowned with a circlet of thorns for the amusement of the mob. His clothes were won at dice. The cup of wine and the dish at the Last Supper, the lance point or the bowl that caught His Blood on the Cross, these became part and parcel of the demeaning of the divine. The Quest for the Grail and for the Ark was turned into parody and special effects by Stephen Spielberg, who surpassed even the mischievous tricks of the wizard Merlin. In *Indiana Jones and the Last Crusade*, the Vessel was described as 'the greatest artefact of mankind', also as 'a cup which gives everlasting life'. After a book-burning in Berlin and some attacks by Zeppelin and Panzer, the father and son Jones reached a desert pillared temple and discovered two Grails, one a jewelled and false chalice, the other a simple and true bowl. An appalling adventurer was converted into a suppurating zombie by taking the wrong draught, while father Jones was saved by quaffing from the right Grail, before dropping it down an abyss. And so, the most significant medieval illumination ended as a silly projection on a silver screen.

The life of Christ was filmed as a practical joke by the Monty Python team as the romp of a nobody who got it all wrong. The sense of the sacred legend was moribund, although John Boorman's film *Excalibur* did confuse Arthur with the wounded Grail King in a rich evocation of the myth. And the trite romantic musical of *Camelot* was moving enough to inspire Jacqueline Bouvier Kennedy to try and re-create a cultural court around her and the martyr President in the White House. But the final facetious nonsense of the musical *Spamalot* was a penny whistle piping into thin air.

In its many transmutations from the eternal to the ephemeral, from marvel to mockery, from courtly love to kitsch, the legend of the Grail abides because it remains the universal symbol of the Gnostic desire to strike a spark from the divine intelligence. *From Ritual to Romance* by Jessie Weston has explained its enduring appeal:

> No theory of the origin of the story can be considered really and permanently satisfactory, unless it can offer an explanation of the story as a whole . . . and of the varying forms assumed by the Grail: why it should be at one time a Food-providing object of unexplained form, at another a Dish; at one moment the receptacle of streams of Blood from a Lance, at another the Cup of the Last Supper; here 'something' wrought of no material substance, there, a Stone; and yet everywhere and always possess the same essential significance; in each and every form be rightly described as *The Grail*?

Why haven't we seen a photograph of the whole Earth yet?

PRINTED AS A PUBLIC SERVICE BY EAST WIND PRINTERS, SAN FRANCISCO

Above: *Why haven't we seen a photograph of the whole earth yet?*, Stewart Brand, begetter of *The Whole Earth Catalog*, *1965*.

Left: Poster for John Boorman's *Excalibur, 1981*.

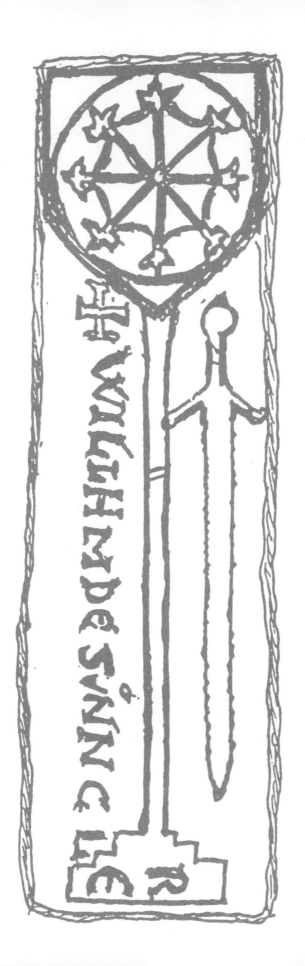

EPILOGUE

To know that any revelation is from God, it is necessary to know that the messenger that delivers it is sent from God, and that cannot be known but by credentials given by God himself.

John Locke, *A Discourse of Miracles*, 18th century

The problem with most Grail studies is to refer to 'the Grail'. When the Holy Vessel was first viewed by Perceval in the original romance by Chrétien de Troyes, the knight observed 'a Grail'. In personal visions, folk symbols and religious constructs, there are more appearances of Grails than at the miracle of the loaves and the fishes, the feeding of the multitude, or of manna falling as dewdrops from heaven. In the individual quest for divine grace, the image of a Grail among a host of other Grails depends on the period in which it is seen or made. But in its universal sense, which binds together its myriad roles, it is an essence that infuses life in all Creation.

That is the message of this book, which attempts to demonstrate the significance and show the images of the many Grails. As the chameleon, the Holy Vessel may, in dream or representation, have plural aspects, as one dish or cup or stone or whatever. The many visions of those who have dared to describe the sight of the Grail are markers and symbols of the search for divine grace. And in the old romances and texts, the witnesses told of what appeared to be the truth of their inspirations and experiences.

We are beset now by false prophets. They claim what they cannot show or prove. Their names are innumerable and inconsiderable, as the angels counted as standing on a pinhead. If Jonathan Swift were still with us, he would call them the What-if Facticides. After some research, which is usually taken from the original and serious work of other people and rarely acknowledged, these fantasists put forward a hypothesis.

Was Christ or the Grail buried under a mountain in the south of France? We will prove it by mystic graphs spread over the Massif Central and the Pyrenees. Did Jesus marry Mary Magdalene and provide the blood line of the Merovingians? We will show it by a spurious Priory of Zion and a wealthy priest from an obscure mountain village. Diagrams on Poussin paintings demonstrate where the Holy Blood is and how the Grail crossed the Atlantic. What if, as Swift suggested, we seek to make sunshine out of cucumbers?

Each speculation by these writers of historical fiction is supported by an array of glittering and separate facts curiously linked together, rather like the little jade plates covering the corpses of ancient Chinese princesses. Within a few pages, the assertion becomes the actual, the idea is changed into the proof. These authors are less historians than alchemists. They seek to find the Holy Vessel and the Holy Blood in a Philosopher's Stone of their imagination, although that only produced brass and no gold.

Yet the Quest for the Grail remains a personal voyage. The question is the choice of a guide. My own journey was begun in Rosslyn Chapel with the discovery of the Templar tombstone with its chalice containing the Rosy Cross and the crusading blade. And yet many months passed before I noticed that the whole building was a Grail chapel, that its roof was the stone fallen from heaven of the Ka'aba and *Parzival*. Looking above me, I saw that the ceiling was divided into five sections stretching from east to west. In the first four segments, the flowers of Creation opened in all their glory, particularly the rose of the Virgin Mary. Then in the west, the stars of the sky clustered on high.

To the south, I could see the sun that gives light and life, then the head of Jesus Christ, and then the dove flying down with the host in its beak. Below this sign of the Holy Spirit was carved the symbol of the Grail. It looked like the bowl of a cup or a crescent moon, the emblem of Islam. From it poured God's grace and bounty, seen as waves or flow. Frozen in stone with algae on the heaven behind it, this Grail seemed to let fall all the green things of the Third Day of Creation. As I solved the mystery of this sacred place by finding the Grail among the constellations above, I heard Marlowe's Doctor Faustus plead in my ear:

> See, see how Christ's blood streams from the
> firmament!
>
> One drop would save my soul!

As the Grail legends declared, each of us may only attain a holy vision, if we already know what we should see and are fit to do so. By research and circumstance, I discovered the Grail trails, places, shapes and signs that are the matter of this book. There are many more to be found, particularly by those who follow in the steps of the cult of St Mary Magdalene. But every person may discern the Holy Vessel only in the form that each of us is able to perceive. As the old command went: 'Seek, and ye shall find.'

Living in this sceptical age, I found it difficult to believe that all of the intense faith of the Middle Ages came from nothing and went into oblivion. I have studied some of the remains. The crypts and the spires, the blazing glass windows and the stone reliefs, all reflect the secrets and the aspirations of

Jesus Christ with the Grail at the Last Supper. *(From the Church of St Lawrence, Nuremberg)*

Rosslyn Chapel, Scotland, where the discovery of a Templar tombstone inspired the author to embark on his Quest for the Grail.

the Grail. If we have souls, then each of us will continue to reach for a kind of transcendence.

In the century of a new millennium, we may join in an individual quest for divine guidance. If there is a life after death, the Grail persists as our goal. We do not wish to see the Holy Spirit through a glass darkly, but in fire, face to face.

I may only sketch a few of the ways there. I have tried to describe my guides on that path and what they have said. I have told you of the signs and the symbols on the forking paths of my quest for the Holy Vessel. All I can hope is that I may have followed occasionally the words of Robert de Boron in his *Joseph of Arimathea*:

> He spoke the blessed words,
> So sweet and precious,
> Gracious and merciful,
> That are rightly called and named
> The secret of the Grail.

NOTES

CHAPTER ONE

Although his interpretation of the word 'Grail' restricts its origins and significance to the medieval romances, Richard Barber in *The Holy Grail: Imagination and Belief* (London, 2004) is scholarly and informative. Theodore de la Villemarqué wrote *Contes populaires des anciens Bretons* (Paris, 1842), while this author wrote *The Discovery of the Grail* (London, 1998). See also John Hardyng, *The Chronicle of John Hardyng* (ed. Henry Ellis, London, 1812).

CHAPTER TWO

I acknowledge gratefully the book by Jeremy Black and Anthony Green, with illustrations by Tessa Rickards, *Gods, Demons and Symbols of Ancient Mesopotamia* (London, 1992) for the insights in this book; the drawing of the fish man-god is by Sir Austen Henry Layard. I have used the text of *The Histories* by Herodotus translated by Baehr and Henry Cary (Frome, 1992). Robert Graves, *Greek Myths* (London, 1955), is still incisive on the ancient Greek myths of Creation.

George St Clair, *Myths of Greece Explained and Dated* (2 vols, London, 1901), and C.H. Moore, *The Religious Thought of the Greeks* (Cambridge, Mass., 1916), have been helpful on the Orphic and Mithraic cults. Charles Bertram Lewis, *Classical Mythology and Arthurian Romance* (Oxford, 1932), stresses the Greek origins of the Arthurian cycle, while G.R. Levy, *The Sword from the Rock: An Investigation into the Origins of Epic Literature and the Development of the Hero* (London, 1953), is original and compelling.

On Zoroaster and the 'Grail' Temple of King Chrosroes the Second, essential is Lars-Ivar Ringbom, *Graltemple und Pardies: Beziehungen zwischen Iran und Europa im Mittelalter* (Stockholm, 1951). I have used John Dryden's translation of *The Aeneid*, first published in London in 1697. Brian Branston's *The Lost Gods of England* (London, 1957) and *Gods of the North* (London, 1955) are stimulating and essential reading, particularly on *The Dream of the Rood*. Twelve Arthurian Norse works including the Merlínusspá are listed in 'Scandinavian Literature', an essay by Phillip M. Mitchell in *Arthurian Literature in the Middle Ages* (ed. R.S. Loomis, Oxford, 1959). Useful on Celtic sacred cauldrons is Stuart Piggott, *The Druids* (London, 1968). Peter Berresford Ellis, *The Druids* (London, 1994), is excellent on the religion of the Druids. The quotation from Roger Sherman Loomis derives from his *Wales and the Arthurian Legend* (Oxford, 1956).

CHAPTER THREE

The Gnostic Scriptures by Bentley Layton (London, 1987) is seminal, as are two books by Elaine Pagels, *The Gnostic Gospels* (New York, 1979), and *Adam, Eve, and the Serpent* (New York, 1988). Also valuable is the concise survey by Benjamin Walker, *Gnosticism: Its History and Influence* (London, 1983). I am also grateful to Malcolm Lee Peel for his edition of *The Epistle to Rheginos: A Valentinian Letter on the Resurrection* (London, 1969).

John Passmore's excellent work on *The Perfectability of Man* (London, 1970) suggested the connection between the Pelagian heresy and Arthurian literature and Protestantism. St Augustine's *Confessions* showed that he was a heretic and a Manichean before his conversion to Christianity and the doctrine of original sin. Essential in studies of the historical truth of Arthur are John Morris, *The Age of Arthur: A History of the British Isles from 350 to 650* (London, 1973), and Leslie Alcock, *Arthur's Britain: History and Archaeology, AD 367–634* (London, 1971), which is particularly significant on excavations at Iron Age hill forts and hanging bowls of the 6th century.

In his cited works, Roger Sherman Loomis is the authority on the Irish and Welsh origins of the Grail theme. There is a fine Penguin Books edition of Geoffrey of Monmouth, *The History of the Kings of Britain* (tr. and intro. by Lewis Thorpe, London, 1966). There was even an Anglo-Saxon version of Geoffrey's Latin *History* and of Wace's French *Brut*, written by a priest in Worcestershire named Layamon. It was brutal but poetic, particularly about slaughter. Strangely, it supported the Celtic resistance to the Anglo-Saxons, as though the enemies had become one British people by the time of the Norman Conquest. For the West Country traditions of the visit of Jesus, I am indebted to the Revd C.C. Dobson, *Did Our Lord Visit Britain as they Say in Cornwall and Somerset?* (rev. edn, Glastonbury, 1947).

I am again grateful to Roger Sherman Loomis, 'The Oral Diffusion of the Arthurian Legend', in the book edited by him, *Arthurian Literature in the Middle Ages: A Collaborative History* (Oxford, 1959). His magisterial treatment of this subject and of the Celtic roots of Arthurian literature leave all scholars in his debt. Also admirable on its subject is James P. Carley, *Glastonbury Abbey* (rev. edn, Glastonbury, 1996). See also Adamnan, *De Locis Sanctis* (ed. D. Meehan, Dublin, 1958).

CHAPTER FOUR

Inspirational in his treatment of the origins of alchemy and ecstasy is Dan Merkur, *Gnosis: An Esoteric Tradition of Mystical Visions and Unisons* (New York, 1997). The translation of Zosimos, *The Visions*, is taken from that book, also the expert opinion from the valuable S. Angus, *The Mystery-Religions and Christianity* (London, 1925). For the translation of the Emerald Tablet, see Julius Ruska, *Tabula Smaragdini* (Heidelberg, 1926); also C.J.S. Thompson, *The Lure and Romance of Alchemy* (New York, 1990); C.A. Burland, *The Arts of the Alchemists* (London, 1967); Jacques Sadoul, *Alchemists and Gold* (London, 1972); and Derek and Julia Parker, *A History of Astrology* (London, 1983).

The *Autobiography* of Carl Gustav Jung talks about his first experiences with active imagination, as does his article of 1916, 'The Transcendent Function', and his Tavistock lectures of 1935. His preoccupation with Gnosticism is curiously revealed in his 'Seven Sermons to the Dead' of 1916, republished in *The Gnostic Jung* (ed. Robert A. Segal, London, 1992). Three volumes of his *Collected Works* particularly deal with the Grail: vol. 6, *Psychological Types*, vol. 12, *Psychology and Alchemy*, and vol. 14, *Mysterium Coniunctionis* (London, 1953–71). The quotation from Hippolytus comes from his *Elenchos*, V, 8:5–6. The quotation for the Apocryphal IV Ezra, 14:39–40, is taken from *The Apocrypha and Pseudepigrapha of the Old Testament in English* (ed. R.H. Charles, 2 vols, Oxford, 1913). *The Grail Legend* by Emma Jung and Marie-Louise von Franz was published in Boston, Mass., in 1986. The 'guardian of her sex' was Helen Luke, writing on 'The Return of Dindrane' in *At the Table of the Grail*, edited by John Matthews, who also published his *The Holy Grail: The Quest for the Eternal* (London, 1981). *The Chalice and the Blade* by Riane Eisler was published in 1987 in New York.

CHAPTER FIVE

I am indebted to John Armstrong, *The Paradise Myth* (London, 1969); Germain Bazin, *Paradeisos: The Art of the Garden* (London, 1990); B.S. Childs, 'Garden of Eden': The Interpreters of the Bible (New York, 1962); Jean Delumeau, *Mille ans de bonheur: Une histoire du paradis* (Paris, 1995); Eleanour Sinclair Rohde, *Garden-Craft in the Bible* (London, 1927) and *The Story of the Garden* (London, 1932); and, of course, John Milton, *Paradise Lost* (London, 1667), and John Dryden, *The Aeneid* (London, 1692). Also important are R.W.T. Gunther, *The Greek Herbal of Dioscorides* (Oxford, 1934); Theophrastos, *History of Plants* (ed. A.F. Hort, London, 1916); Mary Lascelles, 'Alexander and the Earthly Paradise in Medieval English Writings', *Medium Aevum*, V (1936); and Sylvia Landsberg, *The Medieval Garden* (London, 1995). The translations from Homer and Horace are my own, while this author has also written *Jardins de gloire, de délices et de Paradis* (Paris, 2000). The quotation from the King James Bible is from the Gospel of St John, 20:15–17.

CHAPTER SIX

As a summation, *The Oxford Guide to Arthurian Literature and Legend* (Oxford, 2005) by Alan Lupack is most instructive. I am indebted to the introduction by Robert Kehew of *Lark in the Morning: The Verses of the Troubadours* (Chicago, 2005). The poems in the bilingual edition are translated by Kehew, Ezra Pound and W.D. Snodgrass. I have also quoted from the excellent translation of *Perceval, or, The Story of the Grail* by Ruth Harwood Cline with introduction and notes (Athens, Ga., 1985). Jean Frappier's works on *Perceval* are most important, particularly his *Chrétien de Troyes et le mythe du Graal* (Paris, 1972). William A. Nitze, *Perceval and the Holy Grail: An Essay on the Romance of Chrétien de Troyes* (Berkeley and Los Angeles, 1949), emphasises the importance of the Byzantine ritual of Chrysostomos in the Grail procession, while Eugene J. Weinraub, *Chrétien's Jewish Grail: A New Investigation of the Imagery and Significance of Chrétien de Troyes's Grail Episode Based upon Medieval Hebraic Sources* (Chapel Hill, NC, 1976) is also significant.

A brilliant pamphlet by Leonardo Olschki, *The Grail Castle and its Mysteries* (Manchester, 1966), alone stresses the power of the Grail as representing the Light of God, deriving from the Gospel of St John and Gnostic heresies in the 12th century. The remarkable *Visio Pacis: Holy City and Grail* (State College, Pa., 1960) by Helen Adolf relates the Grail Quest to the loss of Jerusalem and the search for a heavenly city. I have also quoted Abenezra's poem from the excellent Ellen McCaffery, *Astrology: its History and Influence in the Western World* (New York, 1942). See also *The Elucidation: A Prologue to the Conte del Graal* (ed. A.W. Thompson, New York, 1931) and Gerbert de Montreuil, *La Continuation de Perceval* (3 vols, ed. M. Williams and M. Oswald, Paris, 1922, 1925, 1975).

Eleanor of Aquitaine may also have inspired an earlier lost Grail romance by the troubadour Rigaut de Barbezieux, who wrote before 1160: 'Just as Perceval, when he was alive, was lost in wonder at the sight, so that he could never ask what purpose the lance and grail served, so I likewise, *Mielhs de Domna* (arguably Eleanor of Aquitaine), for I forget all when I gaze on you.' See Rita Lejeune, 'The Troubadours', *Arthurian Literature in the Middle Ages* (ed. R.S. Loomis, Oxford, 1969). The quotation from the Gospel of St John is from 1:8–9.

CHAPTER SEVEN

The authority on the Lancelot or Vulgate cycle is Jean Frappier, who wrote an article on the subject in *Arthurian Literature in the Middle Ages: A Collaborative History* (ed. R.S. Loomis, Oxford, 1959). I have used the Penguin edition of Gerald of Wales's works, edited and translated by Lewis Thorpe (London, 1978). Helen Adolf, in her *Visio Pacis: Holy City and Grail*, already cited, is stimulating on the subject of the *Joseph of Arimathea* of Robert de Boron. I have used the Penguin edition of *The Quest of the Holy Grail* (London, 1969). It was edited and translated by P.M. Matarosso, whose introduction is illuminating, and who particularly quotes the works of Jean Marx, *La Légende arthurienne et le Graal* (Paris, 1952), and Albert Pauphilet, *Études sur la Queste del Saint Graal* (Paris, 1921). Matarosso's *The Redemption of Chivalry: A Study of the Queste de Saint Graal* (Geneva, 1979) is also excellent.

Étienne Gilson, in *La Théologie mystique de Saint Bernard* (Paris, 1947), stresses the mysticism and divine grace in *The Quest of the Holy Grail*. P.M. Matarosso is quoted on the grave ambivalence between primitive belief and Christian faith in his edition of *The Quest*. *The Grail Legend* by Emma Jung and Marie-Louise von Franz is already cited. Norma Lorre Goodrich, *The Holy Grail* (New York, 1992), was particularly struck by *The History of the Grail*, which she preferred to call the *Grand-Saint-Graal*. I have used the King James Bible for the Gospel according to St John, 3:14–16, 6:48–50, 53; 19:40–41, and 21:5, 6, 9, 12. The leading French authority quoted on the *Lancelot* cycle was Ferdinand Lot, *Étude sur le 'Lancelot en Prose'* (Paris, 1918).

CHAPTER EIGHT

I deal with the connection between the Cistercians and the Knights Templars in *Jerusalem: The Endless Crusade* (New York, 1995), in *The Sword and the Grail* (New York, 1992) and in *Rosslyn* (Edinburgh, 2005), particularly over the question of weapons as well as faith. I have quoted from J.A. MacCulloch, *Medieval Faith and Fable* (London, 1932), on the importance of relics as well as the Host in the Middle Ages. The brilliant book by the librarian at Montségur, Raimonde Reznikov, *Cathares et Templiers* (Toulouse, 1993), proves that the Knights Templars both attacked and supported the Cathars in the Langue d'Oc. Michel Roquebert, in *Les Cathares et le Graal* (Toulouse, 1995), considers the Grail texts as orthodox and Catholic, and so he denies the title of his book, stating that the Cathars as heretics had nothing to do with the Holy Vessel. Zoé Oldenbourg, *Massacre at Montségur: A History of the Albigensian Crusade* (New York, 1961), remains magisterial on the subject.

The translation from the *Chanson de Roland* is my own. William Preston wrote *History of Masonry*, published in 1804 in London. Particularly significant on St Bernard is *Vézelay et Saint Bernard* (ed. Jacques d'Arès, Croissy-Beaubours, 1985), and *The Second Crusade and the Cistercians* (ed. Michael Gervers, New York, 1992). For St Bernard's views on the crusades, see G. Constable, 'The Second Crusade as seen by Contemporaries', *Traditio*, 9 (1953), and J. Leclerq, 'L'Encyclique de St Bernard en faveur de la croisade', *Revue bénédictine*, 81 (1974).

Most interesting of recent works on the Knights Templars are Gérard de Sède, *Les Templiers sont parmi nous* (Paris, 1962); Louis Charpentier, *Les Mystères Templiers* (Paris, 1967); Guy Tarade, *Les Derniers Gardiens du Graal* (Paris, 1993); Michel Lamy, *Les Templiers* (Bordeaux, 1997); Patrick Rivière, *Les Templiers et leurs mystères* (rev. edn, Paris, 1997); Raimonde Reznikov, *Cathares et Templiers* (Portet-sur-Garonne, 1993); and Alain Desgris, *L'Ordre des Templiers* (Paris, 1994). The quotation on the Knights Templars by St Bernard of Clairvaux comes from his *De laude novae militiae*, contained in *Patrologia Latina*, clxxxii. Farhad Daftary puts the revisionist case in *The Assassin Legends: Myths of the Ismai'ilis* (London, 1995).

CHAPTER NINE

The quotations about the endeavour to destroy the Host and other examples of miracles come from the admirable

J.A. MacCulloch, *Medieval Faith and Fable* (London, 1932), Manly P. Hall, *The Adepts in the Eastern Esoteric Tradition: The Mystics of Islam* (Los Angeles, 1994), and Dan Merkur, *Gnosis: An Esoteric Tradition of Mystical Visions and Unisons* (New York, 1997), from whom the quotations of the Koranic verses are taken. J.D. Anderson and E.T. Kennan translated St Bernard's *Advice to a Pope, De Consideratione Libri Quinque ad Eugenium Tertium* (Kalamazoo, 1976). F. Bogdanow made an excellent comparison in his essay, 'The Mystical Theology of Bernard de Clairvaux and the Meaning of Chrétien de Troyes' *Conte du Graal*' in *Essays in Memory of the Late Leslie Topsfield* (ed. Peter S. Noble and Linda M. Paterson, Cambridge, 1984). The Rule of the Templars is published in Henri de Curzon, *La Règle du Temple* (Paris, 1886). Most useful is Benedicta Ward, *Miracles and the Medieval Mind: Theory, Record and Event, 1000–1215* (London, 1982).

CHAPTER TEN

See Peggy McCracken, 'Damsels and Severed Heads: More Linking in the Perlesvaus' in *Por le soie amiste: Essays in Honor of Norris J. Lacy* (ed. K. Busby and C.M. Jones, Amsterdam, 2000); also Thomas E. Kelly, *Le Haut Livre du Graal: Perlesvaus: A Structural Study* (Geneva, 1974). *Le Haut Livre du Graal Perlesvaus* was edited by William A. Nitze and collaborators in a definitive text and commentary, published by the University of Chicago Press in 1937. For the translations, I have also used *The High History of the Holy Graal*, translated from the old text by Sebastian Evans (London, 1910).

I am again indebted to Robert Sherman Loomis for his original and brilliant *Celtic Myth and Arthurian Romance* (New York, 1927). The article on 'Gereint, Owein, and Peredur' by Idris Llewelyn Foster in *Arthurian Literature in the Middle Ages: A Collaborative History* (ed. R.S. Loomis, Oxford, 1959) is also excellent. The leading Welsh commentator on *Peredur*, from whom I have quoted, is the admirable Glenys Goetinck, *Peredur: A Study of Welsh Tradition in the Grail Legend* (Cardiff, 1975). The text of *Peredur* in *The Mabinogion* was translated by Gwyn and Thomas Jones (rev. edn, London, 1974).

CHAPTER ELEVEN

Illuminating analysis and the modernised translation from William Wey come from N.H. Wethered, *The Four Paths of Pilgrimage* (London, 1947); J.A. MacCulloch, *Medieval Faith and Fable* (London, 1932), is again invaluable on the subject of miracles and provided the quotations from Theodoret, St Columba and Pope Gregory. On the subject of the relics in Constantinople and in Rome, Ian Wilson provides expert advice in *Holy Faces, Secret Places: The Quest for Jesus' True Likeness* (New York, 1991). An original Travellers' Guide by Ean and Deike Begg, *In Search of the Holy Grail and the Precious Blood* (London, 1995), provides unique research into the sites of the sacred relics of Europe. The translation from Dante's 'Paradiso', Book 31, lines 103–8, is my own. Teddy Kollek and Moshe Pearlman, *Pilgrims to the Holy Land* (London, 1970), is most useful on its theme, while a recent fine work on the subject is Simon Coleman and John Elsner, *Pilgrimage: Past and Present* (London, 1995).

CHAPTER TWELVE

The extensive journeys and observations of the abbeys, churches, monasteries and shrines of southern and northern Europe have been undergone by this author. He is indebted to the brilliant essay 'Le Trésor au temps de Suger', by Danielle Gaborit-Chopin, in *Le Trésor de Saint-Denis* (Dijon, 1992); also to Pierre-Marie Auzas, *Eugène Voillet le Duc: 1814–1879* (Caisse Nationale des Monuments Historiques et des Sites, 1979).

Again I am grateful to C.J.S. Thompson, *The Lure and Romance of Alchemy* (New York, 1990). Richard Barber's *The Knight & Chivalry* (London, 1970) is penetrating on the actual effect of the Grail romances on knightly behaviour. The quotation is taken from the translation of Gottfried von Strassburg's *Tristan* by A.T. Hatto (London, 1960). W.H. Jackson deals with *Chivalry in Twelfth-Century Germany: The Works of Hartmann von Aue* (London, 1994). The text of *Parzival* is analysed in my own *The Sword and the Grail* (London,

1999); also in David Blamires, *Characterization and Individuality in Wolfram's 'Parzival'* (Cambridge, 1966), and in Margaret F. Richey, *Studies of Wolfram von Eschenbach* (London, 1957). The translations from the original are largely mine.

I am indebted to Walter Johannes Stein, *The Ninth Century and the Holy Grail* (Temple Lodge Press, 1988), for the quotation from the Twelve Keys of Basilius Valentinus. Hugh Sacker, *An Introduction to Wolfram's 'Parzival'* (Cambridge, 1963), is excellent on the subject of the Grail. Otto Springer's essay 'Wolfram's *Parzival*' is important in *Arthurian Literature in the Middle Ages: A Collaborative History* (ed. R.S. Loomis, Oxford, 1959), an excellent compendium.

All scholars are indebted to *The Middle High German Poems of Willehalm by Wolfram of Eschenbach* (tr. and intro. Charles F. Passage, New York, 1977). *Wolfram von Eschenbach, Titurel and the Songs* (tr. and intro. Marion E. Gibbs and Sidney M. Johnson, New York, 1988) is also essential. As always, Helen Adolf, in her *Visio Pacis: Holy City and Grail* (State College, Pa., 1960), has striking insights, while Roger Sherman Loomis, *The Grail: From Celtic Myth to Christian Symbol* (New York, 1963), identifies the *Alexanderlied* as a source for the stone Grail in *Parzival*.

Most important in the understanding of *Parzival* are Linda B. Parshall, *The Art of Narration in Wolfram's Parzival and Albrecht's Jüngerer Titurel* (Cambridge, 1981), and Henry and Renée Kahane in collaboration with Angelina Pietrangeli, *The Krater and the Grail: Hermetic Sources of the Parzival* (Campaign, Ill., 1965), to whom I am grateful for their translations of *Parzival* and the *Corpus Hermeticum*. See also Hartmann von Aue, *Iwein* (ed. F. Benecke and K. Lachmann, Berlin, 1959); Arthur C.L. Brown, 'The Bleeding Lance', *Publications of the Modern Language Association of America*, 25 (1910); A.T. Hatto, 'Y a-t-il un roman du Graal de Kyot le provençal?', *Les Romans du Graal au XIIᵉ et XIIIᵉ siècles* (Strasbourg, 1954); Henry Kratz, 'The Prologue to Wolfram's *Parzival*', *Journal of English and Germanic Philology*, 65 (1966), and *Wolfram von Eschenbach's Parzival: An Attempt at a Total Evaluation* (Francke Verlag Bern, 1973); Jean Marx, *La Légende arthurienne et le Graal* (Paris, 1952); and W. Scott, *Hermetica* (4 vols, Oxford, 1924–36).

CHAPTER THIRTEEN

The two classic works by J. Huizinga, *The Waning of the Middle Ages* (London, 1924) and *Homo Ludens* (London, 1949), were my inspiration for this chapter, and the quotations are from these works. Norman Housley, *The Later Crusades: From Lyons to Alcazar, 1274–1580* (Oxford, 1992), is excellent on the requiems of the movement. M. Keen, in *Chivalry* (London, 1984), translated the passage on the Teutonic Knights from Jean Cabaret d'Orville, *La Chronique du bon duc Loys de Bourbon* (Paris, 1872). On pilgrimage, I am again indebted to N.H. Wethered, *The Four Paths of Pilgrimage* (London, 1947), and to *Pilgrimage: Past and Present*, already cited, as well as to Donald R. Howard, *Writers and Pilgrims: Medieval Pilgrimage, Narratives and Their Posterity* (Berkeley and Los Angeles, 1980).

CHAPTER FOURTEEN

The most important recent book on frontier conflicts is *Medieval Frontier Societies* (ed. Robert Bartlett and Angus MacKay, Oxford, 1989): the work is particularly fine on the *reconquista*, and the quotations derive from that work. Always useful for the geography of the Grail situation are *The Atlas of the Crusades* (ed. Jonathan Riley-Smith, London, 1991) and Ean and Deike Begg, *In Search of the Holy Grail and the Precious Blood*, already cited, the only Baedeker on the subject. The quotation about the Christian conversion of Aragon comes from the Revd Professor Robert Burns, *The Crusader Kingdom of Valencia* (2 vols, Cambridge, Mass., 1967). There is an excellent article on 'Arthurian Literature in Spain and Portugal' by Maria Rosa Lida de Malkiel in *Arthurian Literature in the Middle Ages: A Collaborative History* (ed. R.S. Loomis, Oxford, 1959), and Walter Stein wrote an intriguing appendix on the legend of St Lawrence and the Roman Grail in his cited *The Ninth Century and the Holy Grail*, which quotes St Gertrude. The quotation from Fernand Braudel comes from his seminal work, *The Mediterranean and the Mediterranean World in the Age of Philip II* (2 vols, London, 1972).

I have generally used the Modern Library translation of *Don Quixote* by Samuel Putnam after the Castilian of Miguel de Cervantes (New York, 1949). Yet, as Cervantes himself wrote about the problems of translation: 'Translating from one language into another, unless it be from one of those two queenly tongues, Greek and Latin, is like gazing at a Flemish tapestry with the wrong side out: even though the figures are visible, they are full of threads that obscure the view and are not bright and smooth as when seen from the other side.'

CHAPTER FIFTEEN

Norman Housley, *The Later Crusades: From Lyons to Alcazar*, already cited, is excellent on the papal misuse of pardon money collected for crusades. The quotations from Erasmus are from *Opus epistolarum Desiderii Erasmi Roterodami* (ed. P.S. Allen *et al.*, 12 vols, Oxford, 1906–58). E.C. Gardner, *Arthurian Legend in Italian Literature* (London, 1930), is essential reading, as is Antonio Viscardi, 'Arthurian Influences on Italian Literature from 1200 to 1500' in *Arthurian Literature in the Middle Ages: A Collaborative History* (ed. R.S. Loomis, Oxford, 1959), and Ian Wilson, *Holy Faces, Secret Places: The Quest for Jesus' True Likeness* (New York, 1999), who is stimulating on the sack of Rome and quoted the letters on the catastrophe.

On the subject of Italian patronage in that period, Sergio Bertelli, *The Courts of the Italian Renaissance* (Milan, 1985), is helpful; and on the Medici, Edward L. Goldberg, *Patterns in Late Medici Art Patronage* (Princeton, NJ, 1983), is important. Vasari's *Lives of the Artists* and Cellini's *Autobiography* contain remarkable revelations, while W.L. Gurdesheimer, *Ferrara: The Style of a Renaissance Despotism* (Princeton, NJ, 1973), is informative. Harold Acton, 'Medicean Florence' in *Cities of Destiny* (ed. Arnold Toynbee, London, 1967), is an elegant essay on the subject, while Bernard Berenson, *The Italian Painters of the Renaissance* (London, 1952), remains seminal. The translations from the *Divine Comedy* of Dante and *L'Orlando Innamorato* by Boiardo are my own. The critic quoted on *Orlando Furioso* by Ludovico Ariosto is Barbara Reynolds, whose superb translation of the Italian poem is quoted from her rendition of that classic work for Penguin Books (London, 1975). John Hale refers to the Instruction of the Emperor Charles the Fifth in his definitive *The Civilization of Europe in the Renaissance* (London, 1993).

CHAPTER SIXTEEN

Essential reading on Rosslyn Chapel are two books by Robert Brydon, *The Guilds, the Masons and the Rosy Cross* (Roslin, 1994) and *Rosslyn and the Western Mystery Tradition* (Edinburgh, 2003). I deal with the subject fully in my three previous books, *The Sword and the Grail*, already cited, *The Secret Scroll* (London, 2001), and *Rosslyn* (Edinburgh, 2005). Also recommended is Karen Ralls, *The Templars and the Grail: Knights of the Quest* (Wheaton, Ill., 2003). The biblical quotation is taken from the Book of Haggai, 2:7–9.

J. Huizinga, *The Waning of the Middle Ages* (London, 1924), is a supreme example in prose of how to describe the essence of a period. I am grateful to the Scottish and English National Heritage guides to the Cistercian abbeys of Melrose and Newbattle. Also valuable are Hubert Fenwick, *The Auld Alliance* (Kineton, 1971), and Maurice Vieux, *Les Secrets de Bâtisseurs* (Paris, 1975). Lewis Spence wrote 'The Arthurian Tradition in Scotland' for the *Scots Magazine* (April 1926), while *Genealogie of the Sainte-Claires of Rosslyn* by Father Richard Augustine Hay was published in 1835 in Edinburgh.

CHAPTER SEVENTEEN

I have used Walter Scott's translation and edition of the *Hermetica* by Hermes Trismegistus (London, 1924) and John Donne's *Collected Poems* (Oxford, 1970). Vital for an understanding of alchemy in the Middle Ages is the seminal work by Keith Thomas, *Religion and the Decline of Magic* (London, 1971); also Richard Kieckhefer, *Magic in the Middle Ages* (Cambridge, 1989), which gives the quotations from Robert Fludd

and Bishop Latimer and John of Glastonbury. The theory of the woundsalve comes from Sir Kenelm Digby, *A Late Discourse . . . Touching the Cure of Wounds by the Powder of Sympathy* (London, 1658). Jung's work on *Psychology and Alchemy* and on *Alchemical Studies* may be found in *The Collected Works of C.G. Jung* (vols 12 and 13, London, 1953). I have slightly adapted the text of Malory's *Morte D'Arthur*, as edited by Israel Gollancz for the Temple Classics (4 vols, London, 1901). There is an imaginative essay by Adam McLean, 'Alchemical Transmutation in History and Symbol' in *At the Table of the Grail* (ed. John Matthews, London, 1984). Bishop Hooper and Puritan protestors and Martin Luther's hatred of the Pope are chronicled in Bernard McGinn, *Anti-Christ* (London, 1994). Nikolai Tolstoy is particularly good on the political value of Merlin's prophecies in his *The Quest for Merlin* (London, 1985), and he does much to establish Myrddin as a true Welsh bard.

CHAPTER EIGHTEEN

Useful on the early legends of voyages to America is *The Quest for America* (ed. Geoffrey Ashe, New York, 1971). David Blamires, *Herzog Ernst and the Otherworld Voyage: A Comparative Study* (Manchester, 1979), is excellent on his subject. My own *The Sword and the Grail*, already cited, establishes the probability and accuracy of the Zeno Narrative. The account of the expedition of Earl Henry St Clair to Canada in Michael Bradley's *Holy Grail across the Atlantic* (Toronto, 1988) is highly speculative. Well researched and convincing on the Cortereal voyages is E.B. Delabarre, *Dighton Rock* (New York, 1928). The translations from *The Lusiads*, Herrara and the letters of Columbus are mine.

Perry Miller, *Errand into the Wilderness* (Cambridge, Mass., 1956), is seminal on the mission of the Pilgrim Fathers, and he quotes John Winthrop and Cotton Mather. J.H. Elliott, *The Old World and the New, 1492–1650* (Cambridge, 1972), is most stimulating. Essential reading on John Milton is his biography by William Riley Parker (2 vols, Oxford, 1968).

CHAPTER NINETEEN

My inspiration for this chapter was the remarkable anthology *Pandaemonium: 1660–1886*, conceived and compiled by the documentary film-maker Humphrey Jennings and edited by Mary-Lou Jennings and Charles Madge (London, 1985). Also admirable is Francis D. Klingender, *Art and the Industrial Revolution* (rev. edn by Arthur Elton, London, 1968). Anna Seward's poem comes from *The Poetical Works*, edited by Sir Walter Scott in two volumes in Edinburgh in 1810. John Britton's *Autobiography* was also published in two volumes in London in 1850, while James Nasmyth's *Autobiography* was edited by Samuel Smiles and published in London in 1883. T. Ashe edited *The Table Talk and Omniana of S.T. Coleridge*, published in 1884 in London. A superb edition of *The Novels of Thomas Love Peacock* was edited by David Garnett and published in 1948 by Rupert Hart-Davis in London.

There is an erudite survey of the *Rosicrucians* by Christopher McIntosh (Wellingborough, 1987), which tells of the hermetic Order of the Golden Dawn, and quotes the poem by Werner. The Rosicrucian version of the Round Table at Winchester derives from *The Rosicrucians: Their Rites and Mysteries* by Hargrave Jennings (London, 1907). On Sir Walter Scott, I have found particularly interesting the book by Coleman O. Parsons, *Witchcraft and Demonology in Scott's Fiction* (Edinburgh, 1964); the essays by Paul M. Ochojski and R.D.S. Jack in *Scott Bicentenary Essays* (ed. Alan Bell, Edinburgh, 1973); Albert Canning, *History in Scott's Novels* (London, 1905); James Anderson, *Sir Walter Scott and History* (Edinburgh, 1981); and Donald Davie on *Waverley* in *Walter Scott* (ed. D.D. Devlin, London, 1968). Scott's Jacobite feelings come from vol. 3 of *The Letters of Sir Walter Scott* (ed. H. Grierson, 12 vols, London, 1932–7).

Mark Girouard is superb and original in his 19th-century analysis, *The Return to Camelot: Chivalry and the English Gentleman* (New Haven, 1981); he quotes Queen Victoria and J.A. Froude. For Alfred Lord Tennyson, I have used *The Works*, published by Macmillan in London in 1904. The letter of Edward Fitzgerald to Alfred Tennyson was quoted in Hallam Lord Tennyson's *Tennyson, a Memoir* (1897). John

Addington Symonds's invocation of male brotherhood was privately printed in 1875, while Ralph Waldo Emerson's 'The Harp' was published in 1870. Surprising and evocative, Modris Eksteins's *Rites of Spring: The Great War and the Birth of the Modern Age* (New York, 1989) is essential reading for any true understanding of the wellsprings of the First World War.

CHAPTER TWENTY

In their original book, *In Search of the Holy Grail and the Precious Blood*, already cited, Ean and Deike Begg are strong supporters of the claims of Reichenau and Weingarten to many blessed relics. I am indebted to the late Bernard Levin for his advice and loan to me of the librettos of *Lohengrin* and *Parsifal*. Of the many recent books on Wagner, I have found most useful: Ernest Newman, *The Wagner Operas* (New York, 1948); John Chancellor, *Wagner* (London, 1978); Martin Gregor-Dellin, *Richard Wagner: His Life, his Work, his Century* (London, 1983); and Michael Tanner, *Wagner* (London, 1996), who quotes the correspondence between King Ludwig and Wagner, also the criticism by Nietzsche.

CHAPTER TWENTY-ONE

The Economic Consequences of the Peace by John Maynard Keynes was published in 1919 in London. Stephen Spender wrote of the Weimar Republic in the preface to his novel *The Temple* (London, 1988), while Christopher Isherwood's *Christopher and his Kind, 1929–1939* was published in 1977 in London.

On the occult beliefs of the Nazi leaders, the following books are useful: Jean-Michel Angebert, *Hitler y la Tradición Catara* (Barcelona, 1976); J.H. Brennan, *Occult Reich* (London, 1974); Marcel and Willy Brou, *Les Secrètes des Druides* (Brussels, 1970); Francis King, *Satan and the Swastika* (London, 1976); Roger Manvell, *SS and Gestapo* (London, 1969); W.L. Shirer, *The Rise and Fall of the Third Reich* (London, 1960); and particularly Nigel Pennick, *Hitler's Secret Services* (Sudbury, Suffolk, 1981).

Alfred Rosenberg's *Der Mythus des XX Jahrhunderts* was published in 1930 in Munich, while Edward Bulwer-Lytton's *The Coming Race* appeared in 1871 in London. I am indebted for the account of the visit of Dr Fuchs to the Theosophical Society in Edinburgh to Robert Brydon, the historian of the Scottish Knights Templars. Otto Rahn's *Kreuzzug gegen den Graal* was published in 1933 in Stuttgart, and his *Luzifers Hofgesind* in 1937 in Leipzig and Berlin, while the accounts of his researches near Montségur and those of the *Ahnenherbe* may be found in the works of Gérard de Sède, particularly *Le Secret des Cathars*; of Jean-Paul Bourre, especially *La Quête du Graal* (Paris, 1993); and of Guy Tarade, particularly *Les Derniers Gardiens du Graal* (Paris, 1993).

CHAPTER TWENTY-TWO

For an understanding of prophecy and insight, most useful is Michael Lieb, *The Visionary Mode: Biblical Prophecy, Hermeneutics, and Cultural Change* (Ithaca, NY, 1991). Gerald Bullitt is illuminating in *The English Mystics* (London, 1950). Dan Merkur is brilliant in his study of mystical experiences in *Gnosis: An Esoteric Tradition of Mystical Visions and Unisons* (New York, 1997), from which the quotations from Julia of Norwich and Martin Buber are taken. Timothy Leary wrote on sacred drugs in *Open City*, 16–22 June (1967), which also dealt with 'psychedelic therapy'.

ACKNOWLEDGEMENTS

The author and publishers would like to thank all the artists, writers, publishers and literary representatives who have given permission to include the pictures, poetry and prose in this work. While every effort has been made to find copyright holders, this has not always been possible, and the publishers will be glad to make good any omissions in future editions.

IMPORTANT GRAIL TEXTS

Virgil	*The Aeneid*	Anonymous	*Perlesvaus*
Geoffrey of Monmouth	*The History of the Kings of Britain*	Anonymous	*The Quest of the Holy Grail*
		Anonymous	*The Prose Lancelot*
Robert de Boron	*The History of the Grail Joseph of Arimathea Merlin*	Anonymous	*Mort d'Artu*
		Dante	*The Divine Comedy*
		Chaucer	*Canterbury Tales*
Wace	*Roman de Brut*	Sir John Mandeville	*Travels*
Layamon	*Brut*	Sir Thomas Malory	*Morte D'Arthur*
Chrétien de Troyes	*Perceval* or *The Story of the Grail*	Camõens	*The Lusiads*
		Cervantes	*Don Quixote*
Gautier de Doulens	*First Continuation*	Ariosto	*Orlando Furioso*
Manassier	*Continuation*	Spenser	*The Faerie Queene*
Gerbert de Montreuil	*Continuation*	Bunyan	*The Pilgrim's Progress*
Anonymous	*Song of Roland*	Milton	*Paradise Lost*
Anonymous	*Aliscans*	Peacock	*The Misfortunes of Elphin*
Anonymous	*Didot Perceval*	Sir Walter Scott	*The Talisman*
Jacopus de Voraigne	*The Golden Legend*	Lady Charlotte Guest	*The Mabinogion*
Anonymous	*Wartburgkrieg*	Alfred Lord Tennyson	*Idylls of the King*
Hartmann von Aue	*Iwein*	Wagner	*Tannhäuser*
Gottfried von Strassburg	*Tristan*		*Lohengrin*
Wolfram von Eschenbach	*Parzival Willehalm Titurel*		*Parsifal*
		C.G. Jung	*Psychology and Alchemy*
Albrecht von Scharfenberg	*Jüngerer Titurel*	T.H. White	*The Once and Future King*
Heinrich von dem Türlin	*Diû Krône*	Emma Jung and Marie-Louise von Franz	*The Grail Legend*
Anonymous	*Peredur*		

SELECT BIBLIOGRAPHY

Adorno, Theodor W., *In Search of Wagner* (tr. R. Livingstone, London, 1981)

Anderson, Flavia, *The Ancient Secret* (London, 1953)

Ashe, Geoffrey, *Camelot and the Vision of Albion* (New York, 1971)

Barber, Richard, *The Holy Grail: Imagination and Belief* (London, 2004)

Bathélémy, A., *Au XIIe siècle. Le Graal, sa première révélation* (Toulouse, 1987)

Bertrand, M., and Angelini, J., *The Quest and the Third Reich* (New York, 1974)

Bonilla y San Martin (ed.), *La Demanda de Sancto Grial* (Madrid, 1907)

Borst, Arno, *Die Katharer* (Stuttgart, 1953)

Brinkley, R.F., *Arthurian Legend in the Seventeenth Century* (New York, 1967)

Brown, Arthur C.L., *The Origin of the Grail Legend* (Cambridge, 1943)

Bruce, J.D., *The Evolution of Arthurian Romance from the Beginnings down to the Year 1300* (2 vols, Göttingen, 1923–4)

Burdach, Konrad, *Der Gral* (Stuttgart, 1938)

Cavendish, Richard, *King Arthur of the Grail: The Arthurian Legends and their Meaning* (London, 1978)

Currer-Briggs, Noel, *The Shroud and the Grail: A Modern Quest for the True Grail* (London, 1987–8)

Deinert, Willhelm, *Ritter und Kosmos im Parzival* (Munich, 1960)

Domanig, Karl, *Parzivalstudien* (2 vols, Paderborn, 1880)

Emmel, Hildegard, *Formprobleme des Artusromans und der Graldichtung* (Berne, 1951)

Entwhistle, William J., *The Arthurian Legend in the Literatures of the Spanish Peninsula* (New York, 1925)

Evans, Sebastian, *In Quest of the Holy Grail* (London, 1898)

Evola, Guilio, C.A., *Il Mistero del Graal* (Rome, 1972)

Faral, Edmond, *La Littérature Arthurienne* (3 vols, Paris, 1929)

Fouquet, Jean, *Wolfram d'Eschenbach et le Conte del Graal* (Paris, 1938)

Gadal, A., *Sur le chemin de Saint-Graal* (Haarlem, 1960)

Gallais, Pierre, *Perceval et l'initiation* (Paris, 1972)

Gilson, Étienne, *Les Idées et les lettres* (Paris, 1955)

Golther, Wolfgang, *Parzival und der Gral in der Dichtung des Mittelalters und der Neuzeit* (Stuttgart, 1925)

Guyer, Foster E., *Chrétien de Troyes* (Berne, 1958)

Hertz, Willhelm, *Die Sage vom Parzival und dem Gral* (Breslau, 1882)

Holmes, Urban T., *Chrétien de Troyes* (New York, 1970)

Kahanne, Henri, and Pietrangeli, Renée and A., *The Krater and the Grail, Hermetic Sources of the 'Parzival'* (Urbana, 1965)

Kempe, Dorothy, 'The Legend of the Holy Grail, its Sources, Character and Development' in *The Holy Grail or Grand-Saint-Graal* (London, 1905)

Klenke, Amelia, *Chrétien de Troyes and 'Le Conte del Graal'* (Madrid and the Catholic University of America, 1981)

Kolb, Herbert, *Munsalvaesche, Studien zum Kyotproblem* (Munich, 1963)

Kurz, Johann B., *Wolfram von Eschenbach. Ein Buch vom grössten Dichter des Mittelalters* (Ansbach, 1930)

Leroux de Lincy, Antoine J.V., *Histoire de l'Abbaye de Fécamp* (Rouen, 1840)

Lindsay, Jack, *Arthur and his Times* (London, 1958)

Lupack, Alan, *The Oxford Guide to Arthurian Literature and Legend* (Oxford, 2005)

Marx, Jean, *La Légende Arthurienne et le Graal* (Geneva, 1974)

Matarosso, Pauline, *The Redemption of Chivalry: A Study of the Queste del Sant Graal* (Geneva, 1979)

Mergell, Bodo, *Der Graal in Wolframs Parzival* (Halle, 1952)

Micha, A., *La Tradition manuscripte des romans de Chrétien de Troyes* (Paris, 1931)

Nelli, René, *Écritures cathares* (Paris, 1968)

Newstead, Helaine, *Bran the Blessed in Arthurian Romance* (New York, 1966)

Niel, Fernand, *Albigeois et Cathares* (Paris, 1955)

Owen, D.D.R., *The Evolution of the Grail Legend* (Edinburgh, 1968)

Paetzel, Martin, *Wolfram von Eschenbach und Crestien von Troyes* (Berlin, 1931)

Partner, Peter, *The Murdered Magicians: The Templars and their Myth* (New York, 1981)

Pauphilet, Albert, *Études sur la Queste del Saint Graal* (Paris, 1921)

Pollman, L., *Chrétien de Troyes und der 'Conte de Graal'* (Tübingen, 1965)

Ponsoye, Pierre, *L'Islam et le Graal: Étude sur l'esotérisme du Parzival de Wolfram von Eschenbach* (Paris, 1958)

Puech, Henri-Charles, *La Queste du Graal* (Paris, 1965)

Ravenscroft, Trevor, *The Cup of Destiny: The Quest for the Grail* (York Beach, Me., 1982)

Richey, Margaret F., *Gahmuret Anschevin: A Contribution to the Study of Wolfram von Eschenbach* (Oxford, 1923)

——, *Studies of Wolfram von Eschenbach* (Edinburgh, 1957)

Ringbom, Lars-Ivar, *Graltemple und Paradies* (Stockholm, 1951)

Ritchie, Robert L., *Chrétien de Troyes and Scotland* (Oxford, 1952)

Runciman, Stephen, *The Medieval Manichee: A Study of the Christian Dualist Heresy* (Cambridge, 1947)

San Marte, A.S., *Parcival-Studien* (3 vols, Halle, 1861–2)

Schröder, Franz Rolf, *Die Parzivalfrage* (Munich, 1928)

Serrus, Georges, and Roquebert, Michel, *Châteaux cathares* (Toulouse, 1986)

Singer, Samuel, *Wolframs Willehalm* (Berne, 1917)

——, *Wolfram und der Graal: Neue Parzival Studien* (Zürich, 1937)

Sumption, Jonathan, *The Albigensian Crusade* (London, 1978)

Waite, Arthur E., *The Holy Grail: Its Legends and Symbolism* (London, 1909)

Weber, Gottfried, *Der Gottesbegriff des Parzival* (Frankfurt, 1935)

Weston, Jessie L., *The Legend of Sir Perceval* (2 vols, London, 1906–9)

——, *The Quest of the Holy Grail* (London, 1913)

——, *From Ritual to Romance* (Cambridge, 1920)

Wilmotte, Maurice, *Le Poème du Gral. Le Parzival de Wolfram d'Eschenbach et ses sources françaises* (Paris, 1933)

INDEX